YORK NOTES C(

Postcolonial Literature

Wendy Knepper

Longman
is an imprint of

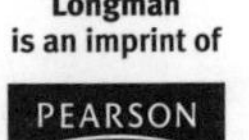

Harlow, England • London • New York • Boston • San Francisco • Toronto
Sydney • Tokyo • Singapore • Hong Kong • Seoul • Taipei • New Delhi
Cape Town • Madrid • Mexico City • Amsterdam • Munich • Paris • Milan

YORK PRESS
322 Old Brompton Road, London SW5 9JH

PEARSON EDUCATION LIMITED
Edinburgh Gate, Harlow, CM20 2JE, United Kingdom
Tel: +44 (0)1279 623623 Fax: +44 (0)1279 431059
Website: www.pearsoned.co.uk

First edition published in Great Britain in 2011

ISBN 978–1–4082–6665–6

British Library Cataloguing in Publiction Data
A CIP catalogue record for this book can be obtained from the British Library

Library of Congress Cataloging-in-Publication Data
Knepper, Wendy.

Postcolonial literature / Wendy Knepper.
p.cm. -- (York notes companions)
Includes bibliographical references and index.
ISBN 978-1-4082-6665-6 (pbk. : alk. paper) 1. Commonwealth literature (English)--History and criticism. 2. Postcolonialism in literature. I. Title. II. Series.
PR9080.K64 2011
820.9'00914--dc22

2011006479

10 9 8 7 6 5 4 3 2 1
14 13 12 11

Phototypeset by Carnegie Book Production, Lancaster
Printed in Malaysia, CTP-KHL

Contents

Part One
Introduction

Postcolonial literature challenges and moves beyond colonialist ways of representing of the world and its peoples. From the onset of colonialism, marked by the arrival of Christopher Columbus in America in 1492, until its decline and demise in the twentieth century, colonisers met with resistance in various political forms: war with indigenous peoples, slave revolts, revolution (such as in Haiti and America), mutiny and anti-colonial liberation struggles. In cultural terms, writers and storytellers from colonies around the world represented the struggle for emancipation in political, cultural, economic or material and ideological terms. After the colonial era, anti-imperial resistance may have, largely, come to an end, but it seems that the need for narrative persisted, perhaps even grew. Postcolonial literature has continued to play an ongoing and essential role in enabling individuals, communities, nations and the world at large to critique and envision identities and socio-political relations. Yet, one may well ask, what is the purpose of postcolonial literature in the twenty-first century? In a world where imperialism can no longer be described in colonial terms as a relationship between centre and periphery or as a contest among competing empires, does postcolonial literature still have a role to play?

This introduction to postcolonial literature seeks to respond to these questions as well as to offer a highly selective engagement with postcolonial literature, including discussions of contributions by leading authors and key theorists. The primary focus of the volume is on postcolonial literature in English, particularly during the latter part of the twentieth century, including accounts of writing from five continents, which were formerly part of the British Empire. Leading postcolonial authors are discussed – including figures such as Salman Rushdie, Toni Morrison, Derek Walcott, V. S. Naipaul and J. M. Coetzee – in order to highlight the diversity and excellence of postcolonial writing from around the world. Moreover, this book discusses lesser known and contemporary figures in postcolonial writing in order to offer a fuller account of postcolonial literature and its emerging themes.

Reading postcolonial literature demands a certain knowledge of history, beginning with Christopher Columbus's 'discovery' of the New World in 1492 to the more recent events of 9/11 and its aftermath. This work begins with a cultural overview (Part Two), which presents contexts for empire, colonisation, decolonisation and new forms of imperialism in the current era. Part Three: 'Texts, Writers and Contexts' examines various modes and genres of postcolonial writing, including discussions of novels, poetry, drama and the short story. Each chapter in this part of the volume offers an extended commentary on a key literary text as a means to highlight and pull together the many concerns raised in the chapter. Works by authors from Africa, North America, Europe, Asia and Australia are discussed in order to give a sense of the range of perspectives evident in postcolonial literature from around the world. Through a comparative analysis of literary forms, this section of the volume aims to highlight both the shared concerns and cultural specificities of postcolonial literature, paying particular attention to national frameworks and transnational issues.

Part Four: 'Critical Debates and Theories' offers an introduction to postcolonial theory and debates. This section of the volume includes an introduction to colonial discourses and strategies for postcolonial writing, debates about the interplay of race, gender and sexuality, an overview of theories of creolisation and hybridity, and a consideration of emerging issues in the field, such as the relationship between postcolonial perspectives and globalisation theory. Works by key thinkers such as Edward Said, Homi Bhabha, Gayatri Chakravorty Spivak and Frantz Fanon, are discussed in these chapters. Moreover, the theory is illustrated by brief accounts of works of postcolonial writing, including works of literature from the colonial period, such as by Jane Austen, E. M. Forster and Shakespeare. Contemporary works of literature by Zadie Smith, Hari Kunzru and Nalo Hopkinson among others are introduced in order to indicate new directions for postcolonial writing. This part of the volume encourages readers to think critically about the work of postcolonial literature in challenging prevailing conceptions of identity and citizenship in the modern world. In Part Five, the inclusion of a timeline helps to situate postcolonial writing from a historical perspective while an annotated bibliography suggests further directions for reading about postcolonial literature and its contexts.

The 'Post-colonial' versus the 'Postcolonial'

Postcolonial critics argue that we need to distinguish between the idea of the 'post-colonial' and the 'postcolonial'. While the term 'post-colonial' is said to designate the period after colonialism comes to an end, the notion of the 'postcolonial' is a more expansive term, referring to ways of conceptualising identity, literature and culture that go beyond imperialist paradigms. Elleke Boehmer observes that postcolonial literature 'is generally defined as that which critically or subversively scrutinizes the colonial relationship'.[1] John McLeod reinforces this point when he remarks that 'we might begin to think about the postcolonial as a *hinged* concept, which articulates together particular historical and material conditions on the one hand, with strategic, often contestatory ways of representing, knowing and transforming such conditions on the other'.[2] Postcolonial literature and criticism seek to explore the relationship between history and culture: authors and literary critics both respond to and critique histories of empire and colonial discourses, or ways of talking about the colonies and its peoples.

Writing and empire have been intimately linked throughout history. Colonial administrators, explorers, missionaries and European writers contributed to a diverse range of colonial discourses or ways of representing the colonies and colonial subjects. Works such as Tzvetan Todorov's *The Conquest of America* (1982), Peter Hulme's *Colonial Encounters: Europe and the Native Caribbean, 1492–1797* (1986) and Mary Louise Pratt's *Imperial Eyes: Travel Writing and Transculturation* (1992) underscore the intimate connections between empire, the language of the coloniser and representation. In colonial contact situations and through colonisation, language serves to mediate, represent and order the colonial world. The imposition of the language of the coloniser is another factor to consider as it is part of a wider process for imposing European culture, particularly as it transformed and/or effaced the local, indigenous or colonised peoples. Works of literature from the colonial period sometimes reflect the ambivalence of the colonial enterprise by showcasing forms of oppression while still perpetuating colonial worldviews. Notable examples that have received considerable critical attention, as well as inspired postcolonial rewriting, include Shakespeare's *The Tempest* (1610–11), Daniel Defoe's *Robinson Crusoe* (1719), Rudyard Kipling's *Kim* (1900–1) and Joseph Conrad's *Heart of Darkness* (1899, 1902).

Resistance to colonialist perspectives and representations of the world is one of the defining attributes of postcolonial literature. A landmark study by Bill Ashcroft, Gareth Griffiths and Helen Tiffin, entitled *The Empire Writes Back* (1989), highlights the many ways in which postcolonial literature has challenged the dominant discourses and practices associated with colonialism through rewriting works of history and culture. Postcolonial literature challenges the ideologies (such as the ideas and beliefs concerning race/ethnicity, culture, gender, the nation and sexuality) and oppressive dimensions of colonialism (such as slavery, indenture, institutionalised racism, genocide and so forth). Bart Moore-Gilbert argues that postcolonial criticism focuses primarily on literary and other forms that 'mediate, challenge or reflect upon the relations of domination and subordination – economic, cultural and political – between (and often within) nations, races or cultures, which characteristically have their roots in the history of modern European colonialism and imperialism'.[3]

A long historical view of postcolonial transition places emphasis on manifestations of ambivalence about empire and resistance to the colonial order on the part of the colonised as well as the coloniser. Intimations of the postcolonial can be found during the colonial era: a moment that looks forward to a real or imagined future when the colony will attain independence and undergo decolonisation. In this context, it is important to highlight the fact that colonisation was not simply a top-down practice. Through cultural and racial intermixtures, colonial culture resisted and transformed the dominant model. The colonies saw the emergence of forms of identity and culture that had not previously existed. The study of postcolonial literature is attentive to all of these approaches to writing, which range freely across cultures, times and places in order to represent the postcolonial moment.

At the same time, postcolonial literature highlights the legacies of colonialism or the ways in which the history of oppression lives on. Colonialism shaped ways of talking and writing about categories of identity, such as race, gender, culture and sexuality. Racism, sexism, the disenfranchisement of ethnic minorities, religious conflicts and other tensions are often among the legacies of colonialism as a process that involved relations of domination and subordination. Thus, any interpretation of postcolonial literature demands that we consider the persistent influence of the colonial past, a past which, often in diffuse ways, has shaped the identity of nations that were formerly colonised as well as that of the colonisers themselves. The legacies of the colonial past continue to influence or 'haunt' the postcolonial world, complicating a sense of when the postcolonial moment begins and ends.

In the modern era, postcolonial societies around the world continue to work through the oppressive afterlife of empire. Specifically, colonial discourses (ways of talking about identity and power relations) and oppressive practices have persisted. Both formerly colonised peoples and colonial powers have had to continue to struggle with the transition to a postcolonial nationhood. Principally, this means challenging the prevailing assumptions of British colonialism, which assumed that an English-speaking, white, patriarchal (male-dominated) and Christian model of socio-political identity should be imposed on peoples elsewhere. In Britain, ongoing debates about the notion of a multiracial, multicultural society have their origins in the changing face of British identity through empire, as peoples, cultures, religions, languages and races from around the world were incorporated and came to complicate a sense of what it means to be British.

Consequently, the study of postcolonial literature raises wider questions about the world we live in today as well as our relationship to a long history of cultural formation that dates back to the fifteenth century. Specifically, we might consider the role of neoimperialism or the ways in which a nation or group of nations influences the economic and/or political life of another country, whether through economic influence, military intervention or some other form of coercion. Moreover, we might investigate how colonisation as a global phenomenon paved the way for the rise of the global economy, migration around the world, transcultural contact, global communications and so forth. Our contemporary world order, with its uneven economic and political relations, such as the extremes between rich and poor countries in the world today, often perpetuates (and extends) the inequities that began during the colonial era. From a global perspective, political instabilities and uneven economic relations in the global economy can frequently be traced back through the long history of colonial relations and struggles among competing empires. The analysis of colonial power relations and dynamics – particularly as represented in literature – can elicit critical and creative perspectives concerning the relations between imperialisms, past and present, particularly in the context of our globalising world.

In summary, this volume aims to offer a selective introduction to the study of postcolonial literature in English, related theory and key debates, including discussions of events in the early period of colonisation to accounts of fiction in a post-9/11 world. Readers are asked to consider the multifaceted dimensions of empires past and present. The inclusion of key concepts and comparative literary perspectives provides an introduction to a field of literary studies that continues to encourage a critical and creative engagement with our changing world and its uneven power dynamics. Readers of this book are encouraged to consider the ways in which postcolonial writing and theory enable us to examine critically a world order that emerged more than five centuries ago, and how it has come to shape the horizons of contemporary life and literature.

Wendy Knepper

Notes

1 Elleke Boehmer, *Colonial and Postcolonial Literature: Migrant Metaphors*, 2nd edition (Oxford: Oxford University Press, 2005), p. 3.
2 John McLeod, *The Routledge Companion to Postcolonial Studies* (London: Routledge, 2007), p. 9.
3 Bart Moore-Gilbert, *Postcolonial Theory: Contexts, Practices, Politics* (London: Verso, 1997), p. 12.

Part Two
A Cultural Overview

This chapter offers a broad overview of the colonial era, post-colonial transition (including the role of anti-colonial and independence movements), and decolonisation (the dismantling of colonial rule and related ideologies).[1] The material is necessarily selective and tends to focus on the contexts for the British Empire and its writing practices. We will take a look at the roles of imperialism (a term that refers to the practice of establishing dominance over a territory and its peoples) and colonisation (a term that denotes the implanting of settlements on a distant territory). The age of empire, associated with exploration, conquest and colonisation, dates back to the fifteenth century and extends well into the twentieth century. Before the nineteenth century, global imperial ambitions were largely dominated by the contending powers of Spain and Portugal, France and Britain. The conscious decision to acquire and maintain colonies for political and economic advantage reached its ideological peak during the nineteenth century when many European nations held colonial territories, including Spain, France, Portugal, Britain, Holland (the Netherlands), Germany, Italy and Belgium.

Following the Second World War, most nations began the process of divesting themselves of colonial holdings, although this took several decades in some instances. At the same time, anti-colonial and independence movements by colonised peoples helped to accelerate the process of decolonisation. Decolonisation, as we shall see, involves more than the attainment of nationhood and independence from colonial rule. Postcolonial critics argue that it is a complex and ongoing process of revealing the tacit assumptions and ideologies about power, identity and culture that persist even after political independence is achieved. The residual influence of colonialism – colonial legacies – must be overcome in order to bring about a truly postcolonial condition.

The Age of Empire: Exploration, Conquest and Colonisation

The era of conquest and colonisation begins with Christopher Columbus's 'discovery' of the New World in 1492. Backed by the Spanish monarchy, Ferdinand of Aragón and Isabella of Castille, Columbus had hoped to find a trade route to the mainland of Asia, but encountered instead the lands and peoples of the American continent and Caribbean basin. Columbus's letters to the monarchs include reports of the voyages and his impressions of the lands he found. Columbus's 'Letter on the First Voyage' (1493) was printed and circulated throughout Spain and it was so popular that it went through three printings. The Spanish monarchs successfully obtained a papal bull* from Pope Alexander VI, which gave them authority and jurisdiction over the territories in the region. While Spain had rights to most of the New World, the Portuguese were granted the rights to colonise Africa, Asia and the territory that would eventually come to be known as Brazil.

Hernán Cortez and Francisco Pizarro played a significant historical role in the conquest of territory by the Spanish in the New World. While Pizarro's efforts focused on South America, Cortés led the forces that defeated the Aztec empire in 1521 (an

* A papal bull refers to a letters patent or charter issued by a pope: it is named after the *bulla* or leaden seal used to authenticate the document. Historically, papal bulls have been drawn up in order to authorise the Crusades, the Inquisition and rights to imperial expansion in certain regions of the world.

indigenous people) and the conquest of the territory now known as Mexico. He is also known for his relationship with an indigenous woman (from the Nahua peoples) named Malintzin (often referred to as 'La Malinche') who was both his translator and mistress. Often maligned for the role she played in bringing about the defeat of the Aztecs, she was branded a traitor by some: during the Mexican Revolution (1910–20), she was often depicted as an evil temptress. Her role as the mother of the hybrid peoples of mixed Spanish and indigenous origin who inhabit Mexico and the United States (Chicanos)* has been celebrated by Chicana feminists, such as Gloria Anzaldúa. Malintzin has been linked to the figure of the Virgin Mary, *La Llorona* (the folklore story of the woman weeping for lost children) and the brave Mexican *soldaderas* (women who fought beside men during the Mexican Revolution). While Malintzin became central to postcolonial writing and nationalist expressions of community, the explorer Cortez played a powerful role in imperial history by representing the New World in his letters to the Spanish court of Charles V. Other notable histories of Spanish conquest include that of Dominican friar, Bartolomé de las Casas, who described the violence of conquest in his *Brevísima relación de la destrucción de las Indias* (*A Short Account of the Destruction of the Indies*), written in 1542. While de las Casas's work presents a significant early critique of conquest, Bernal Díaz del Castillo's eyewitness account of the conquest of Mexico in 1632, *Historia verdadera de la conquista de la Nueva España* (*The True History of the Conquest of New Spain*) defends colonial efforts to serve God and acquire wealth.

France also undertook colonial initiatives during the sixteenth century, beginning with Jacques Cartier's voyages to Canada (as it is known today) between 1534 and 1542. Although accounts of his three voyages were published, the original manuscripts have been lost. Colonisation in 'New France' began at settlements in the eastern part of the country, including the founding of Québec in 1608. During this time, the French presence spread westwards to the Great

* For a discussion of hybridity, see Part Four: 'Cross-cultural Paradigms'.

Lakes and southwards to present-day New Orleans in Louisiana. The French also acquired holdings in the Caribbean basin, notably in Saint-Dominigue (modern day Haiti), Martinique, Guadeloupe and Guyane, and participated in the slave trade and the establishment of plantations. France's shifting territorial holdings during this period, including most notably the loss of control over the lands in Canada, were tied to interimperial histories of strife. For example, the Seven Years' War (1756–63) is often seen as the first global military conflict, involving the great powers (including France, England, Prussia and Spain) during this imperial era. The peace treaties ending the war resulted in the realignment of territorial control over colonial territories. France lost its holdings in Canada. Britain gained New France, Spanish Florida and some Caribbean holdings. Spain exchanged control over Spanish Florida for territorial control over lands west of Mississippi as well as regained control over Cuba and the Philippines. Such exchanges would leave their imprint on the cultures of the colonies, which often resulted in a deepening intermixture of languages, cultures and peoples.

The Rise of the British Empire

Britain's imperial history began closer to home than most, starting with English incursions into Ireland and intervention from the twelfth century onwards. Following the Battle of Kinsale in 1601, England established dominance over Ireland. In Ireland, English was introduced as the official language of government and indigenous economic and social systems were replaced by English ones. The English introduced its own ruling class of administrators who governed over or supplanted the pre-existing aristocracy or ruling figures. This imperial activity set a precedent and pattern for colonisation in more distant parts of the world, which would gradually expand to include holdings on five continents. At the height of its power and influence, the British Empire covered almost a quarter of the world's land surface as well as its population. Under James I, the Atlantic phase of imperial expansion (the 'first empire' or 'mercantile empire') began. In 1607, a colony was established in Jamestown, Virginia. The Atlantic empire encompassed parts of North America and the West Indies. The indigenous populations were overcome through battle or died as a result of contracting diseases from European settlers. Conflict with Spain played a central role with respect to colonial holdings during the seventeenth century. Islands such as Jamaica and Trinidad were taken over from the Spanish. The Seven Years' War, mentioned above, led to a British victory over the French and Spanish and resulted in an increasingly powerful role for Britain.

The Atlantic Slave Trade

The late seventeenth century saw the rise of the triangular Atlantic slave trade, which linked Britain, Africa and the Caribbean. Until 1807, when slave trading was outlawed, the transport of slaves from Africa to the Caribbean was central to the colonial endeavour. Slaves were transported to the Caribbean via the Middle Passage (so named because it was the middle leg of the triangular journey from Britain to Africa, from Africa to the Caribbean, and from the Caribbean to Britain) to labour on the plantations. The Treaty of Paris, following the Seven Years' War, confirmed Britain's role as the dominant imperial power in the Caribbean and North America until the American Revolution in 1775. This marked the demise of influence in the Atlantic region, but Britain soon turned its colonial efforts to other regions of the world.

Australia and New Zealand

The second phase of British imperialism was sparked by James Cook's three voyages of exploration between 1768 and 1799, which led to the colonisation of Australia and New Zealand. In his journals, he offers first-hand observations concerning peoples and places he encountered, including the coast of New Zealand, the east coast of Australia, and detailed descriptions of Tahiti, Tonga and previously unknown islands in the Pacific, such as the Hawaiian Islands. Cook asserted land claims in eastern Australia on the grounds that the area was *Terra nullus* (no man's land) despite the fact that indigenous peoples were already resident in the area. In 1788, Australia became a penal colony with the first transport of convicts and guards to Botany Bay. Following release from prison, convicts became landowners and settlers, establishing a new life. This marked the beginning of a long period of settlement as rebels, criminals and free settlers from England and Ireland came to New South Wales. In 1840, the Maori peoples and islands of modern-day New Zealand were also incorporated under British rule with the signing of the Treaty of Waitangi. During this time period, indigenous peoples were both marginalised and assimilated into settlements. As in North America, many indigenous peoples died as a result of exposure to diseases carried by British subjects. Others were economically disadvantaged and suffered as a result of British assumptions of racial supremacy. Britain's colonial intervention inevitably led to ongoing tensions and hostilities between settlers and indigenous peoples.

India

Elsewhere, in India, the English East India Company had been granted a charter in 1600, but it was not until the eighteenth century that Britain became the dominant European power in the region, extending its control to the subcontinent as well as Burma, Ceylon and parts of Malaysia. Whereas settlement had been the norm in earlier colonisation initiatives, the situation was quite different in South and East Asia. Most of the British peoples who came to the region did so under the employ of the East India Company. Missionaries introduced education, fostering an intermediary class between English-speaking persons and the local peoples. Nonetheless, colonial intervention profoundly changed the existing social structure. During the nineteenth century, the British administration associated with the East India Company gradually began to take over control of territories by invoking the 'doctrine of lapse' (when a ruler dies without a male heir apparent) or claiming that a territory was subject to misrule. In 1857–8, the 'Indian Mutiny' erupted as local peoples attempted to overthrow British rule. When the uprising was stifled, the East India Company's period of rule came to an end and direct rule by Britain was instituted, which was accompanied by the declaration of Queen Victoria as 'Empress of India'. India itself was referred to as the 'jewel in the crown' of the British Empire, which is indicative of its high worth as a colonial territory.

Africa

Certain European powers, such as France, Portugal and Britain, had settlements or protectorates in Africa prior to the nineteenth century, but the nineteenth century saw an unprecedented 'scramble for Africa' (generally referred to as taking place between 1881 and the First World War in 1914) as various European powers sought to gain control over parts of the continent. France gained control over regions of North and West Africa. Italy dominated parts of East Africa, including Somalia and Eritrea. Belgium came to dominate the Belgian Congo, Rwanda and Burundi. German protectorates were established in parts of East (modern-day Tanzania, Rwanda and Burundi, Kenya, and Mozambique), West (modern-day Cameroon and Togo), and South West Africa (modern-day Namibia and Botswana).

On Britain's part, the missionary, explorer and anti-slavery advocate, David Livingstone, offered accounts of his experiences in *Missionary Travels and Researches in South Africa* (1857) and *Narrative of an Expedition to the Zambezi and Its Tributaries* (1865). From the 1880s onwards, British settlement in Africa took on a new importance, as empire began to extend beyond smaller pre-existing settlements in areas such as Gambia, the Gold Coast and Sierra Leone. Egypt, Northern and Southern Rhodesia, Nyasaland, Nigeria and British East Africa came under British rule. The Second Boer War (1899–1902) resulted in the British defeat of the (colonial

Dutch) Afrikaners and the founding of the Union of South Africa. Colonial administration was introduced to oversee local rulers and political institutions. Through indirect rule, indigenous governments were transformed under empire. Cecil Rhodes, a mining magnate and politician who migrated to South Africa, defended British imperialism in his 'Confession of Faith' (1877) where he observed 'that we [the British] are the first race in the world and that the more of the world we inhabit the better it is for the human race'.[2] Rhodes went on to argue that the entire world would be better off under British rule as it would mean an end to all wars. Rhodes thus continued to uphold the imperial ideologies of domination underpinned by a confident faith in Britain's cultural and racial supremacy.

Rising Anti-Colonial Sentiment

By the end of the First World War, the British Empire extended over much of the world. Nonetheless, as the empire expanded, it was susceptible to disintegration from within, which heralded its eventual decline and dissolution. The early twentieth century saw the rise of anti-colonial sentiment and a growing resistance to imperial presence in the form of nationalist movements, labour unrest and anti-colonial protests. The formation of the Anti-Imperialist League (1898), the Indian Independence Movement, espousals of pan-African identity and the Negritude movement (a global movement for black solidarity and anti-colonial resistance in the 1930s), and the growing body of anti-colonialist writings contributed to a climate for change. Notably, we might consider the importance of texts such as W. E. B. Du Bois's *Souls of Black Folk* (1903); the writings of Mahatma Gandhi (a leading critic of colonisation in India and leader during the Indian Independence Movement); the work of the Harlem Renaissance (a movement in African American arts and letters during the 1920s and 1930s), which included figures such as Langston Hughes, Nella Larsen, Claude McKay and Zora Neale Hurston; Caribbean protest, exemplified in texts such as C. L. R. James's *The Black Jacobins*

(1938); and works of Negritude, such as Aimé Césaire's *Cahier d'un retour au pays natal* (*Notebook of a Return to My Native Land*, 1939). At the same time, European writing reflected a growing ambivalence about colonial rule, such as is found in the work of Joseph Conrad and E. M. Forster.* Finally, colonial migration and an emergent cosmopolitanism during the early part of the twentieth century contributed to alternative constructions of identity, negotiated by subjects circulating between metropolitan centres and colonial peripheries.

Post-war Independence Movements and Decolonisation

During the Second World War, British Prime Minister Winston Churchill and US President Franklin D. Roosevelt drew up the 1941 Atlantic Charter in which they declared that the signatories would 'respect the right of all peoples to choose the form of government under which they will live'. Although this declaration was intended to apply to the countries under Nazi occupation, it became a platform for postcolonial independence movements. Members of nationalist movements pointed out that after supporting a struggle against Nazism and fascism, they could not be expected to return to systems of government that were underpinned by white supremacist assumptions. Consequently, the post-war period brought with it a tremendous change in the world order; in the decades that followed, decolonisation movements would take place around the world.

Of course, there had been earlier examples of anti-colonial uprising and independence movements, such as the formation of the first black republic in Haiti (1804) and the American Declaration of Independence (1776), but these were the exception rather than the rule. In America, however, independence from British rule did not mean an end to colonial ideology or influence. The continued practices of slavery and the reliance on the plantation

* See Part Four: 'Postcolonial Reading Practices' and 'Race, Gender and Sexuality' for discussion of these texts.

economy of the South led eventually to Civil War and the abolition of slavery (1865), but the legacies of racism and colonial thinking continued to trouble American society, even after the colonial period. Similarly, Haiti's internal strife led to a massive multiracial exodus from the country, especially by those fearing violence. In the period following the revolution, Haiti endured efforts to reconquer the island (1825), economic isolationism, American occupation (1915–34), and other forms of imperialist intervention and hostility.

Like Haiti and America, many anti-colonial struggles around the world in the post-war era entailed uprisings and revolution, war and ongoing liberation struggles. The Viet Minh quest for independence and the Anti-French Resistance War (1946–54), the Cuban Revolution (1959) and the Algerian War (1954–62) are among but a few examples of violent transition to independence. The 1955 Bandung Conference, led by Jawaharlal Nehru for India, Gamal Abdel Nasser for Egypt and Josip Broz Tito for Yugoslavia served as a catalyst for postcolonial solidarity among nations and colonised peoples. Delegates from twenty-nine countries, representing over half the world's population, participated in the conference, which led to the creation of the Non-Aligned Movement in 1961. In 1966, the Organisation of Solidarity with the People of Asia, Africa and Latin America (Organización de Solidaridad con los Pueblos de Asia, África y América Latina or OSPAAAL) was founded in Cuba with the stated purpose of fighting globalisation, imperialism and neoliberalism as well as defending human rights. The Tricontinental Conference involved delegates from Guinea, the Congo, South Africa, Angola, Vietnam, Syria, North Korea, the Palestine Liberation Organisation, Cuba, Puerto Rico, Chile and the Dominican Republic. One of the main purposes of the organisation, still in existence at the time of writing, is to promote the causes of freedom fighters in the Third World.

Notably, the political struggles and writings of Frantz Fanon served as sources of inspiration for liberation movements. Fanon's emphasis on decolonisation was already evident in *Black Skin, White*

Masks (1952), which examines the psychic effects of colonial subjugation. However, it was the Algerian struggles to overthrow French imperialism which inspired him to write *Les damnés de la terre* (*The Wretched of the Earth*), published in 1961. This book explores the impact of colonial violence, advocates the overthrow of colonial power by violent means if necessary, and sets out a framework for decolonisation. The text offers a critique of nationalism and imperialism, which includes discussions of mental health and the role of intellectuals in revolutionary situations. His discussion of the role of language as a means to mould the 'natives' is especially interesting for literary critics, as is his assessment of the importance of a national literature. Fanon's work would later influence the political thought and action of leaders around the world, including Ali Shariati in Iran, Steve Biko in South Africa, Malcolm X in the United States and Ernesto Che Guevara in Cuba.

Postcolonial America: Civil Rights and Postcolonial Writing

As we have already seen, America's multicultural, multiracial composition reflects the influence of overlapping imperialisms, particularly through English, French and Spanish presences, which were accompanied by the emergence of Creole culture, Chicano identities and anxieties around borderlands in the United States (see Part Four: 'Cross-cultural Paradigms'). Decolonisation in the United States began with Independence and the abolition of slavery, but many of the civil, legal and ideological changes took place in the post-war period in an effort to continue the unfinished work of decolonisation. In the Southern states, the introduction of Jim Crow laws (1876–1965)* was based on the claims of separate but equal status. In reality, these laws institutionalised racism as well as racial

* The Jim Crow laws were named after 'Jump Jim Crow', a song-and-dance caricature of African Americans performed in 'blackface' by white actor Thomas D. Rice in the nineteenth century, in order to mock African American peoples. This pejorative term was subsequently applied to laws of racial segregation instituted in many Southern states.

segregation, ensuring the ongoing disenfranchisement of African Americans living under these laws. The civil rights movement successfully challenged and overturned these racist laws. In 1954, state-sponsored school segregation was declared unconstitutional by the Supreme Court of the United States in the famous *Brown v Board of Education* case. The remaining Jim Crow laws were overruled by the Civil Rights Act of 1964 and the Voting Rights Act of 1965. Decolonisation within America was accompanied by violent incidents, such as the bombing of the Street Baptist Church in Birmingham, Alabama in 1963, the assassinations of Malcolm X in 1965 while he was speaking at the Organisation of Afro-American Unity, and black civil rights leader, Martin Luther King, Jr in 1968. Challenges to racism are evident in works of literature during this era, notably in life writings such as Malcolm X's *The Autobiography of Malcolm X* (1965) and Maya Angelou's *I Know Why the Caged Bird Sings* (1969). In the decades that followed, black women's writing, such as Alice Walker's *The Color Purple* (1982) and Toni Morrison's *Beloved* (1987),* explores the legacies of violence and slavery through fictions about the historical past.

African American efforts inspired the Chicano civil rights movement as well as Asian American writers and other marginalised ethnic communities to express their vision of postcolonial society. The Chicano civil rights movement of the 1960s and 1970s, known as *El Movimiento* (The Movement), addressed concerns about land grants, farm workers' rights, education, voting and political rights and the need to reclaim a collective history. Rodolfo 'Corky' Gonzales's poem entitled 'Yo Soy Joaquín' (1967) refers to America's failure to honour the provisions of the 1848 Treaty of Hidalgo at the conclusion of the American–Mexican War, which protected land grants and guaranteed civil rights. This multilingual epic poem celebrates hybrid Chicano identities, which are neither indigenous nor European, neither Mexican nor American, but a combination of all these facets. In the decades that followed, Chicana feminists

* For a discussion of Morrison's work, see Part Three: 'Magic Realism and Folklore in the Postcolonial Novel'.

would consider not only ethnic discrimination but also issues of gender oppression. Mirta Vidal, Anna Nieto Gomez, Martha Cotera, Gloria Anzaldúa and Cherríe Moraga are among some of the leading figures in this movement. Meanwhile, Asian Americans consider the ways in which racism has perpetuated the marginalisation of Chinese and other Asian members of the nation. Amy Tan's essay, entitled 'Mother Tongue' (1990), examines the many 'Englishes' upon which the author draws in order to express herself. Like Chicano writers, Tan finds that the self cannot be expressed merely through standard English. Writers such as Maxine Hong Kingston and David Henry Hwang set out to subvert Orientalist stereotypes,* but some critics, notably Frank Chin, suggest that their works reinforce racial and cultural stereotypes. In the work of all of these communities of writers, we see a profound commitment to dismantling imperialist discourses of identity and rewriting history from the perspective of the marginalised and oppressed. At the same time, authors offer contested and varied responses to the rich world of the postcolonial imaginary.

Postcolonial India and the Partition Novel

Postcolonial transitions are often challenging. Nineteen forty-seven marks the withdrawal of Britain from India and the partition of India into the sovereign states of the Dominion of Pakistan (later Islamic Republic of Pakistan and People's Republic of Bangladesh) and the secular Union of India (later Republic of India). More than ten million people from the former British Indian Empire were displaced. Violence erupted between Hindus, Muslims and Sikhs, resulting in a significant number of deaths. The dismantling of colonial rule was accompanied by dislocation and division along religious lines, producing a situation of conflict, which has led to

* For a discussion of Hong Kingston, see also Part Three: 'Magic Realism and Folklore in the Postcolonial Novel' and for Hwang, Part Three: 'Performing Race, Gender and Sexuality'. See Part Four: 'Postcolonial Reading Practices', for a discussion of Orientalism.

enduring tensions. Responses to these events have led to the emergence of a new novelistic genre, namely, the Partition Novel, which is written in various languages from the subcontinent, including English, Bengali and Urdu. In English, Khushwant Singh's *Train to Pakistan* (1956), Manohar Malgonkar's *A Bend in the Ganges* (1964), Salman Rushdie's *Midnight's Children* (1981)* and Amitav Ghosh's *The Shadow Lines* (1988) are some of the most famous examples of this novelistic genre.

The Rise of Multiracial, Multicultural Britain

In Britain, the Caribbean poet and folklorist Louise Bennett bore witness to the process of 'colonisation in reverse' as colonial subjects migrated to Britain and began to challenge and transform prevailing assumptions about race, culture and the nation. Nineteen forty-eight was a particularly noteworthy year, which saw the arrival of the SS *Empire Windrush* at Tilbury Docks in Essex. Bearing 492 male passengers from the West Indies, *Windrush* has come to symbolise the rise of multiracial, multicultural Britain. Sam Selvon's *The Lonely Londoners* (1956) offers a representative view of the lives of these men as they struggled to settle into a less than welcoming 'Mother Country'. Nonetheless, Selvon offers a rather optimistic view of the possibilities for social transformation as compared to the next generations of writers who confront the openly racist elements in society.

The 1960s to 1980s would see incidents of overt resistance to migration and racism. In 1968, Enoch Powell's 'Rivers of Blood Speech' represented the views of a certain proportion of the British population who were openly resistant and hostile to migration. A decade later, in 1979, Margaret Thatcher was accused by some of tapping into and exacerbating racial tensions when she discussed fears about New Commonwealth immigrants swamping Britain. Political standpoints such as these, it was sometimes argued, reflected and it

* For a discussion of Rushdie's work, see Part Three: 'Magic Realism and Folklore in the Postcolonial Novel'.

could be said to some extent influenced some of the racist attitudes in wider society, which were reinforced through incidents of police brutality and racially motivated policing activities. The 'sus' (suspicion) laws from the nineteenth century were revived; police specifically targetting black men and bringing them into custody. Linton Kwesi Johnson's anti-sus poem, entitled 'Sonny's Lettah', highlights the ways in which racism continues to produce situations of violence and injustice in British society, particularly for black men. Hanif Kureishi's *My Beautiful Laundrette* (1985)* offers a similarly bleak view of racism in Britain through its representation of interracial tensions, but it also offers a counter-revolutionary presentation of multiracial Britain through a mixed race, homosexual love affair.

Black British women's writing, especially since the 1990s, has confronted the legacies of double colonisation, highlighting the ways in which women suffer from gender and racial oppression. Buchi Emecheta, Andrea Levy, Zadie Smith and Bernardine Evaristo are among those who give voice to the Black British experience from a feminine perspective. Asian British perspectives emerge not only with Kureishi but also through the work of Monica Ali, Hari Kunzru, Meera Syal and Nadeem Aslam. Many of their fictions explore the sense of dislocation associated not only with the colonial past but also the contemporary postcolonial order.

Postcolonial Writing in the Anglophone Caribbean and Beyond

Decolonisation within the Caribbean occured in a highly uneven manner in the post-war period. While Jamaica gained independence in 1962, Antigua did not claim its post-colonial status until 1981. The transition to the postcolonial era has been especially challenging here. Many of the islands are dependent on tourism, which is often accompanied by an intense awareness of economic disjuncture. Trevor Rhone's 1976 film *Smile Orange* and Jamaica Kincaid's *A*

* For a discussion of Kureishi's work, see Part Three: 'Performing Race, Gender and Sexuality'.

Small Place (1988)* are good examples of works that critique the tourist's assumptions about the Caribbean. As a result of political and socio-economic instabilities, many Caribbean writers have migrated out of the region and live in Britain, the United States or Canada. In Britain, Sam Selvon (Trinidad), George Lamming (Barbados), V. S. Naipaul (Trinidad), Linton Kwesi Johnson (Jamaica) and Caryl Phillips (St Kitts) are among the many who migrated to its shores. The United States is or has been home to writers from Cuba (Reinaldo Arenas and Gustavo Perez Fírmat), Jamaica (Kwame Dawes), the Dominican Republic (Junot Díaz and Julia Alvarez), Puerto Rico (Giannina Braschi), St Lucia (Derek Walcott), Antigua (Jamaica Kincaid) and Barbados (Kamau Brathwaite).† Canada has a similarly rich community of writers, including figures such as Dionne Brand, Nalo Hopkinson, Austin Clarke, Makeda Silvera, Shani Mootoo and Lillian Allen. The work of these writers is extremely diverse, reflecting generational differences, and varied approaches to sexual politics and language.

Indigenous Perspectives: Rewriting the Land and its Peoples

In Canada, the United States, New Zealand and Australia, the diverse claims of indigenous peoples have resulted in a richly varied body of literature, reflecting the particularities of culture, geography and colonial relations. To offer a specific example, we will turn briefly to the case of Canada where the term First Nations refers to indigenous peoples who are neither Inuit nor Métis (mixed race, Indian and Francophone Canadian). There are over 600 recognised governments or bands of First Nations peoples. While much of the literature sustains oral storytelling and song traditions, the history of literary

* For a discussion of Kincaid's writing, see Part Three: 'Novels of Exile and Ambivalence'.

† For a discussion of V. S. Naipaul's fiction see Part Three: 'Novels of Exile and Ambivalence'. See Part Three: 'The Transnational Short Story Cycle' for a discussion of Díaz's short stories and Part Three: 'Decolonising the Stage' for a discussion of Walcott's theatre. For a discussion of Brathwaite's poetry, see Part Three: 'Post-colonial to Post-9/11 Poetics'.

production has shifted from anti-colonial protest in the 1970s to life writing and other narratives that reclaim history from an indigenous perspective. Daniel David Moses, a poet and playwright, often focuses on the exploration of historical representation in his work. For instance, in *Almighty Voice and His Wife* (1991), Moses subverts the stereotypical image of the tragic Indian by retelling the history of a nineteenth-century Saskatchewan Cree folk hero from two divergent perspectives: one part is naturalistic while the other offers a parodic vaudeville show that undermines the expectations and assumptions of a white audience. Métis literature tends to focus on the historical legacies of this racially mixed peoples and the quest for a homeland. For example, Maria Campbell's *Halfbreed* (1973) focuses on the life of a racially mixed narrator who addresses a reader, presumably white Canadian, who knows little about her people's history. Jordan Wheeler's *Brothers in Arms* (1989) explores gender and sexuality in connection with Mohawk and Métis identity. Louis Riel, a poet and hero of the Métis people, often figures in literature, including works such as Deon Gutteridge's *Riel: A Poem for Voices* (1968), which brings history, myth and poetry together.

While matters concerning civil rights have been addressed, land claims and issues of territoriality continue to be of importance for indigenous peoples in North America, Australia and New Zealand. Colonisation in all of these places was accompanied by the appropriation of land, especially in favour of gaining control over water, grazing areas and other natural resources. In the United States, the Indian Claims Commission was established in 1946 to hear claims of Indian tribes against the United States; it was especially concerned with claims for monetary compensation for appropriated lands. In Canada, the Office of Native Claims was created in 1974. In Australia, the Aboriginal Land Rights Act was passed in 1976, but it was not until 1992 that the High Court of Australia declared that the previous legal concept of Australia as a *Terra nullius* (no man's land or unoccupied territory prior to colonisation) to be invalid. In 1998, the New Zealand Parliament apologised to the Ngai Tahu for injustices dating back to the 1840 Treaty of Waitangi and offered compensation.

In light of these ongoing concerns about the relation to the land, it is especially noteworthy that the Assembly of the First Nations and the National Congress of Indians recognised a cross-border sense of unity with the 1999 'Declaration of Kinship and Cooperation Among Indigenous Peoples and Nations of North America'. Among its aims, this declaration protects and promotes the right of citizens to move freely across the border of Canada and the United States while retaining full recognition of their status as members of indigenous nations.

Colonial Legacies and Postcolonial Transition in Nigeria and South Africa

Finally, we might consider the situation of Africa. Given the emphasis on the literature of Nigeria and South Africa in this volume, we might contrast the situations of these two very different nations. The territory of modern-day Nigeria brings together the histories of diverse precolonial peoples, cultures and kingdoms, including the Nok people of central Nigeria, the Hausa of Northern Nigeria, the Fulani, the Yoruba kingdoms and the Igbo peoples as well as the associated Kingdom of Nri. Through Atlantic trade, the Portuguese and Spanish as well as British empires had longstanding relations with the coastal peoples of Nigeria during the colonial era. In 1885, Britain's control over the area of Nigeria was recognised by European powers; in 1886, the Royal Niger Company was established. In 1901, Nigeria became a British protectorate and remained under British rule until 1960 when independence was declared. In the post-colonial era, the cultural and political differences between Nigeria's dominant ethnicities, the Hausa ('Northerners'), Igbo ('Easterners') and Yoruba ('Westerners'), created tensions within the newly formed nation. In May 1967, the Eastern Region declared itself an independent state, called the Republic of Biafra. In July 1967, the Nigerian Civil War erupted as the Nigerian side attacked the newly declared Biafran State. By the time the war ended almost three years later in January 1970, more than one million people had died. In the years that followed Nigeria endured military dictatorships, *coups d'état* and counter coups, interrupted only by a short-lived return to democratic government (1979–83), until 1999, when democracy was once again instituted. Nonetheless, the need to address government corruption and institute electoral reforms has been a subject of discussion in recent years. Writers in Nigeria and abroad have responded to this turbulent postcolonial history and/or sought to reconstruct Nigerian history in resistance to colonialist discourses. Among Nigeria's many noteworthy authors, we might consider the work of Wole Soyinka, Chinua Achebe, Ken Saro-Wiwa, Buchi Emecheta, Elechi Amadi, Ben Okri, Chris Abani and Chimamanda Ngozi Adichie.*

South Africa, which had been a self-governing British colony since 1910, attained full independence as a republic in 1961. However, the post-colonial era did not mark a transition towards decolonisation in the form of dismantling colonial ideologies. Instead, South Africa persisted in its adoption of apartheid (an Afrikaans word meaning 'separation'), a form of government that legally instituted racial segregation and white supremacist laws in 1948. Apartheid protected white minority interests and disenfranchised all others. From 1948 until the end of apartheid in 1993, South Africa discriminated against and oppressed all non-white persons, relying on discriminatory laws, forced displacement, confinement, torture, massacre and other forms of domination. In many ways, we can see this racist society as an extension of colonial rule, which had favoured segregation and introduced laws limiting the freedom of the black population since the nineteenth century.† During this era, the work of writers such as

* For a discussion of Soyinka's theatre, see Part Three: 'Decolonising the Stage', and Adichie's short stories, see Part Three: 'The Transnational Short Story Cycle'.

† Earlier examples of discriminatory legislation in South Africa include: the Franchise and Ballot Act of 1892 placing limits on black education and other aspects of life; the Natal Legislative Assembly Bill of 1894 depriving Indians of the right to vote; the General Pass Regulations Bill of 1905, which denied blacks the vote altogether, and limited them to fixed areas; the Asiatic Registration Act of 1906 requiring all Indians to register and carry passes; and the South Africa Act of 1910, which enfranchised whites, giving them complete political control over all other race groups and removing the right of blacks to sit in parliament.

Bessie Head, Alex la Guma and Dennis Brutus[*] attests to the devastating effects of racial oppression, and finds expression in resistance to apartheid and/or its underlying ideologies. Notably, all three writers were forced to flee the country to escape oppression and the threat of confinement. Drawing on his personal experiences, La Guma's *The Stone Country* (1967) depicts the horrors of prison life in South Africa while *In the Fog of the Seasons' End* (1972) tells the history of underground resistance, recounts the events of the Sharpeville Massacre, and highlights the urgent need for revolution. Protest against apartheid emerges in the poetry of Dennis Brutus who was imprisoned for his resistance to the apartheid government and (like La Guma) forced to flee the country. For another perspective, Nelson Mandela's *Long Walk to Freedom* (1995) offers an autobiographical account of life under apartheid and a vision of post-apartheid transition. White South African writing can also be seen as participating in the wider work of challenging apartheid and examining the possibilities for decolonisation in the post-apartheid era. In this context, the work of J. M. Coetzee,[†] Nadine Gordimer and Ingrid de Kok, among others, is especially worth noting.

Postcolonial Horizons: Neoimperialism and Globalisation

While colonialism has come to an end and decolonisation remains ongoing, we might consider what the future of postcolonial literary studies holds. With the collapse of the Berlin Wall in 1989 and the intensification of globalisation since the 1990s, some argue that we are moving into a new era of imperialism.[‡] The flows of capital, peoples and goods around the world and the general tendency to transnational relations of power, negotiated on multiple scales, suggest a new kind

* For a discussion of Brutus's poetry, see Part Three: 'Post-colonial to Post-9/11 Poetics'.

† For a discussion of Coetzee's novels, see Part Three: 'Novels of Exile and Ambivalence'.

‡ See Part Four: 'Postcoloniality in a Globalising World' for a discussion of globalisation.

of approach to spatial governance that is no longer allied with the centre-periphery model of the colonial era. Yet, even in this afterlife of empire, postcolonial writers and critics continue to grapple with the dynamics of decolonisation, which are now complicated by the influence of neoimperial intervention as well as the more diffuse sense of interimperial forms of governance and oppression.

From an economic perspective, the role of the International Monetary Fund and the World Bank have served to complicate postcolonial transition for many former colonies, leaving them with crippling debts and severely constraining the possibilities for self-determination. More generally, the conditions of inequality that characterised colonial rule have made it difficult – nearly impossible in some cases – for post-colonial countries to gain an equal standing in the global economy. Anti-globalisation critics and movements call attention to the ways in which wealthy Western countries maintain a powerful presence in developing countries, exploiting natural resources and local labour forces. Particularly interesting in this regard is the documentary film *Life and Debt* (2001), which traces the impact of global financial institutions on life in Jamaica. Similarly, Arundhati Roy's *The God of Small Things* (1997) offers a compelling fictional representation of globalisation as a new form of imperialism.

Themes of exile and migration are evident in contemporary works of fiction, which move beyond the concerns of the diasporic community* or (post)colonial migration to consider transnational identity more generally. Michael Ondaatje's *Anil's Ghost* (2000) features a globe-trotting forensic specialist, Anil Tissera, who returns to her native land to investigate human rights concerns in Sri Lanka and inadvertently sets into motion further incidents of state-sponsored violence as a response to her inquiry. Caryl Phillips's *A Distant Shore* (2003) examines the role of the refugee

* The term 'diaspora' (meaning dispersion) initially referred to the scattering of Jewish peoples as a result of several forced expulsions from what is now known as Israel, Jordan and parts of Lebanon as well as the State of Palestine. Subsequently, 'diaspora' has come to refer more generally to the movement, migration or scattering of a people away from a settled location or ancestral homeland.

and racism in contemporary British society. Jhumpa Lahiri's *Unaccustomed Earth* (2008) and Junot Díaz's *The Brief Wondrous Life of Oscar Wao* (2007)[*] focus on characters whose lives can only be understood through dynamic explorations of transnational relations in America. Zadie Smith's *On Beauty* (2005) and Hari Kunzru's *Transmission* (2004) explore the connections between globalisation and the lives of the marginalised (see Part Four: 'Postcoloniality in a Globalising World'). All of these works also place emphasis on the persistence of postcolonial perspectives, especially with respect to an identity politics that takes into account the interplay of race/ethnicity, gender, class, age and sexuality.[†]

Post-9/11 fictions highlight the ways in which colonialist modes of thinking continue to trouble and influence cultural relations and power dynamics in a globalising world. Edwidge Danticat's *Brother, I'm Dying* (2007),[‡] explores the connections between American imperialism past and present through its interventions in Haiti and current migration policies. The poetry of Kamau Brathwaite and Meena Alexander[§] explores the connections between the events of 9/11 and imperial dislocation, whether in the form of violent episodes in history or cultural migration. Works such as Ed Husain's *The Islamist* (2007) and Ayaan Hirsi Ali's *Infidel* (2008) challenge prevailing Western misconceptions about Islamic and Muslim identities. Khaled Hosseini's *A Thousand Splendid Suns* (2007) and *The Kite Runner* (2003) explore the ways in which transnational migration and identity are shaped by shifting relations to the global order, especially through the presence of the Taliban in Afghanistan. Kamila Shamsie's *Burnt Shadows* (2009) explores relations among traumatic events such as the bombing of Nagasaki, the Partition of

* For a discussion of Lahiri's and Díaz's short stories, see Part Three: 'The Transnational Short Story Cycle'.

† For more on this topic, see Part Four: 'Race, Gender and Sexuality'.

‡ For a discussion of Danticat's work, see Part Three: 'The Transnational Short Story Cycle'.

§ For a discussion of Brathwaite's and Alexander's poetry, see Part Three: 'Postcolonial to Post-9/11 Poetics'.

India and the events of 9/11. H. M. Naqvi's *Home Boy: A Novel* (2009) offers a comically rendered depiction of the Pakistani migrant experience in New York after the cataclysmic event of 9/11. In summary, postcolonial literature and critical perspectives continue to challenge the legacies of empire with respect to our conceptions of identity, nationhood, transnational and interimperial relations, and governance.

Notes

1 For a helpful definition of decolonisation, see Bill Ashcroft, Gareth Griffiths and Helen Tiffin (eds), *Post-Colonial Studies: The Key Concepts* (London: Routledge, 1998), pp. 63–7.

2 Cited by Bernard Magubane in *The Making of a Racist State: British Imperialism and the Union of South Africa: 1875–1910* (Eritrea: Africa World Press, 1996), p. 102.

Part Three
Texts, Writers and Contexts

Magic Realism and Folklore in the Postcolonial Novel: Rushdie, Hong Kingston and Morrison

Magic realism emerged in the twentieth century as a powerful literary mode: a way to think through and beyond prevailing realities in order to untangle and 'seize the mystery that breathes behind things'.[1] This literary form has played a significant role in postcolonial writing, enabling authors to express political realities in phantasmagorical ways and articulate horizons beyond colonialism and its legacies. According to *The Oxford Dictionary of Literary Terms*, magic realism is defined as follows:

> A kind of modern fiction in which fabulous and fantastical events are included in a narrative that otherwise maintains the 'reliable' tone of objective realistic report ... designating a tendency of the modern novel to reach beyond the confines of realism and draw upon the energies of fable, folktale, and myth while maintaining a strong contemporary social relevance.[2]

A novel written in the mode of magic realism contains fantastic attributes and elements; for instance, a character might exhibit supernatural abilities, such as flight, levitation, telepathic communication or transformation into another form. An excellent example of magic realism can be found in Alejo Carpentier's *The*

Kingdom of this World (*El reino de este mundo*, 1949) which offers an account of the Haitian Revolution. One of the main characters, Mackandal, an escaped slave,* gains the ability to transform himself into various beings (such as bird, fish or insect) as well as to fly, through his communion with African diasporic gods of voudou.† When he is finally captured, the slaves believe that he escapes death by flight. Thus, he provides a link between the histories of revolution and spirituality, or the sacred and the profane in Western terms. Magic realism can serve many purposes: it may elicit a space reflective of cultural diversity, transgress national and cultural boundaries, destabilise normative (standard) assumptions or Eurocentric notions about the world, and foster new ways of apprehending the realities of the present as well as histories of the past, especially as they impinge on the present. In our modern postcolonial era, authors such as Salman Rushdie, Toni Morrison, Maxine Hong Kingston, Isabel Allende, Laura Esquivel, Nalo Hopkinson and Ben Okri are among the many writers who continue to work in this literary mode.

The German art critic Franz Roh introduced the term 'magical realism' in *Nach-Expressionismus, Magischer Realismus* ('Post-expressionism, magical realism') (1925) in order to describe a new kind of painterly aesthetic that arose during the Weimar Republic, which he saw as characterised by its emphasis on the material

* The real François Mackandal (spelled variously) was a maroon (fugitive slave) who escaped from the plantation and went on to become a leader of the resistance to slavery. In 1757, he was captured while carrying out a mass poisoning of whites when he was betrayed by a female slave. Although this attempt to overthrow slavery failed, Mackandal is seen as an important forerunner who prophesied and inspired the Haitian Revolution of 1791–1804, which resulted in the founding of the first black republic.

† The term 'diaspora' (meaning dispersion) initially referred to the scattering of Jewish peoples as a result of several forced expulsions from what is now known as Israel, Jordan and parts of Lebanon as well as the State of Palestine. Subsequently, 'diaspora' has come to refer more generally to the movement, migration or scattering of a people away from a settled location or ancestral homeland. Voudou (or voodoo) is a version of African religious beliefs and practices that developed among slave populations in the West Indies (especially Haiti) and Southern states of America.

object.* In 1927, chapters concerning magic realism were translated into Spanish, appearing as *Realismo mágico. Post-expresionismo: Problemas de la pintura europa mas reciente*, and subsequently had a tremendous influence on the development of Latin American fiction. In this spirit of Roh's analysis, Venezuelan writer Arturo Uslar-Pietri, who wrote magic realist stories during the 1930s and 40s, emphasised the mystery of life and saw magic realism as part of the tradition of experimental and vanguard writing in the New World. Carpentier's *The Kingdom of This World*, as we have seen, contains elements of magic realism, although he adapted the idea as the basis for a literary mode he referred to as 'marvellous realism' (*lo realismo marvailloso*) in his essays. For Carpentier, the improbable juxtapositions and marvellous mixtures of the literary mode were grounded in the Caribbean and 'Latin America's varied history, geography, demography, and politics'.[3] Marvellous realism can be seen as related to but distinct from magic realism through its emphasis on the mixture of differing worldviews and approaches to what constitutes reality from a transcultural perspective.† The development of postcolonial writing in Latin America and the Caribbean from the latter half of the twentieth century onwards, notably in Gabriel García Márquez's *One Hundred Years of Solitude* (*El cien años de soledad*, 1967)‡ can be seen as significantly influenced by the migration and transculturation of aesethetic ideas. Magic realism became a literary mode for articulating the New World and paved the way for other postcolonial articulations.

Maggie Ann Bowers claims that literary magic realism is frequently 'set in a postcolonial context and written from a postcolonial

* Magical realism was used to describe the work of artists such as Max Beckman, Conrad Felixmuller, Georges Grosz, Otto Dix and Christian Schad. These painters were also seen as part of an artistic movement known as *Neue Sachlichkeit* (New Objectivity) during the Weimar Republic (1919–33) in Germany, an era of liberal democracy noted for artistic experimentation and creative exuberance.

† Transculturalism expresses the extension of ideas across many (or all) cultures.

‡ *One Hundred Years of Solitude* tells the story of seven generations of the Buendía Family in the town of Macondo. This family epic offers an allegorical account of the history of Columbia. Throughout the novel, the characters are visited by ghosts who highlight the ways in which the past continues to inhabit the present.

perspective that challenges the assumptions of an authoritative colonialist attitude'.[4] Elleke Boehmer emphasises the political dimensions of postcolonial magic realism when she observes:

> Drawing on the special effects of magic realism, postcolonial writers in English are able to express their view of a world fissured, distorted, and made incredible by cultural displacement ... [T]hey combine the supernatural with local legend and imagery derived from colonialist cultures to represent societies which have been repeatedly unsettled by invasion, occupation, and political corruption. Magic effects, therefore are used to indict the follies of both empire and its aftermath.[5]

Magic realism draws on vernacular tradition or the beliefs, customs, idioms and culture of a local people. By introducing alternative cultural traditions and perspectives, the genre resists and even subverts a monolithic, Western colonial outlook on the world and events in history. Moreover, the genre can play a powerful role in the processes of decolonisation through its reliance on vernacular traditions as the basis for the articulation of conditions and perspectives that go beyond the hegemony (dominance) of empire and its legacies. Stephen Slemon suggests that the constant tension between the magical and the real gives expression to the uneven dynamics at work in (post)colonial societies, particularly the gaps and disjunctions between coloniser/colonised perspectives.[6] Through the inclusion of magical elements, the narrative recuperates fragments of culture and gives voice to forgotten or subsumed histories.[7]

Ben Okri's *The Famished Road* (1991), for example, draws on Yoruba culture and oral storytelling traditions in order to recount the history of Nigeria's transition to independence. The road to nationhood is told through the life history of Azaro, an *abiku*, a spirit-child who is destined to die in infancy and be reborn to the same mother over and over again. Through the life of the *abiku*, Okri is able to move between material and spiritual planes, blending myth and reality. In choosing to live, Azaro accepts the difficult challenge of confronting the colonial past and neocolonial present. As this example shows, the adaptation of oral storytelling traditions or folklore can serve to introduce repressed or marginalised aspects of culture as well as to call attention to the long histories of cultural survival and resistance to domination.[8] The magic at work in these traditions thus serves to incorporate a more comprehensive, inclusive representation of the historical and current realities of a given society. The emphasis on the specificity of culturally derived magical and socio-political as well as economic contexts, which underpins postcolonial magic realism, enables the tradition to be renewed through the writer's own vernacular traditions and (post)colonial contexts. In so doing, the narrative offers a more expansive and inclusive account of history and transcultural formation, which takes into account the experiences, perspectives and beliefs of those who have been colonised.

Authors such as Rushdie, Morrison and Hong Kingston have adapted magic realism to suit their own poetico-political purposes, introducing new elements in terms of both form and content. Where Carpentier and Márquez created a transcultural Latin American tradition, Rushdie, Morrison and Hong Kingston have contributed to the articulation of magic realism in the context of (post)colonial transcultural, multicultural and transnational contexts, specifically in the histories of Indian/Pakistani/British (Rushdie), African American (Morrison) and Chinese American (Hong Kingston) identity formation. Through the incorporation of diverse, often contested voices and perspectives, their work can be read at the interface of a postmodern conception of history, which places emphasis on 'the lack of absolute historical truth and casts doubt over the existence of fact by indicating its link with narrative and stories'.[9] Salman Rushdie observes that the events of history are open to interpretation because facts are hard to establish, which leads him to conclude that '[r]eality is built on prejudices, misconceptions and ignorance as well as on our perceptions and knowledge'.[10] Ludic (or playful) narrative techniques, such as metafictional perspectives and other postmodern literary devices, complement the author's efforts to articulate a more encompassing and inclusive sense of the postcolonial experience.

Salman Rushdie: Towards a Hybrid World*

Salman Rushdie's claim that '[u]nreality is the only weapon with which reality can be smashed, so that it may subsequently be reconstructed' is indicative of the revolutionary potential of his approach to magic realism.[11] Born in Bombay (now Mumbai), India, in 1947, the year of India's partition and independence, the family joke was that Rushdie's birth had prompted the British to withdraw from India. Rushdie was educated in England at Rubgy School and at Cambridge University. He lived in England until 2000, aside from a brief stay in Pakistan (1968), then moved to New York. The experience of growing up in India and England profoundly shaped his worldview and writing, which often explores imperial relations, East–West dynamics and transnational experience more generally. Rushdie is well known for the 1989 *fatwa* – in which the Ayatollah Khomeini demanded his execution for blasphemy, following the publication of *The Satanic Verses* (1988) – as well as for his prodigious literary output, which includes works such as *Grimus* (1975), *Midnight's Children* (1981), *Haroun and the Sea of Stories* (1990), *The Ground Beneath Her Feet* (1999), *Shalimar the Clown* (2005) and *Luka and the Fire of Life* (2010). Rushdie's oeuvre ranges across the modes and genres of speculative fiction, fantasy, epic and magic realism, taking inspiration from world literary figures, such as Márquez, Franz Kafka, Nikolai Gogol† and Günther Grass, as well as folklore traditions. Preoccupied by the ways in which macrocosmic political tensions and conflicts 'are played out microcosmically in the

* For more on the notion of hybridity, see Part Four: 'Cross-cultural Paradigms'.

† Gogol (1809–52) was a Ukrainian-born Russian author noted for his humorous and satirical fictions, such as a short story entitled 'The Nose', which tells the tale of a St Petersburg official whose nose leaves his face and develops a life of its own.

lives of his central characters',* Rushdie has brought magic realism to bear on various scales of postcolonial experience, including conceptions of time and history as well as space, whether embodied by the village, the nation, empire or the globalising world order.[12]

Rushdie's acclaimed novel *Midnight's Children* draws on magic realism as a means to narrate the birth and decolonisation of the post-independence nation, specifically, post-colonial India. The novel can be seen as realistic in its precise emphasis on the moment of the protagonist's birth in Bombay at the stroke of midnight on 15 August 1947, a moment that corresponds to India's independence from Britain. It also shows attentiveness to key events in the history of the nation, including the Bombay language marches (1956), the Indo-Chinese war (1962), the death of Nehru (1964), the Indo-Pakistani wars of 1965 and 1971, and the first Prime Ministership of Indira Gandhi (1966–77). However, it is magical in its embodiment and narration of history. Saleem Sinai is one among 1,001 magical children born at the midnight hour whose fates are linked to that of the nation: 'the children of midnight were also the children of the time: fathered ... by history ... in a country which is itself a sort of dream'.[13] The children possess diverse magical skills or attributes, such as the power to change sex at will, the ability to transform into a werewolf, the capacity to walk through mirrors, and an incredible beauty that blinds the beholder. Through the pairing and opposition of Saleem (a name that means 'peaceful') and Shiva (associated with destruction),† characters who are born at the stroke of midnight and then swapped with one another, the novel dramatises the tensions, debates and conflicts of the nation. While Saleem's telepathic abilities can be seen as placing emphasis on communication and dialogue,

* Macrocosm and microcosm are terms used to refer to events that take place on large and small scales, respectively. In this case, we can see that international and national tensions, anxieties and struggles are also played out in the ordinary lives of individuals.

† The Hindu god Shiva is the third in a triumvirate that includes Brahma and Vishnu. Brahma is the creator of the universe while Vishnu is the preserver of it. Shiva's role is to destroy the universe in order to re-create it. Thus, Shiva is both a destroyer and an enabler of transformation.

Shiva's incredible brute strength and dominance are representative of a desire to rule by force and dictatorship. Notably, Saleem's ability to bring all of midnight's children together in a telepathic mental forum leads to the idea of holding a Midnight's Children Conference. Saleem envisions this coming-together as 'a loose federation of equals' where all points of view are given free expression, but Shiva insists that everyone must do as he says or he will resort to violence to enforce his rule. Such events can be seen as refracting the nation's ascendancy as a military power (evidenced in the defeat of Pakistan in 1971), transition towards a centralist government, and imposition of martial law in 1975 when Indira Gandhi declared a state of emergency.

Although the plot focuses on the clashing and oppositional politics of partition, violence and war, the poetics of the work tend to celebrate fusions, connections and porosity. '"Things – even people – have a way of leaking into each other",' Saleem explains, '"like flavours when they cook"' (p. 44). The porous past, the fusions of identity within the postcolonial nation and the blending of narrative traditions invite the reader to consider the ways in which a sense of community is formed in both organic and relational terms. History pours out of the 'fissured body' of the partitioned subject (p. 45). Similarly, narrative has the power to transform the apprehension of the real through its intermixtures: 'Sometimes legends make reality, and become more useful than the facts' notes the narrator (p. 57). This might be taken as a kind of interpretive approach to Rushdie's own insertion of magic into the human/historical body of truth as incarnated by Saleem. Literally and metaphorically, Saleem's 'nose' contributes to the making and interpretation of history. In the days after 'the death of India's humming hopes', veracity is not presented as a stable, fixed object but as a wafting smell, 'a curious mélange of odours, filled with unease' (p. 64). In other instances, India is described as a collective dream or 'the new myth – the collective fiction in which anything was possible, a fable rivalled only by the other two mighty fantasies: money and God' (p. 150). The tensions between divine power and capital might also be seen as correlative to those of the magical and the real, which are played out in a postcolonial society where sacred traditions and the secular (capitalism) go hand in hand. The sacred and grotesque are embodied by Saleem's nose, which is as elephantine as that of Ganesh* (p. 214) and drips constantly. Just as Gogol's 'The Nose' disrupts prevailing ways of understanding the real, Saleem's nose comes to signify his potential for 'sniffing out' other truths.

The blending of magic realist traditions, postmodern narrative techniques (such as the continuous references to the game of snakes and ladders as an allegory for the rise and fall of fortune), and cultural elements from around the world is expressive of the cross-cultural dynamics or hybridity of Rushdie's poetics and conception of the postcolonial condition more generally. From an intertextual perspective, Rushdie refers to Günter Grass's *The Tin Drum* (1959), a novel that links the magical drumming skills of a child who can never grow up to the historical events that took place in fascist Germany, and Márquez's *One Hundred Years of Solitude* as sources of inspiration for *Midnight's Children*.[14] The magical contexts for the novel derive in part from the Middle Eastern and South Asian stories collected in *The Thousand and One Nights*, as is evidenced by frequent references to this text, including a metatextual† comment on the symbolic potential of 1,001 as 'the number of night, of magic, of alternative realities' (*Midnight's Children,* p. 212). The oral narrative traditions of India can be found not only in the voice of the narrator and the framing of the story, which unfolds as a dialogue between Saleem and Padma (Saleem's fiancée), about the story he is writing (and we are supposedly reading), but also through Rushdie's references to Hindu mythology and legends of the life of the Buddha, which tend to blur the distinction between the real and the fantastical in ways comparable to that of magic realism. Finally, the capacity of

* In the Hindu tradition, Lord Ganesh is the son of Shiva and the goddess Parvati: he is depicted with an elephant's head on a human body.

† The term 'metatextual' refers to a text that offers a critical commentary on one or more other texts.

magic realism to express the discrepancies between worldviews is exemplified by Rushdie's comments concerning the reception of the novel: 'In the West people tended to read *Midnight's Children* as a fantasy, while in India people thought of it as pretty realistic, almost a history book'.[15] Thus, tensions between East and West are also elicited through the very fabric of Rushdie's magic realism.

In Rushdie's writing, magic realism offers a forum for transnational dialogue, which discloses points of connection, fluid but disjunctive relations in the world, and open hostilities between opposing worldviews, through the incorporation of elements drawn from Western and non-Western cultures, modern and premodern ways of life, and sacred and profane textual traditions. In the case of *The Satanic Verses*, the epigraph from Daniel Defoe's *The History of the Devil*, which links Satan to vagrancy and empire and describes the infernal condition as one of homelessness, signals many of the themes of this postcolonial work. The opening sequence to *The Satanic Verses* begins in a realistic mode: the work's two main Indian protagonists, Gibreel Farishta (a Bollywood superstar, partly based on Indian film stars Amitabh Bachchan and Rama Rao, who specialises in playing Hindu deities) and Saladin Chamcha (a voice-over artist working in England) are trapped in a hijacked plane during a flight from India to Britain. The Air India jet explodes over the English Channel, but the two are magically saved from death and, in a miraculous transformation, are metaphorically 'reborn' as twins whose fates are conjoined in Britain and a transnational world more generally. Gibreel acquires a halo and takes on the persona of the Archangel Gabriel, while Saladin takes on the role of the devil. These supernatural identities are linked with historical realities past and present as a means to defy the binary opposition of good and evil as well as challenge discourses about minorities in Britain. For instance, officials mistakenly identify Saladin as an illegal immigrant and put him in a detention centre where he and other migrants face systemic racism and are transformed into nightmarish creatures. As a result of police mistreatment, Saladin is both ideologically and physically changed into a demonic other with hairy legs, hooves and horn-like appendages. Thus, the magic realist perspective comes to express both the disorientating and the brutal aspects of the refugee and migrant experience in postcolonial Britain, particularly during the Thatcherite era. At the same time, we might also consider the meaning of Saladin's last name, Chamcha, which means spoon, and, for Rushdie, refers to the domestication of empire and the role of the collaborators who continued to prop up the colonial status quo in the postcolonial era.[16] In *The Satanic Verses*, however, Saladin Chamcha's fluctuating identity between cultures also foregrounds the need for a new definition of being at home in the world, a new sense of the nation, which welcomes and accommodates – rather than marginalises – the diverse histories and peoples which make up its transcultural, multiracial formation. Thus, Rushdie's use of magic realism indicates the need for mutually transformative relations of understanding between cultures as well as indicates, however satirically, the power of community affiliation as Chamcha becomes a cult figure in the South Asian community in London.[17]

Maxine Hong Kingston: the Phantasms of Diaspora

Like Rushdie, Maxine Hong Kingston blends magic realist and postmodern literary techniques as a means to articulate a deeper understanding of postcolonial identity. In 1984, Hong Kingston and Toni Morrison toured China together, and Hong Kingston recognises similarities in their approach to incorporating magic realistic events in their fiction, particularly through oral tradition and ancestral relations.[18] Chinese American, Hong Kingston was born in Stockton, California in 1940 to parents who were illegal immigrants. Her father operated a laundry and gambling house. Until the age of five, when she learned to speak and write English at school, she spoke Chinese. This dual-language identity is reflected in her writing; her English captures Chinese rhythms, tones and images so that the narrative discourse can be seen as a kind of fusion of linguistic domains. In both form and content, her works reflect a hybrid sense of Asian American identity, which is attentive to identity construction across cultures as well as to generational differences and the dynamic interplay of race/gender from both American and Chinese perspectives. Moreover, the precarious experience of (illegal) migration and its legacies are reflected in Hong Kingston's fiction, particularly through the emphasis on parent–child relationships. The works for which Hong Kingston is best known, and in which elements of magic realism and folklore are present, include *The Woman Warrior* (1976), *China Men* (1980), *Tripmaster Monkey: His Fake Book* (1989) and *The Fifth Book of Peace* (2003).

The phrase 'talk-story' refers to an oral tradition of history, mythology, genealogy, bedtime stories and how-to stories that have been passed down through generations, and which form an integral part of Asian family and community life. *The Woman Warrior* and *China Men* draw on this genre in order to explore the ways in which gender has been constructed across generations and through migration from China to America. For Hong Kingston, the shift between magical and realistic perspectives is associated with the instabilites associated with migration, the formation of diasporic identity, and the Chinese American experience. Chinese folkloric traditions, which often feature supernatural events, as well as the indeterminacies associated with history and testimonial narrative, further destabilise the narrative. *The Woman Warrior* takes the form of a fictionalised memoir or *Bildungsroman*,* loosely based on the education and coming-of-age of the author herself. The work begins in a realistic vein with the story of the suicide of 'No Name Woman', the young girl's aunt, who humiliates the family by becoming pregnant out of wedlock.[19] In response to this, which is seen to shame the community as well as the family, the villagers raid the family house and cause extensive damage. '"Pig." "Ghost." "Pig," they sobbed and scolded while they ruined our house' (p. 12). The aunt gives birth in the pigsty that night, and the following morning Maxine's mother finds both mother and child 'plugging up the family

* *Bildungsroman* is a German word used to describe a novel that focuses on the moral, psychological or emotional development of the protagonist.

well' (p. 14). The story is told as a warning to Maxine to ensure that she remains chaste. As the narrator, she observes that such stories were intended to test her 'strength to establish realities': 'Those of us in the first American generations have had to figure out how the invisible world the emigrants built around our childhood fits in solid America' (p. 13). Thus, the diasporic experience approaches a phantasmagorical state.

Haunting is a common element of diasporic fiction whereby the ghostly presence signifies the persistent and often pervasive influence of the past, and the culture of origin, in the present world of the migrant's new home country. When Maxine recounts the tale, she incorporates details that transform her mother's realistic account into a ghost story, thus highlighting the magic realism of the narrative. The family refer to their daughter as a ghost, someone who will bring death upon them all: '"Aiaa, we're going to die. Death is coming. Death is coming. Look what you've done. You've killed us. Ghost! Dead ghost! Ghost! You've never been born"' (p. 20). The girl gives birth to a child whom she also perceives to be a ghost because s/he (the baby's sex is uncertain) has no line of descent. Thus, the daughter's defiance of social norms and customs is seen as resulting in a form of social death, a spectral presence, which precedes the biological end of the lives of mother and child. The dislocating effects of diaspora are figured through Maxine's account of the after-effects of her aunt's story, which have resulted in textual haunting:

> My aunt haunts me – her ghost drawn to me because now, after fifty years of neglect, I alone devote pages of paper to her ... The Chinese are always very frightened of the drowned ones, whose weeping ghost, wet hair hanging and skin bloated, waits silently by the water to pull down a substitute. (p. 22)

The claims of the past upon the present are not only lived but refigured in writing so that the magic realism of the aunt's spectral presence not only haunts the China of her ancestors but has also been passed down and returns, to make claims upon the generations that follow. In threatening to trade places with the narrator, there is a sense that the magical can potentially displace the so-called 'real'.

Like Rushdie, Hong Kingston's magic realism brings to the surface submerged personal histories and recounts vernacular traditions in order to articulate a new kind of postcolonial condition. Where Rushdie's work is typically seen as epic in scope, seeking to rewrite the history of the nation through a macroscopic–microscopic effect, Hong Kingston's work is more often seen within the tradition of the memoir, which seeks to explore the impact of history on the self. Although Hong Kingston focuses predominantly on the intimate, her inscription of the self often incorporates the rewriting of epic and history, and thus calls attention to the dynamic interactions between large-scale and intimate events. Maxine, the character in the text, claims her status as a warrior by interweaving her life story with that of imagined, legendary, real and historical women, including the stories of her mother as a medical practitioner, her aunt's failed efforts to reunite with her husband, the story of Fa Mu Lan and the Ts'ai Yen, a poetess born in AD 175. Thus, drawing on magic realism Hong Kingston suggests that postcolonial identity might be reconstituted through critical and creative acts of storytelling, which entail adapting, resituating and interweaving narratives in order to express a more comprehensive vision of the world.

In *China Men*, a collection of narratives about marvels and magical events from various cultures serve as a way to speak to the wonders, illusions, traps and transformations of masculine identity across times, places, cultures and gender constructs. 'The great grandfather of the Sandalwood Mountains' juxtaposes a Chinese tale about a prince who has cat ears, a Taoist myth about a man who overcomes all illusions but those of love and so is doomed to morality, and a Polynesian tale about the last deed of Maui the Trickster who seeks to transform the cosmos but becomes trapped inside the vagina of Hina the moon goddess. These stories all touch on the mutations of masculine identity; the latter in particular represents the lethal threat of a return to the womb (which becomes an all encompassing tomb).

The threats to masculinity are most strongly represented in the opening fable of the book, concerning a man named Tang Ao who is looking for the entry to Gold Mountain (America/California), but discovers instead the Land of Women. Joking that they will sew his lips together, the women silence him, literally and metaphorically, through various acts of violence: ear piercing, foot binding, special diets and making him wear a mask. These activities, which symbolically transform a man into a woman, also highlight the gender oppression women experienced under patriarchy. The narrator observes that some scholars locate this country during the reign of Empress Wu (AD 694–705) while others argue that it was found earlier, in AD 441, in North America.[20] In positing a preconquest history of America, with connections to Asia, Hong Kingston suggests an alternative reading of colonial and imperial histories. Similarly, in 'The Laws', Hong Kingston bears witness to xenophobic and racist tendencies in America by documenting the various legal exclusions governing Chinese migration to the United States in recent history (1868–1978). In the closing section to the work, entitled 'On listening', Hong Kingston draws on the oral tradition to introduce a series of contradictory stories about the Chinese quest for the Gold Mountain, Hernán Cortez's presence in the Americas, relations with the Spanish empire and the migration of Cantonese labourers to California. By cross-cutting histories, she destabilises a sense of the known boundaries and communities that shape nations past and present, inviting readers to consider the otherness of America itself.

Hong Kingston uses magic realism to express disjunctures between cultures and the tensions of cross-cultural identity formation. America, as the Gold Mountain, emerges as a space of magic realism in both *The Woman Warrior* and *China Men*. For the migrant, non-Chinese culture is perceived as demonic, particularly when the racial and cultural other is a migration official or member of another ethnic group who threatens their livelihood in America. In *China Men*, migrants describe the United States as 'a magical country' that welcomes them in their letters to those still resident in China, but the narrator provides another view when she describes the 'Immigration Demon' who rejects the citizenship papers of Hong Kingston's father as false documents, consigning his American family members to the status of illegal aliens (p. 59). As with many migrants of Hong Kingston's and earlier generations, access to America could only be gained by suppressing certain facts and constructing an identity that would be acceptable to immigration officials. Many migrated illegally. In *China Men*, the narrator presents competing and conflicting accounts of her father's migration story, which disguise the actual facts surrounding his particular experience but also offer a representative account of the many experiences of the generation. In fact, the dislocations of the narrative were designed to protect Hong Kingston's parents from being deported from the United States, but she also expresses a sense of the failures of communication between migrant parents and their children. For example, in seeking to safeguard the family's status as migrants in America, the parents necessarily avoid sharing certain truths with their children.

Diasporic magic realism speaks to the dislocating experiences of everyday life in a new environment. In *China Men*, for example, the ocean culture of Hawaii is experienced as one articulated through the interactions of magic and realist perspectives: the narrator's grandfather, a field labourer named Bak Goong, defends the view that Hawaiian nightfishers might also be Hawaiian warriors walking the earth and vice versa (p. 111). This sense of the coexistence of magical and real interpretations of events stems from his sense that in 'a new land' it is difficult to identify what is 'normal' (p. 111).

Magic Realism and the Identity Trip

Hong Kingston's 1989 novel, *Tripmaster Monkey: His Fake Book*, takes its title from the Monkey King in Sun Wukong's *Journey to the West*, which was originally published in the 1590s and is considered one of the four great classical novels of Chinese literature. Many people have become familiar with the original narrative in recent years thanks to the acclaimed 'circus opera', entitled *Monkey: Journey to the West*, which was created by Chinese actor and director Chen Shi-zheng together with British musician Damon Albarn and British artist Jamie Hewlett. Hong Kingston's novel tackles issues of textual and cultural authenticity and addresses the ways in which identities are constructed and lived through the whimsy and hallucinatory realism of the (drug) 'trip', especially as represented by the Beat movement of the 1950s and Californian counter-culture.* Wittman Ah Sing, the protagonist of the novel, represents 'the present day U.S.A. incarnation of the King of the Monkeys' who can change into any one of seventy-two transformations.[21] His name is also an allusion to the poet American Walt Whitman, whose *Leaves of Grass* (1855) includes titles such as 'Trippers and Askers' and 'Song of the Open Road', which resonate in the slang of the counter-culture generation. A poet turned dramatist, Wittman is a protean character who resists fixed identities and celebrates the poetics of improvisation. Wittman successfully stages an epic play, which includes ghosts, kung fu, fireworks, sixteenth-century Chinese warriors, senior citizen cancan dancers, Forest Dragon and the Horned Dragon. In the final part of the novel, 'One Man Show', Wittman delivers a monologue to his predominantly Chinese American audience in which he critiques and rejects the Orientalist attitudes found in many of the positive reviews of his play.† For him, 'There is no East here. West is meeting West. This was all West' (p. 308). While Wittman rejects the idea of a hybrid, or fusion American identity, Hong Kingston's improvisational text reworks and interweaves narratives from Chinese and American culture so that something new emerges. West is East and East is West in her disorientating and reorientating fiction. Chinese epic tales, such as *The Water Margin*, *The Three*

* The Beat movement originated in the literary, musical and artistic communites of San Francisco, Los Angeles and New York. 'Beat' originally meant 'weary', but took on other connotations, such as the musical beat and beatific spirituality. 'Beatniks' expressed their alienation from society by adopting alternative dress, manners and vocabulary.

† See Part Four: 'Postcolonial Reading Practices' for a discussion of Orientalism.

Kingdoms, *The Dream of the Red Chamber* and *Journey to the West*, are set within the American context where they are on equal footing with references to pop culture and high-brow culture. Thus, she shows that so-called marginalised cultural references are central to mainstream American culture. As a trickster figure and protest artist, Wittman dramatises and critiques the performance of identities in everyday America. Through a conflation of the hallucinatory and the magical real, Hong Kingston articulates an agonistic vision of multicultural, multiracial America.

Toni Morrison: the Reclamation of Communal Histories

Nobel-Prize winning author Toni Morrison was born Chloe Anthony Woffard in Lorain, Ohio, in 1931. A child of the Great Depression, her formative years were shaped by the socio-economic instabilities of the era, which were particularly challenging for African Americans. Her father took whatever work he could find; his occupations included car washing, steel mill welding, road construction and shipyard work. Her mother worked at home and sang in church. Both parents had strong Southern roots. Morrison's father was from Georgia and had vivid memories of racial violence in his childhood, while her mother's parents were part of the migration of African Americans from Alabama, via Kentucky, who sought to find a better life in the North. As with Rushdie and Hong Kingston, early childhood experiences and education would play a powerful role in shaping her fiction. While her father was deeply mistrustful of the capacity of white America to transcend the colonial legacies of racism, her mother looked to the black community as a source of strength. These two principles of critique and community are fundamental to Morrison's work. She earned degrees from Howard University and Cornell University where she completed an MA dissertation on William Faulkner and Virginia Woolf. These modernist authors would have a formative influence on her own fiction: Faulkner through his investigation of the South and Woolf through her emphasis on women's experience.

Any account of Morrison's fiction needs to consider the history of the plantation, slavery and race in America. From the seventeenth century until the abolition of slavery in 1865, the American South participated in the triangular trade route that linked Europe, Africa and the New World. The plantation was central to this route as it was the site of production for raw materials, such as cotton, and foodstuffs, such as sugar, that would be incorporated into finished goods in Europe and elsewhere. This three-legged journey consisted of transporting goods from the Caribbean Basin, including the South, to Europe, where the ships would unload their cargo and reload with finished goods to take to Africa. In Africa, enslaved people were brought onboard and transported to the New World, where they would be sold to provide labour on the plantations. The Middle Passage, namely the journey from Africa to the New World, was a terrifying and perilous experience for Africans who spent the journey chained in the hold of the ship and were occasionally brought on deck for exercise. Many died en route and were thrown overboard. The Middle Passage not only brought death to many and suffering to those who endured it, but also resulted in a profound disruption of African culture and family life. Families were torn apart and peoples from various linguistic and cultural backgrounds in Africa were introduced to a new language and cultural environment. While Africans held onto healing practices, music (particularly drumming and song) and storytelling, passing down knowledge from one generation to the next through oral traditions, these cultural forms also changed through time as a result of dispersion and creolisation.* For Morrison, the African American vernacular tradition is especially important because it offers powerful resources for decolonisation in the postcolonial era, enabling the reclamation of a history from below as well as the recuperation of what has been ignored or subsumed by the dominant colonial culture of America.

While Morrison's first novel, *The Bluest Eye* (1970), is primarily a realist work of fiction, her subsequent body of work, notably *Sula* (1973), *Song of Solomon* (1977), *Tar Baby* (1981), *Beloved* (1987),

* See Part Four: 'Cross-cultural Paradigms' for a discussion of hybridity and creolisation.

Paradise (1997) and *A Mercy* (2008), often includes magic realistic elements, the supernatural and folklore as a means to articulate the black community's sense of history, identity and place in America and in the wider context of the black Atlantic experience. *Sula* tells the story of a girl whose presence is connected to strange and unusual events, particularly freakish accidents and deaths. She might be seen as a kind of 'ogbanje abiku'* in the tradition of the Nigerian and West African spirit children.[22] By linking the incidents in the community to the presence of Sula, Morrison incorporates African belief systems, calling attention to the survival of cultural memory in resistance to the oppressive effects of the Middle Passage and slavery, which sought eradicate connections to African identity. *Song of Solomon*, which includes people flying, a woman without a navel and dead people who talk, recuperates the forgotten or subsumed histories of African Americans through storytelling and vernacular traditions, typically originating in Africa and having been transformed as a result of the dislocating effects of the Middle Passage and life on the plantation, often as a form of resistance to slavery. Morrison has observed that *Song of Solomon* brings together 'the acceptance of the supernatural and a profound rootedness in the real world at the same time, without one taking precedence over the other'.[23]

In a similar vein, *Paradise* tells the story of relations between two communities: Ruby, Oklahoma, an all-black town (founded by settlers who had been ostracised for racist reasons) and a group of women who are known as the Convent. The novel opens with a scene of violence as the men of Ruby raid the Convent, but the main focus of the story is to explore the events leading up to this brutual episode. The reader learns that the Convent is inhabited by women who practise magic, particularly Connie, and serve the community of Ruby with their medical skills and supernatural abilities. However, at the

* *Ogbanje* and *abiku* are Igbo and Yoruba names respectively for a spirit-child or spirit-children who are said to die early only to be reborn again and again to the same mother. This concept and/or its variants has been found among other Nigerian, West African and African diasporic groups, see for example Okri's specifically Yoruba use of *abiku*, discussed earlier.

same time, the women live in isolation, cut off from Ruby, in ways that seem to sever the magic of Paradise (as the women come to call their community) from the realities of everyday life. The Convent serves as a place of refuge and reconciliation, which enables women who enter to come to terms with the power of narrative and discover the power of voice. In this respect, the presence of magic realism signifies a kind of inner rebirth, especially for women who have experienced oppression, but it also functions through gender exclusions, as men are not permitted to join the Convent. Eventually, the women of the Convent are massacred by the men from Ruby in an act of patriarchal oppression. However, their bodies disappear, seemingly in a magical fashion. This supernatural act of resistance is emblematic of the ways in which these women defy patriarchal forces of oppression. Some might argue that women's afterlives are symbolic of the ways in which they transcend hegemonic power structures, but their failure to find paradise on earth is also suggestive of an inability to achieve gender equality. Here as elsewhere Morrison's use of magic realism highlights the perils and hopes associated with the African American quest for new articulations of self/community. She brings a postcolonial feminist perspective to the reinscription of race, gender and community. Like Rushdie and Hong Kingston, Morrison draws on the tradition of magic realism to explore the legacies of the colonial past and the prospects for change in a decolonising world.

Extended Commentary: Morrison, *Beloved* (1987)

The (post)colonial contexts for *Beloved* are indicated from the outset, beginning with the dedication of the novel to 'Sixty Million and more' as well as the epigraph to the novel: 'I will call them my people,/which were not my people;/and her beloved, which was not beloved.' The number sixty million refers to the approximate number of slaves who died in the slave trade. The number is often interpreted as an allusion and response to the some six million Jews who were killed as a result of the Holocaust in order to indicate the scale and magnitude of African American suffering. The biblical epigraph (Romans 9:25) refers to a community that has been despised and outcast, but is now redefined as acceptable. This quotation is especially significant in a postcolonial context, given the African American transition from slavery to citizenship, but it also calls attention to the difficulties of articulating a sense of self and community following the abolition of slavery. It is noteworthy that Morrison's work refers to a fundamental text of colonial formation and religious education – the Bible – as an introduction to her tale of postcolonial emancipation within the African American community. As we shall see, Morrison's novel interrogates the meaning of this biblical verse in a number of ways, especially through the presence of a figure named Beloved, which can be seen as an instance of magic realism because she represents the spectral return of a dead child to the land of the living.

Beloved tells the story of a woman named Sethe who escapes from slavery and attempts to kill all of her children when she fears that they will be recaptured and enslaved once more. Sethe succeeds in killing one child, who is thereafter referred to as Beloved. Years later, it seems that this child returns from the dead as a young woman who comes to live with her mother and sister (Denver). The narrative of infanticide finds its origins in the history of Margaret Garner, as recorded by the Reverend P. S. Bassett in the newspaper *American Baptist* on 12 February 1856. Morrison's desire to rewrite this account from a fictional perspective can be seen as part of her wider project to reclaim black history, such as prompted her publication of *The Black Book* (1974), which contains materials related to 300 years of African American history, including bills of sale for slaves, photos of lynchings, folk sayings, poetry and so forth. Her emphasis on lived experience and communal history is very much in evidence in this work. Significantly, *The Black Book* contains a copy of Bassett's article, 'A Visit to the Slave Mother Who Killed Her Child', a key source-text for Morrison's novel.[24] Similarly, *Beloved* seeks to situate the life of an exceptional individual within the wider context of the community and ordinary life in the post-abolition period.

In *Beloved*, the presence of the supernatural and the magical is connected to African diasporic memory and culture, the trauma of slavery, and the challenges of decolonisation, both personally and collectively.[25] Morrison's work responds to African American narratives such as the autobiographical *Narrative of the Life of Frederick Douglass, an American Slave* (1845) and Harriet Jacob's *Incidents in the Life of a Slave Girl* (1861), which recount the journey from slavery to freedom and tell the story of overcoming exploitation. While such slave narratives characteristically move in a chronological, linear fashion, and are based on personal memory, Morrison's work is attentive to the mediating, distancing effects of intervening accounts and time. Her work calls attention to its purpose as an act of 'rememory', which seeks to revive the past and breathe life into it once more in a postcolonial context. She never lets the reader forget that *Beloved* itself is haunted by the past. Her work is not a slave narrative, but a neoslave narrative, one which attempts to bridge the gap to the past but also serves to highlight the gaps between past and present horizons, which make it impossible to reclaim (and possess) fully a sense of history. In this respect, Morrison's work, like other neoslave narratives, such as Margaret Walker's *Jubilee* (1966), Gayl Jones's *Corregidora* (1975), Octavia Butler's *Kindred* (1979), Sherley Anne Williams's *Dessa Rose* (1986), J. California Cooper's *Family* (1991), extends the signifying tendencies of African American vernacular traditions. Morrison reconstructs the past from a black feminist perspective.

In *Beloved*, magic realism encodes the traumas of the colonial past as well as enables the postcolonial processes of working through trauma. Through the act of retelling the story of Margaret Garner, the colonial theme of possession and repossession under the Fugitive Slave Act* is reconstituted and extended so that Morrison shifts focus away from the colonial moment of repossession to the claims of the slave past on the lives of those in the post-abolition period. Set in Cincinnati, Ohio in 1873, this nonlinear narrative covers events in the life of Sethe; her

* The Fugitive Slave Law or Fugitive Slave Act of 1850 declared that slave-owners had the right to track down and recapture runaway slaves, including those who had migrated to the North.

missing husband, Halle; her children, Howard, Buglar and Denver; her mother-in-law, Baby Suggs; and others with whom she lived on the Sweet Home plantation, including a fellow slave named Paul D, who arrives on her doorstep after years of wandering. The presence of the ghost in Sethe's home is both personal and representative of wider black experience in America. In the early days of the haunting, Sethe suggests to Baby Suggs that they move, but she responds that there is not much point in doing so: '"Not a house in the country ain't packed to its rafters with some dead Negro's grief. We lucky this ghost is a baby."'[26] While the ghost has been present in the house for many years in spiritual form (prompting Sethe's sons to flee their home), Paul D's arrival coincides with the return of the spirit in embodied form. Soon after Paul D comes to Sethe's home, a young woman arrives on the doorstep. Bedraggled and unable to care for herself, she behaves in an infantile fashion and needs to be cared for like a baby. The young woman, who bears the name Beloved, makes claims on Sethe, Paul D and Denver, all of whom are forced to confront the ways in which the traumatic past still haunts their lives. Sethe confronts her unresolved emotions about the murder of her child. Denver, a withdrawn young woman, learns self-sufficiency and establishes a sense of belonging within the wider community. Eventually, she helps to free her mother from the unwholesome and destructive claims of the past. For Paul D, Beloved is a succubus figure, a demon in female form who has sexual intercourse with men in their sleep. Following an erotic encounter with Beloved, Paul D flees Sethe's house. This incarnation of Beloved can be situated in the African American folkloric tradition of the shape-shifting witch[27] as well as the European tradition of ghost narratives. In such a reading, the figure of Beloved might be seen as a hybrid figure from traditions of magic realism at the interface of European and African diasporic cultures. In prompting others to confront the traumas of the past, especially haunting memories of brutal events, Beloved's presence speaks directly to the African American experience of colonial oppression and the post-abolition search for decolonisation within the lives of individuals, the community and the nation.

As a figure of magic realism, Beloved complicates a sense of past–present relations and thus contributes to the novel's multifaceted presentation of postcolonial haunting. In supernatural terms, Beloved might be seen as a *revenant*, the embodied return of Sethe's baby who has grown up. However, there is an equally plausible, realistic explanation for her sudden appearance: there have been reports concerning a young woman in the area near Sethe's home who has recently escaped from men who had confined her for years. If this is the case, the girl's infantile behaviour can be seen as a realistic by-product of her isolation, lack of education and abuse. In this light, *Beloved* tells the story of two instances of mistaken identity: Beloved is haunted by the loss of her mother while Sethe is haunted by her desire to be reconciled with her dead daughter.[28] Both in a way serve as the other's spectral encounter with an unresolved traumatic past. In figurative and psychological terms, Beloved's presence comes to incarnate a more complicated sense of haunting with respect to the traumatic post-abolition experience.

Beloved's fragmentary narratives draw attention to the ways in which acts of 'disremembering' and 'rememory' serve to articulate traumatic events as forms of haunting. Sethe describes rememory as a ghostly presence in personal memory, which is also potentially visible or palpable in the world:

> 'Some things go. Pass on. Some things just stay. I used to think it was my rememory. You know. Some things you forget. Other things you never do. But it's not. Places, places are still there. If a house burns down, it's gone, but the place – the picture of it – stays, and not just in my rememory, but out there, in the world. What I remember is a picture floating around out there.' (p. 43)

The narrative can be seen as a haunted form through the eruption of repressed memories about the past, including references to the Middle Passage, the 'rememory' of the event when Sethe is held down and assaulted by males who forcibly take milk from her breasts, the torture of Paul D and his suffering on a chain gang, and the account of other incidents that rupture a linear chronicle of the past. Beloved herself bears witness to the history of the Middle Passage when she tells the story of how her mother was captured by men without skin (white slave traders) and subsequently leapt from the ship to escape bondage and suffering through death. Beloved offers her own account of trauma in a chapter, consisting primarily of unpunctuated prose, that is indicative of a stream-of-consciousness reverie. The spaces between the words call attention to the lapses of meaning and gaps in memory through the Middle Passage that destabilise the production of postcolonial meaning and hinder efforts at self-articulation: 'some who eat nasty themselves I do not eat   the men without skin bring us their morning water to drink   we have none   at night I cannot see the dead man on my face' (p. 248). The girl refers to a woman 'with my face' (p. 249), suggesting that this is the face of her mother. Consequently, the fragmented memory of the Middle Passage is further confused through the young child's inability to separate herself fully from her mother. Through the interrelation of various traumatic accounts, enabled by the spectral return and embodied presence of Beloved, the reader gains a different sense of history and temporality, which runs counter to the official histories of colonisation and serves to expand the potential for decolonisation in America.

Together, these reinscriptions of the past through the presence of the ghost across cultures come to signify the ways in which the postcolonial condition more generally is one of haunting. The dissipation of the magical real, as figured by Beloved's departure, may indicate that a process of reconciliation with the past-present horizons* has been realised. Ultimately, however, by making it impossible to resolve the meanings of Beloved as an entity in the

* The phrase 'past-present horizons' is indebted to the work of postcolonial theorists who explore the ways in which the legacies of the colonial past impinge on the present. It also refers to the ways in which postcolonial critics draw attention to the proleptic (forward looking) postcolonial presence in the past. Homi Bhabha's notion of the future anterior or projective past is helpful to consider. The notion of going back to the past in order to write the future, or of a time lag is important in this context.

story and a narrative discourse, the magic realist perspective serves to articulate states of tension and anxiety that continue to resonate through the lives of the individual and the community. Finally, *Beloved* comes to a close with the claim that 'this is not a story to pass on' (p. 324), an acknowledgement of the paradoxes concerning a story that should not be missed or overlooked but which is also impossible to transmit in a transparent fashion. Magic realism, which brings together paradoxical and contradictory elements, thus becomes a vehicle for giving expression to the complicated past-present horizons that constitute the postcolonial condition.

Notes

1 Luis Leal, 'Magic Realism in Spanish America', in Wendy Faris (trans.) and Lois Parkinson Zamora and Wendy Faris (eds), *Magical Realism: Theory, History, Community* (Durham, NC: Duke University Press, 1995), p. 123.
2 Chris Baldick, *The Concise Oxford Dictionary of Literary Terms*, 3rd edn (Oxford: Oxford University Press, 2008), p. 194.
3 Zamora and Faris, *Magical Realism*, p. 75.
4 Maggie Ann Bowers, *Magic(al) Realism* (London: Routledge, 2004), p. 95.
5 Elleke Boehmer, *Colonial and Postcolonial Literature: Migrant Metaphors* (Oxford: Oxford University Press, 1995), p. 235.
6 Stephen Slemon, 'Magic Realism as Postcolonial Discourse', in Zamora and Faris, *Magical Realism*, pp. 407–26.
7 Ibid., p. 418.
8 For a specific example, see Michael Dash's 'Marvellous Realism – The Way Out of Négritude', *Caribbean Studies* 13.4 (January 1974), pp. 57–70.
9 Bowers, *Magic(al) Realism*, p. 77.
10 Salman Rushdie, *Imaginary Homelands: Essays and Criticisms 1981–1991* (London: Granta, 1992), p. 25.
11 Rushdie, *Imaginary Homelands*, p. 122.
12 Andrew Teverson, *Salman Rushdie* (Manchester: Manchester University Press, 2007), p. 219.

13 Salman Rushdie, *Midnight's Children* (London: Vintage, 2006), p. 159.

14 For the importance of *The Tin Drum*, see Rushdie, 'Salman Rushdie on Günter Grass', *Granta* 15 (Spring 1985), p. 180. On *One Hundred Years of Solitude*, see: Abdulrazak Gurnah, 'Themes and Structures in *Midnight's Children*', in Abdulrazak Gurnah (ed.), *The Cambridge Companion to Salman Rushdie* (Cambridge: Cambridge University Press, 2007), p. 100.

15 Salman Rushdie, 'Introduction', (25 December 2005) in *Midnight's Children*, p. xv.

16 Salman Rushdie, 'The Empire Writes Back with a Vengeance', *The Times*, 3 July 1983, p 36.

17 Stephanie Jones, 'Of Numerology and Butterflies: Magical Realism in Salman Rushdie's *The Satanic Verses*', in Stephanie M. Hart and Wen-chin Ouyang (eds), *A Companion to Magical Realism* (Woodbridge: Tamesis, 2005), pp. 265–6.

18 'Maxine Hong Kingston with Maggie Ann Bowers', in Susheila Nasta (ed.), *Writing Across Worlds: Contemporary Writers Talk* (Abingdon: Routledge, 2004), p. 180.

19 Maxine Hong Kingston, *The Woman Warrior* (London, Picador, 1981), pp. 12–13.

20 Maxine Hong Kingston, *China Men* (London: Picador, 1981), p. 10.

21 Maxine Hong Kingston, *Tripmaster Monkey: His Fake Book* (New York: Vintage Books, 1990), p. 33.

22 Many critics have commented on this African diasporic presence in *Sula*. For a close reading, see Christopher N. Okonkwo, 'A Critical Divination: Reading *Sula* as Ogbanje-abiku', *African American Review* 38.4 (Winter 2004), pp. 651–68.

23 Toni Morrison, 'Rootedness: The Ancestor as Foundation', in Mari Evans (ed.), *Black Women Writers* (New York: Anchor Books, 1984), p. 342.

24 Middleton A. Harris (comp.), Toni Morrison (ed.), *The Black Book* (New York: Random House, 1974).

25 For an excellent discussion of Morrison's work in relation to trauma, see Jill Matus, *Toni Morrison* (Manchester: Manchester University Press, 1998).

26 Toni Morrison, *Beloved* (London: Vintage, 2005), p. 6.

27 Pamela E. Barnett, 'Figurations of Rape and the Supernatural in *Beloved*', *PMLA*, 112.3 (May 1997), pp. 418–27.

28 Elizabeth B. House, 'Toni Morrison's Ghost: The Beloved Who is Not Beloved', *Studies in American Fiction* 19 (1990), pp. 17–26.

Novels of Exile and Ambivalence: Naipaul, Kincaid and Coetzee

Ambivalence and exile are typically at the heart of the colonial relationship. On the one hand, colonisation aims 'to civilise' other peoples by bringing them into the fold of empire. On the other hand, colonisation relies on 'emphatically divisive and exploitative'[1] practices, such as stereotyping, 'military conquest, massacres and dispossession, forced labour, and cultural repression', in order to assert power over the other.[2] Colonial relations are typically ambivalent because they are split between a sense of benevolence and exploitation as well as similarity and difference. Specifically, Homi Bhabha points out that ambivalence is part of the colonial process of self/other relations through colonial mimicry, which produces 'a reformed, recognizable Other, *as a subject of difference that is almost the same but not quite*'.[3] Exile occurs through literal and figurative acts of dislocation. In the Caribbean, the Middle Passage and indenture were responsible for dislocating millions of peoples from Africa and Asia, producing a sense of exile.* In *Stranger Shores, Essays: 1986–1999*, J. M. Coetzee identifies the condition of being displaced, unsettled, lacking in independence

* See the section on Toni Morrison in Part Three: 'Magic Realism and Folklore in the Postcolonial Novel' for more about the Middle Passage. Indenture is a process whereby labourers enter into a contract for a set period of time in exchange for their ocean transportation, food, clothing, lodging and other necessities during the term of the contract. They are not, however, paid a wage for their work.

and unsure of which rules to follow as a preoccupation of Caribbean writers.[4] In a country such as South Africa, where forced exile and racial segregation have figured in the colonial and apartheid eras, a sense of dislocation and exile remains pervasive. In the postcolonial era, the decolonising processes of working through the past often produce anxiety and ambivalence for the colonised and colonisers alike, particularly when faced with the challenge of bringing about reconciliation in societies that have been fractured by histories of violence, systemic racism and forced migration.

In response to these socio-political concerns, ambivalence and exile also figure in postcolonial literature, shaping both the form and content of the narrative. In this chapter, we will explore these concerns from three distinctive perspectives. The Nobel Prize winning author V. S. Naipaul offers an uneasy, often vitriolic, critique of empire, colonial subjects and exile during the colonial and postcolonial eras as well as through his own experience as a migrant subject. Born in Antigua and now living in the United States, Jamaica Kincaid explores ambivalence in terms of colonial, postcolonial and neocolonial subject formation in her *Bildungsromane*,* travel writing and narratives about gardening. The white South African writer, J. M. Coetzee, another recipient of the Nobel Prize for literature, examines imperial, apartheid and post-apartheid encounters between oppressors and oppressed peoples as well as the dislocating effects of his own migrant experience. In the very act of writing, these authors bring to life the deeply ambivalent processes of self-inscription and social formation that continue to trouble the postcolonial subject and empire.

V. S. Naipaul: Perspectives on Exile

Born in Trinidad in 1932, Naipaul is the descendant of indentured labourers from India who settled in the Caribbean. He won a scholarship to study at Oxford in 1950 and came eventually to live in

* *Bildungsroman* is a German word used to describe a novel that focuses on the moral, psychological or emotional development of the protagonist.

England. *The Enigma of Arrival* (1987) describes the author's attempts to come to terms with his migrant history and identity: the sense of his own 'strangeness', of himself as 'a man from another hemisphere, another background, coming to rest in the middle of life in the cottage of a half neglected estate ... with few connections with the present'.[5] In *Enigma*, as in *An Area of Darkness* (1964), a travelogue about the author's first journey through India in the 1960s, the colonial migrant experiences a sense of disillusionment when he realises that London – a place he believes he already knows – is actually 'a city that was strange and unknown' (p. 146). He remarks: 'I had come too late to find the England, the heart of empire, which (like a provincial, from a far corner of the empire) I had created in my fantasy' (p. 141). Naipaul has travelled extensively throughout Africa and India as well as the Caribbean, producing volumes of travel writings, which reflect his often acerbic views about the possibilities for decolonisation and the attainment of a sense of belonging.

Homi Bhabha suggests that transcultural contact is associated with ambivalence because of the excesses of meaning it produces, which cannot be easily resolved into a single, coherent sense of self: the 'hybrid location of cultural value – the transnational as the translational, [takes place] in an environment of generalised aporia [doubt], ambivalence, indeterminacy.'[6] A sense of loss, associated with migration and exile, is central to much of Naipaul's early writing, particularly in works such as *Miguel Street* (1959), *The Mystic Masseur* (1957) and *A House for Mr Biswas* (1961), which focus on events in the lives of Indo-Trinidadians. In his early work, we find a blend of comedy, pathos and irony, which gradually tends towards increasing bleakness, as Naipaul describes the conditions of exile and anxiety so characteristic of the Indo-Caribbean community, which has occupied a marginal position within a largely Afro-Caribbean society.

Another of his works, *The Middle Passage* (1962), highlights the difficulties of locating identity and writing a history of the Caribbean. The title of this work is especially noteworthy as it refers to the middle part of the triangular trade route during which enslaved persons were forcibly taken from Africa to the New World. Commissioned by the government of Trinidad and Tobago, led by Eric Williams, to write a book about the West Indies as a region, Naipaul began a journey that would take him to Trinidad, British Guiana, Surinam, Martinique and Jamaica. From the outset, his description of the voyage from London to the West Indies is marked by ambivalence: 'There was such a crowd of immigrant-type West Indians on the boat-train platform at Waterloo that I was glad I was travelling first class to the West Indies'.[7] Naipaul distances himself from his fellow passengers, offering what might be construed as a white, colonial, English vantage point, but he also points out the ironies of such a perspective. One of his fellow passengers remarks: 'Jamaicans were beaten up in race riots, and deservedly, for they were uneducated and ungrateful and provoked the English people' (p. 22). In response to this comment, Naipaul refers to an article from the London *Evening Standard* in which Anne Sharpley gives a Jamaican view of islanders from St Kitts, Montserrat, Antigua and other small islands: '"but when they ask them in London where them comes from … them's got to say Jamaica, 'cos nobody heard of dem islands"' (p. 22). In this passage, Naipaul presents Caribbeans as a people who see their fellow members in racialised, imperialistic terms, but often disavow their own cultural, racial differences. West Indians are shown to be deeply conflicted, engaging continuously in fine processes of cultural and racial distinction, which bear the imprint of imperial racism and disdain for cultural difference. What emerges is a vision of a deeply fractured people: 'As England receded, people prepared more actively for the West Indies. They formed colour groups, race groups, territory groups, money groups' (p. 13). One passenger, a Mr Mackay, disparages '"those black fellers going to England and stinking up the country"' (p. 8), but also 'identified himself with black fellers' when speaking of the race relations in the Caribbean (p. 8). Migration to England exacerbates the dislocation and splintering of identity: 'What had been desirable in the West Indies appeared differently in England' (p. 13). Naipaul's voyage of return emphasises the ambivalence of a migrant self who was once but is no longer quite West Indian and is now almost but not quite English.

Naipaul's account of the West Indies under the British empire may seem equally dismissive: 'For nothing was created in the British West Indies, no civilisation as in South America, no great evolution as in Haiti or the American colonies. There were only plantations, prosperity, decline, neglect: the size of the islands called for nothing else' (p. 19). Yet Naipaul also points out that the British saw these islands as places to be exploited, so a spirit of brutality rather than creativity dominated. One of the men recounts the difficulty of finding housing; the dialogue highlights the ways in which the colonial legacies resurface in the present: 'He say, "Blackie, I am coming up to get my rent or to get you out of that room." I watch him and I say, Good. Come up, *bakra*"' (p. 3). 'Bakra' is the term used to refer to the slave master, ruler or member of the ruling class in colonial days. When the landlord comes up, the tenant kicks him down the stairs in an act of resistance that has been shaped by the oppressive dynamics of the colonial past. Naipaul shows that a sense of ambivalence concerning the West Indian as insider/outsider prevails in the contemporaneous era when he reports that the travel agent who sold him a ticket said: '"You wouldn't want to travel with all them West Indians",' adding that even the dockers are sick when they come off the ship (p. 5). Naipaul does not comment on this passage, but in the context of his voyage of re-entry into the Caribbean, it serves to highlight an uneasy sense of his status as an outsider/insider.

Naipaul's critique of the ambivalence of colonial discourses and mimicry comes to the foreground in the second section of *The Middle Passage*. Naipaul begins his section on Trinidad with quotations from Thomas Mann and Tacitus,* which highlight the

* Thomas Mann (1875–1955) was a German essayist, cultural critic and novelist. Tacitus was a senator and historian of the Roman empire. Naipaul is thus referring to the long history of slavery and imperialism through his intertextual allusions.

psychological and cultural dislocations wrought by slavery and colonialism. This quotation from Mann's *The Tables of the Law* (1944) reveals the ways in which exile shaped identity for the Israelites who were enslaved in Egypt:

> Because several of their generations had lived in a transitional land, pitching their tents between the houses of their fathers and the real Egypt, they were now unanchored souls, wavering in spirit and without a secure doctrine. They had forgotten much; they had assimilated some new thoughts; and because they lacked real orientation, they did not trust their own feelings. They did not trust even the bitterness that they felt towards their bondage. (p. 33)

Naipaul sees West Indians as cut off from their ancestral roots yet without the confidence or resources to forge an identity independent of their former colonial masters: 'the West Indian accepted his blackness as his guilt, and divided people into the white, fusty, musty, dusty, tea, coffee, cocoa, light black, dark black. He never seriously doubted the validity of the prejudices of the culture to which he aspired' (p. 64). In this passage, Naipaul shows that internalised colonial beliefs have created schisms and commodified views of the self, as is indicated by the descriptions of skin colour in terms of tea, coffee and cocoa. However, Naipaul's own mimicry of colonialist discourse does not always seem to echo in an ironic, mocking fashion. Such, for instance, is the case when he observes: 'Like monkeys pleading for evolution, each claiming to be whiter than the other, Indians and Negroes appeal to the unacknowledged white audience to see how much they despise one another' (p. 78). On account of his mimicry of the language of colonialism, Naipaul is frequently accused of having appropriated for himself the values and judgements of white imperialist society. Perhaps Naipaul's discourse reflects an unresolved ambivalence because it both mimics and mocks colonialist discourses, slipping continuously between internalisation and resistance.

Set in Africa, Naipaul's *A Bend in the River* (1979), takes its inspiration in part from Joseph Conrad's *Heart of Darkness* (1899, 1902) and recent events in Zaire (formerly the Belgian Congo) in order to highlight another kind of exile and ambivalence. Naipaul has expressed admiration for Conrad, and like him, he explores the ways in which colonialist discourse seems to undermine its own authoritative projections. Naipual's novel about post-colonial Africa, modelled on the lives of Indian Africans, Europeans and native Africans living in Mobuto Sese Seko's Zaire, examines anxieties and tensions related to the effort to create an identity in a society whose form and history were shaped by European colonisation. Divided into four main sections, entitled 'The Second Rebellion', 'The New Domain', 'The Big Man' and 'Battle', the novel traces the economic boom and collapse associated with the copper industry as well as outlines the corruption of the postcolonial government under 'Big Man', a leader who resorts to violence. The novel focuses on events in the life of Salim, an ethnically Indian Muslim and shopkeeper who is neither European nor fully African. Through his life history and encounters, Naipaul explores the crisis of identity formation in personal, economic and political terms. In critiquing the novel, Helen Hayward observes that Naipaul mystifies the social disarray of Africa, resulting from colonial intervention, so that it is 'portrayed as an inherent characteristic of an eternal Africa'.[8] She observes that Naipaul's descriptions of the landscape and the village life echo Conrad's account of the Congo as menacing, premodern and enigmatic.[9] Similarly, Suman Gupta sees Naipaul's presentation of Africans as 'regurgitating the familiar racial stereotypes and cultural evaluations';[10] as in Conrad's work, Naipaul presents Africans as 'threatening and inscrutable'.[11]

Divided attitudes about colonialism are represented through the novel's references to the past. It opens with a pessimistic observation about the role of power and the position of the oppressed: 'The world is what it is; men who are nothing, who allow themselves to become nothing, have no place in it'.[12] As Salim, the narrator, journeys into the interior of Africa, he imagines the reverse journey made 'in the old days with the slaves' (p. 4). Narcissistically, he likens the slave's ambivalent journey to his own: 'Like the slave far from home, I became anxious only to arrive. The greater the discouragements of the journey, the keener I was to press on and embrace my new life' (p. 4). This reconstruction of a slave's journey as terrible dislocation but inevitably desired arrival is horrifying. Not until the second chapter does the reader discover that Salim is the descendant of Hindus of northwestern India who were slave traders (p. 11). Salim recalls an episode recounted by his grandfather who once shipped a boatful of slaves under the guise that they were a cargo of rubber. This 'unusual event in an uneventful life' is not told as 'a piece of wickedness or trickery or a joke' (p. 11). Yet, Salim suggests that this historical memory must be seen in light of the First World War, when rubber became big business, suggesting that his grandfather has in fact conflated acts of mercantilism. Although it is not possible that the slaves could have been shipped as rubber – for slavery had ended by that period – the event is nonetheless suggestive of the persistence of colonial views in the commodified representation of the slave body. Salim, however, does nothing to undermine his grandfather's account. Rather, the reader can attribute this subversive representation of Salim and his family to Naipaul's representation of colonialist discourse, which is ambivalent only because its authoritative accounts of the past are indicative of a desire to master history and colonial subjects. In memory, the experiences of the oppressed are appropriated for self-gratifying narratives.

The critique of Europe is offered in a more pointed way through Salim's multilayered account of overlapping histories of empire. This imperial history takes into account the rule of Arabs, American neoimperialist attitudes and the Roman empire. The repetition and reversal of imperial dictums is perhaps best represented by the motto on the dock gates: *Miscerique probat populos et foedera jungi* or 'He approves of the mingling of the peoples and their bonds of union' (p. 62). Naipaul's narrator offers this summary of the mimicry and mockery of empire entailed by this motto:

> these were very old words, from the days of ancient Rome. They came from a poem about the founding of Rome. The very first Roman hero, travelling to Italy to found his city, lands on the coast of Africa. The local queen falls in love with him, and it seems that the journey to Italy might be called off. But then the watching gods take a hand; and one of them says that the great Roman god might not approve of a settlement in Africa, of a mingling of peoples there, of treaties between Africans and Romans. That was how the words occurred in the old Latin poem. In the motto, though, three words were altered to reverse the meaning. According to the motto, the words carved in granite outside our dock gates, a settlement in Africa raises no doubts: the great Roman god approves of the mingling of peoples and the making of treaties in Africa. (p. 62)

Through this passage, we get a sense of the contradictory attitudes to empire. Salim views the dock motto as a presumptuous claim to appropriate imperial meaning: 'Twisting two-thousand-year-old words to celebrate sixty years of the steamer service from the capital! Rome was Rome. What was this place?' (p. 63). The European, Father Huismans, sees the motto as emblematic of the rights of Europeans to mingle with Africans. The words attest to his ability to position himself in the immense flow of history rather than in the African bush. Salim observes: 'He was of Europe; he took the Latin words to refer to himself' (p. 63). Once again colonial narcissism surfaces: 'He had his own idea of Europe, his own idea of his civilization' (p. 63). The setbacks of empire, which occur through the destruction of the European town, are seen as only temporary in an era when 'the course of history was being altered' (p. 63). Father Huismans, a man who collects African relics, sees himself as the 'last, lucky witness' to history (p. 65). Ironically, he dies a brutal death when he is captured and killed by bushmen in an act of protest: his head is cut off, spiked and sent down the river as a warning. With this incident, Naipaul invites the reader to consider the intertextual reference to the many heads on spikes of Kurtz's encampment in Conrad's *Heart of Darkness*. The supposedly civilised is consumed by the apparently barbarian in an act that seems to undermine the dictum of the mingling of peoples and making of treaties in Africa. In this respect, the ambivalent rereading of history and colonial discourses seems to suggest a violent rejection of European presence in Africa.

Ultimately, Salim himself is a figure of exile, one among many represented in the novel: there is no future in a country where state-sponsored violence prevails (p. 275). When his store is taken over by the state and handed over to an 'authentic' African, Salim resorts to dealing in illegal gold and ivory. Caught and imprisoned for his unlawful trading activities, Salim manages to escape by steamer, presumably headed for Europe. Thus, *A Bend in the River*, like so many of Naipaul's works, explores the dilemmas of exile and the sense of nihilism that emerges through the chaos of postcolonial transition.

Jamaica Kincaid's Ambivalent Places and Spaces

Elaine Richardson was born in Antigua and completed her education at Princess Margaret School before migrating to New York to work as a nanny. There, she began writing and changed her name to Jamaica Kincaid. Kincaid's writing is often related to events of her life and her ambivalent relationships to her family, particularly her mother. Works such as *At the Bottom of the River* (1982), *Annie John* (1985) and *Lucy* (1990) are *Bildungsromane*, which focus on a coming of age story from a Caribbean feminine perspective. Typically, these stories present ambivalent mother–daughter relationships, which are woven together with ambivalent feelings about empire itself. Partly, the ambivalence about the mother figure can be seen as reflecting Kincaid's own experience, but we might also consider the symbolic meaning of England as the mother country. In *Annie John*, Annie Victoria John, the narrator, progresses from childhood in Antigua through a trying adolescence filled with fierce maternal conflict, which leads to her departure from Antigua for England at the age of seventeen. The girl's middle name, a reference to Queen Victoria, is emblematic of the ways in which the identities of colonial subjects are remapped through empire. In the chapter entitled 'Columbus in Chains', ambivalence about empire emerges through the account of the school lesson on Antiguan history. When a girl from England, named Ruth, is asked to cite the day on which Christopher Columbus discovered Dominica, she is unable to answer the question. Annie John considers the meaning of her ignorance:

> Ruth had come all the way from England. Perhaps she did not want to be in the West Indies at all. Perhaps she wanted to be in England, where no one would remind her constantly of the terrible things her ancestors had done; perhaps she had felt even worse when her father was a missionary in Africa. I could see how Ruth felt from looking at her face. Her ancestors had been the masters, while ours had been the slaves. She had such a lot to be ashamed of, and by being with us every day she was always being reminded. We could look everybody in the eye, for our ancestors had done nothing wrong except just sit somewhere, defenseless. Of course, sometimes, what with our teachers and our books, it was hard for us to tell on which side we now really belonged – with the masters or the slaves – for it was all history, it was all in the past, and everybody behaved differently now; all of us celebrated Queen Victoria's birthday, even though she had been dead a long time.[13]

This passage is indicative of the persistent tensions between the colonised and the coloniser, which are drawn across cultural and racial divides. Ruth's father's profession as a missionary links him to the colonial history of conversion. Moreover, this passage highlights Annie John's sense that a reckoning with the past is required. Ambivalence emerges through the account of colonial education, which serves to mask master–slave relations and encourage a utopian sense of community under empire. Kincaid highlights the role of colonial education, institutions and holidays in effacing the harsh truths of history and encouraging a disavowal of the brutalities of the imperial past. Yet, she also attests to a counter-history, passed down from generation to generation: 'we, the descendants of slaves, knew quite well what really happened' (p. 76). Thus, *Annie John* alludes to a tradition of resistance among the people, which is being eroded through colonial education.

Annie John's ambivalent relations to her mother inform her resistance to colonialism. Her school textbook contains an account of Columbus's journey as a prisoner in chains from the New World to Spain accompanied by a picture. She writes 'The Great Man Can No Longer Just Get Up and Go' (p. 78) in the book, words that mimic her mother's subversive reference to her father, a patriarchal male. When the teacher discovers that she has defaced the textbook, Annie John is punished. The girl repeats what we can take to be the teacher's words to her: 'I had gone too far this time, defaming one of the great men in history, Christopher Columbus, discoverer of the island that was my home' (p. 82). Once again, this passage effaces a key historical moment: for the island is only home to Annie John because her ancestors were forcibly transported to the New World via the Middle Passage and enslaved.

Kincaid offers a similarly damaging account of education in *Lucy*, a story about a young woman who has travelled to work as an *au pair* in the United States. When her employer, a woman named Mariah, expresses her love of daffodils, Lucy experiences an unhappy flashback: she recalls being forced to memorise William Woodsworth's poem about daffodils ('I Wandered Lonely as a Cloud', 1804) at the Queen Victoria School for Girls when she was ten years old. When she finally sees a daffodil, she notes that she had to wait nine years to see a flower that never grew on her island, but that she was forced to commemorate under British rule. Thus, the daffodils come to represent the oppressive legacies of empire through its false domestication of the island as a landscape and culture that is continuous with that of England.

A Small Place (1988) speaks to ambivalence and resistance of a different sort by exploring the role of Antigua (and the Caribbean) in the neocolonial world of tourism. The narrative begins as a second-person address to tourists, but also slides into a more general address to colonial powers. While the narrative is most often read as a vitriolic denunciation of foreign exploitation and domestic corruption, the textual echoes of colonial discourses and histories can also be interpreted in a highly ambivalent fashion. For instance, the narrator suggests that the British empire itself was a product of ambivalence:

> And so all this fuss over empire – what went wrong here, what went wrong there – always makes me quite crazy, for I can say to them what went wrong: they should never have left their home, their precious England, a place they loved so much, a place they had to leave but could never forget. And so everywhere they went they turned it into England; and everybody they met they turned English. But no place could ever really be like England, and nobody who did not look exactly like them would ever be English, so you can imagine the destruction of people and land that came from that. The English hate each other and they hate England, and the reason they are so miserable now is that they have no other place else to go and nobody else to feel better than.[14]

Kincaid touches on a point made earlier in this chapter: the colonisers can never perfectly reproduce the culture and people they love. The result is a sense of ambivalence, which leads inevitably, in Kincaid's view, to an eruption of violence and destruction. Antigua comes to represent a space of resistance she loves and a space of domination she despises. It is an unreal place that she describes as a beautiful prison, which locks people in and out (p. 79). Her work reverses colonial stereotypes, making ironic reference to generalised notions of identity: 'all masters of every stripe are rubbish, and all slaves of every stripe are noble and exalted; there can be no question about this' (p. 80). However, the ambivalence again surfaces in the depiction of what decolonisation must mean:

> Of course the whole thing is, once you cease to be a master, once you throw off your master's yoke, you are no longer human rubbish, you are just a human being, and all the things that adds up to. So, too, with the slaves. Once they are no longer slaves, once they are free, they are no longer noble and exalted; they are just human beings. (p. 81)

Thus, Kincaid suggests that the condition of being human is an ambivalent one, neither denigrated nor exalted. Between these polarities, former slaves and masters must come to terms with a new, shared sense of humanity, which must be something other than what it once was when determined by colonialism and its discourses.

In Kincaid's recent texts, ambivalence remains evident in the complex feelings she expresses for her garden. *My Garden(book):* (1999) is a personal account of her experiences as a gardener and efforts to understand the ways in which the Caribbean was depicted as a new Eden, but came to be a place of terrible suffering through slavery and the plantation system. Her account of the rise of botany is particularly telling as it attests to the transplantation of peoples, commodities and plants from around the world under empire. Kincaid reflects on the temptation to view the garden as a space of conquest: 'But this desire to pin one's garden down, to conquer it, and leave your own imprint, it's so vain, so unavoidable'.[15] Unsurprisingly, some critics argue that Kincaid's relation to the garden takes the form of a quest for spatial control.[16] Jeanne C. Ewert observes that Kincaid's 'passionate acts of collection and appropriation' embody the otherness and hybridity* of the author whose 'voice of the colonized inside herself speaks in the tones of the colonizer'.[17] While double-voicing and ambivalence are certainly characteristic of Kincaid's writing, it could be argued that she finds happiness in the garden because it is a locale that resists her

* See Part Four: 'Cross-cultural Paradigms' for more on hybridity.

intentions, designs and impulses to create a certain kind of order: 'Nothing works just the way I thought it would, nothing works just the way I had imagined it, and when sometimes it does look like what I had imagined (and this, thank God is rare) I am startled that my imagination is so ordinary' (p. 6). Kincaid takes delight in her garden precisely because it is a place that thwarts one's best effort to impose a system of representation, a plan of order and/or an imagined design. The spontaneity of life in the garden defies efforts to conquer space. Thus, Kincaid recuperates the delight of the pre-Columbian garden where 'things were planted for no other reason than the sheer joy of it' (p. 87). At the same time, the allusion to Aztec histories of ritual sacrifice indicates a profound awareness of the contradiction that 'perhaps every good thing that stands before us comes at a great cost to someone else' (p. 113).

While the story of the Garden of Eden deals with the desire for knowledge in the form of an apple that can be consumed, Kincaid's garden story unfolds as a meditative space of enquiry and wonder. For example, when asked about the odd shapes and arrangement of her flower beds, she realises that she is not quite sure what she is trying to accomplish. Eventually, she comes to understand her spatial purpose: the 'garden I was making (and am still making and will always be making) resembled a map of the Caribbean and the sea that surrounds it' (p. xiv). Gardening becomes an exercise in imagined cartography, which enables Kincaid to rework geographic boundaries and transplant the Caribbean imaginary. Through the garden, she navigates a way through the places that shape her identity in the world: as a gardener, she may live at home in Vermont, but she travels to the Caribbean, England and China, among other places. In the concluding chapter to *My Garden(book):*, entitled 'The Garden in Eden', she locates her own identity in relation to 'the plants for which I have no immediate use and grow only for an interest that is peculiar to me, and so this is the part of the garden which carries me to the world' (p. 171). In this respect, the ambivalent space of empire – the garden – now serves as creative space through which Kincaid locates herself in the world.

J. M. Coetzee's Vision of Life in South Africa

Through its histories of settlement, migration and apartheid, the case of South Africa poses issues relating to exile and ambivalence. Prior to the infamous history of apartheid in the twentieth century, the history of the Boers' Great Trek away from British colonial control in the 1830s and 1840s, the migration of religious exiles to South Africa (particularly the Huguenots during the seventeenth century), and conflicts between imperial powers have produced a long history of dissent and exile in the territory. As discussed in Part Two: 'A Cultural Overview', apartheid, an Afrikaans* word meaning 'separation', was introduced to South Africa in 1948 as a 'policy of separate development' that resulted in conditions of exile for nonwhite persons. The Land Acts of 1913 and 1936 had already restricted the amount of land available to black farmers, thus exiling Africans from the land. The Population Registration Act, the Mixed Amenities Act, the Group Areas Act and the Immorality Act institutionalised racism and segregation, which were accompanied by literal conditions of exile through the uprooting of peoples and restrictions on free movement through society. Notably, the so-called Bantustans or native homelands restricted a large proportion of black peoples from the early 1950s until the end of apartheid in 1994, effectively exiling them from wider society. Exile under apartheid became commonplace, whether through restriction and segregation, imprisonment, house arrest or self-exile as many, including writers such as Alex La Guma and Bessie Head, opted to leave South Africa. In the post-apartheid era, the Truth and Reconciliation Commission (TRC), established in 1995, sought to initiate a dialogue between perpetrators and victims in the hope of achieving a community-building process of truth-finding, understanding and forgiveness. In *Writing History,*

* Afrikaans is a West Germanic language spoken mainly in South Africa and Namibia. It developed from the language of Dutch settlers whose descendents came to be known as the Boer (Dutch for 'farmer').

Writing Trauma, Dominick LaCapra observes that the South African TRC 'was in its own way a trauma recovery center',[18] providing a social mechanism for South Africa to work through its oppressive past. The motto on the TRC's home page, 'Truth. The Road to Reconciliation', seemed to suggest that the exposure of truth might bring not only reconciliation but also a sort of justice.[19] Yet, one may wonder to what extent reconciliation and justice are possible given the ruptures caused by centuries of domination under a system rooted in racial and cultural inequality.

J. M. Coetzee's highly ambivalent sense of identity as a white South African man can be seen as tied to this complicated nexus of events as well as his own family history. Although he spoke English at home, he communicated in Afrikaans with his wider family. Dominic Head notes that 'Coetzee's own comments on his ethnic identity show him to be intensely aware of the slipperiness of his position, and of the ambivalence of this site which divides colonial from postcolonial experience.'[20] Coetzee was born in Cape Town, South Africa, in 1940, and grew up in the Karoo desert region of the Cape province. Following the completion of a Master's thesis on Ford Madox Ford, he moved to the United States in 1965 in order to complete a doctorate at the University of Texas at Austin on the work of Samuel Beckett.* Forced to leave the United States, when his application for permanent residency was denied on account of his participation in anti-Vietnam war protests, Coetzee returned to South Africa in 1971. He taught English literature at the University of Cape Town until his retirement in 2002, when he emigrated to Australia.

Coetzee's deceptively simple narratives, which often focus on male characters in crisis, can be seen as shaped by an appreciation of Ford's techniques of unreliable narration and inscription of masculine crisis during the Edwardian period and as a result of the experiences

* Ford Madox Ford (1873–1939) was an English novelist and critic. His *The Good Soldier* (1915) is an excellent example of the use of unreliable narration and intricate flashbacks. Samuel Beckett (1906–89) was an Irish playwright and novelist also known for his experimental style, most famously in the play *Waiting for Godot* (first British production 1955).

of the First World War. The tone and mood of Coetzee's prose reflect his interest in Beckett's writing, which, according to Coetzee, creates 'a rhythm of doubt'.[21] The emphasis on dehumanisation, methods of survival and the evasions of history in Beckett's work resonates deeply for an author who grew up under apartheid. In Beckett's work as in Coetzee's and Ford's, narrative becomes an indirect way of coding historical events. David Attwell phrases the writer's dilemma as follows: 'If history is a determining and circumscribing force, the question remains, what form of life is available to prose narrative as it attempts to negotiate that determination and circumscription?'[22] An ambivalent relationship to history and colonial discourse is characteristic of Coetzee's work.

In *White Writing: On the Culture of Letters in South Africa* (1988), Coetzee notes that South African 'white writing' can only be defined as such in so far as it is written by people who are no longer European but not yet African.[23] Like the white Creole plantocracy of the Caribbean,* the white South African occupies an ambivalent position as an uneasy, distant representative of European civilisation and culture. S/he is at the heart of colonial practices and perpetrates systematic oppression, but s/he is also dislocated by distance and cultural difference from the imperial centre. However, unlike the Caribbean, which as we have seen came to represent a new Eden, Africa was a not a new world, but, according to Coetzee, a distant part of the Old World, a separated garden, distant from, but defined by a Eurocentric perspective (p. 2). Coetzee suggests that this enclosed world, unlike the Judeo-Christian myth of Eden associated with the Caribbean, seemed to offer degeneration rather than regeneration for its people (p. 3). Thus, the African landscape came to represent the frontiers separating the barbarian and civilised. As represented in Conrad's *Heart of Darkness*, colonisers, traders and settlers worried that Africa might turn out to be not an idyllic Edenic garden but an anti-garden threatening wilderness and temptation. Similarly, Coetzee notes that the emergence of pastoral as a mode of

* See Part Four: 'Cross-cultural Paradigms' for discussion of 'Creole'. 'Plantocracy' describes the ruling class or political order dominated by plantation owners.

writing comes to embody the tensions between these two contradictory visions of the garden as blooming and corrupt (p. 4). Yet, these symbolic binaries are complicated by colonial history and discourses of race. According to Coetzee, pastoral in South Africa portrays the white labourer as an ideal, someone labouring against the tendencies of the native land and peoples to degenerate into savagery.* This literary mode, which represents a flight from history, proves to be inextricably entangled with histories of race and racism. On the one hand, the black labourer is excluded from the pastoral scene. On the other hand, the incorporation of the black person as serf in the narrative suggests an ongoing relationship of domination and dependency on black labour. Black presence highlights contradictions about the colonial ideology of the pastoral ideal where the land now defined as a pastoral retreat belonged to the black man not many years before (p. 5). In order to evade this uneasy set of questions, Coetzee argues that there is a blindness to colour endemic within the South African pastoral (p. 5). Race and racism are both present and disavowed in the white South African tradition of ambivalent landscape writing.

Coetzee's *The Life and Times of Michael K* (1983) and *Disgrace* (1999) can be read as attempts to rewrite the landscape in recognition of recent historical events in South Africa. *Life and Times* tells the story of the hare-lipped, nonwhite protagonist, Michael K and his mother, Anna who are forced to leave Cape Town in a South Africa torn apart by civil war. These figures of exile fail to find a safe place to live. Michael's mother dies on the journey to her rural birthplace of Prince Albert. Michael is arrested en route because he does not have the documents that would allow him to traverse the country freely. Subsequently, he is consigned to Jakkalsdrif Camp and forced to work on a railway track. When he is released from labour, Michael becomes a gardener in his mother's home town until the arrival of a relative disrupts his idyll and he flees to the mountains. Michael refuses to eat and becomes delirious. Subsequent returns to

* The traditional farm novel (*plaasroman*) or pastoral tradition is an important genre in Afrikaans literature.

the garden, encounters with revolutionaries, capture by soldiers and treatment in a rehabilitation camp do little to alleviate his fundamental condition of existential angst and exile. Michael K's refusal to eat is often read as a form of resistance, much like that of Franz Kafka's treatment of fasting in the short story 'A Hunger Artist' (1922). While some critics argue that the parable-like aspects of the tale seem to rob the novel of its critical edge, others suggest that its events, spaces and encounters are highly evocative in ways that destabilise colonial discourses. For instance. Jakkasldrif camp 'brings to mind actual relocation camps in which blacks, evicted from white areas, were interned'[24] as well as the concentration camps to which the Boers were consigned during the Anglo-Boer war. This hybrid history – which brings together the sufferings of white and black peoples – can be read as a counter-discourse to the history of apartheid. The ending of the novel is often seen as presenting a new myth of the land as Michael K once again takes on the role of gardener, suggesting that the land be returned to the blacks and itself. This eco-political tale offers an ambivalent poetics that rewrites the colonial discourses of settlement.

Disgrace examines the possibilities for truth and reconciliation in post-apartheid South Africa. The story focuses on events in the life of a professor named David Lurie who enters into a sexual liaison with one of his students, a young woman named Melanie who would have been categorised as coloured (mixed race) under apartheid. When the affair becomes public knowledge, Lurie is asked to make a public statement of confession in order that he might be absolved of his guilty deeds and permitted to remain in his post. Lurie refuses to make a statement and is fired. Many critics read the university's emphasis on the need to make a public confession and be pardoned as a not-so-veiled reference to the TRC's attempts to bring about reconciliation between perpetrators and victims. If this is so, Coetzee offers a rather pessimistic view of official procedures, suggesting that individuals must undergo personal and relational transformations through lived relations and dialogues. Subsequent events highlight the difficulties this internal and social process entails. Let go from the university, Lurie travels to the frontier to spend time with his lesbian daughter Lucy who is making a subsistence living as a farmer. During his stay on the farm, three black men enter the home, lock Lurie in the bathroom, kill the dogs and rape his daughter. By the end of the novel, Lucy has agreed to become the wife of a black African man, knowing that one of his relatives was responsible for her rape. Also, she will inevitably concede her rights of land ownership to her black African husband. Lurie undergoes his own form of reconciliation in rendering services to dogs by caring for the ill and wounded animals before they are put to sleep. Derek Attridge notes that *Disgrace* tends to polarise readers:

> Stating the opposition baldly, Coetzee is either praised (implicitly or explicitly) for unblinkingly depicting the lack of progress South Africa has made towards its declared goal of a non-racial, non-sexist democracy (and Lurie's attitudes towards his lesbian daughter's sexuality may be taken to typify a failure in dealing with homophobia as well) or condemned for depicting a one-sidedly negative picture of post-apartheid South Africa, representing blacks as rapists and thieves, and implying that whites have no option but to submit to their assaults.[25]

Disgrace dramatises the challenges of fostering relations between white and nonwhite peoples in post-apartheid South Africa. While Lucy comes to terms with the reversal of racial hierarchies and comes to accept gender inequity, Lurie chooses to dedicate his life to animals. This is important from a political perspective. In Greek political philosophy, there are two notions of life. The first, *zoe*, refers to the idea of life that is common to all living beings (animals, men or gods); the second, *bios*, refers to the form or way of living proper to an individual or a group. Coetzee seems to suggest that political life (*bios*) in South Africa must first acknowledge man as one among animals (*zoe*). Given that so much of colonialist discourse seems to dehumanise the other as a means to deprive the subject of political rights, it is significant that the post-apartheid state would require a wider conception of political life as well as efforts to defy the kind of binary thinking that severs *zoe* from *bios*. Given the fact that much of the novel is told from the position of Lurie, a compromised character, the reader is left with the uneasy task of trying to imagine alternatives to subordination and domination or mere reversals of power relations. Rather than offering an answer, the novel poses the problems of achieving truth and reconciliation in post-apartheid South Africa.

More generally, the difficulties of deciphering others and discourses of self/other relations feature in all of Coetzee's work. Notably, *Foe* (1986) rewrites Daniel Defoe's *Robinson Crusoe* (1719) and *Roxana: The Fortunate Mistress* (1724) in order to draw attention to the issues of voice/silencing as well as the representation of women and indigenous peoples under empire. In his most recent work, *Diary of a Bad Year* (2008) and *Summertime* (2009), Coetzee explores the role of authorship, memory and history from personal, multiple, shifting and fractured perspectives. Through such devices, the author calls attention to the work of oppressive political situations and empire more generally, which lead to various forms of exile and ambivalence for both perpetrators and oppressors. Ultimately, his work calls attention to the predicaments of decolonisation, offering what might be interpreted as a pessimistic view of the viability of moving beyond imperialist modes of thinking about the self/other and the role of the state. In this regard, his work shares much in common with that of Kincaid and Naipaul.

Extended Commentary: Coetzee, *Waiting for the Barbarians* (1980)

Through allegory, *Waiting for the Barbarians* addresses, indirectly, the colonial dynamics of apartheid, which entailed systematic racism and state-sponsored acts of torture. Published in 1980, the novel can be seen in part as a response to the accounts given by security police concerning the death of Steve Biko in 1977.* Jean Philipe-Wade demonstrates that the justification for torture under apartheid is remarkably similar to the arguments presented for the use of torture in Coetzee's *Waiting for the Barbarians*.[26] The novel tells the story of a magistrate who governs a settlement at the edge of empire in an uncertain time and place. The magistrate takes into his compound a young barbarian woman whose feet have been broken and who has been partly blinded as a result of imperial torture. He anoints her wounded body and eventually decides to take her to her people. Upon his return, he is arrested, tortured and mistreated and thrown on to the streets to live the life of a beggar. The novel traces his crisis of consciousness and attempts to think beyond the defining binary oppositions of empire: the distinction between the barbarian and the civilised. Inspired by Constantine P. Cavafy's poem, entitled 'Waiting for the Barbarians' (1904), and Franz Kafka's 'In the Penal Colony' (1914), a short story about torture, Coetzee examines self/other relations and the role of violence under empire. Cavafy's poem explores the binary opposition of the civilised/barbarian that is central to imperialistic thinking. In a highly ironic fashion, Cavafy points out that empire needs its barbarians in order to constitute a sense of itself and its purposes. The speaker of the poem, a representative of empire, denigrates the barbarians at the same time that he eagerly anticipates their arrival and its outcome. When the barbarians fail to show up, the imperial subject observes: 'And now what will become of us without the Barbarians– / Those people were some sort of solution'.[27] Coetzee's narrative takes this insight as the basis for its dramatic situation, which concerns the empire's desire to capture, interrogate and situate the barbarians as a threat to itself.

The novel traces a shift in its representation of the empire and the binary opposition of the barbarian/civilised by depicting events in

* Steve Biko (1946–77) was a noted anti-apartheid activist in the 1960s and 1970s and founder of the Black Consciousness Movement. He died as a result of injuries sustained during a police interrogation, torture and beatings. The death of such a high profile leader made worldwide news headlines and raised global awareness of the brutal regime in South Africa.

the life of an unnamed magistrate living in an unnamed border town under an unnamed empire. The refusal to name the empire, its territory and its magistrate is significant for it allows the novel to be read as a fable about the workings of imperialism itself. At the outset, the magistrate is sceptical of the rumours that the barbarian tribes are arming for war, believing that fear of the barbarians as savage outsiders stems from the desires of a too-comfortable society. In a key passage from the text, Coetzee illustrates through the magistrate how the imperial subjects imagine the barbarian: as a terrible, but also exoticised Other bringing fire and rape to the civilised household.[28] As in Cavafy's poem, we get the sense that a complacent empire needs to bolster itself by projecting external threats, presumably where none actually exist. Relations between Colonel Joll, the leader of special forces from the imperial centre whose purpose is to maintain imperial rule through patrol, surveillance and torture, if necessary, and the magistrate, who is opposed to the unwarranted use of torture, highlight the ambivalence at work among imperial subjects as duty to the Empire is privileged over love between its servants (p. 6). Moreover, the discrepancy between imperial subjects also shifts through their relations and sense of proximity to the centre. When Joll decides to capture barbarians, the magistrate asks where he is headed in case Joll gets lost and he needs to bring him back to civilisation (p. 13). Both men appreciate the irony of this phrase for the frontier does not correspond to civilisation as represented by the imperial centre: at the edges of empire, it is a rude settlement, bordering on the savage wilderness that lies beyond imperial terrain.

The magistrate's peripheral status enables him to distinguish between various social groups at the borders of empire. When a local fishing people are brought in for questioning, he denies that they are a threat to the Empire (p. 18). The incidents of torture, however, prompt the magistrate to reconsider the meaning of civilised behaviour (p. 25). Turning against empire, he revolts against the ugly injustice and pain of it and wishes to begin again with a new regime (p. 26). In this early passage in the novel, we see that the magistrate is unable to conceive of a world without empire. Rather he desires an apocalyptic ending to the current order and a new start. At the same time, he expresses doubts concerning his desires for the end of empire, fearing the rise of the barbarian race and its lack of civilisation, education and manners (p. 56).

However, the magistrate's relation to empire changes following his return from the journey that reunintes the young woman with her tribe. He reverses the terms and refers to the representatives of empire themselves as barbarian (p. 85). At the same time, he continues to use the word barbarian to refer to the tribes. In this respect, the distinction between the barbarian and civilised is not only reversed but also collapses. The notion of the civilised is exiled: the word finds no reference point in the world. The collapse of the binaries which constitute empire leads him to consider the meaning of a world where civilisation no longer seems possible. Imprisoned, the magistrate notes that a bestial life is turning him into a beast (p. 87). The motif of the man who must get in touch with his animal nature in order to imagine a new kind of politics is of recurring interest to Coetzee. He is a vegetarian and animal rights activist who believes strongly in the politics and rights of animals. We might consider the ways in which his approach to politics revisits a binary of political thought in the West, which distinguishes man's life (*zoe*) from political life (*bios*). As we have seen in relation to *Disgrace*, typically, in Western political thought, *bios* (political life) is the privileged term; this mode of thinking about politics relies on exceptions and we need to consider how certain peoples are stripped of their political lives and reduced to bare life. Coetzee defies this Western attitude and shows that there can be no political life without a conception of the value of life itself: one way forward to a reconstructed politics is to consider the politics of animal life as the basis for establishing human rights and political life more generally. Yet, for a man complicit with torture even the imagination of self as animal is ambivalent. When the magistrate attempts to imagine how the barbarian girl sees him, he is not sure whether he appears as a guardian, like the (white) albatross, or a coward, a black crow who strikes at the already dead (p. 89). As an imperial subject, he is both the guardian and the predator who protects/feeds off the barbarian other.

Nonetheless, he wants to believe that he represents the one man who in his heart was not a barbarian (p. 114). Colonel Joll's forces use charcoal to inscribe the word 'ENEMY' upon the bodies of the barbarians and beat them until the words are smudged with blood (p. 115). A woman in the crowd watching these events is asked to participate in the beating. The magistrate protests vigorously (p. 116). He is beaten badly for his protest, following which he is brought into Colonel Joll's office for an interrogation. Joll comments on the fruitlessness of the magistrate's quest for martyrdom: in this backward place his death will receive no attention (p. 125). Here again we see that Coetzee calls attention to the frontier as a highly politicised zone. Because it stands at the edge of barbarism and civilisation, the frontier is a highly volatile contested space where there is a potential for collapse as well as renewal. Unlike Joll, who feels that border troubles are of no significance, Coetzee shows that the border spaces and histories represent the defining spatial histories of politics and empire.

Throughout the novel, a recurring dream is indicative of the magistrate's obscure change of consciousness. He sees children playing in the snow, building a fort which he recognises as a model of the imperial fortification with its battlements, four watchtowers and gate (p. 56). However, the town is empty and silent, which makes the magistrate long for it to be populated (p. 57). When he tries to cry out, in his dream, he is unable to make any sound because his tongue is frozen in his mouth. This dream of powerlessness in terms of representation and voice runs counter to the illusions of imperial dominance. The ending of the novel offers an entirely different vision of children playing in the snow, building a snowman. In this instance, the magistrate is an observer, but opts not to interfere and to let the children create his snowy body in the ways that they choose; he remarks that the final result is not a bad snowman. The novel closes with his observation that the reality of his life has differed greatly from this vision, and that his doom is to continue on his own directionless path (p. 170). Here the vision of imperial powerlessness has been replaced by a reality in which the magistrate has become peripheral, a witness to the creation of a new kind of body, which will melt away when the spring comes. This act of creating a snow person as opposed to the inscription and defacement of the body suggests an alternative relationship to the imagined body politic, one that returns to nature and art as the basis for its inspiration. Yet, the magistrate's words caution against an overly optimistic interpretation of the future. Instead, we have a vision of exile: a man who progresses along a road that may lead nowhere. But in learning to live in the moment – the now here rather than the nowhere – the magistrate seems finally to have made a productive step forward.

By way of coda to this ambivalent novel, we might turn to Coetzee's *Diary of a Bad Year* (2008), which offers a commentary about the work in a section entitled 'On the hurly-burly of politics'. Coetzee's narrator remarks that he (Coetzee) gave a reading at the National Library in Canberra at which he made remarks about pending security legislation. He referred to the writing of *Waiting for the Barbarians* as a response to South Africa of the 1970s when the police could pick up, detain and torture people with no legal recourse available to victims because of legislation that allowed for the state to take action against those who appeared to pose a threat. The narrator remarks that he is misquoted by the newspaper, *The Australian*, but he is also anxious to tell the reader what was omitted by the newspaper: crucially his observation that the weapons used by the South African state – suspension of the rule of law, torture and kidnappings – rather than being backward, regressive measures were in fact 'progressive' and pioneering, looking forward to the techniques used by governments today.[29]

In this comment on the transposition of historical events into fiction, embedded in a work, *Diary of a Bad Year*, that challenges the boundaries of fiction and testimonial account, Coetzee makes a highly ambivalent remark about the role of laws against terror under apartheid South Africa and in a post-9/11 world, suggesting that the declaration of a state of exception is but a prelude to further acts of terror and abuse. In this barely veiled allusion to the abuses of power associated with the 'war against terror', such as the special measures for surveillance, interrogation and detention introduced in the United States as well as other Western states, Coetzee offers a damning view of the ways in which imperialism continues to operate in the world today. Implicitly, Coetzee prompts his readers to think about the ways in which empires past and present maintain a sense of power and integral identity through methods of exclusion (such as refusing full rights of citizenship to some, whether based on religious, racial, cultural or other differences from the 'norm') and exception (such as stripping people of their rights as citizens and human beings).

Notes

1 Peter Hallward, *Absolutely Postcolonial: Writing Between the Singular and the Specific* (Manchester: Manchester University Press, 2001), p. xv.
2 Benita Parry, 'Liberation Movements: Memories of the Future' *Interventions* 1.1 (1998–9), p. 50.
3 Jamaica Kincaid, *Annie John* (London: Vintage, 1997), p. 76.
4 J. M. Coetzee, *Stranger Shores, Essays: 1986–1999* (London: Vintage, 2002), p. 190.
5 Naipaul, *The Enigma of Arrival* (London: Picador, 2002) pp. 8, 13.
6 Homi Bhabha, 'Postcolonial Criticism' in Stephen Greenblatt and Giles Gunn (eds), *Redrawing the Boundaries: The Transformation of English and American Studies* (New York: Modern Language Association), p. 439.
7 V. S. Naipaul, *The Middle Passage: A Caribbean Journey* (London: Picador, 2001) p. 1.
8 Helen Hayward, *The Enigma of V.S. Naipaul: Sources and Contexts* (Houndmills: Palgrave, 2002), p. 173.
9 Ibid.
10 Suman Gupta, *V.S. Naipaul* (Plymouth: Northcote Publishers, 1999), p. 50.
11 Ibid., p. 51.
12 V. S. Naipaul, *A Bend in the River* (New York: Vintage International, 1989), p. 3.
13 Homi K. Bhabha, *The Location of Culture* (London: Routledge, 1994), p. 86.

14 Jamaica Kincaid, *A Small Place* (London: Virago Press, 1988), p. 24.
15 Jamaica Kincaid, *My Garden(book):* (London: Vintage, 2000), p. 794.
16 Alice D'Amore, 'Kincaid's Garden: A Fourth Garden of Self-Awareness', *MaComère: Journal of the Association of Caribbean Women Writers and Scholars* 7 (2005), p. 153.
17 Jeanne C. Ewert, '"Great Plant Appropriators" and Acquisitive Gardeners: Jamaica Kincaid's Ambivalent Garden', in Linda Lang-Peralta (ed.), *Jamaica Kincaid and Caribbean Double Crossings* (Newark: University of Delaware Press, 2007), p. 125.
18 Dominick La Capra, *Writing History, Writing Trauma* (Baltimore, MD: The Johns Hopkins University Press, 2001), p. 43.
19 Troy Urquhart, 'Truth, Reconciliation, and the Restoration of the State: Coetzee's *Waiting for the Barbarians*' *Twentieth Century Literature* 52.1 (Spring 2006), p. 1.
20 Dominic Head, *J. M. Coetzee* (Cambridge: Cambridge University Press, 1997), p. 6.
21 David Attwell, *South Africa and the Politics of Writing* (Berkeley: University of California Press, 1993), pp. 9–10.
22 Ibid., p. 10.
23 J. M. Coetzee, *White Writing: On the Culture of Letters in South Africa* (New Haven, CT: Yale University Press, 1990), p. 11.
24 Head, *Coetzee*, p. 96.
25 Derek Attridge, 'J. M. Coetzee's *Disgrace*: Introduction' *Interventions* 4.3 (2002), p. 317.
26 Jean-Philipe Wade, 'The Allegorical Text and History: J. M. Coetzee's *Waiting for the Barbarians*' *Journal of Literary Studies* 6.4 (December 1990), p. 281.
27 C. P. Cavafy, *Collected Poems*, Georege Savadis (ed.) and Edmund Keely and Philip Sherrard (trans.) (Princeton, NJ: Princeton University Press, 1975), pp. 17–18.
28 J. M. Coetzee, *Waiting for the Barbarians* (London: Vintage, 2004), p. 9.
29 J. M. Coetzee, Diary of a Bad Year (London: Vintage, 2008), p. 171.

The Transnational Short Story Cycle: Adichie, Danticat, Díaz and Lahiri

Postcolonial literary studies often tend to overlook the short story as a literary form.[1] Critics note that the desire to reclaim history and language, as well as draw on vernacular forms,* finds expression in novels, poetry and drama. Yet, such arguments would presumably also bolster the status of the story, particularly as the oral tradition of storytelling has been especially important in most indigenous and colonised cultures. The short story cycle – a term that refers to a related set of tales – is an especially important literary form, which can give expression to a sense of community and ethnic identity through multiple perspectives. The emphasis on the expression of communal and family identity from an ethnic perspective is evident in works such as V. S. Naipaul's *Miguel Street* (1959), George Lamming's *In the Castle of My Skin* (1953), Amy Tan's *The Joy Luck Club* (1989) and Julia Alvarez's *How the Garcia Girls Lost Their Accents* (1991).[2] Rocio Davis notes the short story cycle faces a twofold challenge: 'the collection must assert the individuality and independence of each of the component parts while creating a necessary interdependence that emphasizes the wholeness and unity of the work.'[3] Many techniques can contribute to a sense of unity in

* The term 'vernacular' means local and refers in this instance to local forms of language and culture, such as dialect, rituals, dance and stories. Such forms typically predate colonialism and/or emerge in resistance to imperial culture.

the short story cycle: recurring characters, an evolving plot, repeating themes and motifs and a developing dramatic situation. Sometimes, however, the connection between the stories is more elusive. They seem to bear relations to one another or share a common orientation; our reading of any particular story shifts in its relation to the collection as a whole. Recurring scenarios, motifs or a sense of related concerns may serve to foster a productive dialogue among the tales.

Recently, the postcolonial short story cycle has undergone something of a revival, especially for writers working in the areas of cosmopolitan and migrant fictions. Innovative in form, these cross-cultural collections reflect the complexity of transnational life, examining the tensions, anxieties and dreams that preoccupy migrants and their children. Such works often proffer a view of those who have come to live with multiple affiliations across literal, metaphorical and psychic borders. This chapter focuses on short story cycles by Nigerian writer, Chimamanda Ngozi Adichie; Haitian American author, Edwidge Danticat; the American storyteller from the Dominican Republic, Junot Díaz; and the Bengali American writer, Jhumpa Lahiri.

Although these collections are quite different in tone, cultural background and themes, they share a connection to America through migration. Their hybrid works[*] follow in the American tradition of minimalism in the story form as exemplified by Raymond Carver (1938–88) whose precise, lucid tales expose disorder and disorientation in the modern world but are also characterised by a careful attention to form. Carver's characters often struggle to live in the present because they are beset by worries about the future and concerns about a past they cannot escape. Through their shared focus on the migrant, diasporic[†] and transnational experience, the authors

* See Part Four: 'Cross-cultural Paradigms' for a discussion of hybridity.

† The term 'diaspora' (meaning dispersion) initially referred to the scattering of Jewish peoples as a result of several forced expulsions from what is now known as Israel, Jordan and parts of Lebanon as well as the State of Palestine. Subsequently, 'diaspora' has come to refer more generally to the movement, migration or scattering of a people away from a settled location or ancestral homeland.

discussed call attention to the disorientating conditions of the contemporary world, especially as reflected in intimate relationships and daily life. These hybrid tales reflect the author's own cross-cultural background and global experiences through the incorporation of storytelling techniques, languages and dialects and other references from around the world. These narratives address and represent the increasingly transnational and globalising tendencies of American identity. The presence of exiles, migrants, tourists and refugees attests to the emergence of what Caryl Phillips refers to as 'a new world order' in which 'there will soon be one global conversation with limited participation open to all, and full participation open to none. In this new world order nobody will feel fully at home'.[4] The complex interplay between race, gender, class, economic disparity and cultural difference comes to the foreground as subjects cross borders and enter into new forms of contact and exchange.

Chimamanda Ngozi Adichie: Between Nigeria and America

Adichie (b. 1977) is a child of Igbo parents, born in Nigeria, whose maternal and paternal grandfathers were killed during the Nigerian Civil War, or Biafran War as it is sometimes known (1967–70). At the age of nineteen, she left for the United States to pursue her studies. Her works reflect both her interests in Nigerian identity and the cosmopolitan perspectives associated with her migrant experience. The Biafran War and its legacies surface in novels such as *Purple Hibiscus* (2003) and *Half of a Yellow Sun* (2006) as well as a play entitled *For Love of Biafra* (1998). Adichie's global interests are reflected in a recent collaboration with Jhumpa Lahiri as editors of a collection of short fiction, entitled *One World: A Global Anthology of Short Stories* (2009).

The Thing Around Your Neck (2009), a collection of twelve stories, brings together tales about Nigeria, colonial encounters and transitions, transnational migration and human rights concerns.[5] Several of the stories attest to the influence of Chinua Achebe

(b. 1930), the author of *Things Fall Apart* (1958) and *Arrow of God* (1964), works that reclaim Nigerian history and explore the effects of colonial intervention.[6] *Things Fall Apart* focuses on the life of Okonkwo, highlighting the effects of Christian missionaries and colonial intervention on the man and his family. In Achebe's novel, the father is disappointed when his son Nwoye converts to Christianity and rejects traditional cultural values and beliefs. The novel ends with the suicide of Okonkwo because he cannot accept the changes happening in society under colonial rule. In the closing pages, a colonial administrator notes that the death of Okonkwo might serve as an exemplary incident in a history he is writing, entitled *The Pacification of the Primitive Tribes of Southern Nigeria*. Like Achebe, Adichie comes from an Igbo background, and shares his concerns about postcolonial transition, but she places emphasis on the mother–son relationship as well as feminist perspectives rather than father and son relationships.

'The Headstrong Historian' can be read as a response to *Things Fall Apart* on account of its critique of imperialistic intervention, particularly the role of missions and violence, and emphasis on the need for the reclamation of history. Adichie's short story depicts events in the life of Nwamgba, a woman born in Nigeria in the late nineteenth century, who marries a youth she loves, even though his family may be cursed by miscarriages. She lives to see her son convert to Christianity and turn against his own culture and beliefs in favour of colonialist discourses. For instance, after attending the Catholic school, he stops eating his mother's food because 'it was sacrificed to idols' and informs his mother that her nakedness is sinful.[7] Increasingly, the mother comes to feel that her son inhabits 'a mental space that was foreign to her' (p. 211). He marries another Christian convert, a woman named Mgbeke, who appears to have become a passive, helpless subject through her mission-school education. However, Nwamgba regains the hope of familial connection when her granddaughter is born. Christened Grace, Nwamgba calls her Afamefuna, meaning 'My Name Will Not Be Lost' (p. 214). Afamefuna lives up to the promise of her name. She rejects the history lesson found in a chapter of her textbook entitled 'The Pacification of the Primitive Tribes of Southern Nigeria' and goes on to research and reclaim the history of Nigeria when she enters university, leading to the publication of her study called *Pacifying With Bullets: A Reclaimed History of Southern Nigeria*. In her resistance to colonial education and the colonialist values of her husband, Afamefuna takes up the cultural heritage of her ancestors, offering a strong anti-imperialist and feminist perspective.

Human rights issues surface in the collection, particularly in the light of recent history in Nigeria. 'Cell One', the opening tale of the collection, highlights lawlessness and the injustices of the prison system as well as calling attention to the influence of American gang violence on youth culture in Nigeria. The Biafran War plays a role in 'Ghosts', a story about an encounter on campus between two men who meet decades after the war. While one man, Ikenna Okoro, managed to escape the country and seek asylum in Sweden, the other, a retired maths professor, was left behind and saw his daughter die as a result of violence. 'A Private Experience' describes how the Biafran War broke out as a result of religious intolerance between the Igbo Christians and the Hausa Muslims of southeast Nigeria. The story contrasts the intimate life histories of two women who form a kind of solidarity across ethnic lines, even as ethnic tensions erupt into violence, leading to deaths in the families of both women. Thus, Adichie suggests alternative possibilities for cross-ethnic dialogue in Nigeria. 'The American Embassy' offers a poignant depiction of a woman who refuses to turn the story of her child's death into a palatable performance for embassy officials in order to obtain asylum. Ugonna, her son, is killed when soldiers enter her home, looking for her husband, a journalist who is wanted by the state on account of his outspoken criticisms of the government. She has been advised to inform the American officials about Ugonna's death in a carefully calculated way: 'don't overdo it, because every day people lie to them to get asylum visas, about the dead relatives that were never born. Make Ugonna real. Cry, but don't cry too much' (p. 134). When confronted with the officials, she finds that she is unable to follow this well-intentioned advice because she cannot 'hawk' her son's story for a visa (p. 139).

The influence of African women's writing is evident in this collection. In 'Tomorrow is Too Far', Adichie focuses on the theme of sibling rivalry and gender roles in a patriarchal society in way that is reminiscent of Tsitsi Dangarembga's (b. 1959) *Nervous Conditions* (1988), a *Bildungsroman** set in Rhodesia (modern day Zimbabwe) during the 1960s and 1970s. Dangarembga's story is told by Tambudzai, a young Shona girl living in a small village in Rhodesia, who reflects on her inability to mourn her brother's death. Adichie's story focuses on a young girl in Nigeria who comes to realise that her young brother, Nonso, is favoured in this patriarchal society because he is 'the one who would carry on the Nnabuisi family name' (p. 188). The girl's cousin, a boy named Dozie, is less favoured because he is merely a *nwadiana*, a daughter's son. The story reveals that the girl played a role in her brother's death and that Dozie has helped her to conceal the truth about this incident from the family.

The work of Nigerian author Buchi Emecheta (b. 1944), can be seen as another important influence on Adichie's collection. The themes of female identity, migration and marriage surface also in earlier work by Emecheta, such as *Kehinde* (1994), which focuses on the relationship between Kehinde Okolo and her husband. Kehinde has been living in London for nearly two decades when her husband decides to return to Nigeria. She follows him after a period of two years only to discover that he has taken another wife. Like Emecheta, Adichie is interested in women's struggles for self-articulation in the face of patriarchal values and cross-cultural relations. Transnational concerns emerge especially in the context of stories about women living in America and struggling to come to terms with their own cross-cultural identities and experiences as well as their husbands or lovers who continue to espouse conservative, patriarchal conceptions of gender and sexuality. Spatial dislocation and emotional distance intersect in these stories. 'Imitation' focuses on events in the life of

* *Bildungsroman* is a German word used to describe a novel that focuses on the moral, psychological or emotional development of the protagonist.

Nkem, the wife of a Nigerian businessman, named Obiora. While Nkem lives in Philadelphia, where she is raising their children, Obiora spends most of his time living and working in Nigeria. Nkem learns that her husband has entered into an affair and moved the girlfriend into their house in Lagos. Nkem adopts the short hair style of Obiora's mistress, and tells her husband that she will return to Lagos. Although Nkem does not directly confront him about the affair, her decision to adopt the style of the mistress – to imitate her – sends her husband a clear message about her demands that he remain faithful in their marriage. Further discussions of Adichie's engagement with the issues of sexual politics and freedom of expression are explored in the extended commentary on the title work of this collection.

Edwidge Danticat: Between Haiti and America

Danticat was born in Haiti in 1969. Her father immigrated to the United States two years later in search of work, and her mother followed him in 1973. Danticat remained in Haiti for eight more years where she was raised by relatives. At the age of twelve, she emigrated to live with her parents in a predominantly Haitian American area of Brooklyn. She received a degree in French Literature from Barnard College and an MFA from Brown University. Much of her fiction deals with the transnational family experience, with a particular emphasis on the lives of women and girls. Her short stories have appeared in more than twenty periodicals (including the journal *Callaloo*) as well as anthologies. Danticat's *Krik? Krak!* (1996) is a collection of nine stories and an epilogue, dealing with the lives of Haitians in the modern era. *The Dew Breaker* (2004), another short story cycle,*

* *The Dew Breaker* offers various perspectives on the life of a Haitian American family man and barber who turns out to be a 'dew breaker' or torturer under the dictatorial regime of François Duvalier. Metaphorically, the term is suggestive of the rupture of the early morning, but it also often refers quite literally to the breaking of the dew as the military police came to drag people from their homes in the night or early morning.

interrogates the enduring effects of torture. Novels include *Breath, Eyes, Memory* (1994), which examines the mother–daughter relationship and sexuality in transnational contexts, and *The Farming of Bones* (1998), which presents a history of Haitian genocide in the Dominican Republic. *Brother, I'm Dying* (2007) takes the form of a post-9/11 memoir in honour of Danticat's father and uncle, a migrant and asylum seeker respectively.

The title of Danticat's collection, *Krik? Krak!*, derives from the Haitian call-and-response storytelling tradition. The storyteller exclaims 'Krik' and the audience responds with 'Krak'. This interactive dialogue brings the teller and listener into a dynamic relationship. Many of the narratives explicitly invoke this storytelling ritual, thus providing a method for interlinking the tales from a stylistic point of view. Set in the modern era, the stories of living Haitians bring transnational histories past and present into dialogue in order to convey a sense of enduring cultural and socio-political identity.

The role of women in history is another linking motif. Rocio Davis remarks that '[t]he telling of stories heals past experiences of loss and separation; it also forges bonds between women by preserving tradition and female identity as it converts stories of oppression into parables of self-affirmation and individual empowerment'.[8] Yet, conflicts between mothers and daughters also surface, suggesting the need to consciously negotiate and establish bonds between generations. In the Epilogue, 'Women Like Us', while the narrator's mother believes that each woman should aspire to 'be the best little cook and housekeeper who ever lived', [9] the daughter wonders why she cannot be a kitchen poet: a woman who both writes and cooks. Issues of silencing are evident both in women's lives and more generally in the lives of those who have lived under dictatorial governments. When the narrator's aunts wonder how the narrator's passion for cooking will manifest itself, the mother laments her daughter's rebellious desire to waste time writing. '"Her passion is being quiet," your mother would say. "But then she's not quiet. You hear this scraping from her. Krik? Krak! Pencil, paper. It sounds like someone is crying"' (p. 220). The mother sees her daughter's acts of orature (forms of writing that draw on the oral storytelling of the community) as a failure to move beyond the mournful past, as a form of ingratitude for the sacrifices made by previous generations.

The first story in the collection, entitled 'Children of the Sea', presents the reader with a tale about past-present horizons in an account of Haitian boat refugees bound for Miami, Florida. The story of a young man's journey, who witnesses the death of a mother and child at sea, incorporates textual fragments in the form of excerpts from unsent letters written by the young man and his fiancée. These letters cannot be sent because he has no fixed address while at sea so he can neither receive nor send correspondence. However, the lovers persist in writing to one another in order to alleviate the pain of separation. Stylistically, this narrative technique creates a somewhat disorientating effect because it shifts from land to sea, from a masculine to feminine perspective. Nonetheless, this technique of narrative dislocation is appropriate for the subject matter of the tale: the story of refugees who have fled from a state of terror on a boat that appears to have become lost at sea.

While the young man comes to apprehend the long history of sea journeys that have shaped Haitian identity, the young woman's letters bear witness to state-sponsored violence in modern Haiti. She notes that members of the youth federation (an association to which her fiancé belonged) have disappeared; she is not sure whether they are dead or in prison (p. 5). Subsequent letters attest to torture and killing, such as the account of the neighbour 'mandan roger' (Mrs Roger) who collects her son's decapitated head from the police (p. 7). They also make reference to the threatening presence of the secret police, known in Haiti as the 'Tonton Macoutes'.* Her stories

* This name refers to the Haitian paramilitary force, established in 1959 under François Duvalier (known as Papa Doc) and in existence until 1986 under Duvalier's son (known as Baby Doc). The name *Tonton Macoute* comes from a Creole story about 'Unce Gunnysack' who abducts children, which was seen as a fitting tale because the members of the paramilitary force seized citizens, many of whom never returned because they had been killed by the state police. See Part Four: 'Cross-cultural Paradigms' for a discussion of 'Creole'.

of events in the present interrupt the tale of the young man's experiences at sea, which highlight African diasporic cultural connections and link present-day sufferings to a longer history of colonial oppression.

Spatial disorientation at sea opens up memories of earlier maritime journeys and cultural references that are central to Haitian history: '[t]here are no borderlines on the sea. The whole thing looks like one. I cannot tell if we are about to drop off the face of the earth. Maybe the world is flat and we are going to find out, like the navigators of old' (p. 6). The narrator evokes accounts of the age of discovery, such as those that prompted the explorers to come to the Caribbean and eventually led to the colonisation of Haiti. Some of the refugees see themselves as the Children of Israel, believing that God will part the sea for them, just as he did for the Israelites who fled slavery in Egypt. Such memories speak to Haiti's history of slavery and the ongoing yearning for the discovery of a Promised Land as a place of belonging and refuge. As the journey continues, the man's skin becomes blacker under the sun, prompting him to note: 'Yes, I am finally an African' (p. 11). The passengers tell stories in the call-and-response tradition, which hearkens back to the oral traditions of slaves on the plantations. The young man imagines that they are making a return journey to Africa, a dream of many African slaves (p. 14). He likens their conditions on the boat to those of slaves on the Middle Passage journey from Africa to the Caribbean (p. 15). Onboard the vessel is a teenage girl, named Célianne, who gives birth to a child at sea. The man learns that she was raped by soldiers in Haiti, who also abused and took away her brother. This raped mother at sea also brings to mind memories of those women who were raped under slavery, suggesting that violence in Haiti persists as a legacy of colonialism. When the infant dies, Célianne throws her dead child and herself into the sea, another reminder of the deaths of enslaved peoples during the Middle Passage. As water seeps into the leaky vessel, the youth doubts he will ever see land again: he visualises himself 'among the children of the deep blue sea, those who have escaped the chains of slavery to form a world beneath the heavens and the blood-drenched earth where you live' (p. 27). The young man imagines his fate is to join Agwé, a voudou spirit (*lwa*) who presides over the sea.* As the story comes to an end, the young woman writes to her fiancé, telling him of 'a sea that is endless like my love for you' (p. 29). This emotionally rich and pathos-ridden tale speaks to the history of migration and exile in Haiti past and present.

The theme of mother–daughter relations serves as a linking device between many of the tales. 'Between the Pool and the Gardenias' presents the tale of a young woman who is arrested for matricide when she is found attempting to bury a dead baby. However, through the narrative, the reader learns that the corpse of the infant girl is one she picked up on the streets of Port-au-Prince, Haiti. She has miscarried on several occasions and is haunted by the memories of her unborn infants. Danticat focuses on the perspective of the woman, who describes the child as if it were still living. Only gradually does the reader come to recognise that she is carrying around a dead child. This individual tale of woe is placed in a wider familial and social context. The narrator of the story remarks that when she first came to the city she was stunned to discover the difference between the urban and rural experiences of motherhood. In the country, the afterbirth is named and buried 'near the roots of a tree so that the world won't fall apart around you (p. 93). In the city, 'a lot of poor women throw out their babies because they can't afford to feed them' (p. 92). The main character of the narrative dreams of her deceased mother, who introduces her to her ancestors, including her 'great grandmother Eveline who was killed by the Dominican soldiers at the Massacre River. My grandmother Défilé who died with a bald head in a prison, because God had given her wings. My godmother Lili who killed herself in old age because her husband had jumped out of a flying

* Voudou (or voodoo) is a version of African religious beliefs and practices that developed among slave populations in the West Indies (especially Haiti) and Southern states of America.

balloon and her grown son left her to go to Miami' (p. 94). These accounts of the lives of dead foremothers and daughters create a living link with history as well as to the collection of tales.

Links between stories reinforce the relations between them. For instance, the attentive reader will recognise that 'Nineteen Thirty-Seven' presents the mother's tale of flight from the Dominican Republic under dictatorial rule by Rafael Trujillo. In 1937, the dictator ordered the massacre of Haitians living in the nation, an act of genocide that would later be referred to as the Parsley Massacre because the soldiers were reported to have thrown parsley at people and asked them to identify the plant. Those who pronounced the word in French or Haitian Creole (*Kreyòl*) rather than Spanish were killed. In Danticat's story, a young woman visits her mother (Défilé) in prison where she learns of the massacre and the death of her grandmother. To offer another example, the story 'A Wall of Fire Rising' offers an account of Lili during her youth prior to her husband's suicide. The interlinking of these narratives allows the reader to experience the ways in which the tales form part of a wider narrative of history that can only be grasped as fragments of a greater whole. By juxtaposing tales from various generations within the short story collection as a whole, Danticat elicits a living present so that events which occurred in the distant past coexist with those in recent times. Events in Haiti are brought close to those which take place in America. In this sense, the 'Krik?, Krak!' tradition of call-and-response narration applies not only to the teller–audience relationship of exchange but also to the sense of living relations among the tales themselves.

Junot Díaz: Dominican American Horizons

Born in the Dominican Republic in 1967, Junot Díaz came to the United States as a child in 1974. This transnational experience – and early separation from his father who had migrated to America several years earlier in search of work – shapes his fiction, which includes a collection of short stories, *Drown* (1996) and the Pulitzer Prize winning novel, *The Brief Wondrous Life of Oscar Wao* (2007).

The ten short stories in *Drown* depict the lives of Dominican and Dominican American boys and adolescent males as they struggle to survive in the harsh and often violent world of poverty, drugs and petty crime. Five of the ten stories focus on Ramon de las Casas, called Yunior, whose father seemingly abandons his wife and children when he migrates to the United States. Years later, following a marriage to an American to gain citizenship, he returns to the Dominican Republic in order to bring his family to New Jersey. Other stories dwell on the experiences of young Latino male narrators who may or may not be Yunior. The presence of a macho, sometimes violent, father figure and/or absence of male role models suggests that these Latino youths may well be doomed from childhood to lives of conflict, itinerant work and possibly crime. Metaphorically, the characters in *Drown* appear to be going under because they are out of their depth in perilous waters, whether in the Dominican Republic or living in the diasporic Latino communities of America.

These gritty coming-of-age stories, typically told in the first person, have something of the comically despairing tone of Holden Caulfield from J. D. Salinger's *The Catcher in the Rye* (1951), an American *Bildungsroman* in which the alienated child struggles to come to terms with his environment. Salinger's work makes use of colloquial and profane language, represents teen angst and alienation, interrogates sexuality, and focuses on the quest for a sense of belonging. All of these facets are present in Díaz's work, but they are both updated and intensified through his focus on the contemporary Dominican Republican cultural context. Specifically, the question of belonging is posed in terms of language at the outset of the collection. The work begins with an epigraph from Cuban American writer, Gustavo Pérez Firmat who observes that the act of writing in English falsifies the work, but it also provides a space of belonging for a writer who, paradoxically enough, does not belong to English, but belongs nowhere else. Throughout the collection, the various first-person narrators 'speak' in English, but their discourse is punctuated by Spanish words that are rarely defined in the narrative. The opening sentence to the first story in the collection, 'Ysrael', reads as follows: 'We were on our way to the colmado for an errand, a beer for my tío, when Rafa stood still and tilted his head, as if listening to a message I couldn't hear, something beamed in from afar'.[10] The word 'tío' (meaning 'uncle') might be familiar to English speakers, but 'colmado' (meaning 'grocer's') is probably not so familiar. Through contextual reference and the provision of a Spanish–English glossary, Díaz effectively draws the English-only reader into a bilingual, bicultural world.

The tales emphasise the effects of being a transnational family, consisting of members living in the Dominican Republic and the United States. In 'Ysrael', Yunior and his older brother, Rafa, have been sent to live in the campo (the countryside) during the summer months because their mother, who works in a factory, does not have time to care for them. Their father is absent because he is working in the United States. More or less unsupervised, the boys soon look for trouble. Rafa decides that they should pay a visit to Ysrael, a boy who was disfigured by a pig when he was an infant. Ysrael wears a mask in order to prevent people from staring at his face, but Rafa is determined to satisfy his curiosity about it. He does not, however, share his plan with Yunior. When the boys encounter Ysrael, they note that he is wearing American clothes (p. 11) and flying a kite, which he tells them his father sent him from Nueva York (New York). Yunior and Rafa tell Ysrael that their father is also in New York, but they are dismayed because theirs only sends them 'letters and an occasional shirt or pair of jeans at Christmas' (p. 12). Ysrael tells them that he will be sent to America to receive an operation to mend his face, but Rafa refuses to believe this. Suddenly, Rafa brings a bottle down on Ysrael's head, knocks him to the ground and removes his mask. While Ysrael is lying unconscious, Rafa examines his face. The boys flee the scene. Yunior, who is seemingly worried about Ysrael, affirms that he will be okay. But Rafa once more affirms that nothing will be done to repair the damage to the boy's face. The absence of the paternal figure as a protector and guide for his children is shown to engender risks, both for the wounded Ysrael and for Rafa and Yunior, who are given insufficient attention. In both cases, however, it is the economic disparity between the Dominican Republic and America which has led to the father figure leaving in search of a better life.

According to David Gates, the theme of masking and unmasking identity – evident in 'Ysrael' – surfaces also in other narratives, such as 'No Face', which recounts Ysrael's memory of the pig's attack, and 'How to Date a Browngirl, Blackgirl, Whitegirl, or Halfie'.[11] In the case of the latter, Yunior provides tips on dating, often in the form of the imperative, which are directly connected to the discourses of racial hierarchies and cultural difference. The disavowal of cultural difference is evident when the narrator observes, 'Take down any embarrassing photos of your family in the campo, especially the one with the half-naked kids dragging a goat on a rope leash' (p. 111). On the date, the youth may talk about the 'loco' (crazy man) in the neighbourhood who stockpiles canisters of tear gas, but he is not supposed to tell his date that his mother 'recognized its smell from the year the United States invaded your island' (p. 113). This is a reference to the American intervention in the Dominican Republic in 1965–6 as a response to civil unrest following the collapse of the Trujillo regime. Thus, the history of American neoimperialism is concealed in order to avoid potential conflicts. Racial difference is suppressed where possible. For example, the youth instructs that any photos depicting the young male with an Afro hairstyle need to be taken down (p. 111). When feeling panicky, the male should run his hand through his hair 'like the whiteboys do even though the only thing that runs easily through your hair is Africa' (p. 112). Racial hierarchies shape the youth's sexual desires: 'The white ones are the ones that you want the most, aren't they' (p. 113). Thus, colonial discourses about racial and cultural supremacy are seen to render problematic the dating experience, producing a comic sense of unease concerning the pitfalls of dating.

'Negocios' (referring to negotiations or a business deal), the final story in the collection, follows the sexual and financial misadventures of Yunior's father in the Dominican Republic and America. Ramón decides to leave the island following a number of disputes with his wife on account of his sexual infidelity. The theme of capitalist aspirations and the exploitation of migrant labourers provides a link between past and present for Ramón, who arrives in America dreaming of 'gold coins, like the ones that had been salvaged from the many wrecks about our Island, stacked high as sugarcane' (p. 130). However, the reality is quite different as he works long hours for low wages, struggles to learn English, and discovers that at least one of his fellow migrants is taking advantage of his ignorance and overcharging him for rent. The precarious nature of his existence is reinforced when he migrates from Miami to New York and is offered a ride by the local police. Afraid of being identified by the police as an illegal immigrant and deported, this leg of the trip is a terrifying experience. During his first year in New York, he works nineteen and twenty hour days, seven days a week. When an accident occurs in the workplace, leaving him in severe back pain, Ramón dreams of suing his employer, envisioning that he will be recompensed and achieve his dreams of owning 'gold rings and a spacious house with caged tropical birds (p. 159). It turns out that these dreams of turning exploitation into financial gain are inspired by his own father, who attempted to swindle a company by damaging his toe. His lawsuit proved unsuccessful, and he ended up having to have the toe amputated. Thus, the family's history of financial disadvantage emerges through the cross-currents of the story about life in the Dominican Republic from the colonial past, through post-colonial transition, to the present in America.

Familial and financial negotiations intersect in the story. The risky path to citizenship entails entering into a new marriage: 'Find a citizen, get married, wait, and then divorce her. The routine was a well-practiced and expensive and riddled with swindlers' (p. 138). Ramón enters into negotiations to find a wife, but he loses his eight-hundred dollar investment. Eventually, he meets, seduces and marries a woman named Nilda. His friend, Jo-Jo, advises him to form a business of his own, bring over his family from the Domincan

Republic, buy a nice house and expand the business because that is 'the American way' (p. 148). Yunior, as narrator, observes: 'Papi wanted a negocio of his own, that was his dream, but balked at starting at the bottom' (p. 149). Eventually, Jo-Jo's accounts of business success, which are linked to notions of family loyalty, sway Ramón: 'Papi had difficulty separating the two threads of his friend's beliefs, that of negocios and that of the family, and in the end the two became impossibly intertwined' (p. 149). Ramón deceives Nilda; he finds a job on the side in order to send money to his wife and children in the Dominican Republic. Yet, when he returns to the island, he cannot muster the will to go and visit the family. Yunior's description of this nonevent elicits a sense of pathos: 'His absence was a seamless thing to me. And if a strange man approached me during play and stared down at me and my siblings, perhaps asking our names, I don't remember it now' (p. 156).

Eventually, Ramón leaves Nilda and brings his family to America, but Yunior grows up filled with anxiety about his relationship with his father as well as about his father's precarious life history. His visits to Nilda to reclaim a sense of his paternal and wider familial history – for he has a half-brother also named Yunior – do little to alleviate his worries and doubts concerning his own existence as well as that of the family and the wider community.

Jhumpa Lahiri: Bengali American Perspectives

Born in England in 1967 to Bengali parents, Lahiri's family migrated to the United States when she was still a child. She grew up on Rhode Island and the Eastern seaboard features as a recurring location in much of her work. Lahiri won the Pulitzer Prize for her first collection of short stories, *Interpreter of Maladies* (1999). Subsequently, she published a novel, *The Namesake* (2003), which was adapted for the screen. With *Unaccustomed Earth* (2008), Lahiri returns once more to the short story. In these works, she tends to focus on the lives of expatriate Bengalis and their children, exploring generational differences, diasporic identity and transnational relations in the contemporary era. Natalie Friedman notes:

> Today's immigrant characters, particularly the children of immigrants, like their creators, belong to a world of cosmopolites that Tim Brennan described as 'exempt from national belonging' and who are perennial migrants 'valorized by a rhetoric of wandering'.[12]

Cosmopolitan issues* of affiliation and issues of belonging surface in most of Lahiri's fictions, which test the possibilities for identity in the borderlands between cultures, particularly American and Indian. While some readers are critical of her work for its focus on the lives of middle class families, Lahiri is also critical of the elitist assumptions that often govern the lives of the upwardly mobile and affluent.

Noelle Brada-Williams offers an incisive reading of *Interpreter of Maladies* as a short story cycle.[13] She notes the balancing and counter-balancing of stories, including ones that contain accounts of unfaithful spouses, such as 'Interpreter of Maladies' and 'Sexy', and others that offer contrasting views of the Indian community, notably in 'A Real Durwan' and 'The Treatment of Bibi Haldar'. While the first story in the collection, 'A Temporary Matter', records the breakdown of a marriage, the final story focuses on events in the life of a migrant who leaves India for England and comes to live in Finsbury Park in North London. The collection consists of nine stories about people living in America, India and England, which offer suspenseful accounts of moments of intimacy related to transnational encounters and/or cosmopolitan experiences. Lahiri highlights the minor events in daily life that trigger personal catastrophes, turning points and transitions. These are not tales that focus on epiphanies so much as the moments when relations come together or tear apart.

In 'A Temporary Matter', set in Boston, a young couple are informed that their electricity will be cut off for one hour each day, over a period of five days, so that repairs to an electrical line, torn

* See Part Four: 'Cross-cultural paradigms' for a discussion of cosmopolitanism.

down during a storm, might be made. This mundane event proves to be the tipping point, breaking the couple's routine for avoiding one another following the stillbirth of their first child. Shukumar, the husband, has taken over cooking, one of the household tasks his wife, Shoba, no longer undertakes on account of depression. As he prepares a meal of lamb, he recalls happier times when Shoba was still pregnant and she held a surprise birthday party for him with over one hundred guests, 'crammed into the house – all the friends and the friends of friends they now systematically avoided ... [Shoba] had made a vanilla cream cake with custard and spun sugar. All night she kept Shukumar's long fingers linked with hers as they walked among the guests at the party.'[14] As the couple eats their candlelit dinner of *rogan josh* (a curry lamb stew that originates in Kashmir), they come to terms with the absences that have come to fill their lives. The loss of electricity reminds Shoba of power outages in India. She tells Shukumar about a time when she attended a rice ceremony in honour of a newborn baby. During this event, which took place in the dark, the baby cried and cried. Shukumar reflects that '[t]heir baby had never cried' and 'would never have a rice ceremony' (p. 11). This sad reflection is a melancholic reminder of the absence of the child and India in their lives. Inspired by her memories of telling stories in India during power shortages, Shoba suggests they exchange accounts of incidents. She tells him that she peeked in his address book in the first few weeks of their relationship to see if there was an entry with her contact details. He tells her a story of forgetting to tip a waiter at a restaurant when he first realised he might marry her, and of returning to give the tip the next day. This Indian ritual of storytelling appears to bring the couple together.

However, absence also plays a role in their tale telling exchange. The stories Shakumar chooses not to tell are equally significant: the night of their first meeting when they attended a Bengali poetry recitation, which he couldn't understand. During the evening, he also reflects on how little he knows of India because his parents went there without him. Over several nights they share intimate details and make love. However, when the electricity is once again working, Shoba tells Shakumar that she is going to move out. As a parting gesture, Shakumar tells her that he had arrived at the hospital and held their dead son, whose fingers had been curled tight just like hers when she slept (p. 22). He had not told her about this incident earlier because he knew that Shoba wanted the sex of the child to be a secret revealed at birth. In telling her the story, Shakumar is also revealing that he has given up hope for their marriage, for he has only withheld the story out of love for her (p. 22). As the tale ends, the couple weep 'for the things they now knew' (p. 22). Storytelling, rather than bringing them together, marks the end of their relationship. Moreover, it highlights differences that separate the pair. Despite their shared Indian diasporic background, they have different relationships to their cultural heritage, differences which have brought them together but also kept them apart. The 'temporary matter' – of withholding electricity for one hour each evening – serves to evoke an Indian diasporic spatio-temporality that allows them to explore the tenuousness of their own relationship to one another.

While 'A Temporary Matter' offers a investigation into diasporic intimacies, some of the stories offer more explicitly political accounts of transcultural difference and postcolonial divisions. 'When Mr. Pirzada Came to Dine' refers to civil war in Pakistan in the early 1970s, especially the conflict in Dacca, a city which 'had been invaded, torched, and shelled by the Pakistani Army' (p. 23). Lilia, the child narrator of the story, learns that these events are related to colonial history when her father explains that 1947 marked not only independence from British colonial rule but also the partition of Indian and Pakistan, which resulted in ongoing divisions within the nation-states as well as across borders: 'He [the father] told me [Lilia] that during Partition Hindus and Muslims had set fire to each other's homes. For many, the idea of eating in the other's company was still unthinkable' (p. 25). The father is incensed to discover that his daughter knows little about the colonial history, and its legacies, which have shaped the life of her family. He wonders aloud what she learns at her Boston school: she reflects on her education, which focuses primarily on American history and geography. Thus, when Lilia sees the map of India and Pakistan, she translates the geographic terrain via the American cartography she knows. When her father points out that India is orange and Pakistan yellow in order to differentiate the national territories, she notices that there are two distinct parts toPakistan, separated by Indian territory: 'it was as if California and Connecticut constituted a nation apart from the U.S.' (p. 26). Thus, she remaps the territory of India and Pakistan onto America, creating an imaginary palimpsest that brings the two regions of the world together into a knowable terrain. While she knows so little about Indian colonial history, at school, she can fill in the missing details about the thirteen colonies of America with ease.

At Halloween, when Mr Pirzada (a visiting research fellow from Dacca) comes over for dinner, he helps to carve a pumpkin for a jack-o'-lantern, but he mistakenly cuts too deeply when he hears a televised newscast announcing that India might go to war with Pakistan. Lilia's father takes over carving the pumpkin, and is forced to give it a large gaping mouth in order to accommodate the area slashed out by Mr Pirzada. The resulting expression on the jack-o'-lantern's face is not so much menacing as astonished, symbolically reflecting Mr Pirzada's own reaction to the menacing news of war. For Lilia, the encounter with Mr Pirzada forms an initiation into world politics as the Indo-Pakistanti War of 1971 breaks out. It also introduces the girl to a sense of the loss that accompanies separation from loved ones in distant parts of the world: she bears witness to Mr Pirzada's separation from his family in Pakistan and comes to experience a sense of loss herself when he returns to Pakistan. Orange is a symbolic colour, the gashed face of the pumpkin representing an eerie double for the orange India on the map. Moreover, Mr Pirzada's habit of bringing treats for Lilia, sweets that she savoured as she prayed for the safety of his family, become part of a childhood ritual. The American tradition of 'trick or treat' resonates in an entirely novel and disturbing way for the child who finds her own life to be related to histories of colonial and post-partition violence in the contemporary world.

The contemporary world of circulating persons, entailing contact across cultures, surfaces in the collection. The title story, 'Interpreter of Maladies', focuses on an exchange between a family of American tourists named Das, and Mr Kapasi, a local Indian guide. Aspects of the tale echo themes and concerns found in E. M. Forster's *A Passage to India* (1924),* such as the possibilities for mutual comprehension, intimacy and sexual attraction between the visiting female tourist and the local Indian man.[15] Kapasi also works as an interpreter or translator for a doctor, speaking on behalf of Gujarati patients when describing their symptoms (hence the title of the tale). Mrs Das suggests that the role of an interpreter of maladies is important and even romantic. She and the guide seem to share a moment of intimacy when she tells him a secret about an act of infidelity she committed, and asks him to interpret her emotional maladies. He cannot help but compare her dissatisfaction with her marriage to the extreme cases of physical illness that he witnesses. He suggests to her that she feels guilt rather than pain on account of her adulterous past. She takes offence. As the story comes to an end, the American woman's child (born as a result of the adulterous affair) is assaulted by monkeys in the forest. In this tale, we see the neocolonial values still circulating in the world. Where Forster examines British imperial prejudices, Lahiri offers a satirical view of American imperialism and tendencies to exoticise the other. By telling the story from Kapesi's point of view, Lahiri highlights the differences between a first-world economic viewpoint and the lives of those who are struggling to eke out a living and find a way of surviving in the global economy.

Extended Commentary: Adichie, 'The Thing Around Your Neck' (2009)

Through her short stories, Chimamanda Adichie illustrates the challenge life in modern America presents for Nigerian women as

* For a discussion of *A Passage to India*, see Part Four: 'Race, Gender and Sexuality'.

they struggle against patriarchal values in transnational and transcultural contexts. 'The Arrangers of Marriage', published in her 2009 collection, *The Thing Around Your Neck*, explores the alienation experienced by a woman who moves to America to live with a husband who is a stranger to her. Although her husband wants her to assimilate and adopt American customs, he has chosen to marry her because he wants an obedient Nigerian wife (p. 184). The young woman forms an alliance with another woman, named Nia, living in the apartment building. She discovers that her husband had a sexual liaison with Nia in the past. Ironically, Nia helps the young woman to realise that she may have a more independent life in America: '"You can wait until you get your papers and then leave," Nia said. "You can apply for benefits ... and then you'll get a job and find a place and support yourself and start afresh"' (p. 185). As the story comes to a close, it is apparent that it is the husband who will be disappointed by this arranged marriage, as his young wife plans to leave him at the first opportunity.

Gender relations across cultures are no easier, as the title work of the collection, 'The Thing Around Your Neck' examines. This rich and engaging story explores the emotions of a young Nigerian woman, named Akunna, who comes to feel as though she is choking when she moves to America. Written in the second person, Adichie's story compels the reader to experience a sense of dislocation and disenfranchisement through the use of 'you', which implicitly conflates the identities of Akunna and the reader. The opening of the narrative gives a sense of Nigerian expectations about the promise and perils of life in America, including stereotypes about violence and the mythology of the American Dream:

> You thought everybody in America had a car and a gun; your uncles and aunts thought so too. Right after you won the American visa lottery, they told you: In a month, you will have a big car. Soon, a big house. But don't buy a gun like those Americans. (p. 115)

Akunna goes to live in Maine with an uncle through marriage and his wife, but she is forced to leave when he sexually assaults her. Thus, the real risks of life in America turn out to be something other. The transnational family which is meant to protect Akunna from dangers in American society turns out be a source of exploitation as traditional patriarchal values enable him to take advantage of her.

At the same time, Akunna learns about racial segregation in America: her uncle works for a company that hires mostly white people and has hired him as a token gesture toward racial and cultural diversity. He and his family live in a predominantly white area so that his wife has to 'drive an hour to find a hair salon that did black hair' (p. 116). She becomes an object of wonder for curious white Americans, many of whom believe she is Jamaican on account of her foreign accent. She learns that she is viewed as an exotic other, associated with elephants and safaris (p. 119). The American tendency to view Africa in monolithic terms, to confuse events in Botswana with those in Nigeria, is indicative of a lack of awareness about national and cultural differences as portrayed by Adichie in her work. Consequently, when a customer in the restaurant where Akunna waits tables asks if she is Yoruba or Igbo because she doesn't have a Fulani face, she is astonished (p. 119). She discovers that she can share her racial and gender politics with the young man:

> You knew that you had become comfortable when you told him that you watched Jeopardy on the restaurant TV and that you rooted for the following, in this order: women of colour, black men, and white women, before, finally, white men – which meant you never rooted for white man. He laughed and told you that he was used to not being rooted for, his mother taught women's studies. (p. 122)

Through their relationship, Adichie critiques liberal American assumptions. The boyfriend's notion that he can understand her worldview eventually irritates her, as does his inability to recognise incidents of racism when they occur. Adichie describes the inevitable confrontation as follows:

> He said you were wrong to call him self-righteous. You said he was wrong to call only the poor Indians in Bombay the real Indians. Did it mean he wasn't a real American, since he was not like the poor fat people you and he had seen in Hartford? (p. 125)

The ability to speak her mind lessens Akunna's sense of cultural asphyxiation: 'The thing that wrapped itself around your neck, that nearly choked you before you feel asleep, started to loosen, to let go' (p. 125). Nonetheless, tensions in the relationship persist. When the young woman learns that her father has died during her absence, she decides to return to Nigeria. As the story ends, it is unclear whether she will return to life in America and/or her relationship with the American boyfriend.

Adichie's story highlights the hopes, anxieties, risks and challenges that accompany life in a transnational era of border crossing. As noted at the beginning of this chapter, Caryl Phillips suggests that we live in an era of global migration and communication when the possibilities for contact, exchange and communication with peoples from distant parts of the world have become commonplace. In the contemporary era, the transnational experience is reshaping a sense of intimacy, kinship, friendship, domesticity and relations among neighbours. Yet, this is also a world where racism, gender discrimination and xenophobia persist and the legacies of empire surface, often unexpectedly. Together, the contemporary short story cycles of authors such as Danticat, Díaz and Adichie bear witness to our changing world order where the local and the personal are often shaped by events and persons in far-flung parts of the world. Unexpected intimacies often spring up between strangers while the old certainties about a sense of belonging and connection no longer seem to bind marriages, families and peoples together. Where earlier tales of migration in the post-colonial era often focused on a sense of exile and the hope of hybrid fusions in the context of the nation, this new era of transnational exchanges and dialogues is characterised by a heightened awareness of both the possibilities and perils of proximity and distance.

Notes

1 For a helpful account of the postcolonial short story, see Jacqueline Bardolph's edited collection of essays: *Telling Stories: Postcolonial Short Fiction in English* (Amsterdam: Rodopi, 2001). See also the entry on the short story cycle in John Charles Hawley's *Encyclopedia of Postcolonial Studies* (Westport, CT: Greenwood Press, 2001), pp. 406–7. Paul March-Russell's *The Short Story: An Introduction* (Edinburgh: Edinburgh University Press, 2009) includes a chapter on the postcolonial story.

2 For a good discussion of the American ethnic short story cycle, see James Nagel's *The Contemporary American Short Story Cycle: The Ethnic Resources of a Genre* (Baton Rouge: Louisiana State University Press, 2001).

3 Rocio G. Davis, 'Oral Narrative as Short Story Cycle: Forging Community in Edwidge Danticat's "Krik? Krak!"', *MELUS* 26.2 Identities (Summer 2001), p. 66. Davis draws on Forrest L. Ingram's *Representative Short Story Cycles of the Twentieth Century: Studies in a Literary Genre* (The Hague: Mouton, 1971).

4 Caryl Phillips, *A New World Order: Selected Essays* (London: Vintage, 2002), p. 5.

5 For a particularly insightful review of the collection, see Bernardine Evaristo's book review in *The Times* on 17 April 2009 accessed from http://entertainment.timesonline.co.uk on 16 September 2010.

6 For an excellent account of the influence of *Things Fall Apart* on Adichie's writing, see Chimamanda Ngozi Adichie, 'African "Authenticity" and the Biafran Experience' *Transition* 99 (2008), pp. 42–53.

7 Chimamanda Ngozi Adichie, *The Thing Around Your Neck* (London: Fourth Estate, 2009), p. 210.

8 Davis, 'Oral Narrative', p. 68.

9 Edwidge Danticat, *Krik? Krak!* (New York: Vintage, 1996), p. 219.

10 Junot Díaz, *Drown* (London: Faber & Faber, 1996), p. 1.

11 For an excellent review of *Drown*, see David Gates, 'English Lessons' in *The New York Times* on 26 September 1996 accessed from http://query.nytimes.com on 30 September 2010.

12 Natalie Friedman, 'From Hybrids to Tourists: Children of Immigrants in Jhumpa Lahiri's The Namesake' *Critique: Studies in Contemporary Fiction* 50.1 (Fall 2008), p. 114.
13 Noelle Brada-Williams, 'Reading Jhumpa Lahiri's *Interpreter of Maladies* as a Short Story Cycle', *MELUS* 29.3/4 (Fall 2004), pp. 451–64.
14 Jhumpa Lahiri, *Interpreter of Maladies* (London: Flamingo, 2000), p. 9.
15 Simon Lewis offers an interpretation of the story's relation to Forster's work in 'Lahiri's *Interpreter of Maladies*' *Explicator* 59.4 (2001), pp. 219–21.

Decolonising the Stage: Davis, Wilson, Walcott and Soyinka

In *Post-Colonial Drama: Theory, Practice, Politics*, Helen Gilbert and Joanne Tompkins define postcolonial performance as follows:

- acts that respond to the experiences of imperialism, whether directly or indirectly;
- acts performed for the continuation and/or regeneration of the colonised (and sometimes precontact) communities;
- acts performed with the awareness of, and sometimes the incorporation of, post-contact forms; and
- acts that interrogate the hegemony that underlies imperial representation.[1]

In this chapter, we will look at how these facets of postcolonial drama contribute more specifically to decolonising the stage or producing new forms of theatricality that give expression to postcolonial culture. Specifically, we will consider four very different postcolonial contexts: Wole Soyinka's drama in Africa, Derek Walcott's Caribbean theatre, August Wilson's reconstruction of African American performance and Jack Davis's restaging of

Australian performance traditions from an aboriginal perspective. These four playwrights challenge the legacies of colonialism and settlement while seeking to recuperate indigenous or precontact forms as a means to regenerate the community as a whole. Vernacular traditions, such as folklore and ritual, play an especially important role in this form of theatre, but these works are also highly critical of colonial oppression. In this respect, these dramatists can be seen as decolonising the stage by drawing through critique, reclamation and renewal.

Jack Davis: Australian Aboriginal Perspectives

Aboriginal and indigenous drama plays a powerful role in dramatising the concerns of native peoples whose own cultures and traditions predate colonial contact, but have undergone tremendous oppression through colonialism and continue to experience various forms of marginalisation in the postcolonial era. Indigenous drama often expresses concerns about postcolonial identity, claims to the land and acts of injustice, both historic and contemporaneous. In Australia, Jack Davis (1917–2000), Wesley Enoch (b. 1969) and Jane Harrison (b. 1960) are among some of the best known aboriginal playwrights. Where indigenous peoples of North America have been represented in often stereotypical terms through Hollywood cinema and popular culture, the Aboriginal peoples of Australia have been 'less often mythologised in/through popular representation than simply ignored, especially in visual media'.[2] As such, Aboriginal drama is less often concerned with countering popular stereotypes than with the reclamation of history and calling attention to acts of dispossession and exile associated with white invasion and settlement. Notably, the histories of genocide, forced resettlement, separation and dispossession have shaped Aboriginal culture. White Australians attempted to deal with the 'Native Question' by systematically destroying the cultural identity of the Nyoongah peoples, an indigenous group in the southwest of Western Australia, first by using violent action to subdue Aboriginal rebellion and then by absorbing Aboriginal children into white culture or marginalising Aboriginal families on isolated settlements. Jack Davis's own life was shaped by these contexts. Under the Aboriginal Protection Acts (1909–43), indigenous peoples were forced to live on reserves and prohibited from speaking with whites. Black families were often separated so that children could be taught to reject their heritage and embrace white values instead. Early in his youth, Davis was sent to Moore River Native Settlement for just such an 'education'. Later he would dramatise such experiences as well as incorporate the Nyoongah language in an effort to resist the imperialistic culture of Australia. In this context, theatre plays a decolonising role by highlighting social injustice, but more than this it offers a forum for giving expression to a suppressed culture. Helen Gilbert argues that a theatre of decolonisation:

> can be effected through a series of theatrical counterevents, or rather counterprocesses, that allow the remapping of space, the reframing of time, the relocation of sightlines, and the repositioning of the colonial subject/body in representation.[3]

In this respect, a theatre of decolonisation goes beyond protests about exploitation and engages in a complex and nuanced investigation of postcolonial cultural formation and individual life choices.

The work of Jack Davis is particularly noteworthy because he has played a foundational and leading role in Australian Aboriginal drama. His first play, *Kullark* (1979), chronicles events in Western Australian Aboriginal history from white settlement to the present, interweaving the past and present, particularly through the lives of the Yorlah family, which consists of Alec, Rosie and their son Jamie. The play traces the shift from relatively peaceful encounters between white and Aboriginal peoples to violence. The murder of Yagan* and

* Yagan (*c.* 1795–1833) was an Australian Aboriginal warrior from the Nyoongar tribe who played a key part in early indigenous Australian resistance to British settlement and rule in the area of Perth, Western Australia. He led a series of burglaries and robberies across the countryside, during which white settlers were killed. In response, the government offered a bounty for his capture, dead or alive.

the massacre of Aborigines at Pinjarra serve as warnings that the 'white man will not tolerate murder'.[4] This hybrid work mixes English and Aboriginal language in the dialogue (for more on hybridity, see Part Four: 'Cross-cultural Paradigms'). These scenes of violence are cross-cut with representations of dependency and pessimism in modern Aboriginal life. Alec, an alcoholic, dependent on welfare payments from the state, comes into conflict with his son, a university student who is critical of his father's passive acceptance of white domination. The historical drama provides a wider historical context for the father's alienated condition, showing how he (along with his parents and sibling) were forcibly transferred to the Moore River Settlement. In the postwar period, Alec confronts racism in a society that continues to marginalise Aboriginal peoples. The continuous history of cultural resistance is dramatised through Yagan's indigenous chant and dance when he calls forth Warrgul the Rainbow Serpent, the creator of earth and life in Aboriginal mythology. Brian Crow and Chris Banfield observe the effect of cultural and racial collisions as represented in the drama:

> Warrgul retains an emblematic visual presence during the performance of the play through the painting of the Rainbow Serpent in the shape of a map of the Swan River. But when the invading white characters enter they do so through revolving screens that 'cut' segments of the Serpent and replace it with European images of Australia. By such means, together with the alteration of past and present day, Davis is able to convey the continuity of white Australian racism and its effects on Aborigines, but also the history of black resistance and its spiritual basis.[5]

The staging of the Serpent, however, might also suggest a more subversive interpretive perspective. Despite the fact that it is fractured through the excisions associated with settlement, the

Serpent as a symbol of Dreamtime* invokes a mythological notion of time and space, which reframes Western chronological and cartographic apprehensions of time and space. The cross-cutting of scenes suggests that an achronological, dialogic approach to narrating the nation is required from a postcolonial perspective. Moreover, the very title of the play, *Kullark*, which means 'home' in the Nyoongah language, domesticates Australian history, grounding it in Aboriginal language and culture.

Davis's 'First Born' trilogy, comprising of *The Dreamers* (1980), *No Sugar* (1985) and *Barungin* (*Smell the Wind*) (1988), explores the richness of Aboriginal cultural traditions alongside concerns about land rights and the deaths of indigenous peoples as a result of white racism. *The Dreamers* is a two-act play that subverts European realism through its inclusion of supernatural aspects, characters and situations found in Aboriginal storytelling. The figure of Worru, a dying Aborigine, comes to symbolise the decline of the culture as a whole. During the play, the audience witnesses his descent into senility, which is accompanied by a retreat into memory and flights of the imaginary. The theme of Aboriginal dispossession dominates the play, which focuses on the lives of hard-drinking, unemployed men, imprisonment and the erosion of Nyoongah language and culture. In the first act, a drunken Worru begins to dance to disco music, performing a clumsy version of a partly remembered tribal dance. The scene ends with the introduction of didgeridoo and clap sticks as musical accompaniment rather than disco. Thus, the presence of indigenous dance and song highlight the long history of Aboriginal culture, but, at the same time, these forms are represented as part of a dying culture, which appears to be heading towards extinction.

No Sugar focuses on the Millimurra family in the depression years following the stock market crash of 1929. Rounded up by state authorities, they are transferred to the Moore River Settlement.

* For the Australian Aboriginal peoples, 'Dreamtime' (also called 'The Dreaming') refers to the era of creation before the physical world existed, but Dreamtime still exists in parallel to the physical world. Aboriginal songs, dances and visual arts commemorate Dreamtime.

Racist discourses and practices are dramatised in this work, which includes speeches by A. O. Neville,* the Chief Protector of Aborigines, and highlights incidents of sexual abuse perpetrated against Aboriginal females by Mr Neal, the superintendent of the settlement. However, Joe Millimurra and his lover Mary eventually escape from the confines of the settlement with the hopes of attaining a measure of autonomy and freedom. Song and dance, particularly through *corroboree* (a ceremonial meeting during which Aborigines interact with the Dreamtime through dance, music and costume), enable resistance, offering Aboriginal peoples a way to express their rejection of a white supremacist culture.

The final play in the trilogy, *Barungin*, offers a deeply pessimistic portrayal of poverty, alcoholism and Aboriginal deaths in custody, all in the context of Australia's bicentennial. The work opens and closes with a funeral service; the closing scene, following the death of Peter in police custody, is particularly noteworthy. At Peter's funeral, his sister, Meena, reads a list of names of those who have died in custody, ending with the name of John Pat who died in a police cell after an alleged fight with four officers. The image of the tribal Dancer whose movements are accompanied by the didgeridoo creates a unifying sense of loss through time. This lament for a dying culture offers an elegiac representation of Aboriginal presence and absence in Australia.

August Wilson: Reclaiming African American Culture and History

African American playwright, August Wilson (1945–2005) was born to a black mother and a white father, a German baker who had little contact with his son. He was raised by his mother on The Hill, a black ghetto of Pittsburgh, left school at fifteen, and spent his days

* Auber Octavius Neville (1875–1954) emigrated from England to Australia where he served as Chief Protector of Aborigines in Western Australia. The film *Rabbit-Proof Fence* (2002), directed by Philip Noyce, contains a powerful portrayal of Neville by Kenneth Branagh.

on the streets as well as reading at the public library. He became interested in the work of Langston Hughes, Ralph Ellison and Richard Wright. Coming of age in the 1960s, he was especially influenced by the Black Consciousness and the Black Power movements, both of which were aimed at articulating a strong sense of black, nationalist identity. In 1965, he discovered the music of Bessie Smith and the blues, developing an interest in black cultural expression that would come to shape his theatrical work. In the 1960s, Wilson cofounded the Black Horizons Theatre, aimed at raising black consciousness. Arguably the most important African American playwright of the twentieth century, this Pulitzer Prize winning dramatist is best known for *The Pittsburgh Cycle*, which consists of ten plays: one for each decade of the twentieth century. This body of work depicts the traumatic legacies of slavery and dramatises the challenges of decolonisation in America. The plays comprise *Gem of the Ocean* (2003) for the first decade of the twentieth century; *Joe Turner's Come and Gone* (1988) for the 1910s; *Ma Rainey's Black Bottom* (1984) for the 1920s; *The Piano Lesson* (1990) for the 1930s; *Seven Guitars* (1996) for the 1940s; *Fences* (1987) for the 1950s; *Two Trains Running* (1992) for the 1960s; *Jitney* (1982 and 2000) for the 1970s; *King Hedley II* (2001) for the 1980s; and *Radio Golf* (2005) for the 1990s. All but one – *Ma Rainey* being the exception – are set in Philadelphia.

Wilson argued that the reclamation of history was essential for African Americans, but stressed that an investigation of the past needed to be done in a highly critical fashion so that informed choices could be made about the best way forward:

> blacks in America need to reexamine their time spent here to see the choices that were made as a people. I'm not certain the right choices have always been made. That's part of my interest in history – to say 'Let's look at this again and see where we've come from and how we've gotten where we are now.' I think if you know that, it helps determine how to proceed in the future.[6]

Wilson's cycle of plays can thus be seen as an attempt to investigate critically the history of African American life. At the same time, as Bonnie Lyons notes, his work is deeply satisfying on an emotional plane and gives a full range of expression to tragic and comic dimensions of everyday life:

> While his plays are scorching indictments of racism and often include disclosures of past traumatic racial incidents which have scarred the characters, his work also celebrates the joy of music, food, stories, humor, and love. Wilson's most obvious strengths as a playwright are his ability to create vivid, fully realized characters and to provide them with rich, graphic, metaphorical language.[7]

Wilson's drama draws its inspiration from African American history, culture and everyday life. In his critique of racism, reclamation of history and renewal of cultural forms, Wilson employs strategies for decolonising the stage that are comparable to those of Davis and other dramatists who seek to represent the perspectives of oppressed peoples.

Set in Chicago, *Ma Rainey's Black Bottom* focuses on events in the life of a black blues singer, Ma Rainey, during the 1920s. Rainey's white manager, Irvin, and the recording company, Sturdyvant, both seek to exploit her talents. Ma Rainey is clearly aware of the exploitative aspects of this arrangement, as is evident when she describes her working relationship. She argues that the management 'don't care nothing about me. All they want is my voice. Well I done learned that, and they gonna treat me like I want to be treated no matter how much it hurt them. ... As soon as they get my voice down on them recording machines, then it's just like if I'd be some whore and they roll over and put their pants on. Ain't got no use for me then.'[8] For Ma Rainey, the blues is an expressive art form that gives voice to African American experience. She claims it as a force for cultural expression that can renew and enrich the world and which white people don't understand. 'You don't sing to feel better.

You sing 'cause that's a way of understanding life ... This be an empty world without the blues. I take that emptiness and try to fill it up with something' (pp. 194–5). Paradoxically, this Mother of the Blues,* is actually more of a child of this vernacular form because the blues has always been there, prior to her entry to the world. She is a Mother of the Blues to the extent that she participates in the reproduction of this art form: she is able to participate in the rebirth and regeneration of African American life through song. The blues is a way of talking about and understanding life, enabling her and the African American community more generally to come to terms with the African American experience.

In Wilson's oeuvre, African American culture offers many resources for self-expression and serves as a means to confront and overcome the suffering of the slave past and its legacies. *The Piano Lesson*, set in the 1930s, takes its title from a collage work of the same name by Romare Bearden.† An heirloom piano is at the centre of this play about a conflict between siblings and their views of the past. For the sister, Berniece, the piano links the family to their slave past: her grandfather had seen his 'owners' sell his wife and son to acquire the musical instrument. For the brother, Boy Willie, the piano is a commodity that can be sold in order to raise funds to purchase the land on which his ancestors had been enslaved. When the ghost of the recently deceased white landowner, Sutter, returns to reclaim the piano, brother and sister are literally and metaphorically prompted to exorcise the ghosts of the past. The ending of the play features:

> a musical call-and-response moment that channels the past in particularly African fashion as the sister, Berniece, sits at the piano and pleads to her ancestors to come to the aid of her brother, Boy Willie.[9]

* Historically, Gertrude Pridgett, otherwise known as Ma Rainey (1886–1939) is commonly referred to as the 'Mother of the Blues'.

† Bearden's *The Piano Lesson* depicts a black girl playing the piano with an older woman, presumably the piano teacher, standing over her shoulder. This brightly coloured collage work is thought by some to represent jazz pianist Mary Lou Williams, who spent her childhood years in Pittsburgh.

Joe Turner takes up the themes of forced migration and labour, which separated African Americans under slavery and in the post-abolition period, and depicts the challenges of reuniting individuals, family and community. Set in Seth Holly's boarding house, the play dramatises the lives of many people passing through in search of better prospects, and shows that freed slaves and their descendants are in a state of exile, separated from Africa and alienated in racist America. This loss of identity results in wandering, as peoples search for an identity, an occupation, family and a home. This drama offers a multifaceted response to the sense of alienation experienced by African Americans through its acts of cultural, spiritual and spatio-temporal reclamation. Inspired by African American vernacular culture, specifically a Bearden artwork of 1978, entitled *Mill Hand's Lunch Bucket*, and the blues song 'Joe Turner's Come and Gone', the play calls attention to the resources of culture, which enable black Americans to survive and find meaning in their lives. The song, recorded by blues artist W. C. Handy, was first sung by many estranged black women who had lost their husbands, fathers and sons to Joe Turner – a plantation owner who illegally enslaved blacks in the early twentieth century.

As the play opens, Seth and his wife Bertha are discussing the unusual behaviour of Bynum, a man who engages in African diasporic spiritual practices.* Bynum talks about his encounter with a 'shiny' man who enables Bynum to contact the ghost of his father. Following his father's advice to find a song in his life, Bynum discovers the Binding Song, which gives him a sense of purpose. Moreover, he uses his song to bind people to one another, thus extending the healing powers of music to the wider community. A white peddler, named Selig, enters the scene and explains that he is a people finder. Audience

* The term 'diaspora' (meaning dispersion) initially referred to the scattering of Jewish peoples as a result of several forced expulsions from what is now known as Israel, Jordan and parts of Lebanon as well as the State of Palestine. Subsequently, 'diaspora' has come to refer more generally to the movement, migration or scattering of a people away from a settled location or ancestral homeland.

members later discover that Selig's grandfather participated in the forced migration of Africans to the New World, and that Selig's father was employed tracking and capturing runaway slaves in order to return them to the plantations. Ironically, Selig himself – heir to the legacies of colonialism – uses these same skills to reunite separated African American families in a post-slavery world. In this sense, he profits from the legacies of slavery by reuniting people (for a fee) who have been separated in the past by his kin. In significantly different ways, the presence of Bynum and Selig attest to the need to find and bind oneself to others in the present and throughout history. In terms of decolonisation, the presence of Bynum is especially significant for he enables African Americans to overcome the traumas of the past and achieve a deeper emotional and spiritual post-abolition reunification of self, family and society.

Bynum's personal narrative intersects with those of Herald Loomis and his daughter Zonia, who also come to stay in the boarding house. Herald is a wanderer, searching for his wife, Martha, from whom he has been separated. His gruff and somewhat erratic manner tends to cause anxiety for those staying in the boarding house. In Act I, Scene IV, the boarders and owners of the house participate in a call-and-response song and dance, called Juba, which is reminiscent of the Ring Shouts of African slaves. Ring Shouts derived from the meshing of Christian doctrine with African spiritual traditions; thus they represent a hybrid cultural form, enabling African Americans to ground their New World identities. The temporary moment of communal entertainment is broken, however, when Herald enters the room in protest. He begins to mimic their dancing, but events soon take a turn as Herald is possessed by a vision of the Middle Passage and collapses. In his vision, he re-experiences the terrifying journey from Africa to slavery in the New World, during which many Africans died from illness, overcrowding and mutiny. The horrors of death and burial at sea (Africans, living and dead, were tossed overboard) are represented by bones rising up out of the water. The bones – the African slaves – arrive on the shores of America and are subject to slavery; they become flesh, but are zombified or not fully alive under the dehumanising conditions of slavery. Emancipation is symbolically represented when the black bodies begin to breathe and stand up. However, Herald's inability to stand up – during the vision and immediately after it – indicates that he is not yet spiritually emancipated from the conditions of slavery and forced labour. Thus, his alienation from members of the boarding house is shown to be a symptom of a much more radical sense of rupture and exile, resulting from slavery and its legacies.

In the second act, the audience learns that Herald was a member of Joe Turner's chain gang. During his years of forced labour, he lost contact with his family. Although he subsequently managed to locate his daughter, he found it impossible to locate his wife (who had migrated North in the meantime). Bynum sings: 'They tell me Joe Turner's come and gone / Ohhh Lordy / Got my man and gone'.[10] When Herald asks Bynum to stop, he remarks: 'Now I can look at you ... and see a man who done forgot his song. Forgot how to sing it. A fellow forget that and he forget who he is. Forget how he's supposed to mark down life' (p. 71). He adds that he was once in a similar position himself; he tried singing his father's song until he discovered that it had to come from inside of him. Bynum guesses that Herald participated in the chain gang, which the latter confirms, stating that he was forced to labour for seven years. Following his release, he has been 'wandering a long time in somebody else's world' in search of the making of his own life (p. 72). Herald eventually finds and confronts Martha, who tells her own story of wandering and exile, but she has managed to come to terms with separation and grief, unlike her husband. She has renamed herself Martha Pentecost in honour of her spiritual rebirth. Herald slashes his chest in the climactic ending of the drama and claims his freedom from the bonds of the past. As the play ends, with Herald having finally found his song and his identity, Bynum observes that Herald is 'shining like new money' (p. 94). Ironically, it would seem that commodified images of African Americans have not entirely been overcome. However, there is nonetheless a new kind of symbolic currency in place: for in having found his shiny man, Bynum also finds release. When he encountered the shiny man on the road, he discovered that 'there was lots of shiny men and if I ever saw one again before I died then I would know that my song had been accepted and worked its full power in the world' (p. 10). In binding his fate to that of Herald Loomis, Bynum extends the influence of song and its recuperative potential, suggesting that the fostering of communal bonds depends first on individual and collective regeneration.

Derek Walcott: Reclaiming Caribbean Culture and History

Born in St Lucia, Caribbean playwright, painter, critic and poet Derek Walcott (b. 1930) won the Nobel Prize for Literature in 1992. Walcott's mother encouraged her son to become involved in a local theatre group, which set the stage for his lifelong interest in drama. Walcott has written approximately thirty works of drama during his career; this brief discussion can only highlight a few of these. At twenty, he wrote and staged *Henri Christophe: A Chronicle* (1949), a play based on the life of the Haitian leader, and cofounded with his brother the Santa Lucia Arts Guild. The guild gave Walcott a means of producing and directing his own plays, such as *Robin and Andrea* (1950), *Three Assassins* (1951) and *The Price of Mercy* (1951). In 1959, he founded the Little Carib Theatre Workshop, later known as the Trinidad Theatre Workshop, which he led until 1976. His performance work, which draws on Caribbean folklore from the Anglophone and Francophone Caribbean, reflects his upbringing on an island that was colonised by both the French and the British. Walcott's theatrical work is highly varied, reflecting different strategies of decolonisation.[11] He has rewritten canonical works of Western literature through Caribbean forms, based performance in folk culture, protested against colonial and neocolonial presence, and forwarded nationalist aspirations. Walcott's rewritings of Western literature include such plays as *The Joker of Seville* (1974), from *El burlador de Sevilla* (1634) by Spanish playwright Tirso de Molina, for the Royal Shakespeare Academy. *Pantomime* (1978) revises Daniel Defoe's *Robinson Crusoe*, presenting the tale through the perspectives of a hotel manager and his assistant. *Branch of the Blue Nile* (1986) opens with a group of West Indian actors rehearsing a scene from William Shakespeare's *Antony and Cleopatra*.

Plays such *Ti-Jean and His Brothers* (1957) and *Dream on Monkey Mountain* (1967) draw on creolised* folk culture and language in order to depict struggles for survival, often in mythic terms. *Ti-Jean and His Brothers* offers a dramatic account of a popular folktale from the Francophone Caribbean concerning a mother and her three sons, each of whom goes off to confront a diabolical plantation owner. Gros Jean, the eldest brother, is very strong, but physical strength alone proves inadequate. Mi-Jean, the middle brother, is an intellectual, but he too fails. Only the wily youngest boy, named Ti-Jean, succeeds through instinct and common sense. Consequently, the play is often said to celebrate the triumph of native resourcefulness over colonialist power rather than resistance through revolt or assimilation into dominant colonial culture. Along the way, the drama offers a scathing indictment of slavery as a devouring, evil force, which decimated the lives of many Afro-Caribbean people. The play's hybrid opening, which begins with a frog chorus that might be read as an allusion to Aristophanes's *The Frogs* (405 BC), playfully reworks the interfaces of Western and Creole cultures:

> FROG
> Greek-croak, Greek-croak
> CRICKET
> Greek-croak, Greek-croak.
> [The others join]
> FROG
> Aeschylus me!
> CRICKET
> The moon always there even fighting the rain

* See Part Four: 'Cross-cultural Paradigms' for a discussion of creolisation.

Creek-crak, it is cold, but the moon always there
And Ti-Jean in the moon just like the story.[12]

The phrase 'Greek-croak' can be seen as a kind of parody of the chorus in classical Greek theatre, as can the phrase 'Aeschlyus me' for excuse me, which is an allusion to another Greek playwright. At the same time, this opening offers a playful reworking of 'cric-crac', the call-response mechanism that figures in Caribbean storytelling traditions, whereby the storyteller shouts 'cric' and the audience responds 'crac'.* When the cricket says 'creek-crac', he is moving from Greek parody towards Creole culture; the presence of a man in the moon, suggests another reworking of the nursery rhyme tradition of English culture, infusing it with the Creole presence of Ti-Jean.

Another of Walcott's plays, *Dream on Monkey Mountain*, is often considered to be among his most successful. Set in the Caribbean, it focuses on events in the life of an old charcoal burner, named Makak, who comes down from his hut on the mountain to sell his wares in town, gets drunk and lands in jail, where he hallucinates about being the king of a united Africa. However, things soon fall apart as life in Africa proves to be full of conflict and intrigue. The play thus resists an idealised notion of a return to Africa as a way of healing the wounds of the past and leading to unity. Instead, Walcott shows that Caribbeans must come to terms with the realities of life on the islands in the present. Through the interplay between dream and reality Walcott highlights the dangers of replacing the actualities of Caribbean cultural diversity with a romanticised vision of Africa.

Walcott's dramaturgy offers a pan-Caribbean critique of Western imperialist intervention in the region while highlighting the various strategies of resistance. His musical, *O Babylon!* (1976), portrays Rastafarians in Jamaica at the time of Haile Selassie's 1966 visit,†

* Compare this to Edwidge Danticat's *Krik? Krak!*, discussed in Part Three: 'The Transnational Short Story Cycle'.

† Haile Selassie (1892–1975) was Emperor of Ethiopia from 1930 to 1974. Claiming to be a direct descendent of King Solomon and the Queen of Sheba, he is worshipped in Rastafarianism, a religious movement that developed in Jamaica in the 1930s.

using reggae music as a means of exploring resistant West Indian identity and the rejection of Western culture. Protest against systemic corruption and rampant modernisation can be seen in works such as *Beef, No Chicken* (1982), a two-act tragicomedy about a small town named Couva in Trinidad, which faces the introduction of a six-lane highway. Otto Hogan, the owner of a restaurant serving roti, refuses to accept a bribe and thus delays the building of the highway through the centre of the town. *Remembrance* (1980) focuses on the life and memories of Albert Perez Jordan, a Trinidadian schoolmaster who lost his elder son in the 1970 Black Power uprising. In this play, Jordan moves beyond a sense of failure, consistent with a lifetime of colonial subjugation, and comes to recognise his resistant inner strength and sense of fortitude during a period of nationalistic and racist fervour.

Finally, Walcott can be said to have produced a nationalistic theatre that represents pan-Caribbean aspirations for emancipation throughout the region's history. In 2002 Walcott published his three early history plays – *Henri Christophe*, *Drums and Colours* and *The Haytian Earth* – as *The Haitian Trilogy*, representing the history of the Caribbean as a four-hundred-year cycle of war, conquest and rebellion. The Haitian Revolution is frequently a source of inspiration and anxiety for Caribbean writers because it represents the founding of the first black republic, but also calls attention to the disappointments associated with this early resistance to imperialism and entry into the global economy. *Christophe* chronicles the Haitian Revolution from after the death of Toussaint L'Ouverture* to the death of Christophe.† The characterisation and language of the play tend to elevate and perhaps even romanticise the Haitian Revolution. Written in free verse, the language of the play is modern, but, as Edward Baugh notes, it owes much to

* Toussaint L'Ouverture (1743–1803) was the leader of the Haitian Revolution. In 1801, he oversaw the introduction of a new constitution. In 1802, the French arrested L'Ouverture and deported him to France where he spent the remainder of his life in prison.

† Henri Christophe (1767–1820) was a key leader in the Haitian Revolution who rose to power after L'Ouverture was deported.

Renaissance English drama in both language and situation.[13] *Drums* offers a similarly heroic view of the past, this time in a nationalist vein. The West Indian Federation commissioned Walcott to write the play in honour of its inauguration in 1958. He chose 'to begin with a school boy's view of the past, remembering certain pictures in primary school books, such as Columbus in chains, Raleigh and Gilbert at the foot of the old Sailor in the Millais painting, the portraits of Toussaint'.[14] The play represents five personal tragedies in Caribbean and New World history, including those who represent imperialism and colonialism (Columbus and Raleigh), resistance and revolt (Toussaint L'Ouverture and George William Gordon),* and the struggles of the common man (a shoemaker named Pompey). *The Haytian Earth* (1984) was also written for a celebration: Walcott was invited by the St Lucian government to do a revival of *Henri Christophe* to celebrate the 150 years after slavery in 1984. Walcott proposed instead to write a new play. Perhaps even more than *Drums*, this work reclaims the histories of common people and sets them alongside well known historical figures. Through his emphasis on the betrayals and exploitation of the common people, Walcott offers a critique of the failures of the Haitian revolution and proffers a more democratic political vision of revolutionary politics.

Wole Soyinka: Decolonisation in Nigeria and Beyond

Nigerian playwright, poet, novelist and critic, Wole Soyinka was the first black African to receive the Nobel Prize for Literature in 1986. Together with Chinua Achebe, he is one of Nigeria's most famous and influential authors. Akinwande Oluwole Soyinka was born in

* Born to a white planter and a slave, George William Gordon (1820–65) was declared a national hero of Jamaica on the centenary of his death. Gordon was a leader of the native Baptist movement and was elected to the House of Assembly for Saint Thomas. On account of his association with Paul Bogle as well as his criticism of Governor Eyre, Gordon was falsely accused of playing a leading role in planning the Morant Bay rebellion. He was court-martialled and executed at Morant Bay.

Western Nigeria in 1934, then still a British colony, and raised as a member of the Yoruba tribe. He pursued university studies in Nigeria (University of Ibadan) and England (University of Leeds). His drama, particularly his theory of tragedy, is derived from Yoruba culture; his works refer to Yoruba gods, spirits, rituals and festivals. The Yoruba language influences Soyinka's rhythmic use of English. At the same time, Western influences are evident in his work as a result of his largely Western-based education. Reference to the Bible and Western literature, particularly an appreciation of classical Greek theatre, comes together with Yoruba mythology and cultural references in his theatrical work. In the late 1950s, he wrote *The Invention* (1955), *The Swamp Dwellers* (1958) and *The Lion and the Jewel* (1959). In the 1960s, he founded two influential theatre companies, The Masks Company (1960) in Lagos, and the Orison Theatre Group (1964), which staged plays that contributed to the articulation of postcolonial Nigeria through drama.

Social justice has long been a key theme in Soyinka's work, shaped in part by the author's experiences as a detainee in prison during the Biafran War (1967–9), activism and responses to dictatorships and misrule in Africa more generally. From 1970 to 1975, the author lived in exile, and his works during these years, notably *Madmen and Specialists* (1970), *Jero's Metamorphosis* (1973), *The Bacchae of Euripides* (1972) and *Death and the King's Horseman* (1975), mark a turn towards an increasingly pessimistic view of decolonisation. *Requiem for a Futurologist* (1983) focuses on the story of a con artist who exploits a gullible populous, while *A Play of Giants* (1984) presents a thinly veiled critique of Idi Amin of Uganda, Macias Nguema of Equitorial Guinea, Jean-Baptiste Bokassa of Central African Republic and Mobuto Sese Seko of Congo/Zaïre. Three plays written in the 1990s, *A Scourge of Hyacinths* (1991), *From Zia, with Love* (1992) and *The Beatification of Area Boy: A Lagosian Kaleidoscope* (1995), offer direct and critical responses to the military dictatorships and irresponsible government of Nigeria. The author's exile and death sentence for treason began after Nigeria's General Ibrahim Babangida annulled the June 1993 presidential elections.

Soyinka fled Nigeria and lived in exile in France and the United States until 1998.

As already suggested, Yoruba culture and ritual play an important role in Soyinka's major works of theatre, especially the tragedies. In a critical work entitled *Myth, Literature, and the African World* (1976), Soyinka defines 'the fourth stage' as a realm that links the worlds of the dead, the living and the unborn. Many of his works aim to bring the audience into this sphere through rites of transformation, divine possession and symbolic rebirth. Soyinka suggests that directly or indirectly, Ogun, the god who risked the perils of the abyss and created a sphere between the spirit and the human world, enables this transition. *A Dance of the Forests* (1960), written for the Nigerian independence celebrations and performed by The Masks, focuses on characters – Adenebi (a lost soul), Rola (a prostitute) and Demoke (an artist who has murdered his rival) – who are all guilty of a crime or act of immorality. They leave the public festivities of the Gathering of the Tribes in order to retreat to the solitude of the forest where they undergo a transition, passing from the world of the living to the world of the dead and the gods. Here they meet Dead Man and Dead Woman, figures of suffering and grief. In the fourth stage, the characters experience or witness a series of conflicts and challenges, which are embroiled with the struggles between Ogun and Eshuoro, representing the forces of creation and destruction respectively. Through its focus on the seemingly inescapable and recurring cycles of human history, the play seems to offer a warning against repeating the mistakes of the past rather than a celebration of national culture. Notably, the presence of an *abiku* (a child that dies repeatedly in childbirth) or Half-Child, 'neither living nor dead, neither body nor spirit, neither recognised nor forgotten' augured an ambivalent sense of Nigeria's prospect for post-independence rebirth.[15] Indeed, Soyinka himself claims that the play 'takes a jaundiced view of the much-vaunted glorious past of Africa', describing the political scene as a kind of '*danse macabre*'.[16] Instead, through the figure of Demoke, the artist who saves the Half-Child while putting his own 'life' in jeopardy, Soyinka places emphasis on individual confrontations with history and personal efforts to bring about social justice through personal redemption.

In addition to epic encounters with the past and works of tragedy, Soyinka has written comedies and plays in a much more satirical, biting vein. In 1960, he staged *The Trials of Brother Jero* in Ibadan, the capital city of Oyo State, Nigeria. This satirical play explores the hypocrisy of Brother Jero, an unscrupulous preacher motivated by greed who appears to be a holy figure but is actually a trickster. This dramatic work offers a critique of the Western introduction of Christianity to Africa, and might fruitfully be read in dialogue with a similar critique of earlier missionary presence: Achebe's *Things Fall Apart* (1958), a novel that traces the transitions of Igbo peoples through colonial contact. In *Jero's Metamorphosis* (1973), Soyinka returns to this character, but the drama is considerably less lighthearted in tone, reflecting the changing socio-political conditions. The plays of the 1980s on dictatorships and con men, *Reqieum* and *A Play of Giants*, owe much to the scenarios represented in the *Jero* plays. In such works, the failures of colonial intervention and postcolonial rule are equally highlighted. Thus, Soyinka, like Walcott, Wilson and Davis, draws on the resources of local culture in order to give expression to a sense of history and identity that runs counter to dominant colonial perspectives. In so doing, however, these playwrights also present dramatically the struggles of oppressed peoples to achieve decolonisation.

Extended Commentary: Soyinka, *Death and the King's Horseman* (1975)

Death and the King's Horseman takes the form of a one-act play, broken into five scenes, which includes stage instructions to run the drama without an interval. The action is based on events that occurred under colonial rule in Oyo, western Nigeria, when a British colonial officer by the name of Pilkings intervened in the ritual suicide of Elesin Oba (whose name derives from the words for 'horseman' and 'king' respectively) in order to prevent him from fulfilling his duty to follow Alafin, his lord, into the afterworld. In Soyinka's drama, the emphasis is less on colonial intervention and more on the individual's personal choices under extremely challenging circumstances. Elesin is taken into custody and eventually manages to kill himself, but not before his son does so. These ritual deaths call attention to the importance of ritual in the life of the community, a theme that is more widely explored through other communal rituals. Moreover, African ritual juxtaposes colonial rituals, thus highlighting the cultural differences and tensions of the colonial era.

The opening scene focuses on Elesin as he prepares for his ritual death and thus emphasises the meaning of this event for the self and community rather than from a colonialist perspective. Elesin encounters women in the market and chants the tale of the 'Not-I' bird, which deals with various fears and denials of death, and that he will welcome death. Soyinka shows that the community depends upon Elesin to join his lord in the afterworld in order to keep their world in balance. Elesin's self-sacrifice will bring into proper balance the three levels of existence in traditional Yoruban cosmology: the worlds of the living, the ancestors and the not-yet born. Thus, the ritual suicide has a regenerative function in maintaining the community's identity through time. However, Elesin delays his death, claiming that he must sleep with a beautiful young girl that he sees passing through the market. Permission is granted for him to do so by Iyaloja, the leader of the women in the market, but Elesin is also warned that he must not place the community in jeopardy.

Set in the District Officer's bungalow, the second scene dramatises the colonialists' lack of understanding of African culture and indifference to local perspectives. Simon Pilkings and his wife Jane practise dancing the tango while wearing *egungun* masks – ritual masks that represent the spirits of dead ancestors – which they plan to wear to a fancy-dress ball in honour of a visit from the Prince of England at an exclusive event for elite English, white colonial subjects only. This misappropriation of sacred traditions for frivolous, colonial entertainment is seen as a blasphemous act. Sergeant Amusa, a 'native' colonial administrator, is horrified when he discovers the pair wearing the masks. Even though he is Muslim, and therefore not a participant in Yoruba rituals, he still respects Yoruba spiritual tradition. Amusa is a particularly interesting character for he represents the native administrator class who typically are seen as not belonging wholly to either the local community or Western culture. In this case, his Muslim identity is probably the result of his family having converted from a traditional Western African religion to Islam during the earlier period of Muslim colonisation. We get another sense of colonial hierarchies through the presence of the house-servant, Joseph, who is a Christian. As a convert and servant in a colonial household, he has distanced himself from the community, believing himself to be superior to his fellow Africans. However, in this scene, we also see that he remains an inferior figure from a colonial perspective because he is racially other (black). Moreover, we see that Jane and Simon are far more secular than their Christian servant and look down on him for his ardent faith, which is the product of 'the preaching of the missionaries' (*Six Plays*, p. 170). Joseph functions as a native interpreter who explains local customs to the colonials. In this instance, he explains why Elesin must join the king in the afterlife as well as why his eldest son, Olunde, is bound to take over the tradition of horseman. As drumming is heard in the background, Simon becomes enraged with 'those bloody drums' and claims that he will prevent this death from taking place (p. 166).

Scene three returns to the market, where tensions erupt when Sergeant Amusa attempts to impose colonial order, and comes into conflict with the women and girls congregated there. They insult him, calling him a 'white man's eunuch' and suggest that under his 'government knickers' all there is is a 'handle which the white man uses to summon his servants' (p. 174). This comic interchange highlights the intersections between gender, sexuality and resistance to empire as the local participant in colonial administration is presented as an emasculated figure. Conflict of duty emerges as a key theme in this scene as Amusa declares he is just doing his job while Iyaloja ('Mother' of the market and leader of the women) explains that Elesin must fulfil his obligations to the community. They imply that Amusa does not understand the 'official business' that takes place between a groom and bride on the wedding night. Implicitly, masculinity is thus associated with Elesin as a figure who represents community and colonial resistance.

Colonialism itself is subverted when the girls – who have received a colonial education – band together to defend the culture of 'the mothers of the market' (p. 176), suggesting that Amusa is not sufficiently respectful of the matriarchal aspects of Yoruba culture. The girls surround the constables and enter into a dialogue that mimics and mocks colonialist stereotypes of natives as tractable, loyal, restless, untruthful, as well as subverting English customs and rituals, such as drinking whiskey, playing golf and referring to one another as 'old chap' (p. 178). When the girls, speaking in the colonial voice, call Amusa, he snaps to attention, much to the amusement of the people in the marketplace. After the constables depart, the scene switches from this parody of colonialism to the rite of the Horseman who must confront his fated end. The Praise Singer, who follows Elesin Oba and sings praises of his deeds, becomes a vehicle for the voice of the dead king who questions Elesin in order to make sure that he will carry out his duty. The scene ends with music and dancing, which are prominent elements in traditional African drama. Thus, we see the interplay between colonial and local culture as well as the shift from anticolonial resistance to local expression of ritual meaning. Nonetheless, Soyinka does not present an idealised, nationalistic view of these events, but rather dramatises the ambivalence and tensions at the heart of colonial African society.

Scene four takes place during the fancy dress ball held at the Great Hall of Residency in honour of the Prince of England; the band plays 'Rule Britannia', badly, in the background (p. 186). The Pilkings, wearing the ritual masks, mimic ancestral ritual dance in order to entertain the Prince. This act of mimicry, unlike the school girls' performance in the previous scene, once again highlights their lack of knowledge of African culture as they clumsily try to replicate a cultural ritual that they fail to understand. Two conflicts dominate the scene. Olunde returns from England to bury his father only to discover that efforts are underway to prevent his suicide. He enters into conversation with Jane, during which their opposing worldview erupts into an argument. At the end of the scene, Olunde confronts his father, whom he disowns because he has failed to fulfil his communal duty. These two distinct plot lines are linked through the dialogue between Olunde and Jane, which touches on the question of self-sacrifice for the good of the community as a whole. Olunde finds inspiring the story of an English captain who goes down with his ship in order to save the lives of others (pp. 192–3). When Jane accuses Olunde of defending a barbaric custom – ritual death – Olunde calls attention to the barbaric qualities of white imperialists, arguing that '[by] all logical and natural laws this war [the Second World War] should end with all the white races wiping out one another, wiping out their so-called civilisation for all time and reverting to a state of primitivism the like of which has so far only existed in your imagination when you thought of us'. His only plea is that they 'at least have the humility to let others survive in their own way' (p. 195). When Jane protests that ritual suicide cannot be interpreted as an act of survival, Olunde retorts that Western civilisation is engaged in the mass suicide of global warfare; he has witnessed hordes of wounded people as a medical practitioner in hospital wards. For Olunde, contact with the Western world has allowed him to understand his role in both Western and African cultures. By comparing rituals across cultures, he emerges as a mediating figure, but his loyalties are tested when his father is imprisoned, having failed to fulfil his duty. As the scene comes to a close, Elesin is taken, sobbing, to be imprisoned in a room that formerly was used to hold slaves.

Scene five culminates in the tragic downfall and deaths of Elesin and Olunde, both of whom suffer when their cultural values fail to be acknowledged by the colonial order. Pilkings claims to be saving Elesin's life, but Elesin protests that Pilkings has destroyed it and brought disaster upon the community (p. 204). The theme of colonial resistance on the part of the younger generation once again comes to the foreground as Elesin observes that his son has obtained 'the secrets of his enemies' (p. 205) and will seek vengeance. Soyinka shows that the colonial situation produces personal, intimate conflicts through his depiction of Elesin as a compromised figure who confesses to his young bride that his 'weakness' comes 'not merely from the abomination of the white men who came violently into my fading presence' but that 'there was also a weight of longing on my earth-held limbs. I would have shaken it off, already my foot had begun to lift but then, the white ghost entered and all was defiled' (p. 207). His yearning to remain alive, his sense of duty and colonial presence all come together to produce a situation of dishonour and ultimate downfall. When Pilkings asks Elesin to give him his word of honour that he will try nothing foolish, such as taking his life, Elesin replies that his 'honour' is already 'locked up in that desk in which you will put away the report of this night's events. Even the honour of my people you have taken already; it is tied together with those papers of treachery which make you masters in this land' (p. 209). Elesin calls attention to colonial control through bureaucracy, representation and documentation. In the closing to the play, with Olunde and Elesin both dead, Iyaloja reproaches the colonials for playing with strangers' lives: 'The gods demanded only the expired plantain but you cut down the sap-laden shoot to feed your pride' (p. 219). Thus, Olunde's untimely death and Elesin's belated entry into the otherworld are tainted by colonial intervention.

Culturally and textually, *Death and the King's Horseman* reflects the hybrid Nigerian identity. While the plot highlights the struggle of two distinctive cultural traditions, the work shows the inescapable entanglements of English and Yoruba cultures. Yoruba words appear throughout the drama, and Soyinka includes a glossary at the end of the play in order to assist the English-only reader to understand the meaning of Yoruba terms and cultural references. Significantly, these words highlight the importance of ritual in the community: examples include the words *egungun* (ancestral masquerade), *etetu* (placatory rites or medicine) and *gbedu* (a deep-timbred royal drum) (p. 220). At the same time, colonial voices and the mockery of those voices produces a sense of both colonial oppression and resistance during the colonial period. Shifts between standard and nonstandard English as well as lyrical utterances, inflected by Yoruba speech, produce a resonant English that reflects the various facets of colonial contact and exchange. In this respect, this work of theatre engages in decolonisation by examining critical imperial legacies as well as reviving and paying homage to Yoruba rituals for individual and collective articulation.

Notes

1 Helen Gilbert and Joanne Tompkins, *Post-Colonial Drama: Theory, Practice, Politics* (London: Routledge, 1996), p. 11.
2 Ibid., p. 209.
3 Helen Gilbert, *Sightlines: Race, Gender, and the Nation in Contemporary Australian Theatre* (Ann Arbor: University of Michigan Press, 1998), p. 2.
4 Jack Davis, *Kullark and The Dreamers* (Sydney: Currency Press, 1982), p. 38.
5 Brian Crow with Chris Banfield, *An Introduction to Post-Colonial Theatre* (Cambridge: Cambridge University Press, 1996), p. 71.
6 Kim Powers, 'An Interview with August Wilson' *Theatre* 16 (Fall/Winter 1984), p. 52.
7 Bonnie Lyons and August Wilson, 'An Interview with August Wilson' *Contemporary Literature* 40.1 (Spring 1999), p. 2.
8 August Wilson, *Fences and Ma Rainey's Black Bottom* (London: Penguin, 1988), p. 191.
9 Harry J. Elam Jr, 'The Dialectics of Wilson's *The Piano Lesson*', *Theatre Journal* 52.3 (October 2000), pp. 363–4.
10 August Wilson, *Joe Turner's Come and Gone* (London: Penguin Books, 2010), p. 67.
11 John Thieme offers a very good introduction to Walcott's theatre in

Derek Walcott: Contemporary World Writers (Manchester: Manchester University Press, 1999), pp. 42–76.

12 Derek Walcott, *Dream on Monkey Mountain and Other Plays* (New York: Farrar, Straus and Giroux, 1970), p. 85.

13 Edward Baugh, 'Of Men and Heroes: Walcott and the Haitian Revolution' *Callaloo* 28.1 (2005), p. 49.

14 Bruce King, *Derek Walcott and West Indian Drama* (Oxford: Oxford University Press, 1995), pp. 19–20.

15 Gilbert and Tompkins, *Post-Colonial Drama*, p. 219.

16 Bidoun Jeyifo, 'Introduction', in *Wole Soyinka: Six Plays* (London: Methuen, 1984), p. xiii.

Performing Race, Gender and Sexuality: Dattani, Kureishi and Hwang

Postcolonial theatre not only reclaims history and draws on the resources of vernacular culture, but as a dramatic tradition also engages directly with colonialist discourses of race, gender and sexuality. It challenges and transforms received paradigms through strategic representations, which defy the heteronormative* tendencies of empire and call into question the hierarchies associated with the colonial order. In so doing, there emerges a dissident form of postcolonial theatre, which is often highly politicised and provocative in its staging of the postcolonial. This chapter focuses on this strand of performance, which derives its critical edge from explorations of those who have been the most marginalised under empire. In turning to the work of postcolonial writers for the stage and screen, Mahesh Dattani, an Indian writing in English, Hanif Kureishi, a Britisher of Anglo-Pakistani background, and David Henry Hwang, a Chinese American, we might consider the ways in which their culturally hybrid perspectives come to shape the postcolonial stage.† While challenging prevailing imperialist and heteronormative constructions of gender and sexuality, these writers also invite us to consider the possibilities for queering identity, citizenship and society. More

* The term 'heteronormative' refers to the notion that heterosexuality is seen as a norm against which all other practices are deemed aberrant.

† See Part Four: 'Cross-cultural Paradigms' for a discussion of hybridity.

widely, they challenge prevailing assumptions about the interplay of race, gender and sexuality, calling attention to the 'role' of postcolonial identities in the contemporary world.

One of the popular misconceptions about queer theory is that it refers narrowly only to gay and lesbian culture. However, queer theorists point out that the field engages with these issues in the context of a much more expansive critique of discourses of knowledge and power: how we come to understand, 'perform' and defy normative ideas of gender and sexuality. At its most productive, queer theory helps theorists to confront ways of knowing, experiencing and living one's gendered and sexual identity. Since the 1990s, the work of theorists such as Judith Butler, Eve Kosofsky Sedgwick, Michael Warner and Judith Halberstam has proved influential in enabling literary critics to consider the ways in which the queer can destabilise dominant ways of thinking about gendered and sexual identities. As noted in Part Four: 'Race, Gender and Sexuality', the postcolonial queer has come to play an especially important role in challenging imperialist approaches to gender and sexuality, which tend to privilege the heteronormative and the patriarchal. When speaking about the postcolonial stage, the work of Judith Butler is especially worth considering because she places emphasis on the performativity of gender.

Butler's *Gender Trouble* (1990) introduced the notion of gender performativity, which refers to the ways in which gender is socially constructed. She offers the example of drag: when someone adopts the role of a masculine or feminine identity and performs it in a highly self-conscious way, s/he calls attention to the way society regulates these identities in everyday life. In *Bodies That Matter*, Butler asks: 'Is there a way to link the question of the materiality of the body to the performativity of gender? And how does the category of "sex" figure within such a relationship?'[1] She argues that bodies should be seen as the effect of the dynamics of power and in relation to the norms that regulate behaviour (p. 2). Performativity refers to the notion that individuals enact certain normative patterns or 'scripts' of accepted behaviour, which serve to regulate and constrain expressions of gender and sexuality (p. 2). She argues that subjects come into being through the process of 'assuming' a sex (p. 3), especially through socialisation. Prevailing discourses, assumptions and norms related to sex and gender shape the subject's self-knowledge and actions. This poses questions of identity in relation to discourses of knowledge and the workings of power. As a esult, subjects and identities that do not conform to prevailing discourses are situated as 'abject': they represent '"unlivable" and "uninhabitable" zones of social life' (p. 3). In this instance, queer theory might then examine the ways in which the self is constituted through exclusion and abjection, processes which are at work within society as well as internalised by the self, as someone whose sexuality is deemed not the 'norm' struggles to come to terms with his or her identity. Here we might think about the ways in which the practices of exclusion and abjection at work through empire intersect and overlap with the more general processes of regulating sexuality and gender. Queer theory highlights the exclusions present in discourse and practice as well as calling attention to the ways in which the queering of gender and sexuality might also serve to challenge prevailing paradigms for conceptualising the body, identity and citizenship more generally.

These concerns about the performativity of gender and sexuality as well as the queer postcolonial are amplified and extended through the artistic potential of contemporary drama. In the introduction to *Performance and Cultural Politics*, Elin Diamond argues that 'theater was [once] charged with obeisance to the playwright's authority, with actors disciplined to the referential task of representing fictional entities', but she notes that experiments and writing about performance since the 1960s have dismantled textual authority and a notion of a canonical performance.[2] Partly as a result of transformations in playwriting practices as well as theoretical challenges to the primacy of the text, the opposition between dramatic studies and performance studies has largely been eroded. The text is no longer seen as sacrosanct: offering a blueprint for performance that emerges primarily from reading, interpreting and staging the script. W. B. Worthen remarks that '[p]erformance studies has developed a vivid account of nondramatic, nontheatrical, nonscripted, ceremonial and everyday-life performances'.[3] Among these changes, theatre has come to embrace a wider set of performance practices, often staging, parodying or highlighting the performative aspects of everyday life. Finally, critics such as Robert Schechner argue that theatre has become a subset of performance, a much broader and more encompassing conception of dramatic possibility.

Contemporary theatre, which often tends towards the meta-theatrical,* has been particularly amenable to the examination of the performative dimensions of gender and sexuality. Staging transgender and alternative sexualities can serve as a means to interrogate postcolonial society more generally. Notably, the mid-1970s to the 1990s saw the rise of a wide range of queer and gender bending performances in mainstream culture, including the films *The Rocky Horror Picture Show* (1975), *La Cage Aux Folles* (1978), *Victor/Victoria* (1982), *Tootsie* (1982), *Kiss of the Spider Woman* (1985), *The Crying Game* (1992) and *The Adventures of Priscilla, Queen of the Desert* (1994) (many of which are themselves based on plays or novels). When considering the work of contemporary postcolonial performance writers, for the stage and cinema, we can situate it in this history of Western and global performance histories. Yet, these transformations in Western theatrical traditions alone are insufficient to explain the emergence and work of postcolonial queer drama. The performance traditions of indigeneous and colonial peoples tend not to adhere to Western models of theatre with their emphasis on the script and strict divisions between secular and sacred modes of performance. Indeed, many vernacular forms of theatre, such as the carnivalesque, parades or ritual, provided a framework and models for performance, but relied on the improvisational skills of the actors and performers in order to script the actual performance. Moreover,

* Meta-theatre (from the Greek 'meta' meaning beyond) describes plays or performances that draw attention to the fact that the work is an artifice, often in a playful way.

non-Western dramatic traditions have often been more expansive, embracing what might be understood as a total performance, including dance, music, costume, chorus, audience participation and other performance traditions.

Mahesh Dattani: Performing Modern India

Born in Bangalore, India in 1958, Dattani comes from a Gujarati background. He received his early education at Baldwins Boys High School, an English-speaking Christian school. In 1984, he founded the theatre company, Playpen. In 1988, unable to find plays in translation that suited his purposes, he wrote his first theatrical work, *Where There's A Will*. This early work introduces the themes of gender and sexuality which surface in all of his writing, including such notable works as *Dance Like A Man* (1989), *Tara* (1990), *Bravely Fought the Queen* (1991), *Final Solutions* (1993), *On a Muggy Night in Mumbai* (1998) and *Seven Steps Around the Fire* (1999). He regularly receives commissions of his work from BBC Radio; he has adapted and sometimes directed his plays for the screen, notably *Mango Soufflé* (2002, an adaptation of *On a Muggy Night in Mumbai*) in English, *Dance Like A Man* (2003) and *Morning Raga* (2004) in Hindi. Notably, he is the first playwright in English to be awarded the Sahitya Akademi award, a literary prize that is normally awarded to a writer working in one of the main languages of India. The awarding of this prize is indicative of the ways in which the playwright has both challenged and revised the definition of national Indian theatre.

Situating Mahesh Dattani's place in Indian theatre is complicated by the realities of national identity and its associated myriad theatrical traditions. Asha Kuthari Chaudhuri notes:

> ... the spectrum of India's cultural fabric is decidedly complex and difficult to encompass. Hence, when one talks of 'Indian theatre', one enters a vast and intricate arena ... It is extra-

> ordinarily inclusive – encompassing the classical (like the Kathakali, or some Bharatanatyam pieces), the ritual (such as the Raas, the Ramlila, or the Theyyam), the devotional (many of the musically dominant performances), the folk (like the Chhau or the Therukuttu) and the modern, partaking of sundry traditions, forms and lore, sometimes unique, and sometimes bewilderingly intermingling with each other. Dance, drama, mime, song, instrumentation, puppetry, the orally delivered narrative all combine happily, almost seamlessly in a performance by an ensemble of artistes working simultaneously.[4]

Dattani's modern theatre can be seen as related to this vernacular performative tradition, but his work also belongs to modern Indian drama, which has emerged in large urban centres and derives from India's colonial background. As an adolescent Dattani saw Gujarati and Kannada plays so that he came to understand the rich tradition of Indian theatre. Modern Indian theatre in English is typically influenced by Western dramatic traditions and Dattani's work is no exception. He fuses Indian drama with Western models, such as Henrik Ibsen, Arthur Miller and Tennesee Williams, creating a hybrid performance that freely mingles Eastern and Western performance traditions.

Here we might note a few distinctive features of Dattani's hybrid approach to performance, which clearly show his postcolonial perspective. Dattani sees writing in English as a viable form of national theatre, but he argues against a theatre of English mimicry. While some Indians continue even to this day to mimic British English accents and associate Englishness with England, Dattani believes it is important to accept that the English language has been incorporated by India as part of its own cultural identity. Thus, his theatre, written in English, challenges preconceptions about Indian national theatre. Yet, writing in English entails writing for an elite audience, which typically consists of members who are university educated and/or have longstanding historical affiliations with hegemonic English presence. At the same time, this playwright's approach to performance is closer to Indian than to Western-derived practices. While Western theatre is largely centred on the text, and the same might be said of much modern Indian drama, Dattani takes a hybrid approach. He begins working on a play with the actors, even before the script is completely written. In the very act of rehearsing the script, playing out the scenario, the play finds form. This dynamic approach to theatre leaves room for collective performance and communal creation, shaped by lived moments and dialogic exchange.

Although Dattani's hybrid plays are strongly rooted in Indian culture, he resists the notion that his works should be staged for non-Indian audiences in ways that would exoticise the Indian body and culture more generally. He observes that theatre should not function as a kind of touristic experience that merely gratifies the need to see certain kinds of well known site and image:

> the audience should take a journey from the universal to the specific and not straight into something exotic, because that's a journey never taken, that's an imagined journey. It's the same with tourists in India: they're never here, because they're looking for images they've seen already ... they get their dose of nirvana and go back, and they've never been to India. It's the same with a theatrical experience, it's very important that the intention should be to take the audience on a journey – it need not be a journey to India, it could be a journey into themselves, [from a stance] outside their cultural viewpoint, because they're interacting with a viewpoint that's outside their culture, which can have very profound effects in different ways.[5]

The notion of theatre as a journey – a way of learning something profoundly new about the world and the self – can be seen as related to Dattani's approach to theatre more generally. This emphasis on performativity is also evident in his staging of the intersections of race, gender and sexuality. Dattani aims, as we shall see, to show the ways in which performing identity serves as a means to go beyond the legacies of the colonial Indian body. He defies the hierarchies of race, gender and sexuality that were part of the colonial formative process, which valued a white, patriarchal, heteronormative ideal.

Dattani observes that Nitin in *Bravely Fought the Queen* offers the first sympathetic representation of a gay figure in Indian theatre:

> I would say the only time a homosexual character has been treated with sympathy. There have been caricatures. If we look at the statistics of a gay population in any given society, even if you look at it as a conservative five per cent (people put it at ten, but even if you take five per cent), with a population of 850 million we're talking about almost 50 million people, and I think it's a real invisible issue. Almost all gay people are married in the conventional sense, so I think there are invisible issues which need to be brought out and addressed. In this case, it wasn't such a conscious attempt to say 'look, here is an invisible issue, let's talk about it,' I think it's there, and since it is very much a part of our society, very much a part of my society, it happens to be there.[6]

According to Dattani, invisible issues need to be brought into public consciousness: staging the lives and dramas of queer characters is one way of achieving this aim.

As we have seen, queer theatre need not necessarily be associated with gay culture. The defiance of gendered binary oppositions and heteronormative ideologies can be seen as queer. Thus, Dattani's *Tara* offers an example of a play that questions the opposition of masculinity and femininity while highlighting the masculinist values at work in Indian culture. *Tara* is about boy and girl twins who are conjoined from the chest down, but undergo surgical separation. The play focuses on the anxiety and emotional separation that result, especially as the twins – each of whom has only one leg of his or her own – were born with a shared third leg. The third leg belonged to the girl, but the grandparents manipulated the operation in such a way that the boy would get two legs. However, the leg didn't survive on the boy. When the twins discover this family secret, they find it impossible to continue their relationship. Wracked with guilt, the son flees to London and tries to start his own life. Tara, the girl child, wastes away as a result of knowing that she was not actually loved the way she thought she was. In many ways, the play might be read as a postcolonial response to the Platonic ideal of the hermaphrodite: the notion that at one time all humans were both male and female. Split apart, the masculine and feminine search for one another in order to embrace once more a sense of identity that defies binaries. Yet, Dattani complicates this vision by highlighting the fundamental ways in which gender hierarchies can destroy the ability to love and maintain relationships. More generally, the playwright shows the need to value the feminine self, whether one is biologically male or female.

On A Muggy Night in Mumbai is one of Dattani's best known and most frequently performed plays, which has reached a global audience thanks to its film adaptation. The play tackles a number of gay issues, such as homosexual marriage, lifestyle choices, attitudes towards monogamy and promiscuity, and queer self-presentation. Through the drama of Kamlesh, a successful fashion designer, the audience gets a glimpse into the diverse lifestyle choices and attitudes of the gay community. In *Seven Steps*, Dattani focuses on the *hijra* (or transsexual) community with a plot that involves the killing of a *hijra* because of her relationship with a government minister's son. This emphasis on the sexual politics of queer characters once again attests to Dattani's ongoing interest in non-normative, marginalised sexualities. In summary, Dattani queers Indian and postcolonial English theatre in his work; his perspective on Western works of literature suggests that issues of invisibility might be found within the English canon itself. He observes:

> All the great writers were English or at least Anglo Irish. Shakespeare, Yeats, Whitman (I don't think it occurred to any

> of my teachers that the great writers they eulogized with missionary zeal were either gay or bisexual or considered completely immoral in their times!).[7]

In this respect, the author's work revises English culture and thus restages postcolonial drama in a more expansive sense.

Hanif Kureishi: Restaging Postcolonial Identities

Hanif Kureishi was born in 1954 in England and raised in suburbia. His work focuses on events in the lives of migrants and their children, typically from Pakistani or mixed race backgrounds, such as his own culturally and interracially mixed parentage. Kureishi's texts challenge racial and ethnic identities and redefine what it means to be British. Often, he focuses on the lives of those who are marginalised, often on account of their sexual preferences, racial or ethnic background, and/or position in the class system. In many instances, the lives of migrants and the homeless are central to his work. Frequently families and lovers struggle to maintain relationships in the face of violence, socio-political divisions or conflicts related to sexuality. Two of his most recent projects, *Venus* (a 2006 film starring Peter O'Toole, published as a play in 2007) and *The Mother* (a 2003 film adaptation of his play of the same title), deal with sexuality in the lives of aging characters. An earlier work, the screenplay *My Son the Fanatic* (1997) deals with events in the life of a cab driver named Parvez, who faces a crisis when his son embraces a fundamentalist sect, while *London Kills Me* (1991, screenplay and direction by Kureishi) represents the lives of homeless people in London. Perhaps still Kureishi's best known films, *My Beautiful Laundrette* (1985) and *Sammy and Rosie Get Laid* (1987), respond to the kind of racism represented by Enoch Powell in his infamous 'Rivers of Blood' speech (1968) and the party platforms of the National Front and the British National Party. Margaret Thatcher's 1978 televised speech concerning fears of being 'swamped' by 'people of other cultures' contributed to her electoral success and expressed the xenophobic sentiments of many in Britain at the time. Black people, particularly men, were picked up under the 'sus' (suspicion) laws, ostensibly for vagrancy, but actually, it could be argued, as part of a systemically racist policing of the population. Many racist attacks occurred, such as the 1981 firebombing that resulted in the deaths of thirteen black youths. As unemployment grew during the 1980s, migrants became the targets of increasing hostility. While many black British subjects advocated separatism, Kureishi's own family background and sense of ethnic identity suggested that the instability of race and the emergence of multicultural Britain demanded a different kind of politics. While Kureishi's work is frequently grounded in the London experience, it is nonetheless attentive to the legacies of colonialism, the role of diasporic* communities and transnational political contexts.

Ironically, both *My Beautiful Laundrette* and *Sammy and Rosie* were funded by Channel 4, a TV channel created under Mrs Thatcher to respond to 'minority' interests. Referring to Stuart Hall's critique of Kureishi's work, Ruvani Ranasinha remarks that the works 'mark the movement from black groups asserting their right to represent themselves and countering negative images with positive ones to a more complex agenda of a new "politics of representation"'.[8] With the introduction of gay and lesbian characters from white English, Asian and Afro-Caribbean communities, Kureishi explores the complex intersections of ethnicity, sexuality and gender in postcolonial Britain. His work challenges ethnic stereotypes and offers a varied depiction of diverse political and economic interests within diasporic communities and the nation as a whole. Bart Moore-Gilbert observes that:

* The term 'diaspora' (meaning dispersion) initially referred to the scattering of Jewish peoples as a result of several forced expulsions from what is now known as Israel, Jordan and parts of Lebanon as well as the State of Palestine. Subsequently, 'diaspora' has come to refer more generally to the movement, migration or scattering of a people away from a settled location or ancestral homeland.

> the utopian implication of Kureishi's films is that contemporary Britain has within its grasp the possibility of expanding traditional conceptions of national identity to create for the first time a genuine and revolutionary, though always contradictory unity-in-diversity.[9]

In his view, the films proffer 'a new sense of national community built on the idea of pluralism and of non-hierarchical conceptions of difference'.[10] These arguments are certainly true, but the works also offer an equally bleak view of tensions, inequity and violence at work in society.

Set in London during the 1980s, *My Beautiful Laundrette* tells the story of a gay romance between Omar, the son of Pakistani migrants, and Johnny, a white Englishman and former member of the National Front. At the opening of the film, Omar is a naive young man who lives with his ailing father in a flat overlooking a noisy tube line. Yearning for success, he welcomes the opportunity to work for his uncle Nasser, an entrepreneur, who seems to have made his fortune as a businessman and slum lord, as well as another relative, Salim, who traffics in drugs. Omar convinces his uncle to allow him to take over managing a rundown laundromat, which he and Johnny renovate. Nasser admires his nephew's initiative and attempts to arrange a marriage between Omar and his cousin Tania, but these plans soon go awry because of Omar's relationship with Johnny. The interracial homosexual relationship serves as a nexus for crises within the family and community. When Omar's father learns that his son has reconnected with Johnny, he objects: 'He [Johnny] went too far [in reference to his activities in the National Front]. They hate us in England. All you do is kiss their arses and think of yourself as a little Britisher!'.[11] Nasser warns his nephew that he has 'too much white blood' so that he is 'weak like those pale-faced adolescents that call us wog' (p. 31). Meanwhile, Johnny's friends are angered by Johnny's increasing intimacy with the Pakistani community. They refer to Omar as a 'wog boy' (p. 31). Genghis, one of Johnny's friends who has adopted an imperialist nickname (ironically that of an Asian ruler), demands: 'Why are you working for them? For those people? You were with us once. For England' (p. 45). When Johnny replies that he wants to work, Genghis protests: 'I'm angry. I don't like to see one of our men grovelling to Pakis. They came over here to work for us. That's why we brought them over. OK?' (p. 45). 'Don't cut yourself off from your own people. Because there's no one else who really wants you. Everyone has to belong', he observes (p. 46). Genghis represents an 'us–them' mentality, which expresses the racial oppositions at work in Britain at the time.

The questions of belonging and longing are central to the relationship between Omar and Johnny, neither of whom conforms to the heteronormative ideals of their respective cultures. Tensions surface in the erotic relationship, which encompasses both desire and antipathy. Omar says to Johnny: 'I want big money. I'm not gonna be beat down by this country. When we were at school, you and your lot kicked me all round the place. And what are you doing now? Washing my floor. That's how I like it. Now get to work. Get to work I said. Or you're fired' (p. 65). More than Omar, Johnny becomes caught up in the cross-fire between communities, especially when he is asked to take over the management of one of Nasser's slum buildings. When he throws out Pakistani tenants who have failed to pay the rent, working on behalf of a Pakistani landlord, they hurl insults at him: 'You are not human! You are cold people, you English, the big icebergs of Europe' (p. 66). Ethnic tensions are seemingly unavoidable.

Set against these tensions are scenes of Johnny and Omar making love in the back room of the laundrette and embracing, representing an alternative representation of relations in multiethnic Britain. Thus, the film stages queer desire as a force for change in bringing about interracial reconciliation. Yet, this queer potential is offset by eruptions of violence, which neither Omar nor Johnny can prevent. Salim's views are as oppositional as those of the National Front. Salim refers to the white lads as 'a waste of life' (p. 79). He calls for vengeance: 'All over England, Asians, as you call us, are beaten, burnt to death. Always we are intimidated. What these scum need ... is a taste of their own piss' (p. 79). After Salim runs over a white punk's foot, Genghis and his gang nearly beat him to death in retaliation. When Johnny tries to intervene and save Salim, he is beaten 'by his own kind'. Omar arrives on the scene to find that his laundromat has been trashed. Thus, it seems that racial opposition is unavoidable in Thatcher's Britain. Worse still, it seems that the middle ground or reconciliatory perspectives are likely to be pushed to the side in an increasingly violent opposition of competing nationalist agendas.

Nonetheless, the film ends on a positive note as Omar and Johnny wash and splash one another. In staging the questions of familial and national belonging, the gay relationship appears to offer a viable alternative for a different kind of society. Yet, the potentially emancipatory potential of this relationship has to be seen against the pessimistic representation of the prospects for achieving decolonisation in Britain.

More generally, the gay romance enables a critique of patriarchal culture and the role of women in society. Omar's mother has committed suicide. Nasser's wife Bilquis uses magic to bring down a curse on her husband's mistress, a white woman named Rachel. Tania, to whom Omar is supposed to be betrothed, flees from the family's attempt to control her life. She is last seen standing on a train platform. Her image is swept away and she disappears from the film. Thus, a critical feminist perspective and voice is effectively silenced and exiled. The wider critique of gender highlights the difficult situations for women under patriarchy. No matter what their age, race, class or sexual proclivities, whether English or part of the Pakistani diaspora, the conditions for women are shown to be oppressive and stifling, leaving women as individuals isolated.

While the film version of *My Beautiful Laundrette* was an enormous box-office success, winning awards and raising the profile of both Kureishi and the director (Stephen Frears), *Sammy and Rosie Get Laid* received a more lukewarm reception. Nonetheless, the screenplay and film offer an intelligent and devastatingly bleak representation of the intersections of race, gender and sexuality in Britain. While the film ostensibly centres on the mixed race, open marriage of Sammy, a

British Asian, and Rosie, a white English social worker in her thirties, its queer potential and critical edge derives primarily from the presence of outspoken lesbian feminists named Vivia and Rani. Through the open marriage – which could be seen as queering ideals of monogamy – the audience comes into contact with Sammy's lover, Anna, an American photographer who is working on a project called 'Images of a Decaying Europe' and Rosie's lover, Danny, a British Afro-Caribbean squatter who believes in Gandhi's philosophies of nonviolent protest. Through these various sexual entanglements, we get a sense of overlapping dissident perspectives about gender and sexuality. Sammy informs Anna that Rosie doesn't believe in '[g]etting the dinner on and sexual fidelity' (p. 96) while Anna has had the letter W tattooed on each of her buttocks so that when she bends over her bottom spells the word 'wow' (p. 95). Unlike *Laundrette*, this screenplay signals from the start the powerful role of women's voices and perspectives: where Tania and Rachel disappear from sight, these women's voices and views are foregrounded.

Tensions between queer, feminist and patriarchal perspectives are evident throughout the work. Sammy's willingness to embrace feminine perspectives is linked to a resistance to patriarchal power, represented by his father (Rafi) whom he describes as 'a great patriarch and a little king, surrounded by servants' (p. 97). When Rafi comes to visit his son, having travelled from Pakistan, he encounters Vivia and Rani. Rafi is clearly put off by the women's queer relationship (p. 97). Rani wants to interview Rafi for her paper, but he declines. When Rosie tells Rani that her father-in-law claims to be 'a friend of Mao Tse-tung' (p. 103), Rani promises to dig up materials that might suggest otherwise. When it transpires that Sammy's father is guilty of more than just 'paternalism, greed, general dissipation, mistreatment of [... his] mother and vicious exploitation' (p. 125), Sammy, Rosie and Rafi come into conflict when they go out for dinner together. Rafi gives his son a cheque. While Sammy is willing to accept money from his father, Rosie refuses on ethical grounds. At the same time, she admires a drag queen passing by, which prompts Rafi to say that she's 'talking like a damn dyke' (p. 131). Consistently, Rafi links feminism to lesbianism. When Rosie challenges his record of human rights abuses, he protests: 'You are only concerned with homosexuals and women! A luxury that rich oppressors can afford! We were concerned with poverty, imperialism, feudalism! Real issues that burn people!' (p. 133). His homophobia and misogyny are clear in this scene, for Rafi suggests that the rights of women and gay people are of less consequence than other issues of justice. Rafi's sexualised account of politics equates violence with the loss of virginity: 'A man who hasn't killed is a virgin and doesn't understand the importance of love' (p. 134). When Rosie tells Sammy that Rani and Vivia have found information about his father's unethical political activities and human rights violations, she highlights the link between political protest and queer perspectives. She also suggests that they should invite 'the usual social deviants, communists, lesbians and blacks, with a sprinkling of mentally sub-normal' people to the party for Rafi (p. 137). In this passage, and others, Rosie's liberal feminist perspective takes on a disturbingly narcissistic tone for she draws on the language of racism and homophobia in order to bolster her own rebellious stance.

Sammy and Rosie's open marriage and queer household provide a space for otherwise improbable political encounters and dialogues. Danny (who ironically refers to himself as Victoria, a gesture that queers the identity of one of England's queens) meets Rafi in Sammy and Rosie's apartment, where they exchange ideas about the role of violence in the process of decolonisation:

RAFI — Victoria, what's wrong?

DANNY — For a long time, right, I've been for non-violence. Never gone for burning things down. I can see the attraction but not the achievement. OK. After all, you guys ended colonialism non-violently. You'd sit down all over the place, right? We have a kind of domestic colonialism to deal with here, because they don't allow us to run our own communities. But if full-scale civil war breaks out we can only lose. And what's going to happen to all that beauty?

RAFI — If I lived here ... I would be on your side. All over the world the colonized people are fighting back. It's the necessity of the age. It gives me hope.

DANNY — But how should we fight? That's what I want to know. (p. 122)

On another occasion, the juxtaposition of sexual encounters in the household further complicates a sense of political perspectives. While Sammy and Rosie discuss their lack of desire for one another, which they liken to the divisions of the Berlin Wall during the Cold War, Vivia and Rani comment ironically on the limitations of heterosexual performance: 'You know, that stuff when the woman spends the whole time trying to come, but can't. And the man spends the whole time trying to stop coming, but can't' (p. 141). The queering of London itself takes place in the screenplay, which describes how the image of three couples copulating is intercut with scenes of homelessness and images of people dressed in carnivalesque costumes:

> *Now there is a collage of the three couples coupling. This is cut with the kids and the straggly band outside the caravan dancing in celebration of joyful love-making all over London. Some of the straggly kids play instruments or bang tins. Others are dressed in bizarre variations of straight gear – like morris dancers, pearly queens, traffic wardens, naval ratings, brain surgeons, witches, devils, etc.* (p. 157)

Interracial, straight and gay sexual pleasure and a celebration of marginalised peoples are interlinked in the film's climactic moment of anti-imperialistic visual and sonic rhetoric, which is queered through the inclusion of lesbian lovers. In Sammy and Rosie's apartment, Rafi enters into conflict with Rani and Vivia: while he condemns them as 'peverted half-sexed lesbians cursed by God', they threaten to castrate him (p. 159). Queer, feminist and postcolonial perspectives intersect, but they do not necessarily offer a synthetic political perspective. Ultimately, Rafi, pursued by a ghost who reminds him of the human rights violations he has committed, takes his own life in Sammy and Rosie's flat. While the queer space of the flat and the counter-politics it represents seem to undermine the patriarchal, the misogynistic and the imperialistic, the screenplay evades facile depictions of sexual politics.

David Henry Hwang: Chinese American Perspectives

Chinese American playwright, Hwang sees his work as contributing to the wider postcolonial critique of race and culture in America. In 'Evolving a Multicultural Theater', he describes the development of his own theatrical practices and examines the question of modern theatre more generally. He observes that his theatre represents a hybrid mixture of perspectives, garnered from reading works of Asian and African American literatures in dialogue with Western theatre:

> Directly as a result of people like Frank Chin and Maxine Hong Kingston and other non-Asian writers like Ntozake Shange [a black feminist], I became aware of the possibility of opening up this side of myself [issues of race] in my work. When I wrote my first play, F.O.B., to some extent it was an attempt to validate the existence of a previous Asian American literary tradition, through an exploration of two mythological characters: Fa Mu Lan, from Maxine Hong Kingston's book *The Woman Warrior*,* and a character named Kwan Gung, the

* See Part Three: 'Magic Realism and Folklore in the Postcolonial Novel' for a discussion of Maxine Hong Kingston's *The Woman Warrior*.

> god of the writers, warriors, and prostitutes from Frank Chin's play *Gee, Pop*.* I thought it was interesting to try to bring these two characters together in Torrance, California, in the same way that Stoppard took *Rosencrantz and Guildenstern* from *Hamlet* and made another play out of it, bringing about a certain cross-fertilization.[12]

FOB (1983) stages the tensions between those who are 'American Born Chinese' (ABCs) and FOBs ('Fresh Off the Boat') through its focus on three main characters: Dale (an ABC), Grace, a first-generation Chinese American, and Steve (an FOB). The action takes place in a restaurant owned by Grace's family where Dale and Steve vie for Grace's attention. This love triangle allows for Grace to consider facets of her Chinese and American identity. Grace and Steve embrace alternative identities, with Grace adopting the persona of Fa Mu Lan, the cross-dressing woman warrior, and Steve taking on the identity of Gwan Gung, 'the god of fighters and writers'.[13] Role-playing these characters enables them to challenge both American and Chinese American stereotypes about Chinese peoples. Dale finds that he does not fit in either the American world or the Chinese diasporic one. However, Dale's account of his attempts to fit into life in America reveals the extent to which he has internalised racism and negative ethnic stereotypes: '[s]o, I've worked real hard – real hard – to be myself. To not be a Chinese, a yellow, a slant, a gook. To be just a human being, like everyone else. ... I'm making it in America' (p. 32). Dale mocks a Chinese accent and makes fun of FOBs (p. 34). Meanwhile, Steve provides access to longer historical memories about Chinese culture, indenture in America and the persistence of racism (pp. 36, 48). Grace and Steve leave Dale behind to go off dancing together while the latter is left alone to consider his animosity towards recently arrived Chinese migrants.

* Frank Chin is a noted Chinese American author and playwright who is often critical of ethnic stereotyping in America, especially by Asian Americans themselves. Notably, he has been extremely critical of Hong Kingston's work as well as that of Amy Tan and Hwang himself.

Yellow Face (2009), for which Hwang won an OBIE (the Off-Broadway Theater Awards), is a mockumentary drama that features the playwright himself as a leading character. In real life, Hwang was among those who protested against the casting of Jonathan Pryce as a Vietnamese pimp in *Miss Saigon* the musical in 1990. He argued that this was an example of 'yellow face', which is comparable to the black face tradition whereby a white actor adopts a black role (often mocking black identity in the process) and paints his or her face black in order to do so. The play responds to a longstanding Hollywood tradition of casting white actors in Asian roles, as Hwang explains: 'From Mickey Rooney playing Japanese in *Breakfast at Tiffany's* to Bruce Lee being passed over in favour of David Carradine for a TV series called *Kung Fu*, Asians have been consistently caricatured, denied the right even to play ourselves'.[14] Hwang refers to his resistance to the casting of Pryce in the play, blending fact with fiction, in order to comment on his own changing attitudes to race. Initially, he protests: 'did someone suddenly turn the clock back to 1920? Are we all going to smear shoe polish on our faces, and start singing "Mammy"?' (p. 9). Thus, histories of racist representation surface in the drama itself.

The motif of 'yellow face' also serves to disclose other conceptions of race in America. Hwang's attitudes towards race undergo change when he casts a Eurasian in one of his plays and is forced to cover up the racial identity of the actor in order to 'save face'. He claims that the white actor is a Siberian Jew, suggesting that he might be interpreted as racially Asian. Yet, ultimately, he discovers that his own face has become a mask and that he too has been 'running around in yellow face' (p. 68). This is when he decides to create the play the audience is watching with the following aim: 'To take words like "Asian" and "American," like "race" and "nation," mess them up so bad no one has any idea what they even mean anymore' (pp. 68–9). In so doing, he not only fulfils the aspirations of those who believe in a postracial America but also comes to embrace the vision of his own migrant father: 'Cuz that was my Dad's dream: a world where he could be Jimmy Stewart. And a white guy – can even be an

Asian' (p. 69). In this respect, Hwang takes up and fulfils his father's interpretation of the American dream as a place where migrants might achieve success and forge their own indentities.

Extended Commentary: Hwang, *M. Butterfly* (1988)

David Henry Hwang's *M. Butterfly* opened to rave reviews in February 1988 at the National Theater in Washington, DC and subsequently opened on Broadway at the Eugene O'Neill Theatre where it enjoyed a long run. The play can be seen in the postcolonial tradition of rewriting history and canonical works of Western culture. *M. Butterfly* refers to Giacomo Puccini's opera, entitled *Madame Butterfly* (1898). The opera tells the story of B. F. Pinkerton, a lieutenant in the American army, who seduces and impregnates a young Asian woman, named Cio-Cio-San, only to abandon her. The opera ends with the suicide of Cio-Cio-San. At the same time, *M. Butterfly* rewrites recent events in political history. Set against the backdrop of the Vietnam War, China's Cultural Revolution and the events of May 1968 (when student protests in Paris led to a general strike), *M. Butterfly* replays events that took place in the life of French diplomat Bernard Bouriscot during his twenty-year affair with a Beijing Opera performer. Stationed in Beijing, China, during the years of the American war in Vietnam (1965–75), Bouriscot met, fell in love and began an affair with a male, Chinese spy who had disguised himself as a woman. When the lovers tried to enter France, they were both charged with espionage. Only then did the diplomat discover that his mistress was a spy for the Chinese government and also a man. M. Bouriscot was tried, found guilty of espionage and sentenced to prison, from which he was released in 1988. Unlike *Madame Butterfly*, which ends with the death of Cio-Cio-San, and events in real life (Bourioscot was released from prison), the play stages a very different ending. In Hwang's play,

Rene Gallimard (the dramatic counterpart for Bouriscot) dies by committing ritual suicide, (mis)appropriating Eastern cultural traditions – in this case the Japanese ritual of *hari kari* – in death. Thus, Hwang's play can be seen as a parodic reversal of *Madame Butterfly*.

In telling a story about a man who falls in love with another man, playing the role of an Asian woman, Hwang explores the intersections of gender, sexuality and interracial relations. The title of the work cleverly signals the ambiguities of gender, for the designation 'M.' is the French short form for Monsieur (Mister). The play, as we shall see, strategically represents (post)colonial history, racist Orientalist* stereotypes and colonialist constructions of gender and sexuality. In rewriting the opera as well as the recent history of Bouriscot, Hwang subverts the Orientalist tradition of constructing the West as rational, masculine and dominant and the East as exotic, passive and feminine (or effeminate).

> I wrote M. Butterfly, [says Hwang,] as an attempt to deal with some aspects of orientalism. I assumed that many in the audience would be coming to the theatre because they hoped to see something exotic and mysterious, but what exactly is behind the desire to see the 'exotic East'?[15]

In the play, Hwang calls attention to the ways in which Puccini's work not only reflects Orientalist stereotypes but also propagates them. For instance, Gallimard refers to *Madame Butterfly* as his favourite opera and to Pinkerton as 'good-looking, not too bright, and pretty much a wimp', highlighting the unheroic qualities of the Western protagonist whom he nonetheless admires.[16] Moreover, the subversive restaging of the opera is particularly evident when Song Liling (Butterfly) highlights the racism inherent in *Madame Butterfly* as an Orientalist text:

* For a discussion of Edward Said's *Orientalism*, see Part Four: 'Postcolonial Reading Practices'.

> Consider it this way: what would you say if a blonde homecoming queen fell in love with a short Japanese businessman? He treats her cruelly, then goes home for three years, during which time she prays to his picture and turns down marriage from a young Kennedy. Then, when she learns he has remarried, she kills herself. Now, I believe you would consider this girl to be a deranged idiot, correct? But because it's an Oriental who kills herself for a Westerner – ah! – you find it beautiful. (p. 17)

Hwang's Gallimard may be presented sympathetically, but he proves to be as racist as Pinkerton: embracing a fantasy Asian woman who will fulfil his desires and reinforce his sense of masculine dominance over the East. John Louis DiGaetani notes that the operatic source, *Madame Butterfly*, is itself ambivalent about Western attitudes towards the East and might be said to offer a critique of Eurocentrism alongside its Orientalist perspectives: 'Pinkerton is one of the great heels in all opera. Puccini presents the West as oafish and insensitive.'[17] In this context, Hwang amplifies the sense of ambivalence already present in the operatic work through his metatextual representation of *Madame Butterfly*. In *M. Butterfly*, Gallimard embraces a sexist, racist and culturally insensitive vision of 'slender women in chong sams [Chinese dress] and kimonos [Japanese dress] who die for the love of unworthy foreign devils' (p. 91). Racism and misogyny intersect when he observes that Asian women can 'take whatever punishment we give them, and bounce back, strengthened by love, unconditionally' (p. 91). In this context, it is not surprising that he fails to distinguish the differences in gender and culture that separate his fantasy Asian woman from the actual man with whom he is having a relationship. Finally, the distinction between male/female as well as self/other collapses when Gallimard dons the costume and wig of Butterfly in order to kill himself/herself. Prior to plunging the knife, s/he says: 'And I have found her at last. In a prison on the outskirts of Paris. My name is Rene Gallimard – also known as Madame Butterfly' (p. 93). The imperialist and patriarchal violence inflicted on the other also strikes at the self.

James S. Moy remarks that 'Gallimard's fantasy merge[s] the Orient into one indistinguishable mass, eliminating the differences among Chinese, Vietnamese and Japanese'.[18] For Hwang, an Asian American, the critique of this monolithic mode of Orientalism is especially relevant given America's tendency to conflate various Asian nations. Significantly, the play responds to the Orientalist and imperialist assumptions underpinning the long history of American military attacks on Japan, Korea, Vietnam and China. Just as Gallimard fails to understand M. Butterfly (Song), Western nations fail to understand that their overtures are not embraced but seen as hostile and violent acts of assault. Gallimard observes:

> And somehow the American war went wrong too. Four hundred thousand dollars were being spent for every Viet Cong killed; so General Westmoreland's remark that the Oriental does not value life the way Americans do was oddly accurate. Why weren't the Vietnamese people giving in? Why were they content to die and die and die again? (p. 68)

Song, a queer character who embodies both masculinity and femininity, makes explicit the underlying gendered and sexual politics at work in the use of military force against a culture perceived as feminine. Song explains:

> The West has a sort of international rape mentality. ... The West thinks of itself as masculine – big guns, big industry, big money – so the East is feminine – weak, delicate, poor ... but good at art, and full of inscrutable wisdom – the feminine mystique.
> Her mouth says no, but her eyes say yes. The West believes the East, deep down, wants to be dominated – because a woman can't think for herself. (pp. 82–3)

Thus, Song subverts the Asian cultural stereotype of a passive nation because she speaks out, openly protesting against the sexualised imperialistic attitudes of the West.

Hwang draws on culturally hybrid performative tradition in order to highlight patriarchal and imperialist attitudes as well as contradictions in thinking about the intersections of race, gender and sexuality. Song appears in Kabuki theatre,* dressed as a woman; traditionally, the female roles are played by men in this type of performance. The fact that Gallimard does not know this reveals his cultural insensitivity. It also enables Hwang to critique sexism in the East:

> I also wanted to explore why it is that in Asian theatre and also in Shakespearean theatre men play women's roles. It's just touched on briefly. Song Liling says, 'Why are women's roles played by men?' And the answer is: 'Because only a man knows how a woman should act.' Let's look at that in kabuki terms because in kabuki it's expressed much more clearly. In kabuki they say that a woman can only be a woman whereas a man can be the idealization of a woman. This is obscene, and it's inherently sexist. What it's saying is that only a man can be a man's idealization of a woman.[19]

The play explores the disavowals and contradictions of sexuality and gender in other ways. Many have questioned how it could be possible for a man not to know that he has been having sexual relations with another man. Gallimard claims that it is because he never saw his lover naked, assuming that she was a modest Chinese woman, but this is a cultural stereotype rather than a reality of Chinese culture. Hwang notes that the events took place during a homophobic era so that the actions of Bouriscot/Gallimard can be read as examples of self-censorship. Hwang calls attention to the

* Kabuki is a traditional Japanese form of theatre with its roots in the Edo period of the seventeenth century. It comprises stylised elements of music, dance, drama and interaction with the audience, and, as in Elizabethan England, developed at a time when women were forbidden to perform.

belief found in many cultures that having sex with another man is only an act of homosexuality if one is the passive ('feminine') partner. Thus, he suggests another layer of complexity to the construction of sexuality in a cross-cultural context: the disavowal of homosexuality can be seen as part of a colonialist legacy. Overall, the play confronts Western imperialistic attitudes, actions and representations in history and culture. In queering *Madame Butterfly*, the play delivers a far reaching exploration of gender and sexuality in the postcolonial world. Hwang deftly brings together neoimperialistic histories, highlighting American acts of interventionism in Asia as well as the underlying racism and cultural insensitivity that inform these actions.

Notes

1 Judith Butler, *Bodies That Matter: On The Discursive Limits of 'Sex'* (London: Routledge, 1993), p. 1.
2 Elin Diamond, 'Introduction' in *Performance and Cultural Studies* (London: Routledge, 1996), p. 3.
3 W. B. Worthen, 'Drama, Performativity and Performance', *PMLA* 113.5 (1998), p. 1093.
4 Asha Kuthari Chaudhuri, *Mahesh Dattani: Contemporary Writers in English* (New Delhi: Cambridge University Press India, 2008), p. 1.
5 Ibid., p. 22.
6 Erin B. Mee, 'Mahesh Dattani: Invisible Issues', *Performing Arts Journal* 19.1 (1997), p. 20.
7 Raj Ayyar, 'Mahesh Dattani: India's Gay Cinema Comes of Age', *Gay Today* 8.48 (2004), p. 49.
8 Ruvani Runasinha, *Hanif Kureishi* (Tavistock: Northcote House, 2002), p. 40.
9 Bart Moore-Gilbert, *Hanif Kureishi* (Manchester: Manchester University Press, 2001), p. 92.
10 Ibid.
11 Hanif Kureishi, *Collected Screenplays I* (London: Faber and Faber, 2002), p. 26.
12 David Henry Hwang, 'Evolving a Multicultural Tradition', *MELUS* 16.3 Ethnic Theater (Autumn, 1989–Autumn, 1990), p. 16.
13 David Henry Hwang, 'Playwright's Note' in *FOB and Other Plays* (New York: Penguin, 1990), p. 3.

14 David Henry Hwang, *Yellow Face* (New York: Theatre Communications Group, 2009), p. 8.
15 David Henry Hwang and John Louis DiGaetani, '"M. Butterfly": An Interview with David Henry Hwang', *TDR* 33.3 (Autumn 1989), p. 141.
16 David Henry Hwang, *M. Butterfly* (New York: Penguin, 1989), p. 5.
17 Hwang and DiGaetani, 'Interview', p. 142.
18 James S. Moy, 'David Henry Hwang's "M. Butterfly" and Philip Kan Gotanda's "Yankee Dawg You Die": Repositioning Chinese American Marginality on the American Stage' *Theatre Journal* 42.1 (March 1990), p. 50.
19 Hwang and DiGaetani, 'Interview', p. 146.

Post-colonial to Post-9/11 Poetics: Brutus, Alexander and Brathwaite

Postcolonial poetry experiments with form and language as a means for moving beyond the legacies of colonialism and articulating new socio-cultural horizons. As a result of colonisation and the colonial education system, the English language itself often represents a necessary but ambivalent medium for postcolonial communal and self-expression. Inspired readings of postcolonial poetry and wider accounts of the tradition can be found in Rajeev S. Patke's *Postcolonial Poetry in English* (2009) and Jahan Ramazani's *The Hybrid Muse: Postcolonial Poetry in English* (2001) and *A Transnational Poetics* (2009). Patke approaches the postcolonial as a transitional category, a term that 'covers the gap between political self-rule and cultural autonomy'.[1] This chapter explores the work of three postcolonial poets whose poetic techniques and geo-political perspectives represent various possibilities for communal and self-expression, especially in response to oppressive socio-political conditions and exile, namely Dennis Brutus from South Africa, Meena Alexander, a migrant born in India and now living in the United States, and Kamau Brathwaite, a Barbados-born poet who has lived in England as well as Ghana and now splits his time between New York and the Caribbean.

Dennis Brutus as Protest Poet

Protest poetry is one of the most important and diverse traditions to emerge through the poetics of decolonisation around the world, but particularly Africa and its diaspora.* Resistance to apartheid has played an important role in the tradition of performance poetry within South Africa and elsewhere. Rajeev S. Patke notes that the 1970s marked 'the heyday of protest against apartheid' but that the 'political and ethical fallout from apartheid continues to affect contemporary poets in South Africa, where the racial dimension of violence has tended to blur the distinction between colonial and postcolonial predicaments'.[2] Some are critical of protest writing – poetry in particular – because the tendency to polemic can sometimes be at the expense of artistic rigour. Patke poses the question as follows: 'How does a poet keep the edge of protest alive, without letting poetry succumb to considerations that dismiss or marginalize the aesthetic dimension?'[3] This question is relevant not only for those working in the protest tradition; it is fundamental to postcolonial poetry, which is so often concerned with oppression and the articulation of political alternatives.

Dennis Brutus (1924–2009) grew up in a segregated ghetto for 'coloureds' in Port Elizabeth, South Africa. Growing up in a supportive family environment, he became a teacher and went on to play a leading role in the anti-apartheid movement. Education, activism and poetry were central to his life's work. As a teacher, he participated in fighting against the government's erosion of educational standards for black children. In 1958, Brutus set up the South African Sports Association (SASA) which lobbied international sports federations to withdraw recognition of whites-

* The term 'diaspora' (meaning dispersion) initially referred to the scattering of Jewish peoples as a result of several forced expulsions from what is now known as Israel, Jordan and parts of Lebanon as well as the State of Palestine. Subsequently, 'diaspora' has come to refer more generally to the movement, migration or scattering of a people away from a settled location or ancestral homeland.

only South African affiliates. In 1961, he was banned for five years from all political and social activity, which meant that he could not be quoted or published in South Africa. His poetry was thus published abroad, including *Sirens, Knuckles and Boots* (1963) by Mbari Publications (Ibadan, Nigeria). In 1970, Troubadour Press published *Thoughts Abroad* under the pseudonym of John Bruin so that the book could be distributed in South Africa. In 1963, Brutus was arrested, but escaped while on bail. Rearrested by the Portuguese police, he was extradited to South Africa. During another escape attempt, Brutus was shot, and subsequently sentenced to eighteen months hard labour on Robben Island in a cell next to that of Nelson Mandela. Following his release, Brutus lived in exile for more than twenty years. During this time, he continued to speak out as a poet and activist against injustice. Notably, as president of the South African Non-Racial Olympic Committee (SANROC), he led efforts to exclude South Africa and Rhodesia from the Olympic Games. In the post-apartheid era, Brutus was often critical of failures to address the inequalities associated with global capitalism and the controlling interests of an all-white minority in South Africa. Despite government opposition to economic imperialism – what Thabo Mbeki* referred to as 'global apartheid' – economic policy in post-apartheid South Africa remained largely under the sway of foreign investment interests and in line with the 'Washington consensus' with its emphasis on privatisation, free trade and labour policies that benefit business development. Beyond South Africa, Brutus was active in the global justice movement, helping with campaigns against the International Monetary Fund and World Bank, whose role in encouraging Third World debt has been seen as enabling new forms of imperialism in the post-colonial era through economic interventionism. In 2002, Brutus's critique of global capitalism and neoimperialism took the form of resistance to the New Plan for Africa's Development (NEPAD), an economic development

* Thabo Mvuyelwa Mbeke (b. 1942) served almost two terms (June 1999 to September 2008) as the second post-apartheid President of South Africa (after Nelson Mandela).

programme of the African Union that had been adopted at the thirty-seventh session of the Assembly of Heads of State and Government in 2001. Until his death in December 2009, the poet and social critic remained active in his efforts to foster global justice.

'Letters to Martha', written in 1965 and published in 1968, reflects on Brutus's prison experience. Addressed to his sister-in-law, this epistolary (in the form of a letter) poem in itself represents an act of protest, for the prisoners were forbidden to write poetry. The content of the poem also speaks out against the conditions of the prisoners in both literal and metaphorical terms: the work documents incidents of sexual abuse, the sense of privation experienced because all forms of music were forbidden (including a ban on whistling and singing), and the struggle to hold onto a measure of freedom while imprisoned. Yet, his poetry is full of the echoes of music, with references to Western classical works such as *Eine Kleine Nachtmusik* (Mozart, 1787) and *Music for the Royal Fireworks* (Handel, 1749), and poetic voices that will not be silenced. Protest finds voice in the following lines:

> So one grits to the burden
> and resolves to doggedly endure
> the outrages of prison.
> Nothing of him doth change
> but that doth suffer a seachange[4]

In Shakespeare's *The Tempest* (1610–11), Ariel sings the verse, 'Nothing of him doth fade / but that doth suffer a sea-change', alluding to a radical and mystical transformation of the body, but his words are also a falsehood, which deceive Ferdinand (Act 1, Scene ii). Brutus misquotes Shakespeare, changing the word 'fade' to 'change', emphasising the radically transformative aspects of change in prison. Through the reference to Ariel, Brutus invokes an ambivalent poetics of threatening and comforting sounds made by a figure who is both capable of flight and a prisoner on an island, a slave to Prospero. References to *The Tempest* recur in postcolonial writing (such as found in the work of Octave Mannoni, Aimé

Césaire, George Lamming and Kamau Brathwaite), especially as Ariel and Caliban are frequently interpreted as slaves to the colonising figure of Prospero. While many postcolonial writers favour Caliban as a figure of resistance, Brutus chooses the more ambivalent figure of Ariel, a figure who has been imprisoned by Sycorax (the witch who formerly ruled the island) and then bound in servitude to Prospero. Like Ariel, Brutus is a figure of accommodation and resistance who comes to embrace the status of prisoner and then resist it, but discovers that 'the acceptance / once made / deep down / remains' (p. 113). Yet, just as Ariel gains his freedom through his powers of song and flight, Brutus finds his own measure of freedom in poetic flights. The reference to birds reinforces the linkages between the powers of song and flight:

> In prison
> the clouds assume importance
> and the birds
>
> With a small space of sky
> cut off by walls
> of bleak hostility
> and pressed upon by hostile authority
> the mind turns upwards
> when it can – …
>
> the complex aeronautics
> of the birds
> and their exuberant acrobatics
> become matters for intrigued speculation
> and wonderment ...
>
> and the graceful unimpeded motion of the clouds
> – a kind of music, poetry, dance –
> Sends delicate rhythms tremoring through the flesh
> (pp. 113–14)

The clouds and birds can be seen as offering a shared language, visible to those in prison and outside, potentially linking the prisoner to his family. Motion, music, poetry and dance come together as the birds fly. Ultimately, though, the poet does not offer a transcendent flight from the conditions of imprisonment through poetic flights of fancy or escapist lyricism. In the closing stanza of the poem, the poet recalls a night when he yearned to see the stars and shut off the light in his cell in order to do so. However, a 'brusque inquiry' from the machine-gun post and the menace of the guards thwart his sense of delight so that it is the threat rather than the stars he recalls from that night. Nonetheless, the poem ends with the word 'stars', suggesting that this vision of the sky has in voice – if not in memory – survived.

As a protest poet, Brutus's work not only speaks to his own experiences, but attests to the need for solidarity in opposing acts of injustice. The editors of *Poetry and Protest: A Dennis Brutus Reader*, Lee Sustar and Aisha Karim, observe that Brutus lays out his approach to transnational injustice and protest in a 1974 speech:

> It is not resistance to oppression; it is not even liberation merely in the sense of freedom to govern yourself. It has penetrated beyond that to an understanding that what we are engaged in is a struggle against imperialism. It is not a local, nor even a national struggle. We see ourselves as an element in the global struggle against imperialism. This seems to me the truly revolutionary element in our struggle for cultural liberation.[5]

Brutus's poems from the 1970s are particularly suggestive of this anti-imperialistic stance. In an untitled poem from 1973, the poet confronts 'the dim and unavowed specter of a slave, / of a bound woman, whose bound figure pleads silently / and whose blood I must acknowledge in my own' (p. 247). Thus, the poet elicits connections between his own 'rebel blood' and that of the enslaved spectre (p. 247). In 'Across the Mediterranean: Cairo to Frankfurt', the poet exclaims: 'all the world is mine and to love / and all of its humankind' (p. 247). This declamatory assertion may lack the poetic grace of some of Brutus's other verses, but it reflects his sense of the need for greater solidarity in the world.

Brutus's invocations of elegies and commemorative poems as well as of sites of memory, landscapes and cityscapes embody a sense of relational poetics. Brutus visited Algiers for the Panafrican Arts Festival in 1970. While there, he spoke on behalf of the ANC (African National Congress) and PAC (Pan Africanist Congress) at an Organisation of African Unity meeting. He also composed poems, which were published in *Poems for Algiers*. One of these depicts the walled citadel in paradoxical terms as a wounded site of impenetrable resistance: 'only in the Casbah / where the bombed structures gape / in mute reminder of the terror of the French / is the tenacious, labyrinthine and unshatterable heart / of resistance / truly known' (p. 248). The city is wounded and mute. Yet, it also bears witness to terror; its maze-like streets offer a logic that runs counter to the desire to raze and lay bare the Algerian city. Resistance thus is given voice in the residual structure of the city, which articulates another kind of truth, another way of being in the world. 'Munich poem: At the time of the Munich Olympics' (1972) speaks out against the Holocaust, contrasting the pristine German countryside to the acts of genocide carried out at Dachau. In a poem on Bristol (1970), Brutus refers to the chocolate-maker, Fry's, which, he suggests, continues to produce and profit from a long history of exploitation: 'the bean still coalesces a swollen gleam – / sweatdrops globed on salt black flesh / lambent like blooddrops fresh and red' (p. 265). The oil of the dark bean, the sweat of the enslaved black labourer and the production of both chocolate and blood are evoked in these verses, which metonymically* link the product to the methods of production.

* A metonym is a figure of speech or trope used in rhetoric in order to refer to an idea, person or thing by substituting another term. For instance, the word 'sail' might be used to refer to a ship or the word 'crown' might be used to refer to the monarchy.

Bristol's local production of chocolate is resituated via the embodied history of 'sweatdrops globed on salt black flesh', implicitly contrasting the sweetness of sugar to the salty sweat of labourers. In these and other similar poems, Brutus expresses his resistance to racist oppression in all forms.

Exile is a particularly important theme for the poet, especially in the light of his own experience as well as others of his generation who were force to flee South Africa as a result of apartheid. The bitter experience of exile is reflected in this untitled poem from 2005:

> Exile, exile,
> you are a bitter word
> I eat with you my bread
> I drink with you my tea
> you are the bitter word
> that makes the world bitter to me (p. 369)

Exile is personified or embodied as a person with whom the poet dines and lives. In subsequent verses, Brutus refers to the stars as witnesses to his exile from 'a place / where I cannot be' (p. 369) so that even the stars are implicated in the poet's bitter apprehension of his place in the world. 'Inscriptions for a copy of *Road to Ghana* by Alfred Hutchinson' (1978) refers to the South African writer's 1960 memoir documenting his journey to Ghana following his release from prison and acquittal for charges of treason on account of his opposition to apartheid. In this poem, Brutus refers to 'our caged bird' who 'has sung for us' (p. 271). Brutus's reference to the caged bird may be familiar to many readers on account of Maya Angelou's 1969 autobiography entitled *I Know Why the Caged Bird Sings*, which recounts the African American writer's transformation as she overcomes racism. However, there is an earlier reference for Angelou and Brutus, namely Paul Laurence Dunbar's 1899 poem, 'Sympathy'. For Dunbar and Angelou, both African American writers, the image of the imprisoned bird is symbolic of slavery and the desire for free flight. Yet, such an image is also fitting for those who have experienced racial oppression and prison under apartheid. Through this intertextual reference to the work of Dunbar, Brutus evokes a trans-African consciousness. Brutus's poem makes reference to the nightingale, a bird noted for its beautiful singing voice, but the final line of the poem mentions the 'Phoenix'. This allusion is suggestive in metaphorical terms: those who have suffered under racial oppression will rise from the ashes to be reborn.

Meena Alexander's 'Poetics of Dislocation'

Born in India in 1951 to a family of Syrian Christians, Alexander migrated with her mother from Allahabad to join her father in the Sudan where he was working. From the age of five until her late teens, she spent part of the year in the Sudan and part in Kerala in south India. In the Sudan she received an English education. At the age of thirteen, she went on to study English at Khartoum University. Here she wrote her first poems in English, which were translated into Arabic and published in a local newspaper. At eighteen, she travelled to England to undertake doctoral studies, following which she returned to India to teach. In 1979, she migrated to the United States, where she lives today. Although she writes in English, her poetry tends to be inflected by her knowledge of other languages and cultures. Alexander notes:

> I was born a few years after Indian independence and learned English both in India and North Africa. The English I learned in India was always braided with other languages; Hindi, for I was born in Allahabad and spent my earliest years there; Malayalam, the language of my parents; Tamil, which was spoken by my friends; Marathi, for I spent a year in Pune. In contrast, the English I learned from a Scottish tutor in Khartoum and then perfected in the Diocesan School for British children was strict, and given the sternness of colonial

> pedagogy, cut away from the Arabic that flowed all around, from French, and from my mother tongue Malayalam, even from the sort of English I spoke with my parents and friends.[6]

The process of tearing away at language, English in particular, has been central to her poetics in order to release something of that experience not shaped by her postcolonial formation. In addition to the linguistic overlay, she felt strongly the need to express a sense of her gendered, ethnic and cultural otherness.

As a poet and scholar she read widely, drawing on the work of Caribbean, African American, Middle Eastern, African and Asian writers. Ngugi wa Thiong'o's *Decolonising the Mind* (1986) was particularly influential because it called attention to the violence that attends the imperial process of linguistic and cultural acculturation and deculturation. Alexander notes that she never learned formally to read or write in Malayalam, her mother tongue, but instead in English. As a result, she has learned to become 'comfortable with bends and sways to the other of other territories, other languages' (*Shock*, p. 11). At the same time, she lives in poetic exile from Malayalam poets whom she would love to read in the original, but cannot because she lacks the requisite reading knowledge. In 'Alphabets of Flesh', Alexander writes of this experience of inhabiting a no man's land, which is a 'no woman's land' also (p. 13), alienated from a child that might have been in another language. The wounds of language are evident as the poet invokes a brutal vocabulary to describe her suffering (p. 15). The association with what is dumb and bleeding is fundamental to the articulation of a self that has somehow been lost – nearly extinguished – through the filtering of language.

Like Dennis Brutus, Alexander has engaged in epistolary poetics as well as expressions of protest against the injustices of the (post) colonial order. In the collection entitled *Raw Silk* (2004), 'Letters to Gandhi' reflects her response to visiting Muslim survivors of the Godhra massacres. In 2002, inter-religious bloodshed broke out after fifty-nine Hindu pilgrims returning from the holy city of Ayodhya were killed in a train fire in Godhra, Gujarat. More than one thousand people, mainly Muslims, died in retailiatory riots. Alexander's poem is divided into four sections, entitled 'Lyric with Doves', 'Slow Dancing', 'Bengali Market' and 'Gandhi's Bicycle (My Muse Comes to Me)'. She offers a series of reflections on acts of political injustice through time and across continents. Alexander's interest in Mahatma Gandhi's nonviolent strategies of resistance is a longstanding one, shaped in part by her grandparents' politics as supporters of the political leader in his struggles to decolonise India. Alexander stresses the importance of migration in Gandhi's life, arguing that:

> he couldn't have done what he did in India without travelling away. He was a creature of the diaspora, an extraordinary man. It seems to me that he could never have invented *satyagraha* [passive or nonviolent resistance] if he hadn't encountered the race laws in Pretoria. And it made him open his eyes to the horrors of the caste system in India.[7]

Alexander is referring to Gandhi's years in South Africa (1893–1914) during which he experienced racial discrimination as well as the negative effects of racialised hierarchies. Travelling with a first-class ticket, he was thrown off a train for refusing to move from a first-class to a third-class coach. Various other incidents, entailing violence, caused Gandhi to consider the adverse aspects of imperialism. He stayed in South Africa to oppose a bill that aimed to deny Indians in South Africa the right to vote. In 1894, he helped to found the Natal Indian Congress in order to foster political solidarity; when assaulted in 1897 by white settlers, he refused to press charges in court as this was contrary to his principles for achieving justice. On 11 September 1906, when the Transvaal government passed a law to force Indians to register, Gandhi called upon fellow Indians to resist the law by nonviolent means, thus invoking for the first time the principles that would also guide him in his struggles for decolonisation in India.

Turning to Alexander's poem, we can see how a migrant consciousness and pacifist political stance shape its form and content. In 'Lyric with Doves', the poet invokes a symbolic bird of peace – the dove – as a muse for the poet's writing fingers, enabling them to fly metaphorically through sites of violence and trauma.[8] This poem makes reference to Godhra, the city in which Gandhi's Sabarmati Ashram* is located as well as the site of the 2002 massacre. 'Slow Dancing' and 'Bengali Market' are explicitly addressed to Gandhi. Alexander refers to the night when the Sabarmati Ashram gates were shut against Muslims seeking refuge inside. Here she calls upon Gandhi to comment on current events and describe his feelings about the attack (p. 78). The reference to *ahimsa* (meaning kindness and nonviolence, especially to animals) in this poem suggests the poet's outrage that Gandhi's home would not be used to protect those who were under threat. The very act of shutting the gates runs contrary to Gandhian principles, which celebrate ahimsa, as is evident in the collection of Gandhi's writings entitled *All Men Are Brothers* (published by UNESCO in 1958). These acts of violence and injustice are set against the longer history of the partition of India along religious lines, which Gandhi himself protested against. In 'Bengali Market', the poet refers to two million people dead and rivers of blood in reference to the history of violence and unrest in postcolonial India (p. 81). The opening verses of this section of the poem refer to the destruction of the masjid (mosque) (p. 80). The unnamed mosque is the Babri Masjid, a building of religious and cultural significance that was destroyed in 1992. Alexander refers to Kalidasa, the ancient Sanskrit writer, thus evoking a history of Hindu presence, as well as to the work of Russian poet Anna Akhmatova, whose poem entitled 'Requiem' was written in resistance to Stalinist terrorism. In this dense interweaving of references, Alexander's work recalls global cultural histories. The

* Ashram, originally a word describing a religious hermitage, came to mean something more like 'school' or 'studio'. The Sabarmati Ashram was also Ghandi's home, and the place from which he launched the fight for Indian independence.

final section of the poem returns to the iconic image of Gandhi on his bicycle in South Africa as well as refering to Swami Vivekananda's 'Sisters and Brothers' speech with which he introduced Hinduism to America on 11 September 1893. We might also reflect on the allusion to the Akademi, which can be seen as a reference to Gandhi's *All Men are Brothers* as well as to cycling around 'ground zero' (p. 82), which brings together the histories of 9/11 and the September 11 of Gandhi's nonviolent protest. In this dense interweaving of historical and cultural references, brought together through images of spinning wheels, mobility and solidarity across religious divisions, past and present, Alexander calls for a renewal of a pacifist vision in the world.

Like Brutus, Alexander remaps relations to place and space through her writing, especially through migration and its dislocating effects. Alexander's *Fault Lines: A Memoir* (1993) alludes to a term used by geologists to describe a separation or crack in the Earth's surface, particularly as a result of an earthquake or seismic shift. Alexander came into contact with fault lines, which she jumped over, as a child growing up in Allahabad. In her poetry, fault lines have come to symbolise the ruptures associated with transnational mobility and shifting relations to places and identities. The migrant's experience of dislocation finds a poetic correlative in the image of terrestrial tumult. In *The Shock of Arrival* (1996), the poet observes that '[m]igrancy, a central theme for many of us in this shifting world, forces a recasting of how the body is grasped, how language works' (p. 1). She sees the shock of arrival as many-layered because present experience also serves to jostle past memories and recast future horizons. Thus, migration has the potential to unlock new forms of knowledge: 'The shock of arrival forces us to new knowledge ... Race, ethnicity, the fluid truths of gender are all cast afresh' (p. 1). The interplay of race, gender and the migrant imaginary across 'fault lines' comes to the foreground in her poem 'San Andreas Fault'. Split into five parts – 'The Apparition', 'Flat Canvas', 'Funeral Song', 'Package of Dreams' and 'San Andreas Fault' – this poem shows Alexander's acute awareness of transcultural artistic visions. The epigraph comes from the opening verses of Rainer

Maria Rilke's *Duino Elegies*,* a series of poems written between the years 1912 and 1922, spanning years of travel as well as the First World War. Rilke is said to have heard a voice calling to him as he walked near the cliffs of Trieste (located in modern-day Italy but then part of the Austro-Hungarian empire), which in turn inspired him to ask: 'And if I cried, who'd listen to me in those angelic orders?' (cited by Alexander, p. 146). The words of this itinerant poet, spoken in a city at the crossroads of Germanic, Slavic and Latin cultures, provide a fitting entry to a poem that speaks to the transnational experience. The poem incorporates references to other transnational figures, such as Basquiat, a graffiti artist who lived in Puerto Rico and New York and created images that blended various aspects of world culture.† Like Rilke and Basquiat, Alexander is a witness to history from a transcultural, migrant perspective. She alludes to Kali, the Hindu goddess of time and change, and Draupadi (p. 146), a figure whose life story is represented in the *Mahabharata*,‡ when she catalogues acts of racial violence around the world (p. 149). The invocation of Kali is particularly appropriate given her associations with rage and destruction as well as the protective and benevolent aspects of maternal love. The reference to Draupadi, a figure who resisted foreign aggression and patriarchy, suggests a transnational feminist consciousness capable of taking a courageous stand against injustice. Earth shattering events, historic and imagined, are thus brought together in a poem in which the sacred sphere is potential witness to acts of earthly profanity.

Living in New York, the poet experienced at first hand the events of 9/11. In *Raw Silk*, the poet's 'Late, There Was An Island' responds

* Rainer Maria Rilke (1875–1926) was born to a German-speaking family in Prague, which was then the capital of Bohemia. He wrote poems in German and French. As an adult, he travelled widely and lived abroad, including visits to Russia and Italy as well as time spent living in Munich, Paris and parts of Switzerland.

† Basquiat (1960–88) was a child of migrants; his mother came from Puerto Rico and his father from Haiti. He was fluent in French, Spanish and English. As a child, he moved with his family to Puerto Rico for several years, contributing to the artist's sense of dislocation. His work blends Western and Afro-Caribbean cultural and visual references.

‡ The *Mahabharata* is a major Sanskrit epic of ancient India.

to this trauma and its aftermath through a reinscription of the metropolis. This apocalyptic poem is divided into three main parts: 'Aftermath', 'Invisible City' and 'Pitfire'. Where Brutus invokes birds as symbolic of freedom and flight, Alexander's birds are among those decimated by the events of 9/11. At the same time, the birds are part of a dense network of references to song and poetic flight. In this instance, the poet hears a bird cry from the wreckage of the ruined towers, only for this liturgy to be silenced (p. 11). Here the bird's presence links together events in nature, culture and politics, attesting to the damage sustained through multiple registers of experience. The poem cites a phrase, '*Liturgie de cristal*' (Liturgy of crystal), taken from Olivier Messaien's* work of chamber music entitled *Quatuor pour la fin de temps* or 'Quartet for the End of Time'. Messaien composed the piece when he was taken as a prisoner of war by the Germans during the Second World War. The piece premiered in Stalag VIII-A in Görlitz, Germany (now Zgorzelec, Poland) on 15 January 1941, to an audience of fellow prisoners and prison guards. The refernce to the end of time can be interpreted as a nod to both to the apocalyptic dimensions of war as well as to the story of the apocalypse from the Book of Revelation in the Bible. Aesthetically and spiritually, the end of the past and future also marks the beginning of eternity: in this sense, the reinscription of the present as a timeless moment can be said to disclose a sense of eternity. These various ways of interpreting the meaning of the title suggest both the flight from the temporal and the violent potential of history to mark an end to human time. Birdsong plays an important role in this composition for it elicits various ways of understanding the meaning of the flight from temporality and time-bound concerns. In the first movement, the 'Liturgie de cristal', a solo blackbird or nightingale is said to improvise the music, accompanied by trills from other birds, heralding the dawn of a new

* Messaien (1908–92) was a French composer and ornithologist. His music draws on rhythmic influences from various cultures, including ancient Greek and Hindu. His interest in synaesthesia (multisensory mapping, especially colours and music), transcultural compositions and birdsong are important for Alexander.

day. In the third movement, entitled the 'Abîme des oiseaux' (Abyss of the birds), the birdsong represents an opposition to the time-bound and a desire for jubilant flight, yet the birds themselves remain prisoners of time. In Alexander's poem, the reference to birds in the city as well as to music speaks to the theme of apocalypse, flight and the role of lyric. The stifled voice of the bird, however, suggests that she is not composing an artistic work that seeks to transcend time, but rather one that moves through cultural history in search of comfort and an alternative harmony to the discordant voice of the present. Rather than the 'Unreal City' of T. S. Eliot's *The Waste Land* (1922), a reference to London in the aftermath of the First World War, Alexander invokes the memory of a metropolitan landscape that is no longer visible in the wake of 9/11: the city of Manhattan with its twin towers (p. 10). Through the echoes of Eliot's verse as well as the music of Messaien – both works of art composed in resistance to the violence and waste lands associated with war – the invocation of the silenced bird also gives rise to a new kind of lyricism that finds voice in spite of destruction and the loss of life.

Kamau Brathwaite's Quest for a New World Poetics

Born in 1930 in a Barbados still under colonial rule, Brathwaite's work engages with the quest for a decolonising poetics, which entails a critique of imperialisms past and present. Stewart Brown observes:

> Certainly, in terms of his technical experimentation with form and language, as well as in the scale and ambition of his work, he has been more ambitious than the other major poet of the West Indies, with whom he is inevitably compared, Derek Walcott.[9]

While Walcott has engaged with world literary forms,* which he represents from a transnational Caribbean perspective, Brathwaite has

* Walcott is a poet from St Lucia who has won the Nobel Prize for Literature. For a discussion of his theatre, see Part Three: 'Decolonising the Stage'.

been continuously preoccupied with the quest for a New World aesthetic. Following the completion of a BA in history (1953) and a diploma in education in England (1954), the writer journeyed to Ghana where he lived and worked as an Education Officer from 1955 until 1962. These years were especially important for Brathwaite, as he came to understand the importance of African culture in the formation of the Caribbean experience. In 1962, he returned to the Caribbean to work for the University of the West Indies (where he stayed until 1991). From 1966 to 1968, he travelled to England to complete his PhD in history. There, he cofounded the Caribbean Artists Movement as well as writing the poems published in his first trilogy, *The Arrivants* (1973), consisting of *Rights of Passage* (1967), *Masks* (1968) and *Islands* (1969). Upon his return to the Caribbean, he wrote and published a second trilogy entitled *Ancestors*, comprising *Mother Poem* (1977), *Sun Poem* (1982) and *X/Self* (1997). The years 1986 to 1990 are typically referred to by Braithwaite as the 'Time of Salt'. During this traumatic era, Brathwaite's wife, Zea Mexican, died (1986); the poet's home and archive were destroyed by a hurricane (1988); and brigand gunmen broke into his Kingston apartment (1990). *Shar: The Hurricane Diary* (1990), *The Zea Mexican Diary* (1993) and *Trench Town Rock* (1994) respond to events from the 'Time of Salt', while *Words Need Love Too* (2000) can be seen as a 'post-Salt' collection. According to Brathwaite, a recent collection, *Born to Slow Horses* (2005), marks a new phase of writing based on tidalectics or tidal dialectics. This mode of reflection takes inspiration from the back-and-forth of the sea in its cyclical motion rather than eurocentric, linear approaches to thought. Furthermore, tidalectics acknowledges the sea's role in shaping the emergence and formation of the Caribbean transnational consciousness, history, culture and poetics.

In form and content, Brathwaite's work can be situated within the context of the quest for a decolonising poetics, which Kwame Dawes defines as follows:

> The quest for voice, an attempt to tell stories in a language and idiom that is our own, has been at the heart of the

> development of Caribbean writing. This quest has been closely connected to political and ideological development in our region. Central to these developments has been our response to the experience of colonialism and its role as a shaper of culture in our societies.[10]

Brathwaite has contributed to the reclamation of Creole history and aesthetics through his scholarly work, notably *The Development of Creole Society in Jamaica, 1770–1820* (1971). The poet's wide-ranging discussions of nation language and jazz poetics have shaped his poetic practices and contributed to a wider understanding of a New World aesthetic. In *History of the Voice: The Development of a Nation Language in Anglophone Caribbean Poetry* (1979), he traces the development of language through colonialism and the plantation experience. Adopting jazz poetics as the basis for a decolonising aesthetic, Brathwaite has argued for the importance of a postplantation form of articulation, no longer shaped through and by its resistance (and continued engagement) with colonial formation but through folk culture and continuous creativity.[11] However, this does not mean that the poet avoids a confrontation with the colonial past and its legacies. Rather, his work revisits colonialism from a postcolonial perspective, which is not constrained by the ideological and cultural horizons of a Eurocentric view. Brathwaite's own poetic practices show the influence of jazz and Afro-Caribbean music, including works such as *The Arrivants*, *Other Exiles* (1975), *Black and Blues* (1976), *Jah Music* (1986), *Trench Town Rock* (1994) and *Born to Slow Horses*.

Edouard Glissant, a philosopher and creative writer from the Francophone Caribbean, views Brathwaite's poetry as one of broken rhythms: 'A Caribbean discourse finds its expression as much in the explosion of the original cry, as in the patience of the landscape when it is recognized, as in the imposition of lived rhythms'.[12] The attentiveness to rhythm is evident in the poet's *The Arrivants: A New World Trilogy*. The first section of the first book, *Rights of Passage*, entitled 'Work Song and Blues', opens with lines that bring together both punishment and a strong oppositional voice. In this passage, the word 'skin' provides a metonymic bridge between the drum of Africa, covered by a skin upon which the drummer beats out his rhythms, and the skin of the human body, which is beaten by the whip/lash of the master. Between the beating of the drum, an absence made present through Brathwaite's rhythmic language, and the tortured human body under slavery, the poet uses the cutting edge of language as a medium that enables him to bear witness to a counter history of expressive language for singing, shouting, groaning and dreaming about a new kind of life beyond either the absent/present African past or the slave present. The word 'about' opens up a new horizon, which is made more explicit in the stanzas that follow, but in ending the stanza with this word, Brathwaite also evokes a space of possibility, a potential for articulation beyond even the poem and the historical occasion it represents.

Nathaniel Mackey argues that Brathwaite moves from landscape to fractured wordscapes and wordplay as language is thematised and acted upon.[14] Brathwaite creates neologisms or 'calibanisms'* by mixing words to create new meanings. For instance, he introduces the word 'stammament' by combining the words 'monument' and 'stammer' to mark the genesis of language in the Caribbean. Such a language practice could be seen as inspired by creolising processes as well as the plantation practice of speaking in a secret language. Moreover, this practice bears a resemblance to the Rastafarian methods for deconstructing and reconstructing language, such as when the word 'dedication' becomes 'livication' by removing the deadened sound and replacing it with a living one. An example of this stammering speech can be found in 'Negus' from *The Arrivants* (p. 222). Here the word 'it' – a single syllable – provides a fragment of speech, which gains its own sense of rhythm through repetition, like a word beating on a drum. The movement to negation ('it is not') opens up an ambivalent potentiality between being and nothingness, thus

* The word 'calibanism' refers to the language of Caliban from Shakespeare's *The Tempest*, which runs counter to standard English. Caliban's (mis)use of English is a marker of his colonisation and resistance to it.

embodying the creative potential of language to evoke new worlds. In the Bible, the creation of the world occurs through the Word according to John 1:1: 'In the beginning was the Word, and the Word was with God, and the Word was God.' Here the Bible, a text that played a pivotal role in the colonial process, and the role of language as a medium for colonisation come together in the reference to 'your kingdom of the Word'. This earthly kingdom, empire itself, is made manifest in the presence of the red, white and blue associated with the Union Jack as well as that of the dragon, a mythical beast that was killed by St George. St George's cross was adopted as a symbol of the Crusaders and eventually integrated into the Union Jack. The stammering utterance of the 'drag ... dragon' introduces the stanza concerning the need for liberation from worldly powers to the evocation of the kingdom of the Word, a new kind of order beyond the colonial paradigm with its whips, principalities and powers.

Fittingly, *Arrivants* comes to a close with the invocation of a new rhythm in 'Jou'vert', the final poem in the collection. Jou'vert is the Creole word from the French 'jour ouvert' that refers to the opening day of Trinidad's carnival ritual.[15] On this occasion, the poet refers not only to the body that has been beaten by the whip but also to the swaying hips of those dancing in accompaniment to the drum (p. 267). In this case, the rhythmic language and cadence of the drums elicit a counter-history of a people finding new expression in their old rhythms (pp. 269–70). The postcolonial moment finds expression through the rhythms past-present of creolised cultural forms and idioms.

Extended Commentary: Brathwaite, 'Hawk' from *Born to Slow Horses* (2005)

Born to Slow Horses was the 2006 International Winner of the Griffin Poetry Prize, awarded annually in Canada. The work's association with tidalectics or the power of the sea becomes evident when we consider that the white of the sea breaking on the reef as it rushes to the shore is referred to as 'manes of the water' or 'sea horses' in Brathwaite's home of Barbados. The collection of poems refers to events in the life of the poet and contains episodes from the Caribbean as well as New York. The poems in the collection are numbered under headings from i to vii, but the number vi has been replaced by '9/11'. This numeric disruption reflects the dislocating effects of the events of 9/11, which have marked a rupture in history. The accompanying poem, entitled 'Hawk', refers to Coleman Hawkins, arguably the foremost jazz saxophonist of the twentieth century. The poem brings together two histories of 9/11: the concert by Hawkins that took place on 11 September 1967 at Ronnie Scott's jazz club in London, and the terrorist attack on the twin towers in Manhattan on 11 September 2001.

The performance of the song 'Body and Soul' provides the imagined sonic backdrop for a poem that moves through several improvisational movements between London and Manhattan. The opening stanza of the poem describes Hawk as someone 'haunted by twins', a reference that looks forward to the collapsing towers but might also refer to the presence of the Marassa, the sacred twins of voudou in the Caribbean.[*] In a note following the poem, Brathwaite points out the associative connections he hopes to evoke through twinning, suggesting that the audioglyph[†] version of the poem should consist of 'two murals corresponding in spirit to the *Marassa* (Twins) of the twin towers of the World Trade Center' (p. 115). On the one hand, the poet elicits the sound of 'Body and Soul' interacting with World Music, including Portuguese fado, a mournful folk genre; the

* Voudou (or voodoo) is a version of African religious beliefs and practices that developed among slave populations in the West Indies (especially Haiti) and Southern states of America.

† Brathwaite does not define the term 'audioglyph' in this passage. A glyph can be a short form for a hieroglyph or refer to a carving, but here it refers to typeface. He seems to be defying the binary opposition of the spoken/written word through a reference to a performance of the poem as well as the general performative aesthetics of his use of the 'Sycorax video style', which incorporates glyphs of various kinds. In this instance, he seems to be imagining a total performance incorporating murals, music and spoken word.

performance of 'Strange Fruit', a song written about lynching in the American South; Duke Ellington, a jazz bandleader; and songs by Peter Tosh and Bob Marley. On the other hand, he envisions the intoning of the names of the beloved dead referred to in the poem, including those who died as a result of 9/11 as well as the unnamed dead who have been killed through acts of ethnic violence and genocide. The speech will fall 'like breath like leaves like paper spirit of birds' feathers towards the very last & sequence of the moment / monument's beginning' (p. 115). Like Alexander, Brathwaite evokes the shattered landscape of Manhattan in the aftermath of 9/11 by resurrecting silenced voices, including those of birds. Thus, the music of the poem, which refers to 'body and soul', provides a kind of wake for all those bodies and souls lost through acts of racial, religious and ethnic hatred. The pairing of creation and destruction – song and silence – alludes to an intertwined history of trauma/creation.

The typography of the poem and its experimental use of visual symbols further heightens the performative dimension of the work. Brathwaite introduces full stops, unexpected spaces, line breaks in the middle of words, italics, various fonts in varying sizes, text boxes, forward arrows and other visual markers. These textual features prompt the reader to pay attention to shifts in tone and meaning at the lexical and structural levels of the text as well as in terms of tone, voice and register. For instance, the poem includes allusions to other poems and song lyrics, which are in italics, prompting the reader to consider the sound of the words, such as the stammering reference to T. S. Eliot's *The Waste Land*, a poem about the devastating effects of the First World War: '*so so so many . i had not thought death / had undone so many*' (p. 100). The voices of those who mourn the dead at the 'Memorial Tribute to the Heroes of 9/11' are also highlighted through textual shifts. The words of Beth Petrone, a widow mourning the loss of her husband, a fire fighter, are presented in varying fonts. When she refers to the death of her husband, Terry, the word 'incinerated' is in a large, italic font, giving it an explosive force, suggesting the extent of the woman's pain and grief as well as the explosive force of the event (p. 105). A graphic of two figures holding hands, an image of twins, stands at the top of a page where the poem is split into two columns, suggesting that each column of verse is a counterpart to the other. One column or tower of verse refers to great poets and jazz musicians, such as Hart Crane* and Sonny Rollins,† while the other refers to the 343 firemen who themselves became fire: 'howl- / ing ishak meshak & abednegro' (p. 110). This is a reference to the fate of Shadrach, Meshach and Abednego from the Book of Daniel, three men who were thrown into a fiery furnace but saved from death by God. Thus Brathwaite refers to a story of those who were saved and links it to a story of those who died. In misspelling the names of the biblical figures, he alludes to the Bible, but also highlights the difference between those who were saved and those who died (whose names are similar but not exactly the same). Brathwaite is also changing the meaning of the names: placing emphasis on the 'shak' (suggestive of the word shake) and 'negro'.

The use of these typographic devices and sonic techniques is part of Brathwaite's 'Sycorax video style', which explores the potential of computing and word processing to generate new forms of expression. Sycorax is the name of the indigenous 'witch' who Prospero deposes when he takes control of the island in Shakespeare's *The Tempest*. In referring to a Sycorax video style, Brathwaite seeks to renew the power of local language, but he does so through the 'magic' of technology, specifically word processing as a form of writing that relies on light through digital computing. Through experiments with fonts, typeface and symbols as well as spelling, notably as represented in a poem informally known as 'Letter

* Hart Crane (1899–1932) was an American poet who is best known for *The Bridge* (1930), a poem that responds to T. S. Eliot's *The Waste Land* and offers a more optimistic view of the modern era. The poem celebrates The Brooklyn Bridge in America. Such a gesture is important for Brathwaite, who blends trauma and devastation with a more optimistic vision of creation.

† Sonny Rollins (b. 1930) is a noted saxophonist whose work rivals that of Coleman Hawkins in terms of influence. In 1963, Hawkins and Rollins produced a recording together, entitled *Sonny Meets Hawk*. Thus, Hawkins and Rollins can be seen as contributing to the motif of twinning in the poem. Like Crane, Rollins composed a work entitled *The Bridge* (1962). Rollins's work is a jazz piece composed while playing on the Williamsburg Bridge, a bridge that has a view of the New York skyline. In this sense, Rollins might also be seen as paired with Crane.

Sycorax' (a letter from Caliban to his Mother Sycorax),* Brathwaite renews the potential of Caliban's speech, which is traditionally associated with resistance to colonial language, by transforming the appearance of the printed word on the page so that the reader enters into a dramatic encounter with language itself. Thus, the legacies of colonialism and language through transcultural contact resurface in the inscription of new kinds of imperial history and interimperial strife, such as those that have emerged through World War and in the wake of the Cold War, namely through 9/11.

When asked about his response to the events of 9/11, Brathwaite has said:

> Art must come out of catastrophe. My position on catastrophe, as you say, is, I'm so conscious of the enormity of slavery and the Middle Passage and I see that as an ongoing catastrophe. So whatever happens in the world after that, like tsunamis in the Far East and India and Indonesia, and 9/11, and now New Orleans, to me these are all aspects of that same original explosion, which I constantly try to understand.[16]

In this passage, Brathwaite suggests the explosive potential of art as a force that is linked to creation and destruction as well as highlights the need to think about traumatic events in relational terms. This approach to history as a series of interwoven traumas can be seen as an attempt to build bridges. This is a particularly important point with respect to the reading of the poem 'Hawk'. While it explores the falling towers, it also focuses on twins and bridges, suggesting a counter-poetics to the violence associated with world politics. The opening account of Hawk's concert produces a series of musical/poetic connections: 'Rollins Bridge

* Brathwaite has used dubbing techniques in his poetry by performing a poem in a new manner and introducing new poetic techniques to alter the original. For example, 'X/Self xth letter from the thirteenth provinces' has been published four times: the original appeared in *X/Self* (1987), followed by a considerably revised version in *Middle Passages* (1992), which makes use of the Sycorax video style. A slightly revised version appears in the American edition of *Middle Passages* (1993) and another revised version appears in *Ancestors* (2001).

is fallin down / in London . where he arrives / this spinn / -ing golden time' (p. 92). In this verse, Rollins Bridge is probably a reference to Sonny Rollins's 1962 album, *The Bridge*. The title song from this recording includes a musical citation of 'Pop Goes the Weasel', an English nursery rhyme and singing game. Brathwaite's reference to the bridge falling down echoes Rollins because it alludes to another nursery rhyme: 'London Bridge is Falling Down'. The 'spinning golden time' might describe autumn in London, but it is also suggestive of the 'burn / ing time' of Manhattan's 11 September (pp. 92–3, 113), thus suggesting another bridge between London and New York. Throughout the poem, the word 'golden' accumulates meaning: it is associated with the saxophone as a golden horn (p. 94) and the loss of El Dorado (p. 95), the legendary lost city of gold that fascinated New World explorers, and 'the burn- / ing towers of this saxophone' (p. 114). Thus, the saxophone becomes a kind of fiery double for the blazing towers. In the final stanzas of the poem, Brathwaite links the sovereign wars of lust and the love of the saxophone so that he juxtaposes and fuses the twin forces of destruction and creation. In making reference to the green and golden, he perhaps also cites another notion of a golden age, the Edenic moment of Dylan Thomas's elegy for a lost childhood in 'Fern Hill' (1945), which refers to the 'green and golden' time of childhood as an Edenic time and ends with the line, 'I sang in my chains like the sea'.[17] Brathwaite introduces a submerged reference to the sea and the chains of history through this Edenic reference to childhood. His allusion to Dylan Thomas's work asks us to consider the relationship between the metaphorical enslavement of the child and the literal history of slavery that is central to Caribbean formation. In this respect, he participates in the Caribbean tradition of invoking the Marassa twins,* which often involves a reference to a third presence as a marker of plenitude. Thomas's 'Fern Hill' provides a spectral textual presence: the fallen child in Eden who accompanies the twin figures of the Marassa who are pictured, mentioned, metaphorically present and sonically alluded to in 'Hawk'.

* Iconographic representations of the Marassa twins often show a third figure. When they appear as triplets, they are typically associated with faith, hope and charity.

Notes

1. Rajeev Shridhar Patke, *Postcolonial Poetry in English* (Oxford: Oxford University Press, 2006), p. 5.
2. Ibid., p. 44.
3. Ibid., pp. 44–5.
4. *Poetry and Protest: A Dennis Brutus Reader* (Chicago: Haymarket Books, 2006), p. 113. Subsequent citations appear in the text.
5. Cited by Lee Sustar and Aisha Karim in 'Introduction: Dennis Brutus's Ticking Explosives', in *Poetry and Protest*, p. 14.
6. Meena Alexander, *The Shock of Arrival: Reflections on the Postcolonial Experience* (Boston: South End Press, 1996), p. 4.
7. Ruth Maxey and Meena Alexander, 'Interview: Meena Alexander', *MELUS* 31.2 *Varieties of Ethnic Experience* (Summer 2006), p. 28.
8. Meena Alexander, *Raw Silk* (Evanston, IL: TriQuarterly Books, 2004), p. 77.
9. Stewart Brown, 'Introduction', in *The Art of Kamau Brathwaite* (Bridgend: Seren, 1995), p. 7.
10. Kwame Dawes, *Natural Mysticism: Towards a New Reggae Aesthetic* (Leeds: Peepal Tree Press, 1998), p. 14.
11. Kamau Brathwaite, 'Jazz and the West Indian Novel', in *The Routledge Reader in Caribbean Literature*, eds Alison Donnell and Sarah Lawson Welsh (London: Routledge, 1996), p. 337.
12. Edouard Glissant, *Caribbean Discourse: Selected Essays*, trans. Michael Dash (Charlottesville: University Press of Virginia, 1989), p. 109.
13. Kamau Brathwaite, *The Arrivants: A New World Trilogy* (Oxford: Oxford University Press, 1973), p. 4. Subsequent citations appear in the text.
14. Nathaniel Mackey, 'Wringing the Word', in *The Art of Kamau Brathwaite*, pp. 132–3.
15. June D. Bobb, *Beating a Restless Drum: Poetics of Kamau Brathwaite and Derek Walcott* (Trenton: Africa World Press, 1998), pp. 192–3.
16. Joyelle McSweeney, 'Poetics, Revelations, and Catastrophes: An Interview with Kamau Brathwaite', *Rain Taxi, Online Edition*, Fall 2005 accessed from http://www.raintaxi.com on 20 February 2008.
17. Dylan Thomas, 'Fern Hill', *The Norton Anthology of English Literature*, 8th edn, Volume 2, General Editor Stephen Greenblatt (New York: W. W. Norton and Company, 2006), pp. 2448–50, p. 2450.

Part Four
Critical Theories and Debates

Postcolonial Reading Practices

What does it mean to read a text from a postcolonial perspective? What role do texts play in constructing and reconstructing the (post) colonial world? These are among the questions students ask when they first begin to study postcolonial literature. Moreover, they are fundamental questions for any postcolonial literary critic. Colonisation relied on related material and textual practices: the coloniser dominated the colonial world through deeds and words. When Christopher Columbus 'discovered' the New World, he wrote about his encounters in letters and journals. His accounts of the world reflected both his actual experiences in the world as well as his preconceptions and desires about the world he thought he might encounter, which were influenced by his readings of works such as Cardinal Pierre d'Ailly's *Imago Mundi* (1410) and the travel literature of Marco Polo and Sir John Mandeville. This reader-writer role is part of a tradition in colonial and postcolonial literature of constructing and revising a sense of the world order and one's place in it. Empire expressed itself through texts and the propagation of representations about the expanding world it sought to conquer, settle and govern. Literary works such as Thomas More's *Utopia* (1516), a response to Amerigo Vespucci's voyages, Shakespeare's *The Tempest* (1610–11) and Daniel Defoe's *Robinson Crusoe* (1719) and *Roxana: The Fortunate Mistress* (1724), are early examples of the ways in which colonial discovery and expansion began to influence the form, content and course of English literature. Colonial literary texts can tell us something about imperial ways of thinking, particularly about attitudes towards colonisation and processes of settlement. Moreover, these narratives are part of a wider tradition of speaking and writing about colonisation and the relations between the colonised and coloniser, or what we refer to as 'colonial discourse'.

In the postcolonial world, writers challenge colonial discourses through many strategies, such as writing back against imperial history, colonial fictions and other colonialist representations. Such works may be written from the perspective of colonised peoples and as such tend to incorporate alternative ways of perceiving, conceptualising and living in the world. Shakespeare's *The Tempest* has been rewritten and reworked by many postcolonial authors because it represents a fundamental colonial scenario: a white man dominating and governing natives who are coerced into labouring for him. The rewriting of the Caliban and Ariel figures from *The Tempest* has been central to the Caribbean tradition, particularly through the work of George Lamming and Kamau Brathwaite in the Anglophone tradition. Jean Rhys's *Wide Sargasso Sea* (1966) rewrites *Jane Eyre* (1847), providing a back-story for the Creole* history of the 'madwoman' named Bertha who grows up in post-abolition Jamaica before she migrates to England and is locked in the attic of her husband's mansion. V. S. Naipaul's novel *A Bend in the River* (1979) and essay 'Conrad's Darkness and Mine' respond to Joseph Conrad's *Heart of Darkness* (1899, 1902), a story about imperial presence in Africa. J. M. Coetzee's *Foe* (1986) rewrites the story of Robinson Crusoe in order to explore postcolonial perspectives about the silencing of indigenous peoples (represented by Friday). Thus, rewriting canonical works of Western literature is a way of reconstructing the oppressive discourses of the colonial past and imagining new postcolonial horizons.

The rewriting of imperial texts has been part of a larger process referred to as decolonisation: the process of dismantling colonialist

* For more on Creole culture, see Part Four: 'Cross-cultural Paradigms'.

power and discourses. Diana Bryon and Helen Tiffin note that decolonisation 'is not simply to rid oneself of the trappings of imperial power; it is also to seek non-repressive alternatives to imperialist discourses'.[1] The postcolonial literary critic considers how literature is related to colonial power and expansion, domination, ways of thinking about the coloniser/colonised relation, anticolonial resistance and decolonisation. As a vehicle for decolonisation, postcolonial literature critiques colonial ways of thinking, presents alternative cultural views of the world, reconstructs imperial perspectives, expresses anxiety or ambivalence about postcolonial relations, and enables the processes associated with working through the trauma associated with colonialism. In this, local culture, language and vernacular forms often play an important role in moving beyond the dominant forms of expression of the coloniser. To explore these issues related to colonial discourse, representation and decolonisation in more depth and detail, this chapter focuses on three key critics who have played a fundamental role in postcolonial literary theory, namely Edward Said, Gayatri Chakravorty Spivak and Homi K. Bhabha.[2]

Edward Said: the Postcolonial World, the Text and the Critic

Despite the existence of a rich body of writing from anticolonial and decolonising perspectives prior to the work of Edward Said (1935–2001), postcolonial literary theory is generally said to begin with Said's *Orientalism* (1978). Said's approach to analysing representations of the Orient inaugurated an important reading practice in postcolonial literary studies, which is referred to as 'colonial discourse analysis' or the study and critique of discourses for speaking about colonialism. In *Orientalism*, Said examines the ways in which Europe, Britain and France, in particular, represented North Africa, the Middle East and India and gained power over these regions through various means, including scholarship, fiction, colonial intervention and institutions.* He argues that the Western world gained power over the East during the colonial era through a continuum of related activities, which included 'making statements about it, authorizing views of it, describing it, teaching it, settling it, ruling over it'.[3] He sees a profound connection between ways of thinking, writing, visualising and talking about the Orient and the activity of colonising it. Indeed, he argues that representations of the Orient have enabled imperialism because these words and images of it have formed part of 'a Western style for dominating, restructuring, and having authority over the Orient' (p. 3). Influenced by Michel Foucault's analysis of the relationship between power and knowledge,† Said suggests that the exercise of power and the will to knowledge are inextricably linked through Orientalism. Said defines the reality-producing effect of discourse as follows:

> A text purporting to contain knowledge about something actual ... is not easily dismissed. Expertise is attributed to it. The authority of academics, institutions, and governments can accrue to it, surrounding it with still greater prestige than its practical successes warrant. Most important, such texts can create not only knowledge but also the very reality they appear to describe. In time such knowledge and reality produce a tradition, or what Michel Foucault calls a discourse, whose

* Although some critics also refer to the 'Far East' (China and Japan) when talking about Orientialism, Said clearly states that he is not referring to this particular geo-political relationship. Nonetheless, he says we might learn from the specific Anglo-French relationship to the 'Orient' when referring to other East–West relations, such as the American relationship to Palestine or wider engagements with the cultures and territories now understood as Japan, Korea and Vietnam.

† Michel Foucault (1926–84) made a significant contribution to discourse analysis with works such as *Discipline and Punish* (English translation 1977), *Power/ Knowledge* (1972–4) and *The Order of Things* (English translation 1970). Some critics argue that Said misappropriates Foucault's work, but it would be more accurate to say that Said drew on the work of Foucault as a source of inspiration for his critique of Orientalism. For a discussion of Said's relationship to Foucauldian thinking, see Aijaz Ahmad's *In Theory: Classes, Nations, Literatures* (1992) and the excellent summary of debates in Bill Ashcroft and Pal Ahluwalia's *Edward Said* (1999).

> material presence or weight, not the originality of a given author, is really responsible for the texts produced out of it. (p. 94)

With reference to the British occupation of Egypt (1882–1952), Said sees Orientalism as a discourse that justified imperial intervention and authority over territory. As a form of colonial discourse, Orientalism produces the image or stereotype of 'a subject race [Egyptian], dominated by a race [British] that knows them and what is good for them better than they could possibly know themselves' (p. 35). In emphasising the fact that textual representations of the Orient are not natural but constructed, Said opens the way for a critique of the processes whereby representations are constituted through selection and exclusion, gain widespread acceptance, and come to be institutionalised.

Elleke Boehmer defines colonialist discourse as follows:

> Colonialist discourse can be taken to refer to that collection of symbolic practices, including textual codes and conventions and implied meanings, which Europe deployed in the process of its colonial expansion and, in particular, in understanding the bizarre and apparently unintelligible strangeness with which it came into contact. Its interpretations were an expression of its mastery, but they also reflected other responses: wonder, bewilderment, fear. Colonialist discourse, therefore, embraced a set of ideological approaches to expansion and foreign rule.[4]

From the postcolonial critic's perspective, John McLeod observes that theories of colonial discourse analysis 'explore the ways in which representations and modes of perception are used as fundamental weapons of colonial power to keep colonised peoples subservient to colonial rule'.[5] Ania Loomba observes that colonial discourse analysis 'indicates a way of conceptualising the interaction of cultural, intellectual, economic or political processes in the formation, perpetuation and dismantling of colonialism'.[6] In other words, it focuses on the relationship between discourses (ways of talking about the colonial order and its peoples) and imperialism as a set of practices. That said, as John McLeod points out in *Beginning Postcolonialism*, one should not conflate Orientalism with colonial discourse analysis: the latter goes beyond Said's analysis of Orientalism and his own methods of discourse analysis.[7]

Said seeks to understand the role that imperialism has played in the Orientalist tradition. One way he explains this is through a discussion of relations to 'relatively uncommon things, like foreigners, mutants, or "abnormal" behaviour' (*Orientalism*, p. 54). He points out the longstanding practice of differentiating between 'us' and 'them' or the 'civilised' and the 'barbarian'. The term 'barbarian' stems from the Greek word for 'foreign, strange, ignorant', particularly with reference to the unintelligible speech of foreigners. The Romans ('barbarians' themselves from the Greek perspective) took up the word and applied it to tribes or nations that had no Greek or Roman accomplishments. More generally, Said sees the distinction in spatial terms: 'A group of people living on a few acres of land will set up boundaries between their land and its immediate surroundings and the territory beyond, which they call "the land of the barbarians"' (p. 54). For Said, relations between barbarian and civilised are become a means to differentiate between self and other as well as to define a sense of self. Patterns of opposition, differentiation and hierarchies form part of colonial ways of envisioning the world. In Orientalist terms, this way of thinking produces stereotypes whereby the Orient is considered to be timeless, strange, feminine and degenerate while the West is perceived to be historically progressive, rational, normal, masculine and morally upright.[8] In the Western world, these prejudices (ideological constructions of the self and other) served to justify colonial endeavours to civilise the barbarian other. Through an analysis of Orientalism, Said was thus able to show the ways in which colonial thinking, discourses and practices function in complex ways across cultures and through time. He makes this point clear in his conclusion to *Orientalism*, when he observes: 'No one can escape dealing with, if not the East/West division, then the North/South one, the have/have-not one, the imperialist/anti-imperialist one, the white/colored one' (p. 327). He asks his readers to consider the ways in which ideologies are constituted and maintained, encouraging scholars and thinkers to be more reflective about the underlying power dynamics that shape efforts to distinguish between the coloniser and the colonised.

To examine critically the workings of power relations, Said introduces two important terms: 'strategic location' and 'strategic formation'. Strategic location is 'a way of describing the author's position in a text with regard to the (Oriental) material he writes about' (p. 20). Said's own strategic location is shaped by his personal history as a child growing up in the British colonies of Palestine and Egypt and as a migrant to the United States. He notes:

> In many ways my study of Orientalism has been an attempt to inventory those traces upon me, the Oriental subject, of the [Western] culture whose domination has been so powerful a factor in the life of all Orientals. (p. 25)

In postcolonial literary criticism, the concept of strategic location is important because it means that the critic needs to consider his/her own identity, processes of formation and ideological assumptions about the self in relation to the wider world. Strategic formation, on the other hand, is 'a way of analyzing the relationship between texts and the way in which groups of texts, types of texts, even textual genres, acquire mass density, and referential power among themselves and thereafter in the culture at large' (p. 20). For the literary critic, this is a significant concept because it suggests that texts operate in a socio-political sphere because they serve to construct ideas, ideologies and identities, whatever the author's intentions. If a text tends to support prevailing ideas and representations of those in power, it can be said to contribute to a hegemonic perspective, which means that it reflects the interests of the dominant class or culture. Some critics argue that

Orientalism places too much emphasis on the hegemonic aspects of Western discourse, often at the expense of discussing the counter-discursive tendencies or alternative discourses at work in colonial and postcolonial societies. As many critics, including Said in his later work, have pointed out, literary works can also contest or challenge dominant ideas and in doing so offer a counter-hegemonic perspective.

Contrapuntal Reading Practices

Whether or not a text supports, contests or dynamically reproduces imperialist perspectives, the role of the postcolonial critic is to analyse how any literary text relates to the long history of (post) colonial representations, practices and historical events. Arguably, Said's notion of 'contrapuntal reading' represents his most significant contribution to postcolonial reading practices. 'Counterpoint' is a term that derives from the field of musicology where it refers to the relationship between two or more voices, which are typically independent in terms of both melody and rhythm, but often interdependent in terms of harmony. In musical terms, counterpoint does not mean that the voices are harmonious; indeed, the relationship between them is quite often dissonant. Such is also the case when we consider the role of a contrapuntal reading, which is attentive to the relations between the coloniser and colonised, which are interdependent and frequently rife with tensions. In *Culture and Imperialism* (1993), Said transposes the musical term to literary studies as follows:

> In practical terms, 'contrapuntal reading' as I have called it means reading a text with an understanding of what is involved when an author shows, for instance, that a colonial sugar plantation is seen as important to the process of maintaining a particular style of life in England. References to Australia in *David Copperfield* or India in *Jane Eyre* are made because they can be, because British power (and not just the

> novelist's fancy) made passing references to these massive appropriations possible.[9]

In Said's view, postcolonial critical perspectives can and should be applied to the reading of both post-colonial and earlier colonial texts.

Said's readings of Jane Austen's *Mansfield Park* (1814) show that the seemingly intimate and closed world of domestic drama is inextricably related to events occurring elsewhere on the plantations of the Caribbean. The novel tells the story of Fanny Price, an orphaned young girl who is raised by her rich uncle and aunt, Sir Thomas and Lady Bertram, at Mansfield Park. Because Fanny is a poor relative, all of the Bertram children, aside from her cousin Edmund, treat her as an inferior. Fanny responds to Edmund's affectionate behaviour and over time secretly falls in love with him. The children are adults when problems arise on Sir Thomas's plantation in Antigua, which require him to go abroad for a year in order to resolve matters. During his absence, while Sir Thomas is tending his colonial garden, the domestic order starts to come undone. Upon his return, Sir Thomas puts household matters in order once more. Said observes:

> There is nothing in *Mansfield Park* that would contradict us, however, were we to assume that Sir Thomas does exactly the same things – on a larger scale – in his Antigua 'plantations'. Whatever was wrong there ... Sir Thomas was able to fix, thereby maintaining his control over his colonial domain. More clearly here than anywhere else in her fiction, Austen here synchronizes domestic with international authority, making it plain that the values associated with such higher things as ordination, law, and propriety must be grounded firmly in actual rule over and possession of territory. She sees clearly that to hold and rule Mansfield Park is to hold and rule an imperial estate in close ... What assures the domestic tranquillity and attractive harmony of one is the productivity and regulated discipline of the other. (p. 104)

To hold and rule Mansfield Park is akin to lordship over a plantation in the colonies. Moreover, instabilities in the colonies can also disrupt the maintenance of order within the imperial centre. In this instance, the wealth, order and stability of the family and the home are directly related to shifting relationships in the colonial order. For Britain, the late eighteenth and early nineteenth centuries formed a period of instability and change within the Caribbean colonial order, following the Haitian revolution (which saw the overthrow of colonial rule and the emancipation of enslaved persons) and prior to emancipation for colonies under British rule. These interdependencies are not only evident in the socio-political and economic spheres but also come to play a role in intimate relations and the moral fabric of society. According to Said, 'Austen affirms and repeats the geographical process of expansion involving trade, production, and consumption that predates, underlies, and guarantees the morality' (p. 111). From a historical perspective, a contrapuntal reading takes into account the ways in which the processes of imperialism, related instabilities and resistance inform the text.

However, the postcolonial critic should not be constrained by the author's own perspectives and horizons. Said remarks:

> But just because Austen referred to Antigua in *Mansfield Park* or to realms visited by the British navy in *Persuasion* without any thought of possible responses by the Caribbean or Indian natives resident there is no reason for us to do the same. (p. 78)

As Said notes, the interpretation of Austen's work (or any fiction for that matter) 'depends on *who* does the interpreting, *when* it is done, and no less important, from *where* it is done' (p. 111). Here we see him reworking the idea of strategic location, already discussed in *Orientalism*, for the purposes of defining the role of the literary critic. He asks the critic to consider not only the relations between the literary text and the contemporaneous world but also what we make of a text from our contemporary postcolonial perspective. The postcolonial literary critic needs to read critically, often against the grain of the text, and examine whatever colonial assumptions a text or author might hold. Contrapuntal analysis assumes that the history and stories of formerly colonised societies should be told with a view to questioning and revising imperialist assumptions and perspectives.

Said argues that 'contrapuntal reading must take account of both processes, that of imperialism and that of resistance to it, which can be done by extending our reading of the texts to include what was forcibly excluded' (p. 79). For instance, he offers a reading of Rudyard Kipling's India in *Kim* (1900–1), a picaresque* novel about Kimball O'Hara, the orphaned child of an Irish soldier, who grows up on the streets of Lahore, India under British rule in the late nineteenth century. When Kim meets a wandering Tibetan lama, he follows him on a journey covering the whole of India. Kipling's account of Kim's travels throughout the subcontinent includes descriptions of the many peoples and cultures that made up India at this time. Said observes that Kipling's representation of India under British rule highlights facets of empire and resistance, which bears witness to imperial 'history, administrators, and apologists, and, no less important, to the India fought for by Indian nationalists as their country to be won back' (p. 79). An understanding of historical contexts enables the reader to see the work critically in ways that go beyond the particular colonial moment and related tensions it represents. Based on his analysis of *Kim*, Said observes:

> In reading a text, one must open it out to both what went into it and to what its author excluded. Each cultural work is a vision of the moment, and we must juxtapose that vision with the various revisions it later provoked – in this case, the nationalist experiences of post-independence India. (p. 79)

From a postcolonial perspective, the text offers a vision of the world, which is related to other visions and revisions of empire. A

* Picaresque (from the Spanish *picaro*: a wily trickster) describes a subgenre of fiction, often satirical, concerning the adventures of a rogue or rascal.

knowledge of other textual representations can help the critic to gain a more comprehensive sense of the ways in which the colonial world order, in this case India, is represented and re-presented, written and rewritten. Thus, the reading of a literary text might contribute to a wider understanding of the long history of (post)colonial representations.

In this respect, contrapuntal reading plays a powerful role in colonial discourse analysis as it allows the reader to relate the individual literary work to a wide array of colonial and postcolonial histories of representation. Specifically, Said argues that 'one must connect the structures of a narrative to the ideas, concepts, experiences from which it draws support' (p. 79). In his reading of Conrad's *Heart of Darkness* (1899, 1902), a story about an Englishman's experiences in the Belgian Congo, Said shows that the text belongs to 'a huge library of *Africanism*' or lore and writing about Africa. As such, *Heart of Darkness* can be seen as engaging in a struggle with other texts and representations of Africa:

> What we have in *Heart of Darkness* – a work of immense influence, having provoked many readings and images – is a politicized, ideologically saturated Africa which to some intents and purposes was the imperialized place, with those many interests and ideas furiously at work in it, not just a photographic literary reflection of it. (p. 80)

Texts are created in dialogue with the world and existing representations of it, but they also contribute to a repertoire of new images, often provoking responses and dialogues about the text and the world. In the case of colonial literature, Conrad's work can be seen as participating in what Said refers to as the 'scramble for Africa' (p. 80), which can be interpreted in terms of colonial territorial claims to the continent (or part of it) as well as to efforts 'to hold on to, think about, plan for Africa' (p. 80). Thus, Said argues that 'to represent Africa is to enter the battle over Africa, inevitably connected to later resistance, decolonization, and so forth' (p. 80).

Said demonstrates that *Heart of Darkness* can be seen in part as a reflection on the difference between empire and colonialism, especially through Conrad's comparisons of imperialism under the Romans 'who conquered and did little else' (p. 81) and the colonisers who are racially and ideologically motivated to take lands from nonwhite peoples and create settlements that correspond to Western ideas of civilisation. According to Said, Conrad shows that colonialism entails the power to take over territory as well as practices that disguise or obscure these brutal intentions through 'a justificatory regime of self-aggrandizing, self-originating authority interposed between the victim of imperialism and its perpetrator' (p. 82). The self-aggrandising aspects of colonialism are especially evident in the case of Kurtz, who seems to have established a fiefdom in Africa, setting himself up as a god-like figure among the indigenous peoples. Thus, Conrad's literary work exposes something fundamental about colonialism as a process that conceals and justifies its inherent violence.

For most readers, it is easy to understand how and why a novel about colonialism and empire might be read from a postcolonial perspective. However, Said moves beyond thematic approaches to literature and the content of the narrative to consider the ways in which the novel itself as a literary form has been shaped by colonial history. Said argues that many of the canonical novels of English literature – not only those that engage directly with overseas expansion, the act of accumulating riches and territories abroad – need to be considered in relation to empire. In his view, novels such as Samuel Richardson's *Clarissa* (1748)* and Henry Fielding's *The History of Tom Jones, A Foundling* (1749),† which deal with issues of class, marriage and the home, bring narratives about life in England

* *Clarissa* tells the story of a young woman who is tricked into eloping with a suitor named Lovelace. Lovelace takes Clarissa to a brothel where he drugs and rapes her. She eventually escapes from the clutches of Lovelace, but dies as a result of the duress ordeal. Lovelace travels to Italy where he dies in a duel. Thus, a story about domestic crisis takes the heroine out into wider society and the villain to Italy.

† *Tom Jones* tells the story of an orphaned boy who travels widely in the world and undertakes many adventures before he can marry the woman he loves.

and its domestic spaces into dialogue with 'a practical narrative about expanding and moving about in space that must be actively inhabited and enjoyed before its discipline or limits can be accepted' (pp. 83–4).Whether at home or in the colonies, these narratives reflect a common desire to explore and conquer space. For Said, 'the novel, as a cultural artefact of bourgeois society, and imperialism are unthinkable without each other' (p. 84). This argument is an important one for it shows how postcolonial reading practices address issues of content and form in literary works that do not appear to engage directly with colonialism.

Many critics argue that Said's approach to colonial power in *Orientalism* lacks sufficient nuance because he focuses almost exclusively on the role of imperial power and knowledge formation. At times, he seems to ignore resistance to colonial perspectives from within Western society or from outside it; he pays insufficient attention to the tensions within Eastern and Western societies. Despite these criticisms, Said's work has been extremely influential. He raises important questions concerning the dynamic interaction of texts, readers and events in the (post)colonial world. Said highlighted the necessity of coming to terms with the ways in which nations and cultures come to understand themselves, represent relations to the self and other, and engage in political action. His contrapuntal reading methods disclose new strategies for reading the literary text against the grain of imperialist assumptions. Moreover, as we have seen, Said provides a basic critical vocabulary for exploring strategic power relations: he shows how critical theory might be applied to analysing uneven power relations, whether through imperial processes of representation and/or practices.

Gayatri Chakravorty Spivak: the Self and its Others

Born in Calcutta in 1942, Gayatri Chakravorty Spivak migrated to the United States of America where she undertook graduate studies and began her professional academic career. Her theoretically sophisticated and often challenging work draws on deconstructionist,* Marxist† and psychoanalytic theory.‡ While Said places emphasis on the role of the coloniser, Spivak analyses the condition of the colonised. She is particularly interested in the subaltern (a term used to refer to someone who does not belong to the colonial elite), the role of gender and the ethics of reading from a postcolonial perspective. In this respect, her work responds to the question Said poses in *Orientalism* (p. 24): 'how one can study other cultures and peoples from a libertarian, or a non-repressive and non-manipulative, perspective'. Like Said, Spivak asks the postcolonial critic to read both history and literature critically, taking into account multiple interests, desires, power relations, locations, contexts and ideological perspectives that shape any act of representation. Also like Said, she is keenly aware of the political dimensions of representation, but she is more interested in what is unsaid, unspoken and silenced through representation. Where Said seeks to analyse the imperialist assumptions at work in the literary text, Spivak considers how texts represent the oppressed and often re-enact the imperialist tendency to silence the other.

In the words of Ella Shohat, we might say that Spivak points out that 'the struggle to "speak for oneself" cannot be separated from a history of being spoken for, from the struggle to speak and be heard'.[10] Spivak's arguments about the literary text, the role of the postcolonial critic and reading practices are derived in part from an

* Deconstructive reading practices show that the meaning of language and texts is not fixed but susceptible continuously to slippage and contradiction. As a result, differing and even incommensurate interpretations of texts are possible from a literary critical perspective. Spivak translated Jacques Derrida's *Of Grammatology* (published in French in 1967) in 1976. She tends to draw on Derridean methods of deconstruction to interrogate the binary oppositions and dominant ideologies underpinning colonialist discourse.

† Marxist criticism derives from Karl Marx's (1918–83) analysis of capital, class relations and ideology.

‡ Psychoanalysis, beginning with the work of Sigmund Freud (1856–1939), examines the role of the unconscious and dreams. This mode of analysis can shed light on the dynamics that motivate and influence behaviour.

analysis of colonial history and prevailing interpretations of the colonial order. Spivak raises several questions about representation: Who can speak for whom? Who listens? How does one represent the self and others? To explore her approach to these questions in more detail, we can turn first to her approach to the definition of representation in her most famous essay, 'Can the Subaltern Speak?' (1988),* and then consider how these ideas about representation shape her analysis of literary texts in 'Three Women's Texts and a Critique of Imperialism' (1985).

In 'Can the Subaltern Speak?', Spivak offers two definitions of representation. The first is the notion of speaking on behalf of someone, as understood in the context of political representation (*Vertretung*). The second is that of re-presentation (*Darstellung*: portrait) as the term is used in art or philosophy, which takes the form of portraying, depicting or placing someone or something in a particular light. Spivak suggests that these two separate forms of representation (*Vorstellung*) are nonetheless related because representation in political terms (*Vertretung*) is entangled with re-presentation as description (*Darstellung*). In her view, it is both utopian and essentialist to imagine that there is a subaltern subject beyond representation whose identity and interests can be recuperated. Rather, her two-faceted theory of representation can be called upon in order to reveal uneven power dynamics: the ways in which 'the staging of the world in representation – its scene of writing, its *Darstellung*' conceals the operations of power.[11] Representations, in the sense of descriptions, narratives and discourses, need to be looked at closely in order to understand the underlying power dynamics and political perspectives at work.

Spivak explores efforts to represent the subaltern (the nonelite) in

* The subaltern is a term that means 'of inferior rank'. Italian writer, politician and philosopher Antonio Gramsci (1891–1937) adopted the term to refer to the groups who are subordinate to a ruling or dominant class. This group can include peasants, workers and other non-elites (such as those of a lower caste). The Subaltern Studies group uses this term in order to describe and analyse power relations in South Asia. In this context, the subaltern can refer to the marginalised in terms of class, caste, age, gender and so forth.

the context of colonial India. She begins by considering the work of poststructuralist thinkers* Michel Foucault and Gilles Deleuze:

> The participants in this conversation [Foucault and Deleuze] emphasize the most important contributions of French poststructuralist theory: first, that the networks of power/desire/interest are so heterogeneous, that their reduction to a coherent narrative is counterproductive – a persistent critique is needed; and second, that intellectuals must attempt to disclose and know the discourse of society's Other. Yet, the two systematically ignore the question of ideology and their own implication in intellectual and economic history. (p. 272)

Although Spivak agrees with Foucault's and Deleuze's view of the subject (person) as decentred, she does not find it helpful to consider the subject as constituted through networks of power/desire/interest.† Spivak argues that a theory of representation is more promising as a means to explain the construction of subjects: 'radical practice should attend to this double session of representations [as proxy and portrait] rather than reintroduce the individual subject through totalizing concepts of power and desire' (p. 279). While it is important to examine 'the discourse of society's Other', she questions to what extent this can be fully achieved. Rather than try to reclaim the voice of the oppressed, which she does not see as viable, she argues that the

* Poststructuralism is a general term that refers to various critiques of structuralism. Theorists such as Jacques Derrida, Michel Foucault and Judith Butler have contributed to this approach to reading practices. Structuralists identify and examine the foundational structures implicit in all productions of a culture. Poststructuralists are critical of the idea that there is a foundational structure; they approach language, culture and gender as social constructs formed through discursive and material practices.

† The reference to the 'decentred subject' means that the subject is constituted through language and discourses, which serve to structure thought and action. Post-structuralist and deconstructionist theory have been especially important in contributing to theories of decentred subjectivity. The articulation of individuality (the 'I') is seen as problematic because the self is no longer a coherent singular ego, but rather the by-product or effect of multiple, shifting fields of meaning.

postcolonial critic should examine the work of representation through the myriad, uneven, irreconcilable processes for constituting the other. In examining multiple discourses aboutthe subaltern, Spivak highlights the different, often conflicting ways in which the nonelite identity has been constituted throughout colonial history.

To demonstrate her point, she refers to the work of Ranajit Guha and the Subaltern Studies scholars whose work focused (at the time when she wrote the essay) on the nonelites or subaltern figures in colonial India. Guha introduced a taxonomy or series of categories for thinking about the power structure of society, including: dominant foreign groups, dominant indigenous groups at an all-India level, dominant indigenous groups at the regional/local level, and the people or the subaltern. However, Spivak argues that this taxonomy fails to address certain fundamental questions: 'How can we touch the consciousness of the people, even as we investigate their politics? With what voice-consciousness can the subaltern speak?' (p. 285). Instead of establishing a taxonomy, she thinks it is much more useful to consider political consciousness in holistic terms: in terms of the collision of irreconcilable interests that have come to determine what has been and might possibly be known or said about society as a whole and the subaltern in particular. When it comes to the representation of the subaltern, she argues that we need to consider what has been lost, effaced and omitted from the colonial archive.

Postcolonial Feminist Perspectives

The effects of silencing are especially evident when we consider the role of women under colonialism. Spivak remarks: 'If, in the context of colonial production, the subaltern has no history and cannot speak, the subaltern as female is even more deeply in shadow' (p. 287). She calls attention to the 'double colonisation' of women,[12] which refers to the fact that women have been doubly oppressed by colonialism through empire and patriarchy (a society that values men over women). In 1829, the English outlawed the practice of *sati* (referred to as *suttee* by the British), the ritual act of suicide whereby the widow throws herself on the funeral pyre of her deceased husband. For Spivak, this legal intervention highlights the dilemma of the female subaltern situation which is caught between two positions: the imperial and the patriarchal. She describes the intervention as one made by 'White men saving brown women from brown men' (p. 297). Both racism and gender oppression are evident in the imperial desire to speak for the other: to recognise the rights of Indian women, to articulate them on behalf of all Indian women, and thus free them from a repressive society of Indian men. The Indian nativist argument that the women wanted to die is no better in her view. Moreover, Spivak's analysis of British colonial and Hindu discourses highlights the role of cultural difference. Ways of representing and oppressing women, particularly through religious and legal discourses, differ in British and Hindu contexts. The subaltern woman is thus subject to various, often irreconcilable, modes of representation. For Spivak, this complex interplay of factors makes it impossible to retrieve an authentic, coherent representation of the subaltern woman. Instead, she argues that the intellectual or postcolonial critic needs to examine the systems of representation and discourses that try to construct and reclaim the authentic voices of the subaltern woman. In doing so, the postcolonial critic might gain a better understanding of the processes whereby subaltern women's voices have been repressed, excluded and muted. Through her analysis of representation, Spivak explores the complex ways in which the interrelated and uneven power dynamics of empire, patriarchy and cultural difference come to bear on the unstable categories of race, class/caste and gender.

Spivak's influential readings of literary texts reflect her concerns about the relations between imperialism, the representation of women and the problematic role of the postcolonial literary critic. 'Three Women's Texts and a Critique of Imperialism', for example, can be read as a companion piece to 'Can the Subaltern Speak?'. While the latter considers the complex relationships between the political representations of women's interests in colonial India and re-presentations of subaltern women in British and Hindu discourses, 'Three Women's Texts' begins with the question of literary representation in order to understand the politics of female representation under imperialism. In this article, Spivak discusses the relationship between Charlotte Brontë's *Jane Eyre* (1847) and Jean Rhys's *Wide Sargasso Sea* (1966). She begins her analysis with an observation about the role of literature, which echoes Edward Said's remarks on cultural representation and empire:

> It should not be possible to read nineteenth-century British literature without remembering that imperialism, understood as England's social mission, was a crucial part of the cultural representation of England to the English. The role of literature in the production of cultural representations should not be ignored. These two obvious 'facts' continue to be disregarded in the reading of nineteenth-century British literature.[13]

Today, we take it for granted that literature plays a powerful role in the production of cultural representations. The relationship between the nineteenth-century novel and empire has been frequently discussed in the past few decades. However, it is important to note that Spivak, like Said, was challenging critics to read literature from a new, postcolonial perspective. In particular, she was targeting feminist criticism at the time for its blindness to the work of empire. She begins her analysis with *Jane Eyre*, the story of a governess who falls in love with the lord of the house, Edward Rochester. Jane is about to marry Rochester when she discovers that he is already married to a woman named Bertha Mason, who has been imprisoned in the attic due to her insanity. Jane leaves the house, but eventually marries Rochester after Bertha burns down the family estate and plunges to her death. Up until Spivak's reading of *Jane Eyre*, feminist critics, such as Sandra Gilbert and Susan Gubar, saw Bertha as a 'dark double' for Jane, while Marxist critics tended to think about Jane's identity 'in terms of the ambiguous *class* position of the governess' (p. 248). Spivak argues that Jane's transition from a marginalised figure to a member of a community of families takes place through 'the active ideology of imperialism' as a 'discursive field' (p. 247). Bertha Mason is a figure produced by the 'axiomatics of imperialism', by which Spivak means that she is represented in imperialist terms as the other. Jane describes Bertha as a figure whose identity is indeterminate – she is at the frontier of the animal/human divide (p. 247) – while Rochester associates Bertha with the Caribbean as Hell. Spivak argues that the conclusion of *Jane Eyre*, which ends with St John Rivers's self-exile to Calcutta, where he will work as a missionary, represents the culmination of imperialist ideologies. Spivak does not flesh out her analysis in much detail, but she points out that the act of proselytising and saving colonial subjects' souls is entangled with discourses of race, mastery and an oppositional logic that purports to convert war to peace, bondage to freedom and so forth. The irony that colonialism brought war, violence, exploitation, slavery and bondage to the colonised is rewritten through the Christian representation of a pacific mission.

Next, Spivak turns to Jean Rhys's rewriting of *Jane Eyre* in *Wide Sargasso Sea*. Rhys, a white Creole herself,* provides an account of events in the life of Antoinette (later renamed Bertha by the Rochester figure). The work consists of three parts: the story of Antoinette's childhood in post-abolition Jamaica during which the family's plantation home is burned down by former slaves; Antoinette's engagement and marriage to the Rochester figure of the novel; and a narrative of her life in England where she is locked up in an attic. Where Brontë represents Bertha as a snarling dog, Rhys depicts her as a resistant human subject who attacks her step-brother when he claims that he cannot legally interfere in the marriage to Rochester in order to help her. Spivak observes: 'In Rhys's retelling, it is the dissimulation that Bertha discerns in the word "legally" – not an innate bestiality – that prompts her violent *re*action' (p. 250). Rhys also offers a back-story for Eyre's Bertha, which highlights the imperial dynamics at work in the marriage relationship. For instance, the Rochester figure in Rhys's text renames Antoinette, calling her Bertha. Spivak points

* For further discussion of *Wide Sargasso Sea* and creolisation, see Part Four: 'Cross-cultural Paradigms'.

out that 'so intimate a thing as personal and human identity might be determined by the politics of imperialism' (p. 250). Spivak observes that Antoinette, 'a white Creole child growing up at the time of emancipation in Jamaica', is 'caught between the English imperialist and the black native' (p. 250). Rhys's text also includes an account of the 'self-immolating colonial subject for the glorification of the social mission of the colonizer' (p. 251) in the form of the death of Bertha/ Antoinette. However, Spivak argues that Rhys's representation of this death scene differs considerably from the one in *Jane Eyre* because 'the woman from the colonies is not sacrificed as an insane animal for her sister's consolidation' (p. 251). Instead, Rhys reclaims a history for Antoinette, which allows the reader to understand the underlying causes of her mental instability and sense of alienation.

According to Spivak, Rhys's reclamation of history from a feminine perspective does not extend to the position of the black woman. Specifically, the reader never really gains a full picture of the servant, Christophine, a former slave from the Francophone Caribbean. Spivak remarks:

> She [Christophine] cannot be contained by a novel which rewrites a canonical English text within the European novelistic tradition in the interest of the white Creole rather than the native. No perspective *critical* of imperialism can turn the Other into a self, because the project of imperialism has always already historically refracted what might have been the absolutely Other into a domesticated Other that consolidates the imperialist self. (p. 253)

Despite the fact that Christophine is in many ways a figure of resistance to the colonial order, she remains a tangential character in the novel. Although she is an outspoken servant, her views are never wholly recognised by either Rochester or Antoinette. Both resist her efforts to critique imperialism and patriarchy. While Spivak sees the representation of Christophine as tainted by imperialism on account of Rhys's white Creole perspective, we might also argue that Rhys highlights the racism directed towards black women under empire and offers a glimpse (however partial and compromised) of history from an Afro-Caribbean feminine perspective.

Spivak shows the ways in which Rhys brings together the mirroring implicit in colonial relations between the self and other and the textual mirroring between *Jane Eyre* and *Wide Sargasso Sea*. In rewriting *Jane Eyre*, Rhys engages in multiple, entangled representations of British imperial history and literature. Notably, Antoinette plays with a young black servant girl, named Tia, until their racial and class differences surface. Tia is among the crowd of former slaves who burn down the plantation house belonging to Antoinette's family. When Antoinette flees the house she encounters Tia, who throws a rock at her. Looking at Tia, she feels that it is as if she is seeing herself. Years later, as an adult trapped in the attic, she dreams of Tia and the burning house. As the novel comes to a close, it seems that Rhys's Bertha will fulfil the actions of Bertha in *Jane Eyre*: burning down the house and immolating herself in the process. However, Rhys shows us that Bertha's actions can also be seen as an appropriation of colonial resistance. Just as the former slaves burned down the plantation house of the Caribbean – a place that incarnated colonial oppression – Bertha dreams of burning down the house that has become a site of patriarchal oppression for her under Rochester's rule. For Spivak, the reading of Rhys's *Wide Sargasso Sea* affords an opportunity to investigate critically the complex intersections of race, culture and gender from a postcolonial perspective.

Homi K. Bhabha: Ambivalence and Mimicry

Like Spivak, Bhabha focuses on the British presence in India during the colonial period and the legacies of empire in the post-independence period. Born in 1949 in a Parsi family from Mumbai, India, he was educated at the University of Bombay and the University of Oxford. Like Spivak, his work is influenced by multiple theoretical perspectives, such as deconstructionism and psychoanalysis. Bhabha's early criticism engages directly with Said's *Orientalism* and Frantz Fanon's *Black Skin, White Masks* (1952) and *The Wretched of the Earth* (1961),* bringing together the former's emphasis on the role of the coloniser and the latter's emphasis on the role of the colonised. According to Bart Moore-Gilbert, Bhabha sees the coloniser–colonised relationship as:

> more complex and nuanced – and politically fraught – than Fanon and Said imply, principally because the circulation of contradictory patterns of psychic affect in colonial relations (desire for, as well as fear of the Other, for example) undermines their assumption that the identities and positionalities of colonizer and colonized exist in stable and unitary terms.[14]

In his view, relations between the colonised and coloniser are more complicated than an oppositional interpretation of colonial domination and anticolonial resistance might suggest. Whereas Said's theories of representation and colonialism seem to imply a fairly homogenous, top-down approach, Bhabha calls attention to the ambivalent, contradictory and anxious aspects of the colonial relationship.

Ambivalence is a term that comes out of psychoanalytic theory to describe a constant sense of attraction and repulsion towards a person, action or object. In essays entitled 'The Other Question: Stereotype, Discrimination and the Discourse of Colonialism' and 'Of Mimicry and Man', Bhabha argues that this contradictory sentiment characterises the relationship between the coloniser and colonised. Colonial discourse is ambivalent with respect to the colonial subject, who is represented as someone to be nurtured, civilised and educated as well as exploited. Colonisation assumes that

* The psychiatrist and revolutionary, Frantz Fanon (1925–61), was born in Martinique. He served in the French army during the Second World War and subsequently moved to Algeria where he witnessed first hand the Algerian War. An advocate of resistance and revolution, his writings inspired anticolonial resistance movements throughout the latter part of the twentieth century. His critique of race thinking and theories of decolonisation have proved enormously influential.

the colonial subject can be formed and shaped in such a way as to reproduce the values, habits and customs of the imperial order. For Bhabha, the attempt to replicate an imperial original is never wholly possible because the act of repetition introduces differences: 'the colonial presence is always ambivalent, split between its presence as original and authoritative and its articulation as repetition and difference'.[15] Ambivalence emerges as a result of contradictions within colonialism itself, which is characterised by repetition and displacement as well as proximity and distance. In *The Empire Writes Back*, Bill Ashcroft and colleagues observe: 'In order to maintain authority over the Other in a colonial situation, imperial discourse strives to delineate the Other as radically different from the self, yet at the same time it must maintain sufficient identity with the Other to valorize control over it'.[16] Bhabha shows that colonial practices were often carried out in a strategic fashion so as to only replicate those facets of imperial culture that would maintain the status quo.

Colonial discourse and practices encourage the colonised subject to 'mimic' the coloniser by adopting the coloniser's culture, ideologies, language, institutions and values. However, the act of colonial reproduction is never complete, but always partial on account of differences that can be suppressed, but not entirely eradicated. Thus, mimicry entails a sense of similarity and difference. Bhabha argues:

> Colonial mimicry is the desire for a reformed, recognizable Other, as a subject of a difference that is almost the same, but not quite. Which is to say that the discourse of mimicry is constructed around an ambivalence; in order to be effective, mimicry must continually produce its slippage, its excess, its difference. (*Location of Culture*, p. 86)

To demonstrate these points about repetition and difference, Bhabha offers two literary examples: Joseph Conrad's *Nostromo* (1904) and V. S. Naipal's *The Mimic Men* (1967). Conrad's novel is set in an imaginary country in South America following the demise of the

Spanish empire. Martin Decoud, a Frenchified Creole journalist recently returned from Paris, refers to the peoples of 'ungovernable' colonial America as embodying 'the lawlessness of a populace of all colours and races, barbarism, irremediable tyranny' (p. 88). Decoud thus repeats a Eurocentric vision of the Americas, but also highlights the impossibility of achieving a perfect colonial order. Bhabha, too, sees evidence of the ambivalent aspects of repetition and difference in Naipaul's novel about a colonial official, Ralph Singh, who moves to London following his exile from the small (fictional) Caribbean island of Isabella. Bhabha quotes Singh's musings about his colonial identity:

> We pretended to be real, to be learning, to be preparing ourselves for life, we mimic men of the New World, one unknown corner of it, with all its reminders of the corruption that came so quickly to the new. (p. 88)

Bhabha observes that both Naipaul's and Conrad's works introduce characters who are parodists of colonial history. Decoud and Singh write the colonial text 'erratically, eccentrically, across a body politic that refuses to be representative, in a narrative that refuses to be representational' (p. 88). In short, mimicry can be subversive because it both affirms and undermines assertions of colonial power and order.

Mimicry is never very far from mockery; it can appear to parody whatever it mimics. The menace of mimicry stems from a capacity for double vision, which 'in disclosing the ambivalence of colonial discourse also disrupts its authority' (p. 88). There is always already a difference between the coloniser and the colonised: the colonised subject is 'not quite / not white' ('Of Mimicry and Man', in *Location of Culture*, p. 132) on account of cultural and racial difference as well as because of the discrepant power relations. Mimicry like ambivalence can call attention to the gaps, contradictions and instabilities inherent in the colonial enterprise. For the postcolonial literary critic, this means that the identification and analysis of mimicry and ambivalence serve to disclose the ways in which colonisation contradicts and undermines itself.

Postcolonial Reading Practices

For the postcolonial literary critic, colonial discourse analysis assumes that reading practices constitute a political act, which entails a close examination of the power dynamics represented in the text as well as the text's relation to the socio-political production of knowledge and power. The postcolonial literary critic engages in any one or more of the following practices:

- exploring the ways in which colonialism created a way of seeing the world and the order of things and considering how this is reflected in literary and cultural works

- placing emphasis on historical contexts and examining how these contexts influence the production of meaning

- analysing the discontinuities and disruption of meaning with the colonial context and the literary text

- investigating the ways in which literary and cultural works have the power to influence the historical moment

- identifying the legacies of colonial discourse as a means to prevent the continuing of these practices in the present

- reflecting on the ways in which the text speaks to the ongoing processes of decolonisation.

Moore-Gilbert pulls many of these perspectives together when he defines the role of postcolonial reading practices as follows:

> In my view, postcolonial criticism can still be seen as a more or less distinct set of reading practices, if it is understood as preoccupied principally with analysis of cultural forms which

> mediate, challenge or reflect upon the relations of domination and subordination – economic, cultural and political – between (and often within) nations, races or cultures, which characteristically have their roots in the history of modern European colonialism and imperialism and which, equally characteristically, continue to be apparent in the present era of neo-colonialism.[17]

In the post-independence era, it has been important to challenge the legacies of colonial discourse and reconstruct more equitable ways of imagining and living relations between the self and other. Decolonisation (the effort to move beyond the legacies of the colonial past) is one of the important aims of postcolonial literature, particularly in the post-independence period. Writers can challenge colonial discourses, suggesting new ways of envisioning identities and society. Alongside decolonisation, however, postcolonial subjects have had to face other forms of domination, particularly through foreign intervention and global capitalism. Postcolonial literature plays an important role in confronting and working through the traumatic experiences associated with colonialism, but also addresses the challenges contemporary societies face in a changing world. Today, postcolonial literature often addresses the oppressive aspects of globalisation in the contemporary world order as well as through its long history, which overlaps with the circulations of empire during the colonial era (see Part Four: 'Postcoloniality in a Globalising World' for a discussion of globalisation).

Notes

1 Diana Brydon and Helen Tiffin, *Decolonising Fictions* (Sydney: Dangaroo Press, 1993), p. 12.
2 There are several helpful introductions to postcolonial reading practices and literary theory available, including those cited throughout this chapter. See Part Five: 'Further Reading' for more details.
3 Edward Said, *Orientalism* (Harmondsworth: Penguin, 2003), p. 3.

4 Elleke Boehmer, *Colonial and Postcolonial Literature: Migrant Metaphors* (Oxford: Oxford University Press, 2005), p. 51.
5 John McLeod, *Beginning Postcolonialism* (Manchester: Manchester University Press, 2000), p. 17.
6 Ania Loomba, *Colonialism/Postcolonialism* (London: Routledge, 2005), pp. 50–1.
7 John McLeod, *Beginning Postcolonialism*. See chapter two.
8 See John McLeod's discussion for more details, pp. 44–6.
9 Edward Said, *Culture and Imperialism* (New York: Knopf, 1993), p. 78.
10 Ella Shohat, 'The Struggle over Representation: Casting, Coalitions, and the Politics of Identification', in Román De la Campa, E. Ann Kaplan and Michael Sprinker (eds), *Late Imperial Culture* (London: Verso, 1995), p. 173.
11 Gayatri Chakravorty Spivak, 'Can the Subaltern Speak?' in Cary Nelson and Lawrence Grossberg (eds), *Marxism and the Interpretation of Culture* (Urbana: University of Illinois Press, 1988), pp. 271–313, p. 279.
12 Kirstin Holst Petersen and Anna Rutherford use the phrase 'a double colonisation' in their forward to the edited collection entitled *A Double Colonisation: Colonial and Post-Colonial Women's Writing* (Sydney: Dangaroo Press, 1986), p. 9.
13 Gayatri Chakravorty Spivak, 'Three Women's Texts and A Critique of Imperialism,' *Critical Inquiry* 12.1 Special Issue on '"Race," Writing, and Difference' (Autumn 1985), p. 243.
14 Bart Moore-Gilbert, *Postcolonial Theory: Contexts, Practices, Politics* (London: Verso, 1997), p. 116.
15 Homi Bhabha, *The Location of Culture* (London: Routledge, 1994), p. 107.
16 Bill Ashcroft, Gareth Griffiths and Helen Tiffin, *The Empire Writes Back* (London: Routledge, 1989) p. 103.
17 Moore-Gilbert, *Postcolonial Theory*, p. 12.

Race, Gender and Sexuality

Postcolonial identities are intersectional and shifting. Postcolonial gender critics take into account the ways in which various socially and culturally constructed categories of identity (such as gender, race, class, disability, sexuality and religion) intersect and interact with one another. Kimberle Crenshaw first used the term 'intersectionality' to refer to 'the relationships among multiple dimensions and modalities of social relationships and subject formations'.[1] Her work was popularised by the black feminist critic, Patricia Hill Collins, in *Black Feminist Thought: Knowledge, Consciousness and the Politics of Empowerment* (1990), and has become a cornerstone of postcolonial, gender and feminist theories. Intersectionality holds that oppression within society – such as racism, sexism, homophobia and religious discrimination – can best be understood in terms of overlapping and multiple forms of discrimination.[2] Moreover, identities are not unchanging and fixed, but can be seen as shifting and responsive to changing socio-political, cultural and economic dynamics through time and space. Thus, we need to take into account the contexts of a given age or society and how these contribute to a sense of self.

In the postcolonial context, it is important to note that categories of identity have been profoundly shaped by imperialism and its discourses about identity, especially with respect to race, gender and sexuality. From a historical perspective, colonial discourses and practices have created inequities in society. Discriminatory relations have often been evident in institutional practices and legal frameworks as well as through norms, beliefs and prejudices in society more generally. Postcolonial critics, writers and theorists examine critically the alienating effects of colonial discourses and practices as well as seek to articulate new, liberating and equitable constructions of identity. This chapter explores some of the ways in which the interrelationships among race, gender and sexuality have been structured under colonialism before turning to the literature and critical theory of decolonisation as envisioned through responses to black identities, postcolonial and 'Third World' feminisms, and postcolonial queer literatures.

'Race' is a term that refers to the classification of human beings into physically, biologically and genetically distinct groups. This notion of race emerged in connection with the colonial experience and colonial powers relied on theories of race in order to establish dominance and justify imperialism. William Dunbar's 'The Dance of the Sevin Deidly Sins' (1508) is often cited as the first instance of the use of the term 'race' in English.[3] However, he uses the term to denote a class of persons or things with common attributes rather than a categorisation of peoples based on biological traits. In the seventeenth century, Francois Bernier refers to a hierarchy of species of human beings in *Nouvelle division de la terre par les différentes espèces ou races qui l'habitent* ('A New Division of the World According to the Different Species or Races Who Inhabit It', 1764), but, like Dunbar, he does not refer to racial differentiation in biological terms. By the eighteenth century, however, race comes to be understood in terms of physical differences. Notably, Immanuel Kant's *Observations on the Feeling of the Beautiful and the Sublime* (1764) is often cited as one of the first texts to refer to race with respect to physical appearance. The nineteenth century sees the rise of social Darwinism, following the publication of Darwin's *Origin of the Species* (1859), and eugenics or the idea of social planning in racialised terms. Later, eugenics came to be associated with some of the most traumatic events of the twentieth century, particularly the Holocaust. However, the twentieth century also saw many efforts to revisit definitions of race and its underlying racism. W. E. B. Du Bois, a leading African American thinker and author of *The Souls of Black Folk* (1903), declared prophetically: 'The problem of the twentieth century is the problem of the color-line, – the relation of the darker to the lighter races of men in Asia and Africa, in America and the islands of the sea'.[4] In most instances, it took more than just speaking and writing about new ways of conceiving race and countering racism to change prevailing ideas. Social activism and political movements for change have been essential to the process of re-presenting race. At the same time, as we shall see, literature has played a powerful and leading role in helping to foster new ways of thinking about race and other colonial discourses.

When speaking about the legacies of colonialism, it is also important to define what is meant by the terms 'sex', 'gender' and 'sexuality'. When we speak of 'sex' and 'gender', we are referring to the distinction between biological difference, namely sex (male, female, intersexual, transsexual), and the meaning we construct about that biological difference, namely gender (femininity, masculinity, androgyny and so forth). Gender is a social construct: it refers to the various ways in which we think about masculinities and femininities. We could argue that women in particular have been subject to oppression through empire as a patriarchal enterprise. In *Colonial Desire: Hybridity in Theory, Culture and Race* (1995), Robert Young shows that the idea of colonisation itself was grounded in a sexualised discourse of rape, penetration and impregnation. Indeed, Ania Loomba points out that the tendency to feminise the colonial landscape and view it in erotic terms can be seen in John Donne's poem entitled 'To his Mistris going to Bed' (1635):

> Licence my roaving hands, and let them go,
> Before, behind, between, above, below.
> O my America! my new-found-land,
> My kingdome, safeliest when with one man man'd,

My Myne of precious stones: My Emperie,
How blest I am in this discovering thee.[5]

In Donne's poem, America is embodied as a female lover, a territory to be explored and dominated by masculine hands. Her resources – the mine of precious stones – are part of the empire belonging to the masculine subject, which are available to be taken and possessed by him. This allegorical poem tells us that both women and colonial territories are seen as bodies to be explored, dominated and exploited for masculine pleasure.* This poem thus clearly demonstrates the linkages between patriarchal and imperial aspirations in the colonial era.† Moreover, we can see that sexuality is presented in heterosexual terms, as was the case throughout the colonial era. The emphasis on Christianity as the one, true religion of British imperialism also tended to reinforce the importance of conforming to heterosexual norms, imposing these values on cultures where alternative sexualities may have been previously expressed or tacitly permitted.

One of the characteristics of empire, with its emphasis on relations of power and subjugation, is its hierarchical approach to race, gender and sexuality. The white, heterosexual male is assumed to be the dominant subject. Ania Loomba observes:

> Dominant scientific ideologies about race and gender have historically propped up each other. In the mid-nineteenth century, the new science of anthropometry pronounced Caucasian women to be closer to Africans than white men were, and supposedly female traits were used to describe 'the lower races' … Accordingly African women occupied the lowest rung of the racial ladder. When African men began to

* Seamus Heaney's 'Act of Union' from *Selected Poems 1965–1975* (1980) offers a contemporary representation of the female figure in colonial terms.

† Of course, these notions were complicated through historical and lived experience, particularly as Britain 'herself' (a feminised subject) has been ruled by Queen Elizabeth, Queen Victoria and Queen Elizabeth II. However, these female sovereigns are often depicted as exceptional.

> be treated for schizophrenia and confined to lunatic asylums, 'African women … were said not to have reached the level of self-awareness required to go mad, and in colonial literature on psychology and psychopathology, the African woman represented the happy "primitive" state of pre-colonial Africa.' (p. 58)

Scientific discourses offered a supposedly authoritative presentation of facts about the ordering of societies. Sander Gilman's work, particularly *Difference and Pathology: Stereotypes of Sexuality, Race, and Madness* (1985) shows how nineteenth-century medical discourses contributed to the linking of blackness, sexuality and femininity. Notably, in psychoanalysis, Sigmund Freud (1856–1939) refers to the sexual life of women as 'a dark continent', linking the mysteries of female sexuality generally to African territories of colonisation. Earlier examples of colonial discourses linking race and sexuality can also be found. For instance, in ethnographic accounts, such as Richard Head's of 1666, *sati* (the wife's suicide on her husband's funeral pyre) was represented as a barbarian practice but also as an example of wifely devotion worthy of emulation by English women. Colonial discourses also projected 'deviant sexualities', such as sodomy, onto distant cultures and lands. Thus, colonial frontiers and racial others were seen in eroticised terms as presenting possibilities for sexual transgression.

While colonial sexual encounters often exploited inequities and took brutal form, colonisers themselves often presented these events in romanticised terms, such as the account of Inkle and Yarico, given by Richard Ligon in *A True and Exact History of the Island of Barbadoes* (1657). The tale was frequently republished in the seventeenth and eighteenth centuries, including a version that appeared in Richard Steele's *The Spectator* (1711). In Steele's account, Thomas Inkle, an English trader, is shipwrecked in the West Indies, and survives with the help of Yarico, a Carib Indian (who is presented as a Negro maiden in the comic opera version of 1787). They fall in love, but when Inkle returns to his civilisation, he sells Yarico (who is now pregnant by him) into slavery in order to recover his financial losses during the period in which he was a castaway. The production of the comic opera, called *Inkle and Yarico*, attests to the lingering and pervasive interest in this romance based on a colonial scenario of sexual exploitation. More recently, Beryl Gilroy's *Inkle and Yarico* (1996) retells the story from the first-person perspective of Tommy Inkle in order to highlight the imperialist attitudes of the English and thus her work offers a postcolonial Caribbean perspective.

We find an example of intersections of race, gender and sexuality in Joseph Conrad's *Heart of Darkness* (1899, 1902). The novella offers an account of a white trader of ivory, named Kurtz, who 'goes native' and sets up his own fiefdom in the Belgian Congo. He has entered into a relationship with a black woman who is typically believed to be his mistress (although the text does not make this point explicit). Thus, the reader encounters the motif of the dark queen, who seems to have given her body and self to the white man. Meanwhile, at home in England, Kurtz's fiancée, a white woman referred to as the Intended, continues to believe that Kurtz was faithful to her, even after his death in the Congo, because she is deceived by Charles Marlow, a sailor, who heard the dying man's final words. In *Heart of Darkness*, the black, African woman is presented in savage and commoditised terms, which link her to the ivory trade as well as to the 'sorrowful' colonial landscape:

> She must have had the value of several elephant tusks upon her. She was savage and superb, wild-eyed and magnificent; there was something ominous and stately in her deliberate progress. And in the hush that had fallen suddenly upon the whole sorrowful land, the immense wilderness, the colossal body of the fecund and mysterious life seemed to look at her, pensive, as though it had been looking at the image of its own tenebrous and passionate soul.[6]

By contrast, the white woman is presented in idealised terms as someone who needs to be protected from knowing the truth about events that take place in the colonies. When Marlow visits the Intended, he reports that Kurtz died with her name on his lips, although Kurtz's actual last words are 'the horror, the horror'. This act of apparent kindness may seem to protect the Intended from disillusionment concerning her beloved Kurtz, but it also serves to highlight the ways in which the rhetoric and discourses of empire operate through patriarchal complicity. It could be argued that Marlow's actions also serve to conceal the failures of patriarchy and empire as embodied by Kurtz as a masculine figure of authority who suffers a breakdown and fails in his imperialist ventures.

At the same time, fears about miscegenation (the mixing of races) surface in various accounts of sexual encounters between white women and men of other races. Shakespeare's *The Tempest* (1610–11) dramatises such fears when Caliban attempts to rape Miranda, hoping to people the island with Calibans. In the twentieth century, E. M. Forster's *A Passage to India* (1924) (a text we will discuss in more detail later in this chapter) offers an ambivalent account of a white woman who is supposedly raped by an Indian man. Loomba notes: 'Sexuality thus becomes a vehicle for the maintenance or erosion of racial difference. Women on both sides of the colonial divide demarcate both the innermost sanctums of race, culture, and nation, as well as the porous frontiers through which they are penetrated'.[7]

Decolonising Race/Gender: the Black Experience

In the twentieth century, black authors have challenged colonial paradigms concerning race, gender and sexuality. As we have seen, Du Bois foresaw that the twentieth century would be preoccupied to a large extent by the decolonisation of racial discourses and practices. In *The Souls of Black Folk*, he examines and reclaims the identities of black peoples who were oppressed and commodified (economic value assigned to human life) through slavery in the New World.

This work blends history, theory and early psychoanalytic approaches to the effects of colonisation. One of the important concepts he introduces is that of double consciousness:

> It is a peculiar sensation, this double-consciousness, this sense of always looking at one's self through the eyes of others, of measuring one's soul by the tape of a world that looks on in amused contempt and pity. One ever feels his two-ness, – an American, a Negro; two souls, two thoughts, two unreconciled strivings; two warring ideals in one dark body, whose dogged strength alone keeps it from being torn asunder.[8]

As a black person at the beginning of the twentieth century, Du Bois is conscious of the ways in which the legacies of colonial discourses of race and citizenship excluded black persons from full participation and continued to denigrate black identity. Consequently, the body and psyche of the black individual are presented as being in a constant state of tension: torn between a sense of pride in one's black identity and a sense of self-denigration through internalised racism.

In the twentieth century, many black literary texts explored the notion of double consciousness and the malign effects of feeling oneself to be a split subject. For instance, Ralph Ellison's *Invisible Man* (1952) tells the story of an African American man who feels himself to be invisible because this is how he is treated by white America. However, the act of self-inscription (the act of narrating one's own history and identity) makes claims for the recognition of black peoples' identities and rights in America. Toni Morrison's *The Bluest Eye* (1970) tells the story of a young girl named Pecola who believes she is ugly because she and her community base their ideals of beauty on 'whiteness'. She longs for blue eyes. The novel explores the ways in which notions of belonging and identity are racialised in America so that black peoples are marginalised and excluded from full participation. Such texts play an important role in working through the traumatic effects of racism in America and discovering a decolonised perspective concerning racial identities. In this respect, these narratives also follow the model of writing established by Du Bois, who demonstrated that the very act of writing, creating new discourses and storytelling could offer a way out of the conditions of internalised racism and marginalisation. Each chapter of *The Souls of Black Folk* begins with an excerpt from a blues song or hymn, such as 'Nobody Knows the Trouble I've Seen' and 'Swing Low, Sweet Chariot'. In drawing on vernacular culture and the oral tradition, Du Bois speaks and sings of the longstanding traditions of black culture as a source of resistance in the face of oppressive racial discourses and practices.

The psychiatrist Frantz Fanon (1925–61), a noted Martinican thinker and activist during Algeria's quest for independence from French colonial rule, has written some of the most significant works on race and decolonisation in the twentieth century. Fanon argues that black peoples suffer from a sense of self-alienation on account of colonialism and its legacies. In *Black Skin, White Masks* (1952), Fanon highlights and examines the psychiatric ills associated with colonial discourses about race, gender and sexuality. In particular, his chapters on 'The Woman of Color and the White Man' and 'The Man of Color and the White Woman' examine the dynamics of interracial sexual relationships and constructions of race/gender. Speaking of Mayotte Capécia's book *Je suis martiniquaise* ('I am a Martinican woman', published in 1948), Fanon observes that 'Mayotte loves a white man to whom she submits in everything. He is her lord. She asks nothing, demands nothing, except a bit of whiteness in her life.' He suggests that when she tries to decide for herself whether the man is attractive all she sees is that '"he had blue eyes, blond hair, and a light skin, and that I loved him."' Fanon suggests is not difficult to see that a rearrangement of these elements in their proper hierarchy would produce something of this order: 'I loved him because he had blue eyes, blond hair, and a light skin.'[9] In this passage, Fanon attests to the legacies of colonialism whereby the white male continues to be perceived as a lord and master: he represents hegemonic (dominant) masculinity and is therefore desirable. Rather than seeing and desiring the white man as an individual, the black woman continues to engage with the white man in the symbolic and hierarchical terms established during the colonial period. Thus, the black woman's sexual life is shaped by the legacies of colonial discourses of race and gender. Fanon refers to Mayotte's tendency to value whiteness over blackness and how Martinique women live by the simple code that 'the race must be whitened' – not in order to 'preserve the uniqueness of that part of the world in which they grew up', but to 'make sure that it will be white' (p. 47). Fanon's work responds directly to colonial discourses, which, as we have already seen, represented the black woman as unworthy of consideration as a human subject. In the case of neocolonial Martinique,* he observes that the black woman disavows her black identity and also expresses a hatred of (her own) blackness (p. 50). For Fanon, the black woman's desire to be admitted into the white world indicates feelings of racial inferiority or what he calls 'affective erethism'.

Through his critique of race, gender and sexuality, Fanon shows that colonialism has also led to a sense of self-alienation. For the black man, 'there is a constant effort to run away from his own individuality, to annihilate his own presence' (p. 60). He cites the example of a young medical Negro student who wanted to go to the colonies and serve in a colonial unit so that he could 'make white men adopt a Negro attitude toward him' (p. 61). Fanon sees this as a desire for revenge against the image of the frightened black man, abased before a white overlord. Thus, racial hierarchies are both internalised and repressed, but they return in the form of neurotic desires for lactification (becoming white) and revenge as manifest in the desire to appropriate white colonial models of power. In 'The Man of Color and the White Woman', Fanon refers to the 'zebra striping of my mind' in order to indicate the ways in which the

* Unlike Haiti and many Anglophone Caribbean island communities, Martinique has not opted for post-colonial independence as a sovereign nation. Martinique became an overseas department of France in 1946 and remains so today.

binary oppositions of race thinking (white/black) seep through the consciousness of the black colonial subject. For the black man, the desire for lactification is expressed through love of the white woman: 'By loving me she proves that I am worthy of white love. I am loved like a white man' (p. 63). According to Fanon, sexual relations between the black man and white woman enable him to marry white culture and grasp white civilisation in his hands (p. 63). Thus, the black man's relations to the white woman are seen in terms of symbolic access to white, masculine power.

Moreover, Fanon shows that race thinking produces malign effects for both black and white peoples, for those who were formerly colonised and colonisers. Fanon sees neuroses on both sides of the colour line: 'The Negro enslaved by his inferiority, the white man enslaved by his superiority alike behave with a neurotic orientation' (p. 60). Fanon argues that white men and women suffer from a delusional belief in their own superiority and racial supremacy while black men and women internalise this racial hierarchy, which leads to neurotic behaviour for both races as well as complicating interracial sexual relations. Challenging racial discourses and the legacies of colonialism is of vital importance to both the colonised and coloniser. In *Black Skin, White Masks*, Fanon seeks to get beyond the binaries of black/white thinking and the inequities associated with racial hierarchies. As such, he notes: 'Each time a man has contributed to the victory of the dignity of the spirit, every time a man has said no to an attempt to subjugate his fellows, I have felt solidarity with his act' (p. 226). In this passage, Fanon expresses his commitment to solidarity across the colour line in the quest for decolonisation. Rather than look to the past or the recovery of an African diasporic* cultural consciousness as a source of empowerment, as was the case with the

* The term 'diaspora' (meaning dispersion) initially referred to the scattering of Jewish peoples as a result of several forced expulsions from what is now known as Israel, Jordan and parts of Lebanon as well as the State of Palestine. Subsequently, 'diaspora' has come to refer more generally to the movement, migration or scattering of a people away from a settled location or ancestral homeland.

theorists of Negritude,* Fanon declares, 'I am not a prisoner of history. I should not seek there for the meaning of my destiny' (p. 229) and 'I am not the slave of the Slavery that dehumanized my ancestors' (p. 230). He invokes a radical, revolutionary break with the past, claiming that the 'body of history does not determine a single one of my actions. I am my own foundation.' While affirming that the 'disaster of the man of color lies in the fact that he was enslaved' and the 'disaster and the inhumanity of the white man lies in the fact that somewhere he has killed man', he makes one simple request for the future that 'the tool never possess the man. That the enslavement of man by man cease forever. That is, of one by another. That it be possible for me to discover and to love man, wherever he may be.' Both the 'negro' and the white man 'must turn their backs on the inhuman voices which were those of their respective ancestors in order that authentic communication be possible. Before it can adopt a positive voice, freedom requires an effort at disalienation' (p. 231). In this extraordinary passage, Fanon looks forward to what might be described as a post-racial future where humans no longer think of themselves in racialised terms. He looks back to a shared past of disasters where communication was characterised by inhuman voices: inhuman because peoples were seen in essentialist terms or as having an underlying, unchanging essence. Fanon wants to transcend the binaries of black/white and perpetrator/victim. However, he remains a realist because he argues that the acquisition of a positive voice of freedom depends upon an effort at disalienation. Subjects must continue to question and examine the ways in which they continue to be alienated from themselves and one another on account of the history and legacies of colonial race thinking and racist practices. No doubt, this is why the closing sentence to *Black Skin, White Masks* reads: 'O my body, make of me always a man who

* Negritude celebrates black culture and calls for the right to self-determination. The theory is most closely associated with the anti-colonial writing and political views of its founding figures, Aimé Cesairé, Léopold Sédar Senghor and Léon Damas, who met while living in Paris in the 1930s.

questions!' (p. 232). Thus, Fanon speaks to another tradition of decolonising discourses of race and gender, which remains firmly committed to critique, analysis, questioning and revolution.

Investigating Race/Sexuality in Walter Mosley's *Devil in a Blue Dress*

Fanon's work has influenced political thought, decolonisation movements and the course of postcolonial literature. We might consider for example how Fanon's critique of race, gender and sexuality might be brought to bear on the reading of Walter Mosley's *Devil in a Blue Dress* (1990).* Walter Mosley, a writer of African American and Jewish descent, has written a series of detective novels about an African American investigator named Ezekiel ('Easy') Rawlins. *Devil in a Blue Dress*, the first, takes place in post-war California, with a particular focus on the African American community of Watts prior to the escalating tensions and riots of the 1960s. At the beginning of the novel, Rawlins finds himself out of work, when he is fired from a factory because he refuses to work an additional shift. Subsequently, he is employed by a white man, DeWitt Albright, to locate a white girl named Daphne Monet who 'shows a predilection for the company of Negroes'.[10] In racially segregated America, Albright cannot carry out the investigation himself so he needs to hire a black detective who can enter black clubs and speak to members of the community. In the beginning of the novel, we get a sense of the ways in which Easy experiences a sense of 'double consciousness'. When he goes to meet Albright in his office, Easy stutters when speaking to the white doorman wearing a uniform. Easy notes: 'It was a habit I developed in Texas when I was a boy. Sometimes, when a white man of authority would catch me off guard, I'd empty my head of everything so I was unable to say anything' (p. 21). This passage is indicative of the extent to

* Carl Franklin directed the 1995 film adaptation of the novel, starring Denzel Washington, Jennifer Beals and Don Cheadle.

which Easy's experiences growing up in the South in the Jim Crow* era have contributed to a sense of disempowerment. Yet, by the end of the novel, Easy stands up to the factory owner, the corrupt business man and the most powerful white men in the city so that we see a transition from Du Bois's notion of double consciousness to a more nuanced, critical awareness of the perils, risks and possibilities for black masculinity in a racist society.

Easy's quest to locate Daphne enables a wide-ranging investigation into race, gender and sexuality in post-war America. When Easy drives Daphne through Hollywood in the middle of the evening, he reflects on the risks to himself: '[the] canyon road was narrow and winding but there was no traffic at all. We hadn't even seen a police car on the ride and that was fine with me, because the police have white slavery on the brain when it comes to colored men and white women' (p. 98). Daphne's appearance corresponds to that of the *femme fatale* found in hard-boiled detective fiction and the *film noir* tradition: a misogynist image of the seductive woman who can lead a man to his downfall. Her French Creole accent suggests that she comes from the South and is thus a descendant of the colonial plantocracy of Louisiana.† Infatuated, Easy enters into a sexual relationship with her. In the light of Fanon's theories, we might see Easy's desire for Daphne as shaped by his yearning to be on a par with the white man.

Eventually, Easy discovers that Daphne is actually a black woman, named Ruby Hanks, who is 'passing' as white. She has had to end a relationship with a powerful white man, named Todd Carter, because her racial identity has been discovered. Should their relationship be made public, Carter's reputation would be tarnished. When the novel comes to a close, Daphne moves away from California, seemingly in pursuit of a new life. In telling Daphne's story, Mosley is evoking a popular trope

* The so-called 'Jim Crow' laws in nineteenth- and twentieth-century America were those that enforced the segregation of blacks and whites.

† See Part Four: 'Cross-cultural Paradigms' for discussion of 'Creole'. 'Plantocracy' describes the ruling class or political order dominated by plantation owners.

found in African American fiction: the story of the 'tragic mulatta' or mixed-race woman who may attain certain advantages by passing as white but discovers that these benefits come at a very high cost: the constant fear of discovery and the subsequent loss of connection to her family, friends and community, should her secret be discovered.

However, Mosley complicates the novel by bringing the 'passing' narrative together with an incest narrative about Ruby's father who seduces or rapes his daughter following a visit to the zoo where they see zebras mating. In so doing, Mosley highlights the intersections of race, gender and sexuality. In racial terms, the rape is initially represented as an act of abuse perpetrated by a white father on his white daughter. However, Easy (and the reader) are later asked to revisit this event, which is then figured as the rape of a black girl by her father. The zebra motif highlights the confusion about racial identity in a highly sexualised fashion. Here we might recall Fanon's reference to the zebra striping of the imaginary: the notion of black skin, white masks undergoes a complication through Mosley's emphasis on the motif of passing and interracial sexual relations. Specifically, the split psyche of the abused child and the fissures of black/white identity in an America where the 'one drop rule'* prevails produce a complex, indeterminate narrative of self. Ruby says: '"I'm different than you because I'm two people. I'm her and I'm me. I never went to the zoo that day, she did. She was there and that's where she lost her father"' (p. 208). This split white/black self offers two incidents of incest, which cannot be easily reconciled into a single, coherent narrative. The trauma of sexual abuse and racial splitting (into black/white identities) intersect to produce a deeply fractured narrative account.

Rawlins also employs the motif of 'passing' in order to make an important point about Easy's desires for all the trappings of middle-class, white existence. When Easy discovers that Daphne/Ruby is actually of mixed race, he is completely astonished. His

* In America, the 'one drop [of blood] rule' refers to the fact that anyone with black ancestry is considered black.

friend, Mouse, observes that Easy and Daphne/Ruby are similar in many ways – she wants to be white because all her life 'people be tellin' her how she light-skinned and beautiful but all the time she knows that she can't have what white people have. She can love a white man but all he can love is the white girl he think she is' while he too has been heavily influenced by white thinking and culture: 'You learn stuff and you be thinkin' like white men be thinkin'. You be thinkin' that what's right fo' them is right fo' you. She look like she white and you think like you white' (p. 209).* Mouse observes that neither of them can be happy until they accept who they are. This episode is particularly striking in its analysis of the dynamics of passing in literal and metaphorical terms. Mouse offers what might be seen as a Fanonian interpretation of Easy's psychic state: he is a black man who adopts a white mask. For Mouse, Easy, like Daphne, appears to manifest neurotic symptoms of lactification.

Nonetheless, the novel as a whole offers a more complicated presentation of Easy's struggle to articulate postcolonial, black masculinity. Through the investigation, Easy reflects on his vision of a racially integrated America, negotiates with white men of power, eludes the police, earns money and gains insight into the ways in which racism and sexism underpin his desires. His investigation exposes the corruption at the heart of American society as related to brutal capitalism and racism. Women, men and children of colour are seen to be at risk in a society where white men still control economic and political relations. While the plight of the mixed-race society remains very much unresolved, the novel offers a powerful critique of the contradictory discourse and practices of race/gender/sexuality in America.

* 'Passing' brings with it a sense of anxiety about racial identity, but we should also note that the racial hierarchy of America led to many manifestations of anxiety and even self-loathing. For a contrasting account, Gwendolyn Brooks's first novel, *Maud Martha* (1953), focuses on the sense of alienation experienced by a character who feels herself to be 'too black'.

Postcolonial, Black and 'Third World' Feminisms

Postcolonial, black and 'Third World' feminist perspectives have challenged colonial legacies with respect to the intersections of race, class, gender and cultural difference. These various feminist perspectives resist white, middle-class feminism and highlight the ways in which it has often historically excluded racial others. Black feminist, Barbara Smith observes: 'Feminism is the political theory and practice that struggles to free all women: women of color, working-class women, poor women, disabled women, lesbians, old women – as well as white, economically privileged, heterosexual women'.[11] In *Ain't I A Woman* (1981), bell hooks* draws on the real life history of Sojourner Truth (1797–1883) in order to highlight the exclusion of the black woman from white, American feminism. At the Women's Convention in Akron, Ohio in 1851, Sojourner Truth gave a speech in which she expressed her concerns about the ways in which white men and women were constructing a sense of femininity that did not take into account the realities of the black female experience: 'Dat man ober dar say dat women needs to be helped into carriages, and lifted ober ditches, and to have de best places ... and ain't I a woman? Look at me! Look at my arm! ... I have plowed and planted, and gathered into barns, and no man could head me – and ain't I a woman?' She also asserts the strength of motherhood under slavery: 'I have borne five children and seen 'em mos all sold into slavery, and when I cried out why my mother's grief, none but Jesus hear – and ain't I a woman?'[12] bell hooks notes that Sojourner Truth, unlike most women's rights advocates, could refer to her personal life experience 'as evidence of women's ability to function as a parent; do the work equal of man; to undergo persecution, physical abuse, rape torture; and to not only survive but

* Named Gloria Jean Watkins at birth, the author adopted her grandmother's name as her pen name because she admired her bold manner of speaking, but she put the name in lowercase letters in order to distinguish her own identity from that of her grandmother.

emerge triumphant' (p. 160). Truth calls attention to the oppression of institutionalised racism through slavery. She highlights the discrepancies between white women's and black women's experiences, which have been shaped by the intersections of gender and race hierarchies. For hooks and for Truth, racism and sexism must both be eradicated.

As a result of the oppressive tendencies of patriarchy and the shortcomings of white feminist perspectives, many black feminists have sought to reclaim a sense of history, identity and voice on their own terms. Alice Walker's *In Search of Our Mother's Gardens: Womanist Prose* (1983) reclaims the life writings, literature and histories of black women as part of a larger articulation of 'womanism': alongside her consciousness of gender/sexual issues, the black woman needs to consider racial, cultural, national, economic and political matters. Hazel Carby's *Reconstructing Womanhood* (1987) describes the material conditions that shaped the lives and writings of women such as Harriet Jacobs (1813–97), an abolitionist who escaped from slavery and published *Incidents in the Life of a Slave Girl* (1861), and Anna Julia Cooper (1858–1964), an early black feminist. In *Reading Black, Reading Feminist: A Critical Anthology* (1990), Mae Gwendolyn Henderson suggests that the literary critic should consider the 'simultaneity of discourse', a term that refers to 'a mode of reading which examines the ways in which the perspectives of race and gender, and their interrelationships, structure the discourse of black women writers'.[13]

Audre Lorde has made a significant contribution to black feminism as a poet, novelist and critic. A collection of essays and speeches, *Sister Outsider* (1984), and her biomythography,* *Zami: A New Spelling of My Name* (1982), are particularly noteworthy examples of the attempt to reclaim women's sexual history and express a liberating account of the female body politic. In 'Sexism: An American Disease in Blackface', Lorde observes: 'Black feminism is not white feminism in blackface'.[14]

* Biomythography refers to a genre of writing that combines the biographical and the history of myth in one. This is done in order to articulate a more expansive understanding of selfhood.

She notes that black women (in 1979) were still the lowest paid group in the nation (p. 60). She addresses the legacies of colonialism and gender/race hierarchies directly when she observes:

> It would be shortsighted to believe that Black men alone are to blame for the above situations [the raping, brutalizing, and killing of black women] in a society dominated by white male privilege. But the Black male consciousness must be raised to the realization that sexism and woman-hating are critically dysfunctional to his liberation as a Black man because they arise out of the same constellation that engenders racism and homophobia. (p. 64)

Lorde points out that black women and black men need to resist the oppressive interrelations of gender, race and sexuality by rejecting racism and sexism as endemic in white, patriarchal colonialism. In 'Eye to Eye: Black Women, Hatred, and Anger', she addresses the condition of women in America and the Caribbean through references to social history as well as through testimonial accounts drawn from her own life experience. She observes that black women are 'born into a society of entrenched loathing and contempt for whatever is Black and female'.[15]

Like Fanon, Lorde also offers a decolonising and revolutionary perspective, but her arguments are grounded in the politics of sexuality rather than race. In 'Uses of the Erotic: The Erotic as Power', Lorde reclaims the political power of erotic love:

> The very word *erotic* comes from the Greek word *eros*, the personification of love in all its aspects – born of Chaos, and personifying creative power and harmony. When I speak of the erotic, then, I speak of it as an assertion of the lifeforce of women; of that creative energy empowered, the knowledge and use of which we are now reclaiming in our language, our history, our dancing, our loving, our work, our lives.[16]

For Lorde, the power of the erotic is a decolonising one. As a nonrational form of knowledge, it offers an alternative to rationalised, systemic and hierarchical power/knowledge relations through colonial thought. As a loving encounter with the other, a relationship predicated on consent, the erotic offers an alternative model of relations in which the sharing of joy and pleasure forms a bridge and diminishes the threat associated with difference. The erotic is also a form of self-connection that brings energy: it is creative and self-affirming in the face of a racist, patriarchal and anti-erotic society.

Postcolonial and Third World feminists, such as Chandra Talpade Mohanty and Trinh Minh-ha,* indicate the need to go beyond white feminism in order to address the specificities and variety of lived experiences by women of different races/ethnicities, cultures, religions, socio-economic circumstances, nations and classes. Mohanty's 'Under Western Eyes: Feminist Scholarship and Colonial Discourse' (1984) challenges the universalist assumption that women exist as 'an already constituted and coherent group with identical interests and desires, regardless of class, ethnic or racial location'.[17] She rejects the notion of a homogenous Third World feminine identity, especially as constructed by First World patriarchy and Western feminism. In her view, this approach to the oppressed woman replays colonial dynamics in that it objectifies the woman as other. She challenges categorical assumptions about women as victims of male violence, women as universal dependents, married women as victims of the colonial process, women as constrained by familial systems, women as oppressed by religious ideologies, and women's relations to development. In her view, the analysis of gender needs to be flexible and responsive to women's strategic location: to particular socio-economic, racial, cultural and other contexts and circumstances. Nonetheless,

* Filmmaker, composer and theorist, Minh-ha has demonstrated an ongoing interest in issues of representation relating to postcolonial femininities in her influential essay, 'Infinite Layers/Third World?' (1989), and book entitled *Native, Other: Writing Postcoloniality and Feminism* (1989).

Mohanty does not advocate a segregated approach, but suggests that there is a need for strategic coalitions between groups of women, based on the recognition of strategic locations, shared interests and differences.

Reading E. M. Forster's *A Passage to India*

E. M. Forster's *A Passage to India* (1924) offers an early example of a novel that highlights the difficulties of negotiating race, gender and sexuality in a postcolonial context. Set against the backdrop of the Indian Independence movement of the 1920s, the novel tells the story of a woman named Adela Quested who claims that an Indian man, Dr Aziz, sexually assaulted her during a visit to the Marabar Caves (a fictional version of the Barabar caves of Bihar). However, when the case is taken to trial, it appears that she is unsure what has really occurred, whether the rape was imagined or real. In 'The Unspeakable Limits of Rape: Colonial Violence and Counter-Insurgency',[18] Jenny Sharpe responds to feminist critics Elaine Showalter and Brenda Silver, who position the rape as a manifestation of Adela's fears about a loveless marriage to a white man as institutionalised rape. She also notes that some critics view the attack on Dr Aziz's reputation as a symbolic rape. While Sharpe agrees that it is important to situate the rape in terms of women's oppression, she argues that these critical perspectives fail to address 'the historical production of the category of rape within a system of colonial relations' (p. 223). Sharpe reads Forster's novel as 'a narrative that reveals the limits of an official discourse on native insurgency', 'a discourse that racialises colonial relations by implicating rebellion in the violence of rape' (p. 221). She situates Adela as an Anglo-Indian woman who is doubly positioned in colonial discourse as a member of an inferior sex but superior race (p. 225). This contradiction must be addressed when interpreting the assault. She argues that the rape must be understood in terms of colonial hierarchies so that the assault of a white woman who 'belongs' to English men has symbolic value: it is a form of assault on the white, patriarchal, colonial order (p. 230).

Sharpe observes that the incident calls attention to 'the contradictions of gender and race *within the signifying system of colonialism*' (p. 232). In other words, an understanding of the historical contexts can enrich and complicate our understanding of the meaning of the events depicted in Forster's novel (p. 232). Specifically, Sharpe situates the rape in relation to the 1857 Mutiny, which was represented inaccurately as accompanied by the raping of white women. The massacre of English women was represented in sexualised terms: women were objectified as 'eroticized and ravaged bodies' (p. 229). Sharpe observes: 'The sexual nightmare of rape and mutilation remained fixed within the British imagination throughout the nineteenth century, forming an historical memory of 1857 as the savage attack of brown-skinned fiends on defenceless women and children' (p. 234). In the India of the 1920s, the white Anglo-Indian minority was reminded of the events of 1857–8. Sharpe notes that this memory was revived, in part, on account of the 1919 massacre carried out by the English at Amritsar where five hundred Indians were killed and fifteen hundred wounded. According to Sharpe, the misrepresentation of rape in English colonial history and the shadowy presence of the related massacres of 1857–8 and 1919 serve as the basis for Forster's plotting of rape in *A Passage to India*. Ultimately, Adela becomes a sacrifice in a plot that remains focused on the impossibility of friendship between men across the colonial divide. In opposition to such perspectives, the postcolonial feminist critic's task is to 'negotiate between the sexual and racial constructions of the colonial female and native male' without losing sight of the multiple forms of gender and racial oppression evident in the text (p. 239). From a postcolonial feminist perspective, the literary critic needs to remain attentive to the dynamics of imperial power and the histories of violence and discrimination across the colonial divide.

Postcolonial Queer

The 1990s saw the rise of queer theory and its introduction to postcolonial literary criticism. The term 'queer' is often taken to refer to homosexual and lesbian people as well as being related to literature, discourses and theory. As a way of thinking about sexuality, queer theory presents a radical challenge to discourses of knowledge, which Eve Kosofsky Sedgwick refers to as 'the open mesh of possibilities, gaps, overlaps, dissonances and resonances, lapses and excesses of meaning when the constituent elements of anyone's gender, of anyone's sexuality aren't made (or can't be made) to signify monolithically'.[19] Queer theory defies the binary opposition of male/female and resists the tendency to conceive of sexuality in heteronormative terms. In postcolonial contexts, queer theory often explores the intersections of alternative sexualities and/or transgender identities with ethnicity/race. In recent decades, Caribbean fiction has seen a number of important queer fictions, which challenge prevailing homophobic tendencies of the region. These writers confront constructions of Caribbean identity that presume dominant forms of masculinity, heterosexuality and racial/ethnic homogeneity as normative. Cuban dissident, Reinaldo Arenas, remains perhaps the best known gay writer of the Caribbean thanks to his memoir, *Before Night Falls* (*Antes que anochezca: autobiografía*, 1992), which recounts the author's experiences as a sexual and political dissident in Castro's Cuba, time spent in the prison system, migration to the United States as a part of the Mariel boatlift,* and battle with AIDS. This testimonial work was on the *New York Times* list of the ten best books of the year in 1993 and was adapted for the screen by director Julian Schnabel (2000), starring Javier Bardem in the role of Arenas and featuring a cameo appearance by Johnny Depp as a cross-dresser in the Cuban prison system. Arenas is not alone in the investigation of the social contexts for queer identities in Caribbean fiction. In recent years, the work of Michelle Cliff, Patricia Powell, Shani Mootoo, Nalo Hopkinson, Jamaica Kincaid and Thomas

* The Mariel boatlift was a mass exodus of Cubans to the United States in 1980. A number of the exiles had been released from prisons and psychiatric institutions.

Glave, among others, has contributed to a growing recognition of gay, lesbian and queer identity construction in the Caribbean region, its diasporas and transnational contexts.

Certain types of writing tend to express or reinforce particular ways of thinking about gender. Rewriting these kinds of stories (genres) can serve to challenge prevailing constructions of gender. Caribbean Canadian writer Nalo Hopkinson turns to speculative fiction, science fiction and magic realism to explore queer perspectives in novels such as *Brown Girl in the Ring* (1998), *Midnight Robber* (2000), *The Salt Roads* (2003) and *The New Moon's Arms* (2007), and a collection of short stories, *Skin Folk* (2001). She notes that queer traditions from indigenous and other cultures can serve as a means to challenge prevailing paradigms of normative sexual behaviour: '[i]n many of the indigenous cultures of the world, including some African communities, the people who live beyond the borders are cherished. They don't have to live in fear for their spirits, for their very lives.' She describes these people as 'edgewalkers, the winktes, the ones who wear women's clothes when they should wear men's and men's clothes when they should wear women's, or they just mix and match and wear whatever combination pleases them' and comments that 'sometimes they're the ones who claim a gender different to the one they were born in, and they love and marry according to their picture of gender, not the one that we're told our bodies dictate. They become the shamans, the artists, the healers, the visionaries of their communities. They are the ones who envision new ways of being.'[20] Hopkinson observes that the genres of science fiction and fantasy were 'the first literatures I read that wrestled head-on with normativity, a way of being in the world that works for me in some areas and flat out makes me suicidal in others'.[21] The queer potential of the alien and fantastical enables her to give voice to the queer, to explore a range of sexual experiences and envision alternative expressions of gender. Alternative sexualities are often shown to be related to the legacies of colonialism in Hopkinson's works. At other times, she invokes pan-Caribbean or Black Atlantic traditions in order to subvert the oppressive gender roles and sexual histories associated with empire. In *The Salt Roads*, lesbianism, sexual/racial dissidence and revolution come together in Hopkinson's rewriting of the history of slave revolts in Haiti. Haitian revolutionary history is interwoven with the queer sexual history of French poet Charles Baudelaire's mistress, Jeanne Duval (who inspired him to write 'Black Venus'), the life history of Saint Mary of Egypt, and the spiritual birth of the Haitian *lwa* or goddess, Erzulie. *Midnight Robber* introduces the motif of cross-dressing and transgender identity to challenge colonial gender stereotypes. This story recounts events in the life of a child who suffers sexual abuse at the hands of her father. She flees her home and cross-dresses as a robber (traditionally a male figure). Eventually, she is able to confront and overcome early sexual trauma. Hopkinson's queer fictions mobilise science fiction and magic realism – genres associated with alternative worlds and multiple worldviews – to interrogate history and the legacies of colonial identity through exploratory inscriptions of gender/race/sexuality.

Transnational queer perspectives feature in the work of Patricia Powell and Shani Mootoo, especially in Powell's *The Pagoda* (1999) and Mootoo's *Cereus Blooms at Night* (1996). For Powell, a Jamaican American, the politics of location have proven to be especially important with respect to her writing. Reflecting on her decision not to do a reading in Jamaica, Powell states:

> Last year, I was invited to The Bookshop in Kingston, Jamaica, to read. I didn't go. I was completely terrified. All I could think of was that gay march back in the summer of 1992 when I was there researching *The Pagoda*, and reading about the protesters blocking the roads and wielding weapons. And then there were the rabid homophobic articles that spilled out of the newspapers daily. I thought there was no way I could be strong or coherent or calm enough if someone in the audience wanted to be nasty.[22]

Set in the nineteenth century, Powell's novel tells the story of a Chinese woman named Lowe who escapes patriarchal oppression in China by dressing as a man and migrating to Jamaica as a stowaway in the hold of a ship. Her female identity is discovered in the course of the journey by a man who rapes and impregnates her. Following the voyage, this same man helps Lowe to conceal her identity and arranges for her marriage to another woman (also one of his lovers) so that she may bring up her child. In Jamaica, Lowe takes both female and male lovers. Brought together, descriptions of her erotic encounters map the body as a queer site of multiple genders and sexual orientations. Moreover, Lowe bears witness to the lives of indentured labourers* in Jamaica, bringing to life a marginalised historical experience in the national consciousness of the island, which often tends to privilege the histories of African presence over other migrant groups. Thus, multiple forms of marginalised existence in terms of race, culture and sexuality are interwoven in the novel.

Mootoo's *Cereus Blooms at Night* explores the legacies of violence and discrimination associated with colonial discourses of gender and sexuality in the Caribbean context. Set in the town of Paradise, on the fictional island of Lantanacamara, the novel recounts the story of a cross-dressing male nurse, named Tyler, who cares for a madwoman, named Mala. The two form a special bond, which deepens as they explore relations between their sexual histories and experiences. Mala is the child of a lesbian mother who was forced to abandon her daughters when she took flight from her husband, depicted as an enraged patriarch who threatens their lives. With the mother's departure, the daughters are left unprotected to bear the wrath of the father, who sexually abuses his elder daughter, Mala. This genealogy of sexual abuse is accompanied by a more positive investigation of queerness with Tyler. As a man who works in a

* Indenture is a process whereby labourers enter into a contract for a set period of time in exchange for their ocean transportation, food, clothing, lodging and other necessities during the term of the contract. They are not, however, paid a wage for their work.

profession traditionally held by women, Tyler is subject to gender discrimination in the workplace. Moreover, his queer dress and uncertain sexual orientation unsettle those around him. The gender of another character, named Otoh, is also presented as queer: his/her name is short for Otohboto, an acronym for 'on the one hand but on the other'. *Cereus Blooms at Night* subverts normative conceptions of identity through its representations of the pervasively queer Caribbean experience.

Like Hopkinson and Arenas, Thomas Glave takes a dissident view of the intersections of sexuality and politics in works such as *Whose Song? And Other Stories* (2000), *Words to Our Now: Imagination and Dissent* (2005), an anthology entitled *Our Caribbean: A Gathering of Lesbian and Gay Writing from the Antilles* (2008) and *The Torturer's Wife* (2008). In his essay/narrative, 'Whose Caribbean?: An Allegory, in Part', Glave addresses the representation and expression of queer postcolonial Caribbean identity in domestic and global contexts, linking colonial and neoimperial discourses. Glave begins with the description of a child who confounds normative concepts of the gendered, human body: '[t]he child – let us know him/her as "S/He" – possessed a slender penis of startlingly delicate green, the truest colour of the sea that s/he had always loved … s/he also possessed a pair of luminous blue breasts the tone of the purest skies that, on the gentlest days, nuzzled their broad soft chins against the sea.' Instead of nipples the child has 'berries the inflamed colour of hibiscus in its most passionate surrender to the sunsets and dawn that for millennia had washed over that place … [and] … also a vagina and uterus, which, as was common knowledge among all who knew him/her, produced at least twice or three times a year, without assistance from anyone, a race of brazen dolphins.'[23] The 'once upon a time' beginning of the fairytale is rewritten by Glave in an uncertain time as well as in an uncertain place as he describes how 'it came to pass that upon that time, not so long ago, in that part of the world.' Thus, the narrative's indeterminacy is signalled from the outset of the story, and linked to the child's own indeterminate intersexual identity. This identity can be seen as challenging colonial discourses that represent the colonial subject in eroticised terms as coterminous with the land to be dominated. That the child's nipples are berries and s/he gives birth to dolphins, suggests that the child participates in a harmonious way with the biosphere. The sensuous and erotic language does not indicate relations of domination/subordination, but elicits an abundant and mobile fertility, embodied by the currents and waves of the sea, 'which licked and foamed out and back, out and in again.' In this context, we might consider that the sea is often identified with trade and the trafficking of commodities, including human bodies, in the transatlantic histories that link Europe, Africa and the New World. Glave's postcolonial body also challenges notions of race in terms of skin colour (black, brown, yellow, red and white) because the body includes blue breasts and a delicate green penis, which suggest a continuum with the sea and plants respectively. Yet, this child does not escape the legacies of colonialism: his/her dreams link him/her explicitly to the plantation system. S/he dreams of tormented hands vanishing beneath the sea and sugar cane. For Glave, the ambivalent presence of the child bears witness to a long history of exploitation and mobility in and through the Caribbean: the presence of 'stealthy buccaneers or cruise ship companies, slave traders or airline advertisements or a combination of any and all' (p. 672). For Glave personally, the child's presence is conjured up when crossing borders between Jamaica and the United States: this allows him to open up the notion of transnational and pan-Caribbean identity. In the contemporary landscape, the child's body bears evidence of ringworm, and s/he is likely to be propositioned in the context of sex tourism. In this context, the exoticised, eroticised body of the colonial past resurfaces in the contemporary world of neoimperial economic and sexual exploitation. Glave notes that the child yearns to be loved and to be safe from threats, whether in the form of sexual exploitation or gender discrimination, whether foreign or domestic.

In addressing the child's interests and rights, Glave engages in a wider enquiry into Caribbean citizenship at home and in the world. He notes that 'many Caribbean citizens in the twenty-first century ... do not have access to adequate health care, housing, and education' (p. 675). Moroever, he offers numerous examples of discrimination against gay and lesbian culture. In Jamaica, he addresses Prime Minister P. J. Patterson's refusal to do away with the Offenses Against the Person Act and its 'buggery law', which criminalise male homosexuality and contribute to a homophobic culture more generally. Cuba's 1980 Mariel boatlift saw the expulsion of homosexuals, sex workers, drug users, the mentally troubled and AIDS-inflicted people. In the 1990s, the Cayman Islands refused entry to cruise ships loaded with gay and lesbian tourists. The question of 'Whose Caribbean?' addresses discrimination and inequity throughout the region and beyond for citizens and visitors. Glave remarks: 'In an increasingly desperate, balkanized post-September 11th world, that Caribbean needs our energies, against corporate and global hegemonies ... against the destruction and self-destruction of inhumane rhetoric, legislations, and ultimately spurious democracies' (p. 678). Thus, he offers an impassioned plea to attend to the lessons and legacies of colonialism with respect to race, gender and sexuality in our globalising world.

Notes

1 Kimberle Crenshaw, 'Demarginalizing the Intersection of Race and Sex: A Black Feminist Critique of Antidiscrimination Doctrine, Feminist Theory, and Antiracist Politics', *University of Chicago Legal Forum* (1989), pp. 139–67.

2 Patricia Hill Collins, *Black Feminist Thought* (New York: Routledge, 2000), pp. 138–9.

3 Michael Banton, 'The Idiom of Race: A Critique of Presentism', in Les Back and John Solomos (eds), *Theories of Race and Racism: A Reader* (London: Routledge, 2000), p. 53.

4 W. E. B. Du Bois, *The Souls of Black Folk* (New York: Barnes & Noble Classics, 2003), p. 16.
5 Ania Loomba, *Colonialism/Postcolonialism* (London: Routledge, 2005), p. 65.
6 Joseph Conrad, *Heart of Darkness*, Ross C. Murfin (ed.) (New York: Bedford Books, 1989), p. 76.
7 Loomba, *Colonialism/Postcolonialism*, p. 135.
8 Du Bois, *The Souls of Black Folk*, p. 9.
9 Frantz Fanon, *Black Skin, White Masks*, Charles Lam Markmann (trans.) (New York: Grove Press, 1967), p. 43.
10 Walter Mosley, *Devil in a Blue Dress* (New York: W. W. Norton and Company, 1990), p. 26.
11 Barbara Smith, 'Racism and Women's Studies', in Gloria T. Hull, Patricia Bell Scott, and Barbara Smith (eds), *All the Women are White, All the Blacks are Men, But Some of Us are Brave* (New York: The Feminist Press at City University of New York, 1982), p. 49.
12 bell hooks, *Ain't I a Woman* (London: Pluto Press, 1982), p. 160.
13 Mae Gwendolyn Henderson, 'Speaking in Tongues: Dialogics, Dialectics, and the Black Woman Writer's Literary Tradition', in Patrick Williams and Laura Chrisman (eds), *Colonial Discourse and Post-Colonial Theory* (New York: Columbia University Press, 1994), p. 258.
14 Audre Lorde, 'Sexism: An American Disease in Blackface', *Sister Outsider: Essays and Speeches by Audre Lorde* (Berkeley, CA: Crossing Press, 2007), p. 60.
15 Lorde, 'Eye to Eye: Black Women, Hatred, and Anger', *Sister Outsider*, p. 151.
16 Lorde, 'Uses of the Erotic: The Erotic as Power', *Sister Outsider*, p. 55.
17 Chandra Tolpade Mohanty, 'Under Western Eyes: Feminist Scholarship and Colonial Discourses', *boundary 2* 12.3–13.1, On Humanism and the University I: The Discourse of Humanism (Spring–Autumn, 1984), pp. 336–7.
18 Jenny Sharpe, 'The Unspeakable Limits of Rape: Colonial Violence and Counter-Insurgency', *Genders* 10 (Spring, 1991), pp. 25–46. Reprinted in Patrick Williams and Laura Chrisman (eds), *Colonial Discourse and Post-Colonial Theory* (New York: Columbia University Press, 1994), pp. 221–43. All page references are to the reprinted article.
19 Eve Kosofsky Sedgwick, *Tendencies* (Durham, NC: Duke University Press, 1993), p. 8.
20 Nalo Hopkinson, 'The Profession of Science Fiction', *Foundation: The International Review of Science Fiction* (Summer, 2004), p. 7.

21 Nalo Hopkinson and Alondra Nelson, 'Making the Impossible Possible: An Interview with Nalo Hopkinson', *Social Text* 71, 20.2 (Summer 2002), pp. 97–113, p. 111.

22 Patricia Powell and Faith Smith, 'An Interview with Patricia Powell', *Callaloo* 19.2 Emerging Women Writers: A Special Issue (Spring, 1996), p. 327.

23 Thomas Glave, 'Whose Caribbean? An Allegory, in Part', *Callaloo* 27.3 (2004), p. 671.

Cross-cultural Paradigms and the Multicultural Society

From the very first days of empire and colonisation, peoples from around the world came into contact with one another. Languages, cultures, races, religions and peoples mixed together to produce new experiences and concepts of culture, identity and community. The purpose of this chapter is to introduce key concepts for discussing cultural contact and intermixture in colonial contexts – such as the contact zone, transculturation, creolisation, *mestizaje* and hybridity. It also looks at postcolonial culture, including discussions of post-war migration and contemporary debates about the multicultural society.

Colonial Contact and Cultural Transformations

Cristóbal Colón (Christopher Columbus) 'discovered' the New World in 1492, an event which marked the beginning of the exploration of the Americas and inaugurated the era of colonisation. Colonisation brought peoples into contact, but the dynamics of cultural exchange and transformation were experienced in highly uneven ways. While colonisation implies a top-down approach in which the colonising culture imparts its cultural values to the colonised peoples so that they undergo acculturation (the acquisition of culture) and/or deculturation (the loss or uprooting of culture), the lived experience of cross-cultural exchange was often more complex. Processes of selection, subversion and accommodation (of practices, ideas and values) were part of the colonial experience. Furthermore, in the postcolonial era, writers would revisit the dynamics of cultural contact and influence. These dynamics would play an essential role in debates about poetics, the use of the vernacular, and the role of history as well as spark creative responses in an effort to represent decolonising approaches to the postcolonial situation.

Fernando Ortiz (1881–1969), a Cuban sociologist, was one of the first theorists to describe these uneven processes of cultural transformation by introducing the term transculturation. In *Cuban Counterpoint: Tobacco and Sugar* (originally published in Spanish in 1940), Ortiz defines the term 'transculturation' as the reciprocal influences of cultures and modes of representation in various colonies and metropoles.[1] While transculturation may include processes of deculturation and acculturation, it goes beyond loss and acquisition: transculturation involves the dynamic fusion and merging of cultures to produce new identities, cultures and societies. In *Imperial Eyes: Travel Writing and Transculturation* (1992), Mary Louise Pratt introduces the term 'contact zone' to describe the disjunctive processes of socio-cultural and political reproduction. She observes:

> I use [the term] to refer to the space of imperial encounters, the space in which peoples geographically and historically separated come into contact with each other and establish ongoing relations, usually involving conditions of coercion, radical inequality, and intractable conflict.[2]

Pratt calls attention to the fact that cultural transformation is a lived experience and an ongoing process. For postcolonial writers and critics, the contact zone can furthermore be seen through the social spaces where cultures continue to meet, clash and grapple with each other in many parts of the world today. The legacies of the colonial contact zone often persist in post-colonial societies or influence thinking about the meaning of community.

To turn to a specific example of these multiple processes of cultural transformation, we might think of the contact zone of the plantation, which has connections to the triangular trade routes linking the New World, Europe and Africa. Goods and peoples circulated across the Atlantic. Commodities from the Caribbean basin were taken to Europe; ships taking slaves would then make the horrific journey to New World via the Middle Passage from Africa to the Caribbean basin. Many enslaved peoples died while being forcibly transported. Acts of violence were not uncommon. If the captive Africans survived the journey, they were sold into slavery. There they came into contact with fellow slaves and white slave owners. The colonial language was imposed on the slaves (acculturation). Consequently, the Middle Passage is often associated with cultural amnesia (deculturation) for it marked the loss of the specific African culture from which the diverse peoples originated. Nonetheless, forms of dance, drumming, storytelling and other African diasporic* cultural forms persisted. Through mixture with European and indigenous forms, processes of creolisation – in other words, a process of intermixing and cultural transformation that entails deculturation, acculturation and transculturation – took place.

Approaches to Creolisation

The meaning of creolisation has been much debated. The word 'creole' derives from the Spanish *criollo* meaning 'native' or indigenous. Creole originally referred to a white person of European

* The term 'diaspora' (meaning dispersion) initially referred to the scattering of Jewish peoples as a result of several forced expulsions from what is now known as Israel, Jordan and parts of Lebanon as well as the State of Palestine. Subsequently, 'diaspora' has come to refer more generally to the movement, migration or scattering of a people away from a settled location or ancestral homeland.

descent born and raised in the colony, but later came to refer to all those born into Caribbean culture, regardless of the person's racial, ethnic or cultural background. However, postcolonial writers and critics have explored the tensions between what is seen as a tendency to place emphasis on a fixed, essentialist (seen as an unchanging essence) Creole identity versus creolisation as an unfinished, ongoing process. In *The Development of Creole Society in Jamaica, 1770–1820*, Kamau Brathwaite observes that creolisation denotes both a colonial relationship with a 'metropolitan' European power, on the one hand, and a plantation arrangement on the other.[3] He sees creolisation as a cultural action – material, psychological and spiritual – which takes place in a new landscape as individuals from different racial and cultural backgrounds come into contact and begin to form a completely new construct.[4] Brathwaite describes the processes of socialisation, which entailed acculturation, for African peoples who were forced to enter into subordinate relations on the plantation. In his view, one of the tragedies of the plantation system was the emergence of the 'mimic-men', slaves and colonial subjects who imitated white, colonial behaviour (for more on mimicry, see Part Four: 'Postcolonial Reading Practices').[5] Nonetheless, the model of acculturation gave way to a two-way process of mutual influence or interculturation, which is the basis of the creolisation of culture in the Caribbean. Intermixtures occurred through sex, language, religion and culture so that every facet of cultural life came to be fused together to a greater or lesser extent.

The processes of creolisation, the meaning of Creole identities and the tensions within Creole societies are represented by many Caribbean writers. Derek Walcott offers one of the best known depictions of Creole identity in his poem entitled 'The Schooner Flight' (1979), which describes a green-eyed, red-haired sailor known as 'Shabine'.*[6] 'Shabine' is a particularly striking nickname that derives from the Francophone Caribbean word 'chabin', which is used to refer to a racially mixed (black/white) person who often has green eyes and blonde or reddish hair. Interestingly, as the word

* For more on Walcott, see Part Three: 'Decolonising the Stage'.

'chabine' refers to a female identity in French it is also possible to interpret this nickname in transgender terms. The name suggests a further complicating aspect of the character's identity: the intercultural influence of French. Walcott comes from St Lucia, an island which changed hands between various colonial powers, notably between the French and the English, on multiple occasions, which resulted in the intermixing of various European cultural and linguistic influences. As a result of his highly creolised identity, Shabine sees himself as either 'nobody' or 'a nation'. This statement reflects the colonial denigration of creolised identities because they were not racially or culturally pure, but also points the way forward to a new sense of post-colonial identity and nationhood, which celebrates the diversity of identity and the complexities of nationhood for societies where multiple cultures and ethnic groups come together to form a new socio-cultural construct. The notion that creolisation raises questions around the imagining of identity, community and nationhood, which exceed and depart from the legacies of colonisation, is one of the most significant contributions of debates about creolisation.

Nonetheless, it is important to note that creolisation was the product of a profoundly unequal and exploitative system of enslavement and racism. Racial hierarchies and cultural tensions in Creole societies produced a sense of anxiety and sometimes led to incidents of violence in both personal and public spheres. Some representations of creolisation highlight these inequities within Creole society as well as in relation to metropolitan centres. Notably, Jean Rhys's *Wide Sargasso Sea* (1966) represents the shifting hierarchies within Creole society in the post-abolition period as well as the cultural difference and uneven power dynamics that existed between people of English and white Creole descent. The novel also demonstrates the tensions between white and black Creoles, particularly during an era when many members of the white plantocracy* lost their wealth, position and power, which had

* 'Plantocracy' describes the ruling class or political order dominated by plantation owners.

formerly derived from owning slaves. When Mr Mason, an Englishman, marries a white Creole woman, named Annette, he finds it difficult to decipher the culture of the Caribbean. He sees the emancipated blacks as childlike and fails to see their anger when there is a rumour that indentured servants will be brought to the Caribbean and take over the labour carried out by emancipated slaves at reduced wages. Mr Mason fails to heed warnings about his inability to understand Creole culture and is thus helpless to defend his property from incineration when the former slaves burn down the plantation house and threaten his family. Later in the novel, Annette's daughter Antoinette marries an unnamed Englishman (interpreted by critics to be Rochester on account of the intertextual reference to Charlotte Brontë's *Jane Eyre*) who sees her speaking what he refers to as 'debased patois' (a creolised language), and is struck by her otherness: 'Long, sad, dark alien eyes. Creole of pure English descent she may be, but they are not English or European either'.[7] This sense of cultural difference, which is accompanied by an ambivalent recognition of her otherness, contributes to the growing unease in their relationship and eventually leads the unnamed man to come to dislike – even hate – his bride, whom he eventually declares to be mad and imprisons in the attic of his home in England. The novel ends with a dream sequence in which Antoinette sees her childhood home burning down; she awakens and it seems that she will burn down her husband's home in an act of Creole resistance to patriarchal and colonial oppression. The novel leaves unresolved the question of creolisation for the reader: this instance of the cross-cultural imaginary might also be interpreted as an ironic misappropriation of black colonial experience on the part of a white Creole. Specifically, Antoinette envisions her own feminist agenda of emancipation from patriarchy through the quest for freedom from racial oppression. Moreover, we might consider the figure of the husband and the significance of Rhys's refusal to name him. This textual strategy might be said to highlight the colonial temptation to name and describe the world in light of a dominant cultural framework. In this instance, the temptation to impose the template of *Jane Eyre* on *Wide Sargasso Sea* could be seen as a colonising gesture. Overall, *Wide Sargasso Sea* offers a complex depiction of a Creole society in transition as well as its ambivalent relations to colonial power.*

Creolisation as an Ongoing Process

While creolisation first emerged in the context of the Caribbean plantation system, this process has been extended beyond the region, partly through the migration of Caribbean peoples. In the post-war period, Britain encouraged members of the Caribbean and other colonies to migrate in order to meet the growing demand for labourers. Louise Bennett observes that 'colonization in reverse' took place as migrant presence began to transform a sense of cultural and national identity.[8] Trinidad-born Sam Selvon's *The Lonely Londoners* (1956) tells the story of a group of migrants from the Caribbean and Africa in creolised English.† Selvon's use of language forms part of a wider narrative strategy for representing the multifarious ways in which a new kind of contact zone emerges as migrants settle into their new home and undergo processes of acculturation. While some prove to be mimic men, notably a character called Harris who speaks standard English and adopts English mannerisms, others challenge the dominant culture and introduce Creole socio-cultural traditions, such as Tanty who convinces an English store owner to introduce a system of credit practised in the Caribbean. In Selvon's work, the language, space, history and culture of London are seen to be creolised through dynamic processes of encounter, exchange and interculturation.

Since the 1970s, dub and performance poets have continued the processes of creolisation by intermixing Caribbean vernacular idioms

* See Part Four: 'Postcolonial Reading Practices' for more on *Wide Sargasso Sea*.

† The steamship named the SS *Empire Windrush* brought the first generation of migrant workers from the Caribbean to England in 1948. The term 'Windrush Generation' is often used to refer to this post-war generation of migrants.

and forms, particularly those derived from Jamaica. To offer a few examples, works such as Linton Kwesi Johnson's *Mi Revalueshanary Fren* (2002) and Benjamin Zephaniah's *Too Black, Too Strong* (2001) have expanded a sense of what contemporary British culture means in the world through creolised protest poetry that defies deculturation. Thus, creolisation extends its processes beyond the local and time-bound contexts of the colonial periphery, proving to be 'a syncretic process of transverse dynamics that endlessly reworks and transforms the cultural patterns of varied social and historical experiences and identities'.[9] More recently, many critics have come to see creolisation as a process that is unfolding throughout the world through globalisation's tendency to bring peoples from diverse cultures into new forms of transformative contact, especially through disjunctive, uneven power dynamics and flows (for more on globalisation, see Part Four: 'Postcoloniality in a Globalising World').[10]

Hybridity and/or Biculturalism

While the term creolisation was initially applied to specific Caribbean socio-cultural processes of linguistic transformation in the context of slavery and the plantation experience, some critics employ the term with reference to other cultural contexts. For example, outside the Caribbean, Keri Hulme's *The Bone People* (1984), which focuses on the history of the Maori of New Zealand, is sometimes described as a narrative that shows signs of creolising poetics,[11] particularly through its depiction of the child Simon who defies the binary modes of thinking which characterise colonial discourse (see Part Four: 'Postcolonial Reading Practices' for a definition of colonial discourse). Born in 1947, Hulme is of mixed Maori, Orkney Island Scottish and English parentage. The protagonist of the novel, Kerewin Holmes, is part Maori, part European. She lives as a recluse in a tower-shaped house, and undergoes a spiritual renewal through her encounter and relationship with a mute child named Simon P. Gillayley and his step-father, Joe Gillayley. Although *The Bone People* is written primarily in

English, the language of the novel reflects the intonation and style of the Maori language. Maori words and references to culture are incorporated throughout the work. Creolisation is evident in the translingual poetics of the literary work, which freely mixes together European and indigenous forms and idioms.

While it is certainly helpful to introduce terms such as deculturation, acculturation and interculturation when discussing the dynamics of cultural transformation as represented in *The Bone People*, it is perhaps less useful to discuss this work as a fiction about creolisation, particularly as the Maori culture and language, despite its transformation through cultural contact and colonisation, has its own precolonial, persistent and resistant cultural identity (even if that identity was itself shaped by preconquest, cross-cultural contact), which is preservationist in spirit. Linda Moss notes:

> The whole of the first century of contact (1770s to 1870s) was characterised by ambivalent relations: the ferocity of Maori opposition to land seizure by settlers both infuriated and impressed the colonists. Banks, the botanist travelling with Captain Cooke in 1776, like many early visitors to New Zealand, displays a slightly condescending curiosity towards Maori art, but a respect for Maori resistance to the incomers. For the next fifty years, the Maori were in control of cultural borrowings from settlers, who at this date constituted informal groups of traders and whalers, dependant for food and raw materials on the tolerance of their Maori hosts. Like the English in the UK, the Maori were the unthreatened majority who benefited from trade with immigrants, and could choose from their offerings whatever suited their material and cultural needs. It was not until the establishment of formal colonial government in New Zealand in the 1830s and 1840s that the situation changed.[12]

The situation in the Caribbean is not comparable because indigenous populations were decimated through disease, genocide and conflict as well as assimilated into the creolising mixtures of the post-conquest collision of cultures. While indigenous traces are evident in the linguistic, cultural and racial intermixtures of the Caribbean, the preconquest cultures and peoples, the Carib, Arawak and others, have been largely eradicated. Moreover, the ensuing cultural intermixture in the Caribbean was profoundly symbiotic, synthesising various elements into an unforeseen newness.* By contrast, the Maori people in New Zealand only gradually became assimilated within empire, and even then they resisted transculturation, perceiving it to be a form of deculturation.

The Maori experience of cultural transformation highlights the uneven power dynamics that have gradually produced a transformed, hybrid society and bicultural articulation of national identity in New Zealand. Hybridisation has occurred in a limited fashion in New Zealand as a result of colonial hierarchies, the specific colonial history of power, Maori opposition, and various efforts on both English colonial and Maori sides to maintain cultures of difference. Since 1975, the guarantee of Maori sovereignty (*rangatiratanga*) has led to the formal establishment of separate Maori provision for public services (health, education and culture) insofar as these concern Maori affairs. Thus, it is a constitutional requirement in New Zealand to have separate cultural provision for Maori.

In this context, *The Bone People* reflects the complexities of a sovereign but nonetheless hybrid people living in a bicultural but nonetheless hybrid society. Kerewin articulates fears about linguistic contact, intermixture and potential contamination. Specifically, she

* Creolisation is most often associated with the processes of transformation brought about through the plantation system in the Caribbean; it is specific to the region. Although creolising processes have occurred elsewhere, it is important to pay attention to the specific dynamics of cross-cultural transformation. Racially or culturally mixed persons are often referred to as hybrid. The term hybrid places perhaps more emphasis on the contestatory processes of transformation. The very word 'hybrid' carries the historical burden of racism because the term was often applied to a negative account of the union of disparate races. For more on hybridity, see Robert Young's *Colonial Desire: Hybridity in Theory, Culture and Race* (London: Routledge, 1995).

seems to want to keep the 'pure' language of the Maori separate from the profane language of English. She is sitting in a bar when she hears a Maori worker speaking in English; his dialogue is punctured with curse words 'used monotonously, a sad counterbalance for every phrase'.[13] Inwardly, she recoils at this use of language:

> Why this speech filled with bitterness and contempt? You hate English, man? I can understand that but why not do your conversing in Maori and spare us this contamination? No swear words in that tongue ... there he goes again. Ah hell, the ... word has its place, but all the time? ... aue. (p. 12)

The Maori labourer is of course speaking English as a result of both the long history of colonisation, which has brought the language to the people, as well as current labour conditions, which appear to have brought about a condition of alienation, which is reflected in the constant punctuation of curse words. Kerewin envisions the turn to Maori language as a departure from the contaminating influence of English. Indeed, she notes that the Maori language does not contain curse words, thus suggesting that the worker's prevailing mindset is a product of the ways in which English cultural and linguistic contact has profoundly transformed and reshaped the Maori worldview in negative terms. Yet, she also uses an English curse word herself and acknowledges that it has its place and time, suggesting the inescapability of the hybrid postcolonial condition and the impossibility of reversion to a precontact world. Finally, her reflections end with the word 'aue', which is an expression of distress in the Maori language. Thus, Kerewin herself switches from English to Maori in order to express her feelings. Nonetheless, her thoughts, which take place in both English and Maori, are reflective of a hybrid condition where two cultures continue to operate in an ambivalent way in the postcolonial consciousness.

A closer look at the colonial etymology and postcolonial reclamation of the term 'hybridity' highlights the ways in which thinking about racial, cultural and linguistic transformations has been construed through time. Thanks to the critical interventions of postcolonial critics, such as Homi K. Bhabha and Néstor García Canclini, the term 'hybridity' is now commonly used to refer to the ambivalent, mutually transformative dynamics of transcultural transformation. In the colonial era, however, the term finds its origins in botany, horticulture and animal husbandry where it refers to the cross-breeding of two species to form a third, 'hybrid', species. For colonials, the term hybridity was often used to describe in negative terms the union of different species; as such, it was closely connected to fears about the corruption of language and miscegenation (racial intermixing). Robert Young traces the etymology of the word 'hybridity' as follows:

> A hybrid is defined by Webster in 1828 as 'a mongrel or mule; an animal or plant produced from the mixture of two species'. Its first recorded use in the nineteenth century to denote the crossing of people of different races is given in the OED as 1861. Although this is certainly too late (it was used by Josiah Nott in 1843), this date is certainly significant. Prichard has already used the term 'hybrid' in the context of the question of human fertility as early as 1813. ... An OED entry from 1890 makes the link between the linguistic and the racial explicit: 'The Aryan languages present such indications of hybridity as would correspond with ... racial intermixture'.[14]

Young points out that hybridity was part of the racism implicit in colonial discourses as discussions of the phenomenon tended to stress the need to cultivate carefully and control these intermixings for fear that the hybrid would revert to its 'primitive' stock.[15] Thus, in theoretical terms, the colonial usage of the term 'hybridity' reflects the coloniser's desire to rationalise and control the cultural contact situation.

In a postcolonial context, the notion of hybridity is used in a descriptive fashion to refer to the heterogeneous aspects of cultural formation, the intermixtures of language, culture, politics and race, which emerge through contact and uneven exchange. Canclini states: '*I understand for hybridization socio-cultural processes in which discrete structures or practices, previously existing in separate form, are combined to generate new structures, objects, and practices*'.[16] Pidgin and creole languages are often seen as examples of hybridisation as a process of linguistic transformation, but we might also consider the ways in which the so-called discrete structures are themselves already a product of prior hybridisation, so that there is no pure point of origin. Citing contemporary debates as to whether or not Spanglish can be taught in university courses, Canclini rightly points out that Spanish and English culture and language have both been formed through the processes of hybridisation, which emerge from transcultural contact and uneven exchange. Importantly, Canclini points out that a theory of hybridisation 'requires a critical awareness of its limits, of what refuses or resists hybridization'.[17]

In *The Location of Culture*, Bhabha stresses the interdependence and mutual construction of subjectivities through colonial hybridisation, or the ways in which the colonised and coloniser interact. For Bhabha, cultural identity emerges through the 'Third Space of enunciation'; this contradictory and ambivalent space of cultural inscription is one where contact results in the production of something new, which is not simply derived from either one of the pre-existing cultural situations.[18] Cultures and peoples come into contact to create a new hybrid culture through intermixing and mutual influence. When discussing postcolonial hybridity, it is important to differentiate the term from cross-cultural exchange, which implies an even balance of power relations, and pay particular attention to the disjunctive workings of hybridity as shaped through colonisation, which entails an imbalance of powers. Moreover, the specificity of the context and the material factors that shape these uneven dynamics necessarily merit close inspection for the analysis of hybridity to gain its critical edge. While hybridity seems to imply a mutuality, particularly through the emergence of newness, one needs to also consider what is expunged, discarded or unacknowledged through hybridisation processes. This is where Bhabha's emphasis on enunciation gains its power, for it draws the critic's attention to the complex dynamics of articulation. In other words, the critic's analysis of postcolonial hybridity in a literary text needs to be attentive to the specificities of history and location, particularly to the temporal, spatial, geographical, linguistic, socio-economic, political and wider cultural contexts.

Through colonialism, hybridity unfolded in a highly uneven fashion, but postcolonial perspectives enable the critic to identify the oppositional moment (challenges to the dominant, oppressive colonial culture) within the colonial context as well to extrapolate the ways in which postcolonial rewriting serves to interrogate and re-envision the past as part of negotiation of past-present horizons (such as colonial legacies or colonial discourses and their residual influence in the post-colonial era). Through conquest, indigenous and aboriginal peoples of North America, South America, New Zealand and Australia experienced various efforts of deculturation: war, disease and forced migration resulted in the erosion and in some instances extinction of indigenous cultures. Language, customs and indigenous ways of life underwent further deculturation through colonial efforts to assimilate the population. Missionaries encouraged acculturation by teaching the indigenous peoples a colonial language (English, French or Spanish, depending on the colonial power) and providing religious instruction. Labour practices and efforts to control sexual reproduction and intermixing through discourses, practices and laws, also need to be taken into account.

At the same time, the postcolonial critic might want to consider how textual hybridity – such as the mixing of languages and allusions to hybrid cultural forms – might disrupt and challenge oppressive approaches to cultural formation, which stress a top-down approach to exchange (the coloniser's culture dominating that of colonised peoples). Postcolonial narratives can critique power relations and celebrate creative forms of intermixture that serve to offer an alternative vision of transcultural formation. In this respect, Bhabha's example of the 'Third Space of enunciation', drawn from the work of Wilson Harris, is extremely well chosen. Harris's work, from *Palace of the Peacock* (1960) to *The Ghost of Memory* (2006), stages continuously the contact and collision of cultures through space and time, bringing narrative fragments about the hybrid moments of the colonial past into a postcolonial discourse that operates through ongoing processes of contestation and grafting. By reworking the time and space of encounter (as well as other specificities) through an often visionary or dream-like state as well as through metatextual* interventions, Harris introduces a strategic poetics of hybridisation that both challenges and reworks the (post)colonial dynamic. Harris and other postcolonial writers draw on hybrid forms of language and culture – such as creolised English – which typically emerged during the colonial era in order to challenge dominant colonial culture. Thus, postcolonial writing both expresses hybridity as it emerged through colonisation and reshapes identity through dynamic processes of rewriting and renewal.

Mestizaje and Borderlands

Gloria Anzaldúa (1942–2004) is one of the most significant contributors to theories of transcultural/transnational identity from a postcolonial perspective. Born in the Rio Grande Valley of South Texas, her father was a sharecropper, and she was raised on a series of corporate farms. From an early age, she worked in the fields with her family, and this working-class background shaped her postcolonial critique. Her grandmother was a healer, and Anzaldúa's writing practices can be seen as shaped by the shamanic tradition. Her *mestiza* (culturally and racially mixed) identity serves as a point of departure for an investigation of Chicana identity (American citizens of Mexican descent) and postcolonial concepts of cross-cultural

* The term 'metatextual' refers to a text that offers a critical commentary one or more other texts.

experience more generally. In the preface to the first edition of *Borderlands / La Frontera: The New Mestiza* (1987), she states: 'I am a border woman. I grew up between two cultures, the Mexican (with a heavy Indian influence) and the Anglo (as a member of a colonized people in our own territory)'.[19] She grounds her work in a postcolonial feminist critique of *mestizaje* (intermixing) from the Spanish colonisation of the New World to the articulation of Chicano identities in the lands that traverse present-day American and Mexican national borders. In form and content, her writing crosses the borders that separate cultures, languages, races/ethnicities and nations. Fittingly, this mixed text, which might also be seen as an example of textual hybridity, incorporates mixed modes of writing (poetry and prose), genres (including testimonial, history and mythology), languages (English, Spanish, Nahuatl and various dialects, such as Pachuco), and linguistic registers (from slang to academic idioms). Her reclamations of multicultural spaces and histories might be described as a celebration of a consciousness of borderlands:

> The actual physical borderland that I'm dealing with in this book is the Texas-U.S. Southwest/Mexican border. The psychological borderlands, the sexual borderlands and the spiritual borderlands are not particular to the Southwest. In fact, the Borderlands are physically present wherever two or more cultures edge each other, where people of different races occupy the same territory, where under, lower, middle and upper classes touch, where the space between two individuals shrinks with intimacy. (p. 19)

As this conception of borderlands suggests, her critique of (post) colonial formation extends from a critique of historical conditions to a critique of colonial discourses and the articulation of a postcolonial reconstruction of identity.

She recuperates a precolonial history of migration and multicultural identity as the basis for her postcolonial analysis of identity formation and transmutation. In the opening chapter to her work, entitled 'The Homeland, Aztlán / El otro México', Anzaldúa notes that the during 'the original peopling of the Americas, the first inhabitants migrated across the Bering Straits and walked south across the continent' (p. 26). Tracing histories of settlement and migration in America since 3500 BC, she is able to account for indigenous presence in territories now known as Texas, Mexico and Central America. Specifically, the Cochise people of the American Southwest are shown to be the parent culture of the Aztecs who would eventually come into contact with the Spanish in the sixteenth century. The contact and intermixture of Spanish and Indian peoples would produce 'una nueva raza, el mestizo, el mexicano' ('a new race, the mixed one, the Mexican') (p. 27). Continuous intermixing would produce an even greater *mestizaje* in the centuries that followed. Anzaldúa traces the subsequent history of wars at the borders of present-day Mexico and the United States during the nineteenth century, noting the ways in which the conflicts were accompanied by ideologies of white imperialism on the part of Americans. These colonial legacies would of course have a profound impact on the negative treatment of Chicanos in America, which eventually led to resistance in the form of the Chicano civil rights movements in the 1960s and 1970s.

Tracing these colonial legacies is essential for Anzaldúa because she wants to forward a postcolonial reclamation of cultural (and other) intermixtures. Specifically, she recuperates histories of the *mestiza* as the basis for articulating a new kind of cross-cultural consciousness at the borderlands, which is based on a continuous walking among cultures (p. 99). Despite claims that she belongs to all cultures at once and an occasional tendency to romanticise the precolonial past, her model of belonging remains highly ambivalent because it is shaped by the clash of voices and a resulting perpetual state of perplexity and transition, which she refers to as mental nepantilism, 'an Aztec word meaning torn between ways' (p. 100). She positions an (in)tolerance of ambiguity and contradiction as the outcome of the uneven, contested histories across cultures, races and borders. Thus, the 'borderlands' represent the breaking down of cultural boundaries as well as the ambivalent synthesis of different cultures, races and languages. This amalgamation results in a new awareness, the *mestiza* consciousness, which subverts traditional perspectives on cultural identities to create a multicultural paradigm. In terms of her influence, Anzaldúa's theory of borderlands has had a significant impact on the development of Chicano/Latino studies and literature as well as postcolonial constructions of cross-cultural formation, rhetorical practices of code-switching (switching between languages), ways of imagining the nation and theories of spatiality (notably, in the work of geopolitical theorist Edward Soja). Lucha Corpí's writing is heavily influenced by Anzaldúa, and Latin fictions which make use of code-switching might be read in dialogue with her work, such as Giannina Braschi, Gustavo Pérez Firmat and Chiqui Vicioso. Nonetheless, the power of her work derives from the specificities of her analysis. Anzaldúa's *Borderlands* suggests that identity is constructed across difference within the context of culturally specific power relations. Aware of the material conditions of existence, the lived histories of inequity, her auto-ethnographic analysis is attentive to the colonial contexts and legacies that haunt pluralised postcolonial identities, spaces and communities.

Debates about the Multicultural Society

In the postcolonial era, multiculturalism gradually emerged as a paradigm (in some instances, official State policy) for responding to the complex realities of national identity in light of decolonisation and increased immigration. In *Haunted Nations: The Colonial Dimensions of Multiculturalisms*, Sneja Marina Gunew observes that 'the relationship between multiculturalism and postcolonialism is an uneasy one', [20] primarily because the former 'deals with the often compromised management of geopolitical diversity in former imperial centres as well as their ex-colonies'.[21] Gunew argues that a 'critical multiculturalism' is needed in order to confront the ways in which diversity is managed by the State or becomes the basis for including a multiplicity of essentialist identities. Her observations are very much shaped by debates that emerged in the 1990s as well as the acknowledgement that there are various approaches to defining multiculturalism. Generally, multiculturalism implies a relationship between the majority culture and its minorities, which is sometimes seen as implying a white, Eurocentric identity as normative within the multicultural nation. In former British colonies, such as New Zealand, Canada and Australia, multiculturalism is typically categorised along the lines of race, ethnicity and indigeneity. In Canada, the use of the term 'visible minorities' is reflective of the ways in which the language of multiculturalism is often code for thinking in racialised terms. Avtar Brah has suggested that there is a 'minoritising move' inherent to multiculturalism, which often serves to reinforce a sense of marginalisation.[22] While this may be true of multiculturalism, the use of the term is sometimes said to subsume, ignore or marginalise the claims of indigenous peoples. In Australia, Aborigines prefer not to be included in multicultural discourses on the grounds that these refer to cultures of migration. In New Zealand, the Maori sovereignty movement places emphasis on biculturalism as a way to recognise the preconquest rights of inhabitants, their claims to culture and land rights. In Canada, indigenous rights are recognised separately, but also at times subsumed or sidelined by other debates about national identity. Moreover, the institution of multiculturalism as an official policy in Canada has often been seen as an attempt to work around or even disavow the tensions of bicultural French/English identity, which emerged during the colonial era, and later erupted in calls for Québec separatism.

The 1980s and 1990s saw the emergence of literary representations and debates which called into question the role and status of multiculturalism in postcolonial societies. In Britain, critics such as Stuart Hall and Paul Gilroy began calling attention to the prevalence of racism and the need for a politics of recognition and difference that would go beyond superficial constructs of multiculturalism, such as suggested by references to England as a nation of 'saris, samosas and steelbands'. In film, Hanif Kureishi's *My Beautiful Laundrette* (1985) offered a dramatic look at the ways in which the tensions of race, class, gender and sexuality were complicating a sense of multicultural identity under Thatcherism, while Salman Rushdie's novel *The Satanic Verses* (1988) became a touchstone for debates about multiculturalism following the *fatwa* and ensuing protests, book burnings and debates about Muslim identities.[23] Zadie Smith's *White Teeth* (2000), often cited as exemplary of multicultural Britain (or 'new Britain'), alludes to some of the fundamentalist demonstrations against *The Satantic Verses* in that her work includes a farcical scene in which Millat and his crew join protests against a novel they have not read, yet aver is blasphemous.[24] Yet, Smith also shows that the youths' desire to protest represents the return of repressed anger and resentment concerning ongoing ethnic discrimination in Britain. When Millat and his crew try to buy train tickets in order to attend the protest, the ticket man says, 'You little bastards. Can't tell me in English? Have to talk your Paki language?' (p. 231). Millat's response is equally vociferous; drawing on homophobic slang from various cultures to denigrate the vendor (p. 231). Ironically, this scene about multicultural tensions in society highlights shared cross-cultural values in the form of collective animosity towards homosexuality. In this respect, Smith undermines assumptions that the collective values of a multicultural society are intrinsically positive, suggesting the need for a critical, contested version of multiculturalism.

Neil Bissoondath's *Selling Illusions: The Cult of Multiculturalism in Canada* (1994) offered what would subsequently become a hotly debated critique of multiculturalism in Canada. Drawing on colonial history and migrant experience from Trinidad to Canada, Bissoondath argued for the need to foster '[a] nation of cultural hybrids, where every individual is unique, every individual distinct'.[25] His idea of vigorous multiculturalism as opposed to either tolerance or marginalisation emerged from a hybrid critique of colonial legacies within the Caribbean and Canada. The difficulties that nonwhite immigrants in multicultural Canada have faced are not only evident in Bissoondath's novels and stories but also in works by Lillian Allen, Austin Clarke, Michael Ondaatje, Marlene Nourbese-Philip and Dionne Brand, to name a few. Brand's recent novel, *What We All Long For* (2005), offers an ambivalent view of multiculturalism in Canada. On the one hand, Brand celebrates the diversity of multiculturalism in Toronto, a global city that is home to peoples from around the world. On the other hand, Brand calls attention to the ways in which the emphasis on multiculturalism in the contemporary world can serve to conceal and disavow the long history of colonial oppression and violence. For example, in one key passage she highlights the diversity of Toronto as a multicultural city as well as reclaims the largely forgotten history of Canada's indigenous peoples and their claims to the land. There are Italian, Vietnamese, Chinese, Ukrainian, Korean and African communities in Toronto but none of them know or care about the history of the land they stand on 'because that genealogy is wilfully untraceable except in the name of the city itself.' Brand describes them as people 'who are used to the ground beneath them shifting, and they want it all to stop – and if that means they must pretend to know nothing, well, that's the sacrifice they make'.[26] The very grounds of the city, which embody an effaced multicultural history, are disavowed by people who fail to make the connections between their own traumatic histories of transnational experience and those of others. Such a vision is indicative of the continuing need for a decolonising approach to multiculturalism.

By the end of the 1990s, prior to the events of 9/11, many critics claimed that multiculturalism had prevailed over other approaches to diversity, such as the American conception of the 'melting pot'. Neera Chandhoke claimed that the rise of multiculturalism meant the end of the 'grand vision' of the culturally homogeneous nation-state, of national integration.[27] In *We Are All Multiculturalists Now* (1997), Nathan Frazer expressed his regrets about the price Americans have had to pay for the so-called 'failure of assimilation'.[28] While Will Kymlicka celebrated the notion that 'multiculturalists have won the day',[29] Yasmin Alibhai-Brown's *After Multiculturalism* (2000) proposed that multiculturalism was no longer a viable paradigm in a post-multicultural age. The events of 9/11 challenged various assumptions about the attainment of multiculturalism as issues of race, faith and minority rights once again came to the foreground in the 'war against terror', the rise of a new security-conscious era, and the war in Afghanistan. Mohsin Hamid's novel *The Reluctant Fundamentalist* (2007) dramatises the ways in which the legacies of colonialism, particularly with respect to race-thinking, and the limits of American multiculturalism, already evident before 9/11, intensify after the trauma as interethnic tensions increase, racial profiling takes place and regressive forms of nationalism resurface.[30] Postcolonial criticism highlights the need to consider the continuities and discontinuities of race and racisms, imperialism(s) and hostility to the other in (trans)national literatures and political contexts.

From a postcolonial perspective, there has been a growing recognition that the presence of the incommensurate, of differences at play in the world, demands a more complicated engagement with multiculturalism: one that is responsive to the fragmented but interlinked relations among places, spaces and communities in the world. Recent studies in multiculturalism, such as Tariq Modood's *Multiculturalism* (2007) and *Multicultural Politics: Racism, Ethnicity and Muslims in Britain* (2005), approach multiculturalism as a form of political theory and practice. While multiculturalism as a benevolent form of 'tolerance' or a kind of bandage solution to the contradictions, fissures and diversity of the contemporary nation has proven to be an unviable paradigm, we nonetheless need to consider how to respond to the realities of a uneven global order in which societies are now composed of peoples from different histories, backgrounds, cultures, contexts, experiences and positions. Debates about the processes of intermixture, which originated in colonial contexts, are not only of historic and cultural relevance but also enable the kind of critical thinking that is required as individuals, communities and nations continue to come to terms with the meaning of multiculturalism in the long histories of empire and globalisation. This is not to say that the old paradigms will suffice. Increasingly, dynamic relations among peoples and communities around the world as well as within the nation, particularly between generations of migrants, require a more flexible approach to the representation and analysis of the multicultural society.

Notes

1 Fernando Ortiz, *Cuban Counterpoint: Tobacco and Sugar*, Harriet de Onis (trans.) (Durham, NC: Duke University Press, 1995), pp. 102–3.
2 Mary Louise Pratt, *Imperial Eyes: Travel Writing and Transculturation* (London: Routledge, 1992), p. 8.
3 Kamau Brathwaite, *The Development of Creole Society in Jamaica, 1770–1820* (Oxford: Clarendon, 1971), p. xv.
4 Ibid., p. 296.
5 Ibid., p. 300.
6 See Derek Walcott, *Collected Poems: 1948–1984* (New York: The Noonday Press, 1987), p. 346.
7 Jean Rhys, *A Norton Critical Edition: Wide Sargasso Sea*, Judith L. Raiskin (ed.) (New York: W. W. Norton & Company, 1999), p. 39.
8 Louise Bennett, 'Colonization in Reverse', in James Procter (ed.), *Writing Black Britain, 1948–1998: An Interdisciplinary Anthology* (Manchester: Manchester University Press, 2000), p. 16.
9 Kathleen M. Balutansky and Marie-Agnès Souriearu, *Caribbean Creolization: Reflections on the Cultural Dynamics of Language, Literature, and Identity* (Gainesville: University Press of Florida, 1998), p. 3.
10 See Wendy Knepper, 'Colonization, Creolization and Globalization: The Arts and Ruses of Bricolage', *Small Axe* 21 (2006): pp. 70–86; and Michaeline Crichlow, *Globalization and the Post-Creole Imagination: Notes on Fleeing the Plantation* (Durham, NC: Duke University Press, 2009).
11 See, for example, Graham Huggan, 'Opting Out of the (Critical) Common Market: Creolization and the Post-Colonial Text', *Kunapipi* 11.1 (1989), pp. 27–40; Chris Bongie, *Islands and Exiles: The Creole*

Identities of Post/Colonial Literatures (Stanford, CT: Stanford University Press, 1998), pp. 423–5.

12 Linda Moss, 'Biculturalism and Cultural Identity', *International Journal of Cultural Policy*, 11.2 (2005), p. 191.

13 Keri Hulme, *The Bone People* (Auckland: Spiral, 1985), p. 12.

14 Robert Young, *Colonial Desire: Hybridity in Theory, Culture and Race* (London: Routledge, 1995), p. 6. Quotation marks appear in the original as cited.

15 See Young's chapter on 'Hybridity and Diaspora', ibid., pp. 1–29.

16 Néstor García Canclini, *Hybrid Cultures: Strategies for Entering and Leaving Modernity* (Minneapolis: University of Minnesota Press, 1995), p. xxv.

17 Ibid., p. xxxi.

18 Homi K. Bhabha, *The Location of Culture* (London: Routledge, 1994), p. 37.

19 Gloria Anzaldúa, *Borderlands / La Frontera: The New Mestiza*, 2nd edition (San Francisco: Aunt Lute Books, 1999), p. 19.

20 Sneja Marina Gunew, *Haunted Nations: The Colonial Dimensions of Multiculturalisms* (London: Routledge, 2004), p. 8.

21 Ibid., p. 15.

22 Avtar Brah, *Cartographies of Diaspora: Contesting Identities* (London: Routledge, 1996), p 235.

23 For a recent discussion of the post-*fatwa* reception of *The Satanic Verses*, see Ruvani Ranasinha, *The Cambridge Companion to Salman Rushdie* (Cambridge: Cambridge University Press, 2007), pp. 45–60.

24 Zadie Smith, *White Teeth* (London: Penguin Books, 2000), p. 234.

25 Neil Bissoondath, *Selling Illusions: The Cult of Multiculturalism in Canada* (Toronto: Penguin Books, 1994), p. 224.

26 Dionne Brand, *What We All Long For* (Toronto, Vintage, 2005), p. 4.

27 Neera Chandhoke, 'The logic of recognition?', *Seminar* (India) 484 (December 1999), p. 35. See online resource at www.india-seminar.com (accessed 15 August 2010).

28 Frazer observes that multiculturalism 'is not a phase we can embrace wholeheartedly, and I hope my own sense of regret that we have come to this will not escape the reader'. See Frazer's *We Are All Multiculturalists Now* (Cambridge, MA: Harvard University Press, 1997), p. 21.

29 Will Kymlicka, 'Comments on Shachar and Spinner-Halev', in C. Joppke and S. Lukes (eds), *Multicultural Questions* (Oxford: Oxford University Press, 1999), p. 113.

30 For an excellent discussion of multiculturalism in America, especially after 9/11, see Anna Hartnell, 'Moving through America: Race, Place and Resistance in Mohsin Hamid's *The Reluctant Fundamentalist*', *Journal of Postcolonial Writing* 46.3 (July 2010): pp. 336–48.

Postcoloniality in a Globalising World

Since 1989 and the fall of the Berlin Wall, our understanding of the world order and the purpose of postcolonial criticism have both undergone a fundamental shift. The sense that the world could be explained through older conceptions of empire (whether related to the colonial past or to Cold War dynamics) has given way to the notion that we are now living in a complex world order that can no longer be understood in terms of centre–periphery models and nationalistic paradigms. Increasingly, the world is seen as globalised: interrelated and bound together by transnational flows of commodities, peoples, ideas and capital. Roland Robertson observes that '[g]lobalisation as a concept refers both to the compression of the world and the intensification of consciousness of the world as a whole'[1] while Jan Aart Scholte argues that globalisation entails a significant transformation in social space which creates 'links between people located at points anywhere on the earth'[2] and enables global relations 'as exchanges within a planetary realm'.[3] Globalisation manifests itself in virtually every aspect of life: communications, production, markets, finance, organisations, the military, the management of the environment, health, law and consciousness. Scholte notes that globalisation is a distinctly recent phenomenon: it should not be confused with other transnational concepts such as internationalisation (the growth of interdependence among countries), liberalisation (the idea of a borderless economy or global capitalism), universalisation (dispersal of ideas and experiences with an emphasis on a homogenous or universal perspective) and Westernisation. Globalisation introduces a radically new way of thinking about social and spatial relations, identities, economic interdependencies, and imagined and lived communities.

Globalisation may be recent, but the history of how we have come to live in a globalising world is a long one. Colonialism has contributed to the emergence of our globalising world: creating new points of connection and relation among peoples and places as well as enabling the rise of the global economy. In an essay entitled 'Beyond Discipline? Globalization and the Future of English', Paul Jay highlights Roland Robertson's assertion that globalisation 'predates modernity and has been evolving at least since the fifteenth century'.[4] Jay observes that key moments in this long evolution include:

> the collapse of Christendom, the development of maps and maritime travel, the rise of the nation-state, global exploration, colonialism, the creation of citizenship, passports, diplomacy and the entire paraphernalia of international relations, the rise of international communication and mass migration … and a developing sense that communities based on race, ethnicity, gender, sexual preference, and so on, cut across national and state boundaries.[5]

Postcolonial perspectives remain relevant in a globalising world because of this enabling history as well as through the persistence of colonial legacies and the continuation of decolonising processes. Yet, many question the explanatory power of the postcolonial paradigm in a new world order, which can no longer be explained by competing nationalisms or colonial models of expansionism. Thinking about the role of postcolonial literature in a world where notions of empire and world citizenship are changing has been one of the challenges of recent years. This chapter begins with a brief overview of approaches to globalisation and a reading of Hari Kunzru's *Transmission* (2004), a novel about the globalising world of technological, media and migrant flows. The remainder of the chapter focuses on two key debates: the meaning of empire and the definition of world citizenship or cosmopolitanism in a globalising world. The chapter closes with a reading of the 'hood' (neighbourhood) and citizenship in Zadie Smith's *On Beauty* (2005).

Changing Relations to Time and Space

Changing relations to space and time are defining characteristics of globalisation. For Anthony Giddens, globalisation entails 'the intensification of worldwide social relations which link distant localities in such a way that local happenings are shaped by events occurring many miles away and vice versa'.[6] James Rosenau observes that we live in a world of 'distant proximities in which the forces pressing for greater globalization and those inducing greater localization interactively play themselves out'.[7] Rosenau suggests that distance might be defined as follows:

> Distance is not measured only in miles across land and sea; it can also involve less tangible spaces, more abstract conceptions in which distance is assessed across organizations, hierarchies, event sequences, social strata, market relationships, migration patterns, and a host of other nonterritorial spaces. (p. 6)

He observes that there is 'no self-evident line that divides the distant from the proximate' (p. 6). Moreover, in the post-9/11 world, the sense of a barrier to the world outside has been destroyed for many Americans because the destruction of the Twin Towers in Manhattan demonstrated that America was susceptible to attacks. Rosenau sees evidence of a world undergoing 'fragmegration', which suggests 'the pervasive interaction between fragmenting and interacting dynamics unfolding at every level of community' (p. 11). Through travel, broadcast media, internet communications, complex economic interdependencies and the flows of transnational capital, various spatial practices have profoundly destabilised our understanding of borders and distance. To offer an everday example, the use of social network and (micro)blogging technologies, such as facebook and twitter, allow people around the world to be aware of activities taking place in real time. The sense of contact – community – is now enabled by transnational communications. But we also need to consider who is unable to access such technologies, whether as a result of economic or technological challenges, and who is thus shut out of certain aspects of the globalising world. In this respect, globalisation often perpetuates disjunctures and failures to connect and communicate. We might also consider the ways in which global production, for example the import of cheap clothing, tends to exploit certain regions and peoples of the world and favour others, and how our daily engagement with local communities, the nation and transnational communities enables us to relate to place and space in diverse ways.

As a result of technology, the speed at which we travel, communicate and trade has accelerated in the post-war period, especially through the 1990s with the rise of internet culture. David Harvey suggests that time-space compression 'has had a disorienting and disruptive impact upon political-economic practices, the balance of class power, as well as upon cultural and social life'.[8] For the sociologist Manuel Castells, relations to space have changed profoundly in our network society in which a 'space of flows' exists alongside the 'place of spaces'.[9] While the former operates in a deterritorialised fashion (one no longer contained by a region or national boundaries), linking peoples around the world, especially through technology, the place of spaces remains linked to physical locations, such as neighbourhoods. Castells suggests that cultural, political and physical bridges are needed between the space of flows (globalisation) and the place of spaces (localisation) so that we do not head toward life in two parallel universes that cannot meet.[10] We need to find ways to integrate our relationships with neighbourhoods and with the world. Thus, it is important to note that globalisation may be on the rise, but it has not wholly displaced other forms of worldly relations. Any critique of the contemporary world order should thus take into account a plurality of ways of dwelling in the world, examining shifting relations in time, space, place and connection.

In *Modernity at Large*, Arjun Appadurai offers a compelling way of thinking about the changes happening in the world today through his discussion of the importance of the imaginary and the '-scapes' of globalisation. 'The new global cultural economy', Appadurai notes, 'has to be seen as a complex disjunctive order that cannot any longer be understood in terms of existing center–periphery models (even those that account for multiple centers and peripheries'.[11] He identifies five dimensions for examining disjunctive global cultural flows: ethnoscapes (landscape of shifting peoples, including migrants, tourists, refugees, guest workers and so forth), financescapes (the global economy), mediascapes (media circulations), technoscapes (the global flows associated with technology and the IT sector) and ideoscapes (ideas about the state and justice). The suffix '-scape' allows us to point to the fluid, irregular shapes of these landscapes and indicates that 'these are not objectively given relations that look the same from every angle of vision, but, rather, that they are deeply perspectival constructs, inflected by the historical, linguistic, and political situatedness of different sorts of actors'. These actors include: nation-states, multinationals, diasporic communities,* subnational groupings and movements, and intimate groups, such as villages, neighbourhoods and families. Appadurai extends Benedict Anderson's notion of the imagined community. For Anderson, the nation is a socially constructed community, imagined by its members. Even

* The term 'diaspora' (meaning dispersion) initially referred to the scattering of Jewish peoples as a result of several forced expulsions from what is now known as Israel, Jordan and parts of Lebanon as well as the State of Palestine. Subsequently, 'diaspora' has come to refer more generally to the movement, migration or scattering of a people away from a settled location or ancestral homeland..

though we cannot see everyone in the imagined community of the nation, we are brought together by a sense of belonging to a particular kind of collective. Appadurai says that we need now to refer to imagined worlds, 'constituted by the historically situated imaginations of persons and groups spread around the globe'. Through imagined worlds, Appadurai suggests that peoples are able 'to contest and sometimes even subvert the imagined worlds of the official mind and of the entrepreneurial mentality that surrounds them'. For example, members of the antiglobalisation movements, such as the Peoples' Global Action, often protest and demonstrate against exploitative practices of globalisation, particularly at global summits. In doing so, they aim to challenge governments and global organisations, such the World Bank and International Monetary Fund, to change their policies and practices.

Writing in a Globalising World: Hari Kunzru's *Transmission*

Hari Kunzru's *Transmission* (2004) offers a parodic look at globalisation, tracing events in the life of Arjun Mehta, an Indian cybergeek who travels to America on a temporary work visa as a migrant labourer in the IT sector. Global financescapes are invoked as he enters into the boom-and-bust flows of the world economy. He enters a household in a low-income neighbourhood, populated by young migrant workers like himself. Paid a salary of US$500 a week, half of which is deducted for housing, he finds that he has joined the ranks of indentured labourers in the twenty-first century.* This reference to indenture provides a reminder that the global economy has a long history that dates back to colonialism and the coerced migration of peoples under the global imperial economy. This connection is made clear when his colleagues and

* Indenture is a process whereby labourers enter into a contract for a set period of time in exchange for their ocean transportation, food, clothing, lodging and other necessities during the term of the contract. They are not, however, paid a wage for their work.

housemates make the following observation about their recruitment contact: '"When she looks at us," Salim complained, watching out of the window as she started her car, "she sees a bunch of starving coolies"'.[12] Thus, we also get a sense of how ethnoscapes – the flows of migrants around the world – are linked to a long history of global capital, exploitation and ethnic stereotyping.

Culture too is deterritorialised (constructed across borders) and reterritorialised (reformulated at local, regional or national levels) through globalising exchanges, albeit in a superficial manner. Arjun's sister, Priti, works for a global call centre based in India, which teaches her to lose her Indian accent and adopt an Australian one, and requires that she change her name so that she will be more able to serve the local customer base; thus, she undergoes a superficial assimilation into Australian culture as she comes to learn trivia and idioms needed to thrive in the global economy. Meanwhile Guy Swift, an entrepreneur, speaks the language of global branding and marketing: '[h]is communication facilitation stood out from the crowd. Engaging and impactful, for some years he had also been consistently cohesive, integrated and effective over a spread spectrum' (p. 20). This jargon-filled discourse cannot protect him from fears that he will tumble, suffering a fall from grace in the 'constant cycle of fall and recovery' or '[b]oom and bust' (p. 22).

The intersections of mediascapes and technoscapes – underpinned by financescapes and ethnoscapes – are at the heart of the novel's parodic subversion of globality. Arjun's decision to leave India and travel to the United States as a migrant worker is inspired by a Bollywood film, entitled *Naughty, Naughty, Lovely, Lovely* or *N2L2*. Kunzru's satirical account of this film describes events in the life of Dilip, a college-educated youth who is content to 'laze around' (p. 34) on his father's farm in the Punjab until he meets Aparna, 'a beauty from London, back in the old country to visit her relatives' (p. 35). Aparna, played by a legendary Bollywood actress named Leela Zahir, has traditional cultural values but is also an ambitious investment banker. To win her heart, Dilip realises that he must achieve success in the international capital markets, which he does successfully. The volatile nature of global capital and its threats to romance are represented as the hero struggles to win the love of Aparna. This Bollywood fantasy plays an important role in Arjun's life for it inspires him to become a migrant worker, and when that dream is threatened, he seizes on the globally circulating image of Leela Zahir as the source of his salvation. An image of the dancing actress becomes the front-end visual for a computer virus that he unleashes. The virus, which brings down companies around the world, can be seen as satirising what Rita Raley refers to as eEmpire or Electronic Empire: 'the triumphant narrative of technology and capitalism', which 'comprises communicative networks, electronic commerce, modes of production, and global finance markets'.[13] Kunzru undermines the celebratory narrative of eEmpire through his account of Arjun's act of viral terrorism. Arjun creates the virus hoping that he will be able to save his job and generate income for his employer by providing the anti-viral solution. Much to Arjun's dismay, the virus propagates successfully and he is forced to flee because he is being hunted down as an e-terrorist.

Events in the lives of other characters also focus on dramatic encounters in a globalising world. For instance, the lives of Guy Swift and Leela Zahir are deterritorialised and reterritorialised through the intersecting global flows of media, finance, migration and technology. In cyberspace, the viral Leela appears as a dancing figure who is propagated throughout the world, creating havoc wherever she goes. On the set of a new film, Leela, the actress, is beset by reporters once the news of the virus breaks. Eventually, she flees the set, seeking to get away from the trappings of her globalised identity. Her tale of self-exile is juxtaposed against a story of forced migration and protest against rampant transnational capitalism. Global marketer, Guy Swift, who is the head of Tomorrow, 'a truly globalized branding agency, concentrating on the needs of transnational clients' (p. 180), falls from grace. He meets a prospective client, called PEBA, who specialise in transnational security through informatics* and border services. They aim to enable a common border authority in order to prevent the free flow of terrorists and unauthorised circulation of economic migrants (p. 252). Swift envisions rebranding Europe as an exclusive continent, available only to members of Club Europa. PEBA will be positioned as the transnational gatekeeper. Citizens will be encouraged to think of themselves in commodified terms as VIP customers who can gain entry to Europe (p. 257). Ironically, Swift's corporate pitch fails when the Leela virus strikes his computer. Then, Swift himself is mistakenly picked up in one of PEBA's coordinated sweeps aimed at taking 5,000 illegal immigrants off the streets and rehoming them. Branded as an illegal immigrant, Swift is identified as Albanian and deported, but manages to find his way to Italy, nearly drowning in transit. However, he finds that he can no longer fit back into the world order in a complacent fashion. He grows a beard and becomes an outspoken protester against globalisation. Both Leela and Arjun disappear, but their images and the mythology surrounding them live on, circulating freely. Thus, Kunzru calls attention to the disjunctive workings of the global order, leaving the reader to assess what sense might be made of these evacuated lives.

Empire Revisited

For Michael Hardt and Antonio Negri, the meaning of empire has changed profoundly in the contemporary globalising world. In their critical study, *Empire* (2000), they observe:

* Informatics refers to the science of information, the practice of information processing and the engineering of information systems. For instance, it may involve the use of computers and digital reporting tools to manage information and provide services. In the case of *Transmission*, records about illegal immigrants are being used to help workers identify who needs to be rounded up and expulsed from the country.

> Empire is materializing before our very eyes. Over the past several decades, as colonial regimes were overthrown and then precipitously after the Soviet barriers to the capitalist world market finally collapsed, we have witnessed an irresistible and irreversible globalization of economic and cultural exchange. Along with the global order and global circuits of production has emerged a global order, a new logic and structure of rule – in short, a new form of sovereignty. Empire is the political subject that effectively regulates these global exchanges, the sovereign power that governs the world.[14]

For Hardt and Negri, the idea of sovereignty has changed: 'The sovereignty of the nation-state was the cornerstone of the imperialisms that Europe constructed through the modern era' (p. xii). They note that imperialism in this form has represented an extension of the powers and influence of the nation-state beyond their own delimited territorial boundaries to other places in the world. The coding of the world into various imperial holdings under British, Spanish, French and other dominions suggested that sovereignty was still bounded by recognisable territorial concerns and interests. In their view, even neoimperialism, in the form of American power and influence over world economy and politics, no longer suffices as a means to understand the changing world order. By contrast, Empire (which is not the same as imperialism and colonialism for Hardt and Negri) refers to a sense of sovereignty that 'establishes no territorial centre of power and does not rely on fixed boundaries or barriers' (p. xii): 'it is a *decentered* and *deterritorializing* apparatus of rule that progressively incorporates the entire global realm within its open, expanding frontiers' (p. xii). Empire has the following characteristics. Spatially, it encompasses the entire world and is not limited by territorial boundaries. Temporally, Empire is 'not a historical regime originating in conquest' but rather 'an order that effectively suspends history' (p. xiv). It operates on all levels of the social order (p. xv), and is dedicated to peace even though its practices may entail violence. These observations lead the writers to conclude that postcolonial studies has become an historical field, which fails to offer a viable paradigm for interrogating the changing world order.

Specifically, Hardt and Negri observe that postcolonial theory has limited explanatory power:

> The postcolonialist perspective remains primarily concerned with colonial sovereignty. As Gyan Prakash says, 'The postcolonial exists as an aftermath, as an after – after being worked over by colonialism.' This may make postcolonialist theory a very productive tool for rereading history, but it is entirely insufficient for theorizing contemporary global power. ... [Edward Said] charges that 'the tactics of the great empires ... are being replicated by the U.S.' What is missing here is a recognition of the novelty of the structures and logics of power that order the contemporary world. Empire is not a weak echo of modern imperialisms but a fundamentally new form of rule. (p. 146)

Hardt and Negri are critical of the work of thinkers such as Edward Said and Homi Bhabha because they believe that it remains focused on colonial centres of power rather than the modern notion of empire, which is no longer centralised (p. 145). It is debatable whether these observations were entirely accurate at the time, nonetheless, the authors provoked a general reaction in the field of postcolonial studies. Subsequent debates in the field, including contributions by Bhabha himself, have addressed some of these concerns. Indeed, Bhabha has extended his work on ambivalence,* developed as part of a critique of colonialism, to the analysis of the globalising world.[15]

This definition of Empire has been much debated, particularly in light of security concerns and the events following 9/11. The increased patrolling of national borders and the resurgence of American imperialism have tended to undermine Hardt and Negri's claims that Empire is the prevailing modality in the global order. The

* See Part Four: 'Cross-cultural Paradigms', for a discussion of ambivalence.

wars in Iraq and Afghanistan have been cited as evidence that American imperialism continues to shape events in the global order, especially in terms of socio-economic, political and military developments. Nonetheless, Hardt and Negri's *Empire* has fundamentally challenged postcolonial critics and contributed to a shift in the field. The editors of *Postcolonial Studies and Beyond* (2005) pose the question as follows:

> Some scholars view postcolonial methods and vocabularies as out of step with an intellectual scene increasingly carved up by rubrics such as the information age (the so-called digital divide), transnational capital, globalization, and alternative modernities. What, then, is the value of postcolonial studies in our globalizing world, and does it have a viable future beyond its existing life span, identified by Vilashini Cooppan in this volume as the period from Edward Said's *Orientalism* (1978) to Michael Hardt and Antonio Negri's *Empire* (2000)?[16]

Arguably, the most innovative and interesting work in postcolonial literary criticism today attempts to address this question, to which the editors and contributors to this collection offer a number of innovative responses. They 'trace unexpected and uneven developments before, during, and after colonial modernity' (p. 4). Through an attentiveness to the long history of globality, the critics suggest a need to go beyond 'a shallow embrace of the contemporary notion of the global' (p. 4).

Where Hardt and Negri see a clear distinction between two modes of imperialism (colonialism and Empire), Simon Gikandi resituates the debate in his article entitled 'Globalization and the Claims of Postcoloniality' when he observes that writers on globalization and postcolonialism share two common topics of debate:

> they are concerned with explaining forms of social and cultural organization whose ambition is to transcend the boundaries of

> the nation-state, and they seek to provide new vistas for understanding cultural flows that can no longer be explained by a homogenous Eurocentric narrative of development and social change.[17]

Unlike Hardt and Negri, who offer a reductive view of postcolonial theory, Gikandi shows that postcolonial literary critics have long been concerned with the wider questions raised by colonialism, which extend beyond the colonialists' conception of their own imperial and nationalist interests.

Gikandi does not directly address Hardt and Negri's ideas in his essay, but we might consider the implications of his argument. His analysis of disjuncture and difference in the global order shows that postcolonial criticism has a wider scope than Hardt and Negri seem willing to concede. Gikandi points out that globalisation theory draws on the critical vocabulary of postcolonial studies. That said, he highlights the need for new approaches to narrative in the global order by bringing postcolonial perspectives and globalisation into dialogue:

> Is globalization a real or virtual phenomenon? Where do we locate postcoloniality – in the space between and across cultures and traditions or in national states, which, in spite of a certain crisis of legitimacy, still continue to demand affiliation from their citizens and subjects? These questions are made even more urgent by the realization that while we live in a world defined by cultural and economic flows across formally entrenched boundaries, the world continues to be divided, in stark terms, between its 'developed' and 'underdeveloped' sectors. It is precisely because of this division that the discourse of globalization seems to be perpetually caught between two competing narratives, one of celebration, the other of crisis. (p. 628)

The oscillations between celebration and crisis have already been seen in Kunzru's *Transmission*, which dramatises the highs and lows of belonging to and expulsion from the global order. Where Kunzru shows the collapse of middle-class aspiration, Gikandi calls attention to the fate of two Guinean boys whose dead bodies were found in the cargo hold of a plane in Brussels in 1998. They flew to Europe in order to seek asylum and refuge from 'war, sickness, hunger, lack of education' (p. 630). Such a narrative draws attention to 'the disjuncture between the emergence of global images and the global stories of global subjects ... who are not concerned with ideas or images, but are focused on the material experiences of everyday life and survival' (p. 632). Gikandi suggests that media representations and intellectual discussions about globalisation do not always adequately capture the realities of the situation.

Postcolonial criticism can address these shortcomings because it is attentive to the material conditions of life and the lives of the disenfranchised. Here then is the role for postcolonial literature and criticism: 'Postcolonial literature is not, of course, deaf to the disjuncture between its performance of a global culture and the persistence of this other, darker, older narrative of poverty, of failed nationalism, of death, that will simply not go away' (p. 639). For Gikandi, 'the rhetoric of globalization is constantly undermined by the resurgence of older forms of nationalism, patriotism, and fundamentalism' (p. 640). Bringing postcolonial theory and globalisation into dialogue is thus a means to address the discrepancies between the surface rhetoric and branding of globalisation and the realities of living in a global world.

Gikandi is not alone in pointing out the need for new approaches to reading postcolonial and world literatures. In 'East African Literature and Global Reading', Peter J. Kalliney offers a reading of M. G. Vassanji's novel *The Gunny Sack* (1989),* which explores the blind spots of postcolonial criticism and opens up new ways of reading globalisation through its long historical formation. This epic work traces four generations of a South Asian family history, following the migration from India to East Africa in the late

* A gunny sack is an inexpensive bag, typically made of burlap. This bag is normally used to carry grains or other agricultural products.

nineteenth century and subsequently from Tanzania to North America. The novel's attentiveness to the long history of trade in the Indian Ocean highlights events in the long history of globalism. These events show that alternative formations of globality have unfolded alongside and through empire. Kalliney argues that there is a need to be attentive to the drama of unfolding history, which entails unforeseen events:

> The novel's recovery of this other global history is a rejection not only of imperial narratives of conquest, but also of current narratives of globalization that rely on imperial systems of historical knowledge. Foregrounding contingencies and conflicts in the history of empires, past and present, may better equip us for understanding the contemporary world and the range of responses at our disposal.[18]

If our colonial past is not to be read merely as a predecessor to globalisation, the literary critic needs to revisit the (post)colonial from a new angle: attentive to global history and experiences that cannot be explained merely through reference to competition among empires to settle and govern the world.

Postcolonial writers offer divergent views on the globalising era. To offer one example, in 'Of Berlin and Other Walls' (1990), Wole Soyinka points out that the fall of the Wall does not mean the demise of postcolonial perspectives. Indeed, he points out that the legacies of colonialism, inequity and oppression continue to exist alongside new forms of imperialism, both of which require interrogation. He speaks out against religious fundamentalism, citing the *fatwa* against Salman Rushdie, dictatorships, political oppression and continuing economic disparities. Soyinka declares: 'The issue of power – and, its corollary, freedom – will, I believe, occupy the twenty-first century man, on the level at which ideology has preoccupied us, the nations emergent from colonial domination'.[19] Yet, this does not mean a disregard for the lessons of the past, as Soyinka suggests when he observes that 'Africa must remain the elephant of history; her memory should be accounted legendary because she has much to remember. Her scars are not just part of her general history; each scar is labelled, catalogued, and visible' (pp. 211–12). Speaking more generally, he asserts that 'no people can escape their history' and 'it is not merely a geography that is physically invested by conquerors, but a cultural and philosophical actuality that then becomes weakened in turn by the very erosion of its geographical and economic autonomy' (p. 212). In a globalising world, the Berlin Wall serves as a symbolic point of departure, attesting to 'the unnaturalness, the inherent insult and denigration of our humanity, of the very imposition of any form of dictatorship under whatever colour, purpose, or ideology' (pp. 212–13). Perhaps over optimistically, Soyinka declares that '[t]he era of shameless opportunism is over' (p. 213). Yet, as evidence of the 'seemingly global wave of liberation', he points to the figure of Nelson Mandela and argues that apartheid should end. Soyinka's prescient critique of capitalism and fundamentalist ideology ends with a call for an end to global theocratic terror and 'the apparatus of repression embedded in governance without choice' (p. 215) in the twenty-first century. However, the events of 9/11 and the political aftermath, including the wars in Iraq and Afghanistan as well as the detentions at Guantanamo Bay, have proved otherwise.

Cosmopolitanism

The revival and revision of cosmopolitan thinking has informed postcolonial theory in recent years, especially as a means of thinking about citizenship and identity beyond the confines of nationalism, patriotism and empire. Contemporary discourses about cosmopolitanism revive but also revise earlier notions of this concept, which dates back to Diogenes' (*c.* 412–323 BC) claim to be a citizen of the world. The notion of a citizen of the world resurfaces in the work of Montaigne (1533–92) and features widely in Enlightenment discourses, which tend to associate the cosmopolitan with idealised communities of justice and morality. The idea of cosmopolitanism is explicitly found in the works of Immanuel Kant (1724–1804), particularly his *Idea for a Universal History with a Cosmopolitan Purpose* (1784) and *Perpetual Peace* (1795). The Kantian notion of hospitality as a form of cosmopolitanism offers a similar paradigm, suggesting that the world should be home to all. However, critics continue to debate the meaning of the term and question to what extent cosmopolitanism can be recuperated by postcolonial theory. 'Cosmopolitanism,' Anthony Pagden argues, cannot be easily 'separated from some kind of "civilizing" mission', for it is 'a philosophy particularly well suited to the spread of empire'.[20] In calling people to belong to one world, there is often an imperialist agenda, which privileges a particular cultural perspective.

In the contemporary world, Bruce Robbins offers another explanation of why cosmopolitanism might seem unattractive from a postcolonial perspective:

> Beyond the adjectival sense of 'belonging to all parts of the world; not restricted to any one country or its inhabitants,' the word cosmopolitan immediately evokes the image of a privileged person: someone who can claim to be a 'citizen of the world' by virtue of independent means, high-tech tastes, and globe-trotting mobility.[21]

This idea of a kind of jet set figure offers an elitist view of cosmopolitanism, which seems more aligned with financial privilege and the rise of global capitalism than with notions of citizenship. Citing John Stuart Mill, Robbins observes: '"Capital," Mill writes in 1848, "is becoming more and more cosmopolitan." Cosmopolitanism would seem to mimic capital in seizing for itself the privilege (to paraphrase Wall Street) of "knowing no boundaries"' (p. 171).* In this sense, cosmopolitanism not only entails a certain cultural and

* Robbins is referring to the mentality of those who represent New York-based financial interests. Wall Street is the financial district of New York City, which is a global financial centre.

moral perspective, but is dependent on one's position in the globalising economy, which favours some over others.

Yet, Robbins argues, in a globalising world, one can no longer tidily divide subjects into categories of local and cosmopolitan. 'Instead of renouncing cosmopolitanism as a false universal, one can embrace it as an impulse to knowledge that is shared with others, a striving to transcend partiality that is itself partial' (p. 181). By this, he means that all knowledge is partial; we may communicate with each other to learn more, but should still accept that knowledge will never be total and universal. Thus, he argues that we can speak of 'discrepant cosmopolitanisms', which offer differing or varying accounts of this notion of citizenship in the world. Such an approach would recognise that cosmopolitanism is 'neither a Western invention nor a Western privilege' (p. 182). He offers the examples of ancient Egyptian references to the notion as well as indigenous perspectives, such as offered by the author Rigoberta Menchú, a Guatemalan who has travelled the world in order to call attention to the plight of indigenous peoples and their struggle for justice. Other critics express similar views. While Arjun Appadurai suggests that cosmopolitanism needs to be rerouted in order to avoid 'presupposing either the authority of the Western experience or the models derived from that experience',[22] Benita Parry's account of global flows leads her to argue for an 'emergent postcolonial cosmopolitanism'.[23]

To gain a further sense of discrepant cosmopolitanisms, we might look more closely at various debates and critical perspectives. In the twentieth century, the term 'rootless cosmpolitanism' was applied to the Jewish population in Russia who were perceived as being insufficiently patriotic. The notion that cosmopolitanism runs counter to the interests of the nation thus surfaces when it comes to anxieties about citizenship and the presence of diasporic communities. Kwame Anthony Appiah (who has lived in Ghana, the United Kingdom and the United States) has sought to reconcile the ideas of cosmopolitanism and patriotism through 'rooted cosmopolitanism':

> The answer is straightforward: the cosmopolitan patriot can entertain the possibility of a world in which everyone is a rooted cosmopolitan, attached to a home of one's own, with its own cultural particularities, but taking pleasure from the presence of other, different places that are home to other, different people. The cosmopolitan also imagines that in such a world not everyone will find it best to stay in their natal patria, so that the circulation of people among different localities will involve not only cultural tourism (which the cosmopolitan admits to enjoying) but migration, nomadism, diaspora.[24]

Appiah notes that his concept of cosmopolitanism values 'the variety of human forms of social and cultural life' rather than a sense of citizenship in 'a homogeneous global culture'; he recognizes 'local differences (both within and between states)'. Moreover, by grounding his account of cosmopolitanism in personal experience, he suggests that kinship and politicised perspectives can underpin cosmopolitanism. Appiah quotes his father's exhortation to his children to remember that they are citizens of the world, an idea that is grounded in his father's long-term commitment to the United Nations (p. 213). This attempt to balance a sense of transnational belonging with attachments to a nation or community has become one of the defining features of recent cosmopolitanisms. Like Appiah, Rebecca Walkowitz highlights the idea of allegiances that transcend kin and kind, defining cosmopolitanism as 'a philosophical tradition that promotes allegiance to a transnational or global community … [and] an anthropological tradition that emphasizes multiple or flexible attachments to more than one nation or community'.[25]

In 'Unsatisfied: Notes on Vernacular Cosmpolitanism', Homi Bhabha offers a revisionary approach to cosmopolitanism, which he refers to as 'vernacular cosmopolitanisms': a concept that accommodates an appreciation of the tensions between local specificity and global enlightenment. He rejects the idea of a cosmopolitanism that places 'the "self" at the center of a series of concentric circles that move through the various cycles of familial, ethnic, and communal affiliation to "the largest one, that of humanity as a whole"'.[26] Instead, Bhabha remarks that we need to pay attention to the fissures in the social fabric and the impact of economic disjuncture. How do we account for refugees and the disenfranchised from a cosmopolitan perspective? Reference to world citizenship and the respect for human dignity hardly seem adequate. Bhabha suggests that cosmopolitanism must be envisioned from the perspective of the margins: from a sense of the insufficiency of the self (p. 43). Thus, he offers a model for a reconstructed cosmopolitan subject, which is attentive to the lives and identities of the disenfranchised. In this argument, we see a position similar to Simon Gikandi's earlier discussion of postcolonial reading practices as a way of calling attention to the lived realities of globalism. But Bhabha places emphasis on the role of the cosmopolitan imaginary, the ways in which individuals might become unrecognisable to themselves through worldly relations. The translational moment (when one attempts to think through diverse local and global approaches and perspectives) is important to hold onto because it 'does not attempt to harmonize the local and general, the poetic and political as an abstract identity' (p. 45). Vernacular cosmopolitanism acknowledges the singularity of events and peoples in the world.

Paul Gilroy takes up the notion of cosmopolitanism, establishing a black, postcolonial cosmopolitanism as an alternative to Eurocentric conceptions of this phenomenon. In a recent interview, Gilroy notes:

> I want in some ways to return to the notions of world history – of world citizenship – that [W. E. B.] Du Bois* constructs for us, and which of course were carried on in the twentieth century by social scientists and political activists. ... For me, following Du Bois, it's really about thinking of our planet as one place, of understanding the radical relationality of

* W. E. B. Du Bois (1868–1963) was an intellectual leader in the United States who challenged prevailing conceptions of race and racism on national and global levels.

> developments and, through that, understanding the pivotal power not only of European expansion and state-making but also of colonial administration, colonial government, and colonial war. Those processes produce the social relations we inhabit and, against our better judgment, naturalize most of the time.[27]

In *Against Race: Imagining Political Culture Beyond the Color Line*, Gilroy locates another kind of cosmopolitanism, grounded in the lived experiences of migrant African diasporic travellers:

> It involves considering the normative and ethical character of a distinctive cosmopolitan culture manifest in the lives and experiences of wartime black Atlantic itinerants and their successors: workers as well as students. These may have been fugitives from the United States seeking both culture and liberation from Jim Crow;* soldiers in pursuit of their citizenship and recognition they imagined they could find only by staking their lives on the battlefield in defense of their countries; or numerous other postwar travellers.[28]

Not only does he recuperate the lives of 'ordinary' black migrants, Gilroy points to Rhodes scholars as well as famous black wanderers, such as Josephine Baker, Jesse Owens and Joe Louis† as evidence of 'the rootless cosmopolitanism', which becomes 'a catalyst for the multiculture of the future' (p. 297). In a review of Gilroy's *Against Race*, Simon Gikandi offers a different perspective, however, arguing:

* The so-called 'Jim Crow' laws in nineteenth- and twentieth-century America were those that enforced the segregation of blacks and whites.

† The Rhodes Scholarship is an international award for postgraduate study at Oxford University. Josephine Baker (1906–75) was an African American dancer, singer and actress who was especially noted for her cabaret performances in Paris in the early part of the twentieth century. Jesse Owens (1913–80) was an African American track and field athlete who won four gold medals at the 1936 Olympics in Berlin. Joe Louis (1914–81), another African American sportsman, held the heavyweight boxing championship from 1937 to 1949.

> When I hear of cosmopolitanism, I do not think of ... Gilroy's Rhodes scholars, but of Shabine, the sailor in Derek Walcott's 'The Schooner Flight' ... Shabine's claim is that hybridity, cosmopolitanism, and nationalism are not inherently opposed.[29]

For Gikandi, Gilroy's notion of cosmopolitanism is flawed because of its emphasis on European circulation and presence. In the figure of Shabine, shaped by colonial formation, we find an entirely different representative of the multiculturalism of the future, which celebrates a multiracial, cross-cultural vision of a creolising world.*

Do these varying definitions of cosmopolitanism leave us once again so profoundly unrooted as to finally be unable to take a stance on what global citizenship means? Sheldon Pollock, Homi Bhabha, Carol Breckenridge and Dipesh Chakrabarty suggest that indeterminacy is a defining feature of cosmopolitanism: 'specifying cosmopolitanism positively and definitely is an uncosmopolitan thing to do'.[30] By this, they mean that there are multiple experiences and visions of the cosmopolitan experience. Nonetheless, they suggest the ways in which the postcolonial analysis of cosmopolitanism can open up new ways of thinking about shifting relations between peoples: 'Cosmopolitanism, in its wide and wavering nets, catches something of our need to ground our sense of mutuality in conditions of mutability, and to learn to live tenaciously in terrains of historic and cultural *transition*' (p. 580). They offer examples of these transitional moments: such as post-apartheid South Africa, which might be seen as free or as 'caught in the unresolved pursuit for truth and reconciliation' (p. 580). Negotiating the transitional, they argue, means finding 'ourselves in the interstices of the old and the new, confronting the past *as* the present' (p. 580). Working through differences, the tensions between the past and present, can be productive in promoting new forms of dialogue and identity formation.

* See Part Four: 'Cross-cultural Paradigms' for a discussion of creolisation.

Walter Mignolo offers what remains perhaps the most incisive approach to cosmopolitanism from a postcolonial perspective, which he refers to as 'critical cosmopolitanism':

> I see a need to reconceive cosmopolitanism from the perspective of coloniality (this is what I call critical cosmopolitanism) and within the frame of the modern/colonial world. It should be conceived historically as from the sixteenth century until today, and geographically in the interplay between a growing capitalism in the Mediterranean and the (North) Atlantic and a growing colonialism in other areas of the planet.[31]

Crucially, Mignolo notes the difference between cosmopolitan projects with global designs, which are 'driven by the will to control and homogenize', and critical cosmopolitanism, which 'can be complementary or dissenting with regard to global designs'. He traces the development of cosmopolitanism through the colonial period to the present, arguing that we are in need today of a dialogic and critical cosmopolitanism 'emerging from the various spatial and historical locations of the colonial difference' (p. 741). His notion of critical cosmopolitanism entails recuperating history from below, at the margins of hegemonic cosmopolitanism, and embracing diversality.

Diversality refers to the ability to imagine the world from subaltern perspectives (p. 743) (see Part Four: 'Postcolonial Reading Practices' for a discussion of the subaltern). Mignolo offers the example of the Zapatistas who use the word democracy to try and make the Mexican government understand their Mayan notion of a social organisation based on reciprocity, communal values and wisdom (p. 742) rather than representation, individual rights and reason. Border thinking is thus invoked because the Zapatista reference to democracy challenges and displaces Eurocentric ways of conceiving the term (see Part Four: 'Cross-cultural Paradigms' for more on border thinking). A critical cosmopolitan project presumably seeks to recuperate the points of connection, divergence and incommensurability that are at work in the world today.

Citizenship and 'the Hood' in a New World Order

Zadie Smith's *On Beauty* (2005) mobilises rap and globalised Caribbean perspectives as the means to explore the possibilities for transcultural citizenship in a globalising world of migrating peoples and media. In Smith's novel, rap as a musical form and its related genre of performance poetry are brought into dialogue with Haitian music and the migration of media more generally, including the global art market. Rap and hip hop are particularly appealing genres for the discussion of globalisation because they are simultaneously part of world music and also locally contested genres, which embody tensions around identity, authenticity and locality. These musical genres often transcend 'boundaries of class, race, region, and generation in fascinating ways'.[32] Jeffry Ogbar describes the ways in which debates about realness and authenticity are negotiated in terms of racial and class dynamics:

> No song better represents hip-hop's obsession with keeping it real than Ice Cube's 1991 hit 'True to the Game.' Setting a standard for realness in hip-hop, Ice Cube raps about archetypal sell-outs who 'give our music away to the mainstream' by switching from 'hardcore hip hop' to being 'white and corny.' … Fundamentally, a 'real nigga' refers to a tough urban black male who is intimately familiar with and willing to confront the many challenges of the 'hood.' But what exactly are these challenges and how is the hood defined? The hood is generally understood as the urban space occupied by black working-class and poor people. It is not simply 'urban' or 'black.' (p. 6)

For Smith, dialogues and debates about authenticity and genre form the basis for a critique of identity in a globalising world. In particular, she focuses on the question of how the 'hood' is constructed and what kinds of solidarity, both postcolonial and global, are possible from a new world envisioned through the songs, sounds and politics of the local. She examines what Arjun Appadurai terms the 'global production of locality' (*Modernity at Large*, p. 188) or the ways in which interactions with global flows are transforming constructs of the local and the possibilities for a network of solidarities among individuals and neighbourhoods.

On Beauty reworks E. M. Forster's *Howard's End* (1910) in order to examine how its epigraph, 'only connect', might work in the contemporary world. Like *Howard's End*, *On Beauty* focuses on the exchanges between two families, the Belseys (as the Schlegels) and the Kippses (as the Wilcoxes), and the individual members' relations to the world at large. The events of the novel take place in London and Boston as the two families criss-cross the Atlantic. Living in Boston, the Belsey family consists of Howard, a white, English professor of fine arts, his African American wife, Kiki, and their three children, Jerome, Zora and Levi. They enter into dialogue and conflict with the London-based Kippses, including Monty, a Black British professor, his wife, Carlene, and their children, Michael and Victoria. The possibilities for connection and communication are explored through email, migration, media distribution (legal or otherwise), trans-Atlantic travel and yearning for upward mobility, which are enabled in part by the workings of the global economy and infrastructures for contact. While the confusions of the political and the personal are at the heart of this tale about family, the narrative also focuses on the question of how migrating media transform relations in the 'hood.' Two stories of migrating media and mobility from Haiti are told in parallel. The first involves Levi's and Zora's efforts to find an authentic kind of vocation in the world through interactions with rap, hip hop and performance poetry. The second involves the circulation of a painting of Erzulie, the voudou *lwa*, which 'migrates' from Haiti to London and then to

Boston.* Through a series of misadventures, the painting, which belongs to Carlene Kipps, ends up in the hands of Kiki Belsey. These two stories turn out to be entangled as both the music and the art pass through the hands of Haitian migrants who sell illegal copies of urban music, videos and knock-off designer handbags on the street. The rap artists argue for a Marxist redistribution of wealth, which leads to the theft of a Hector Hyppolite painting with the aim of selling it and sharing the proceeds. Unwittingly, the Belseys enter into these circulations and their blindness to history is part of the novel's critique of the 'happy middle class'. Migrants from Haiti and migrating media raise questions about locality, mobility and cultural citizenship, which are eventually banished from the novel's tale of middle-class melodrama (which ends in the kind of ironic happy way we might find in a novel by David Lodge).†

The Haitian presence in the novel plays a fundamental role in the Caribbean rewriting of rap. In an essay entitled 'The Zen of Eminem', Zadie Smith takes up the question of authenticity in contrasting the branding of the rapper and the poetry of rap. According to Smith, most rappers can be branded, with Snoop, Dr Dre, Nelly, Mos Def and Busta Rhymes all marketable to particular moods and audiences. But 'Eminem, like Tupac before him, does a little of all these things. Like 'Pac, he does them with the integrity of an artist. This doesn't mean he's above the vulgar business of entertainment. It's just that elements of these two rappers are, in the sacred terminology of hip hop, kept real.'[33] While many might contest the idea of Eminem as an authentic artist in the field given his lower-middle-class white origins, Smith puts emphasis on the 'integrity of the artist' as the basis for participation in the community. This is an important point because

* Voudou (or voodoo) is a version of African religious beliefs and practices that developed among slave populations in the West Indies (especially Haiti) and Southern states of America.

† David Lodge is noted for his comic tales of misadventure in the lives of academics, which are often transnational in focus. Examples include *Changing Places: A Tale of Two Campuses* (1975), *Small World: An Academic Romance* (1984) and *Nice Work* (1988).

so much of the novel raises questions about integrity, belonging and community.

The Belseys' son, Levi, embodies a rather ironic impulse to keep it real through a mimicry of the hood, which includes putting on a Brooklyn accent (when he is from a privileged suburb of Boston) and leaving his job at a multinational record store to assist migrants selling illegal goods. He calls all of these migrants his people, and refers to them as 'Haitian' despite the fact that they come from Angola, Cuba and other countries. Most of the migrants tolerate Levi's attempts to speak in street language, except for Chouchou, a Haitian whose name Levi cannot bother to learn so he calls him 'Choo'. Smith uses various versions of the name to indicate point-of-view. Choo makes ironic reference to Roxbury as the 'hood', knowing full well that Levi does not come from there. He also debunks Levi's romanticised idea that they are all hustling when he points to Levi's \$125 running shoes and tells him that he worked in the factory where they were produced at a cost of \$15.[34] Levi is the one being hustled in this global economy. When he decides to visit Chou at his home, he has to ask for directions to find his way around Roxbury, an area he hardly knows. There he is shocked to discover that Chou does not even own a TV, which strikes him as 'poignant and unbearable' (p. 359). Listening to the album *Fear of a Black Planet* by Public Enemy, the stoned Choo confesses to Levi that the first time he heard a bootleg version of this album, he realised: '*We were not the only ghetto*. I was only thirteen, but suddenly I understood: America has ghettos! And Haiti is the ghetto of America!' (p. 360). Instead of rap, Choo wants to introduce Levi to Haitian music, which he describes as political like reggae (p. 360); eventually, he demands to listen to Bob Marley. For a moment, music and the migration of rap open up the possibility of a connection. However, this moment passes as Choo expresses rage concerning his status as an underpaid worker in the United States. He is particularly appalled by the hypocrisy of liberal-minded professors who are part of a system of exploitation from which they claim to distance themselves. Specifically, he cites the example of Sir Montagu Kipps who underpaid Haitian artists for their work and has 'stolen' Haitian art in order to promote his own global reputation as a connoisseur and activist (p. 362).

Elsewhere in the novel, contact with the middle class is depicted as perilous. Carl, a spoken word poet, longs to get away from his street background in Roxbury Park. He manages to do so when he gets a job running a hip hop archive at Wellington College and soon forgets about performing rap as part of a poetry group. He turns his back on rap because it's all about 'gangstas', players and ranting, which is no longer 'his scene' (p. 388). When Haitian workers are protesting outside his window, he asks Zora to shut it so that he can work in quiet (pp. 378–9). Eventually, following an argument with Zora, Carl decides to leave Wellington and go back to 'his people' because he begins to see that he is still perceived as other within a system where the middle class believe that he should gratefully accept what has been given to him. This 'othering' perspective is particularly evident when Zara's poetry teacher tells her it is a beautiful thing to be able to talk on behalf of the dispossessed, a group that is taken to include Carl. Carl, to his horror, eventually discovers that his sense of belonging to a community is illusory; he has become part of the imaginary capital of a world that would claim his rapper authenticity for its own pleasure.

Issues of visibility and invisibility constantly resurface in the novel as Smith shows the extent to which awareness of other perspectives is fleeting at best. Globalisation may enhance opportunities for contact and exchange, but this does not necessarily translate to change or mobilise into a new kind of consciousness. At the spoken word café, students learn about the war, American intervention in Haiti and other issues worthy of protest, but this is only a diversion that makes up part of a comfortable existence. In pointing out these failures and moments of loss, the novel accumulates its own moments of fragmentary beauty through epiphanies that lead nowhere. Such is the case with Levi's activism or Howard's walk through up-market Hampstead to multicultural Cricklewood, praising its 'realness' from the perspective of an outsider as he identifies an African woman, Poles and Russians living alongside each other: '[a]t this distance, walking past them all, thus itemizing them, not having to talk to any of them, flâneur Howard was able to love them and, more than this, to feel himself, in his own romantic fashion, to be one of them. We scum, we happy scum! From people like these he had come' (pp. 291–2). The juxtaposition of Hampstead and Cricklewood in London, like the contrasts between Wellington and Roxbury in Boston, returns the reader to the city as a site of contested identities. Howard, like his son Levi, indulges in the romance of the 'hood' and ignores the realities with which he might come into contact. In this sense, both father and son fail to connect.

We might now return to the ways in which Smith's novel responds to Forster's axiom: 'Only connect the prose and the passion and both will be exalted, and human love will be seen at its height. Live in fragments no longer'. In this case, the notion of bringing together pragmatic and poetic perspectives, communicating across borders, and overcoming the divisions of class and cultural difference proves problematic. *On Beauty* suggests that a poetics of fragmentation and recomposition requires the ability to commit seriously, rather than superficially, to the workings of the world. It requires an ability to get beyond personal narratives and to explore the hidden ways in which romance and the personal are latently politicised. In this way, the novel achieves its own sense of integrity through its profound ambivalence about the relationship between beauty and reality. Smith shows us that beauty is defined as the ability to 'keep it real'. As such, the apprehension of the beautiful is often a fleeting experience because the moment of appreciation typically soon turns to a desire to possess and master the beautiful. This desire to dominate runs contrary to the notion of beauty itself. Smith also talks of the silent voudoo of beauty (p. 137). The desire for social advancement through the appropriation of the beautiful leads to various incidents of spiritual dispossession; individuals lose part of their integrity – lie, misrepresent, steal and betray – in the quest for the beautiful. Yet, Smith wears the morality tale lightly, focusing as she does on moments of visibility and invisibility, possession and dispossession. The ending of the novel, a tribute to the silent appreciation of beauty, speaks volumes as Howard muses on the surging, living beauty that lies beneath the vulgar surfaces of the feminine body in Rembrandt's art. Like the beauties of the world, found in Cricklewood or the realities of poverty that coexist with exploitation and migration, Smith points to the need to move from romance to critical realism. She turns to global media circulations to highlight issues about authenticity, belonging and artistry, which focus on the 'hood' as a site that is negotiated through globalisation as well as the residual discourses of race and class. Instead of deterritorialisation, these works posit the need to engage thoughtfully with the local while remaining open to the flows of the globalised world. In this sense, Smith indicates the need for a creolisation of the 'hood' as a space constructed through complex interchanges with other localities around the world.

Globalisation and postcolonial studies offer overlapping but distinct ways of approaching the contemporary world order and its cultural productions. While some critics argue that we have seen the eclipse of postcolonial criticism, others demonstrate that the contemporary critique of race, economic inequities and residual notions of self and society need to be understood within an expanded postcolonial framework, which is attentive to the legacies of colonialism, neoimperialism and shifting conceptions of empire. In a world where the processes of decolonisation continue to unfold, the critical vocabulary of postcolonial literary theory and criticism remains essential to thinking through the construction of identity, power relationships and so forth. As has been shown, the critical vocabulary of postcolonial studies enables the analysis of uneven power dynamics, disjunctures, incommensurabilities, spatial relations, citizenship and cultural transformations at work in the world today. Thus, postcolonial literature and theory remain relevant in representing and addressing the lived concerns of individuals and nations. Through the emphasis on hybridity, ambivalence, historical representation and marginalised perspectives, the field of postcolonial studies remains essential to recovering a sense of globalism from below* and articulating alternative conceptions of worldliness.

Notes

1 Roland Robertson, *Globalization: Social Theory and Global Culture* (London: Sage Publications, 1992), p. 8.
2 Jan Aart Scholte, *Globalization: A Critical Introduction*, 2nd edition (Houndmills: Palgrave Macmillan, 2005), p. 61.
3 Ibid., p. 61.
4 Paul Jay, 'Beyond Discipline? Globalization and the Future of English' *PMLA* 116.1 Special Topic: Globalizing Literary Studies (January 2001), p. 35.
5 Ibid.
6 Anthony Giddens, *The Consequences of Modernity* (Cambridge: Polity Press, 1990), p. 64.
7 James Rosenau, *Distant Proximities: Dynamics Beyond Globalization* (Princeton, NJ: Princeton University Press, 2003), p. 2.
8 David Harvey, *The Condition of Postmodernity* (Oxford: Blackwell, 1990), p. 284.
9 Manuel Castells, *The Rise of the Network Society*, 2nd edition (Malden, MA: Blackwell, 2000), pp. 453–9.
10 Ibid., p. 459.
11 Arjun Appadurai, *Modernity at Large* (Minneapolis: University of Minnesota Press, 1996), p. 32. Other quotations in this paragraph are from p. 33.
12 Hari Kunzru, *Transmission* (London: Penguin Books, 2005), pp. 43–4.
13 Rita Raley, 'eEmpires', *Cultural Critique* 57.1 (2004), p. 111.
14 Michael Hardt and Antonio Negri, *Empire* (Cambridge, MA: Harvard University Press, 2000), p. xi.
15 See, for example, David Held and Henrietta L. Moore (eds), *Cultural Politics in Global Age: Uncertainty, Solidarity and Innovation* (Oxford:

* The phrase 'history from below' is employed by Stuart Hall to talk about the postcolonial rewriting of history through the perspective of the colonised. Globalism from below refers to stories that reflect the experiences of those who have been most disenfranchised by globalisation.

Oneworld, 2009). Chapter three, by Bhabha, is entitled 'Notes on Globalisation and Ambivalence'.

16 Ania Loomba, Suvir Kaul, Matti Bunzl, Antoinette Burton and Jed Esty, 'An Introduction', in *Postcolonial Studies and Beyond* (Durham, NC: Duke University Press, 20005), p. 2.

17 Simon Gikandi, 'Globalization and the Claims of Postcoloniality', *The South Atlantic Quarterly* 100.3 (2001), p. 628.

18 Peter J. Kalliney, 'East African Literature and Global Reading', *Research in African Literatures* 39.1 (2008), p. 10.

19 Wole Soyinka, 'Of Berlin and Other Walls', in *Art, Dialogue and Outrage: Essays on Literature and Culture* (London: Methuen, 1993), p. 206.

20 Anthony Pagden, 'Stoicism, Cosmopolitanism, and the Legacy of European Imperialism', *Constellations* 7.1 (2000), pp. 4–6.

21 Bruce Robbins, 'Comparative Cosmopolitanism', *Social Text* 31/32 'Third World and Postcolonial Issues' (1992), p. 171. See also Pheng Cheah and Bruce Robbins (eds), *Cosmopolitics: Thinking and Feeling Beyond the Nation* (Minneapolis: University of Minnesota Press, 1998).

22 Arjun Appadurai, 'Global Ethnoscapes: Notes and Queries for a Transnational Anthropology', in Richard G. Fox (ed.), *Recapturing Anthropology: Working in the Presence* (Santa Fe, CA: School of American Research Press, 1991), p. 192.

23 Benita Parry, 'The Contradictions of Cultural Studies', *Transition* 53 (1991), p. 41.

24 Kwame Anthony Appiah, 'Cosmopolitan Patriots', *Critical Inquiry*, 23.3, Front Lines/Border Posts (Spring 1997), p. 618.

25 Rebecca Walkowitz. *Cosmopolitan Style: Modernism Beyond the Nation* (New York: Columbia University Press, 2006), p. 9.

26 Homi Bhabbha, 'Unsatisfied: Notes on Vernacular Cosmopolitanism', in Gregory Castle (ed.), *Postcolonial Discourses: An Anthology* (Oxford: Blackwell Publishing, 2001), p. 41.

27 Tommie Shelby and Paul Gilroy, 'Cosmopolitanism, Blackness, and Utopia', *Transition* 98 (2008), p. 117.

28 Paul Gilroy, *Against Race* (Cambridge, MA: The Belknap Press of Harvard University, 2000), p. 288.

29 Simon Gikandi, 'Race and Cosmopolitanism' *American Literary History* 14.3 (2002), p. 614.

30 Sheldon Pollock, Homi K. Bhabha, Carol A. Breckenridge and Dipesh Chakrabarty, 'Cosmopolitanisms', *Public Culture* 12.3 (2000), p. 577.

31 Walter Mignolo, 'Critical Cosmopolitanism', *Public Culture* 12.3 (2000), p. 723.

32 Jeffrey Ogbar, *Hip-Hop Revolution: The Culture and Politics of Rap* (Lawrence: University Press of Kansas, 2007), p. 3.
33 Zadie Smith, 'The Zen of Eminem', *Vibe* (November 2002), p. 92.
34 Zadie Smith, *On Beauty* (London: Penguin Books, 2005), p. 246.

Part Five
References and Resources

Timeline

	Historical events	Literary events
1492	Christopher Columbus 'discovers' America	
1516		Thomas More, *Utopia*
1600	East India Trading Company established	
1610–11		Shakespeare, *The Tempest*
1655	England wins control over Jamaica from Spain	
1670	Hudson Bay Company established	
1688		Aphra Behn, *Oroonoko: or, the Royal Slave*
1719		Daniel Defoe, *Robinson Crusoe*
1756–63	Seven Years War	
1776	American Independence	
1788	Captain Arthur Phillip lands in New South Wales to establish a new colony	
1789	French Revolution begins (–1799)	Olaudah Equiano, *The Interesting Narrative of the Life of Olaudah Equiano, or Gustavus Vassa the African*

	Historical events	Literary events
1804	Haitian Independence	
1807	The Slave Trade Act abolishes the slave trade, but not slavery itself	
1833	The Slavery Abolition Act abolishes slavery in the British empire	
1835	Boers start Great Trek in southern Africa; Maori Declaration of Independence in New Zealand	
1857–8	Indian Mutiny	
1865	Abolition of Slavery in the United States of America	
1867	Independence of Canada	
1876	Queen Victoria declared Empress of India	
1898	Spanish–American War and emergence of US as imperialist power over Philippines, Cuba, Puerto Rico and Guam	
1899	Outbreak of Anglo-Boer War (–1902)	Joseph Conrad, *Heart of Darkness* (1899/1902); Rudyard Kipling, *The White Man's Burden*
1900	Boxer Rebellion, an anti-Western uprising in China; Commonwealth of Australia (–1901); first Pan-African Conference held in London	Rudyard Kipling, *Kim* (1900–1)

	Historical events	Literary events
1903		W. E .B. Du Bois, *The Souls of Black Folk*
1905	Indian *swadeshi* ('of our own country') movement (–1908) in protest against the British partition of Bengal	
1907	Britain grants dominion status to self-governing (white) colonies	
1912		Claude McKay, *Songs of Jamaica* and *Constab Ballads*
1913	Native Land Act in South Africa	Rabindranath Tagore awarded the Nobel Prize for Literature
1914	Outbreak of First World War	
1918	Armistice ends First World War; Declaration of the Irish Republic	
1919	League of Nations founded; German colonies in Africa transferred to Britain, France and Belgium; May Fourth Movement in China for modernism and resistance to imperialism; Montagu–Chelmsford reforms for limited self-government in India; outbreak of Anglo-Irish War (–1921); Palestinian National Congress reject Balfour Declaration and call for Arab independence	Beginning of the Harlem Renaissance, an African American and African diasporic cultural, artistic, literary and political movement

	Historical events	Literary events
1920	Britain gains mandate over Iraq, Trans-Jordan and Palestine; Gandhi launches Non-Cooperation Movement in India	
1921–3	Civil War in Ireland	
1923		Jean Toomer, *Cane*
1924		E. M. Forster, *A Passage to India*
1925		Alain Locke (ed.), *The New Negro*
1926		Ho Chi Minh, *Colonization on Trial*; Langston Hughes, *The Weary Blues* and 'The Negro Artist and the Racial Mountain'
1927	International Conference against Imperialism and Colonial Oppression, Brussels	
1928		Claude McKay, *Home to Harlem*; Nella Larsen, *Quicksand*
1929	Geneva Convention signed to regulate the treatment of prisoners of war	Nella Larsen, *Passing*; Claude McKay, *Banjo*
1930	Gandhi launches Civil Disobedience Movement	Negritude movement begins in Paris; Mao Tse-tung, 'A Single Spark Can Start a Prairie Fire'
1931	British Commonwealth of Nations founded	
1932		Rudolph Fisher, *The Conjure-Man Dies*; Evelyn Waugh, *Black Mischief*

	Historical events	Literary events
1933		Claude McKay, *Banana Bottom*; Mulk Raj Anand, *Untouchable*
1936		C. L. R. James, *Minty Alley*
1937		Zora Neale Hurston, *Their Eyes Were Watching God*
1938		C. L. R. James, *The Black Jacobins: Toussaint L'Ouverture and the San Domingo Revolution*
1939–45	Second World War	
1942–59	*Caribbean Voices* programme on the BBC	
1944		Eric Williams, *Capitalism and Slavery*
1947	India gains independence; partition of India and birth of Pakistan, accompanied by mass migration of 8.5 million refugees crossing borders as well as violence and death	Jawaharlal Nehru, 'Tryst with Destiny'
1948	*Empire Windrush* docks at Tilbury; Sri Lankan Independence; apartheid introduced in South Africa; Gandhi assassinated; Cambodia gains independence; UN adopts Declaration of Human Rights	Alan Paton, *Cry the Beloved Country*
1949		William Faulkner awarded the Nobel Prize for Literature

	Historical events	Literary events
1950	China assumes control over Tibet; Jordan annexes the West Bank; outbreak of US-Korean War (–1953)	Doris Lessing, *The Grass is Singing*
1952	Kenya declares State of Emergency due to anti-colonial uprisings	Frantz Fanon, *Black Skin, White Masks*
1953		Fidel Castro, 'History Will Absolve Me'; George Lamming, *In the Castle of My Skin*
1954	Vietnamese army led by Ho Chi Minh defeats French colonial forces; Algerian War of Independence begins (–1962)	
1955	Bandung Conference of independent Asian and African states leads to declaration of sovereignty, human rights and equality among nations	Aimé Césaire, *Discourse on Colonialism*
1956	Suez Crisis (–1957); Sudan Independence	Sam Selvon, *The Lonely Londoners*
1957	Ghana and peninsular Malaya gain independence	Albert Memmi, *The Colonizer and the Colonized*; Derek Walcott, *Ti Jean and His Brothers*
1958	Guinea gains independence; riots erupt in Sri Lanka leading to the declaration of a State of Emergency	Chinua Achebe, *Things Fall Apart*; Wole Soyinka, *The Swamp Dwellers*
1959	Cuban Revolution	

	Historical events	Literary events
1960	Sharpeville Massacre in South Africa; Benin, Burkino Faso, Central African Republic, Chad, Congo, Gabon, Ivory Coast, Madagascar, Mali, Mauritania, Niger, Nigeria, Senegal, Somalia and Togo gain independence	Wilson Harris, *Palace of the Peacock*; George Lamming, *The Pleasures of Exile*
1961	Bay of Pigs invasion of Cuba by America thwarted; Cameroon, Sierra Leone and Tanzania gain independence; Patrice Lumumba killed while in custody in the Congo	Frantz Fanon, *The Wretched of the Earth*; Ernesto 'Che' Guevara, *Guerrilla Warfare*; V. S. Naipaul, *A House for Mr Biswas*
1962	Jamaica, Trinidad and Tobago, Uganda, Algeria, Burundi and Rwanda gain independence; Cuban missile crisis	
1963	Formation of Organization of African Unity; Kenya gains independence	Dennis Brutus, *Sirens, Knuckles and Boots*
1964	Malawi, Malaya and Zambia gain independence; Nelson Mandela and Walter Sisulu sentenced to life imprisonment; Guyana sees overthrow of Cheddi Jaggan's government; Civil Rights Act of 1964 outlaws racial discrimination in the United States	Oodgeroo Noonuccal, *We are Going: Poems*

	Historical events	Literary events
1965	Mobutu takes power in Congo; White Rhodesian government declares independence	Kamala Das, *Summer in Calcutta*; Derek Walcott, *The Castaway and Other Poems*; Nelson Mandela, *No Easy Walk to Freedom*; Kwame Nkrumah, *Neo-Colonialism: The Last Stage of Imperialism*; Wole Soyinka, *The Interpreters*
1966	Guyana, Barbados, Botswana, Lesotho gain independence; armed struggles in Zimbabwe and Namibia; Tricontinental Conference held in Cuba leads to formation of Organisation of Solidarity with the People of Asia, Africa and Latin America	Jean Rhys, *Wide Sargasso Sea*; Paul Scott, *The Jewel in the Crown*
1967	Nigerian Civil War breaks out	V. S. Naipaul, *The Mimic Men*; Edward Brathwaite, *Rights of Passage*; Derek Walcott, *Dream on Monkey Mountain*; Ngugi wa Thiong'o, *A Grain of Wheat*
1968	Martin Luther King assassinated	Dennis Brutus, *Letters to Martha and Other Poems from a South African Prison*
1969	Britain sends troops to Ireland to stop rioting; US bombs Cambodia	Maya Angelou, *I Know Why the Caged Bird Sings*
1970	Nigerian Civil War ends; Fiji and Tonga gain independence	Tayeb Salih, *Season of Migration to the North*; Merle Hodge, *Crick Crack Monkey*; Ama Ata Aidoo, *No Sweetness Here*; Toni Morrison, *The Bluest Eye*

	Historical events	Literary events
1971	Bangladesh declares independence and civil war in East Pakistan; Idi Amin's dictatorship in Uganda begins; Bahrain gains independence	Christopher Okigbo, *Labyrinths*; Kamau Brathwaite, *The Development of Creole Society in Jamaica, 1770–1820*
1972	'Bloody Sunday' in Ireland; martial law imposed in Philippines	Steve Biko, *I Write What I Like*; Margaret Atwood, *Surfacing*; Walter Rodney, *How Europe Underdeveloped Africa*
1973	Bahamas gains independence; collapse of Bretton–Woods monetary policy and the departure from the gold standard as a guarantee for currency	Toni Morrison, *Sula*; Kamau Brathwaite, *The Arrivants*
1974	Guinea-Bissau and Grenada gain independence	Nadine Gordimer, *The Conservationist*; Bessie Head, *A Question of Power*
1975	Vietnam War ends; Khmer Rouge seizes power in Cambodia; Angola, Mozambique, Cape Verde and Papua New Guinea gain independence; Indonesia invades East Timor; Indira Gandhi found guilty of electoral malpractice in India	Wole Soyinka, *Death and the King's Horseman*; V. S. Naipaul, *Guerrillas*
1976	Student uprisings in South Africa; Seychelles gains independence	Wole Soyinka, *Myth, Literature and the African World*; Maxine Hong Kingston, *The Woman Warrior: Memoirs of a Girlhood Among Ghosts*

	Historical events	Literary events
1977	Steve Biko dies while in police custody in South Africa; Djibouti gains independence; Bhutto ousted in Pakistan	Samir Amin, *Imperialism and Unequal Development*; Toni Morrison, *Song of Solomon*
1978	Vietnam invades Cambodia and ousts Khmer Rouge from power; demonstrations against the Shah in Iran	Edward Said, *Orientalism*
1979	Soviet invasion of Afghanistan; US intervenes in Nicaragua to undermine the Sandanista regime; Islamic Law introduced in Pakistan; revolution in Iran and hostage crisis in American Embassy; St Lucia and St Vincent gain independence; Idi Amin's government brought down in Uganda	V. S. Naipaul, *A Bend in the River*; Linton Kwesi Johnson, *Forces of Victory*; Kamau Brathwaite, *History of the Voice*; Nadine Gordimer, *Burger's Daughter*; Derek Walcott, *The Star-Apple Kingdom;* Buchi Emecheta, *The Joys of Motherhood*; Earl Lovelace, *The Dragon Can't Dance*; Jack Davis, *Kullark*
1980	Zimbabwe, Antigua and Barbuda gain independence; Iran–Iraq War begins (–1988)	J. M. Coetzee, *Waiting for the Barbarians*; Jack Davis, *The Dreamers*; Maxine Hong Kingston, *China Men*
1981	Belize gains independence	Salman Rushdie, *Midnight's Children*
1982		Alice Walker, *The Color Purple*; Audre Lorde, *Zami: A New Spelling of My Name*; Michael Ondaatje, *Running in the Family*
1984	Brunei gains independence	August Wilson, *Ma Rainey's Black Bottom*

	Historical events	Literary events
1985		Jamaica Kincaid, *Annie John*; Hanif Kureishi, *My Beautiful Laundrette*; Jack Davis, *No Sugar*
1986		Wole Soyinka awarded the Nobel Prize for Literature; Amitav Ghosh, *The Circle of Reason*; Ngugi wa Thiong'o, *Decolonising the Mind: The Politics of Language in African Literature*
1987		Toni Morrison, *Beloved*; Gloria Anzaldúa, *Borderlands / La Frontera: The New Mestiza*; Hanif Kureishi, *Sammy and Rosie Get Laid*; Derek Walcott, *The Arkansas Testament*; Michelle Cliff, *No Telephone To Heaven*
1988		Jamaica Kincaid, *A Small Place*; David Henry Hwang, *M. Butterfly*; Salman Rushdie, *The Satanic Verses*; Tsitsi Dangarembga, *Nervous Conditions*; Amitav Ghosh, *The Shadow Lines*; Michael Ondaatje, *In the Skin of a Lion*; August Wilson, *Nat Turner's Come and Gone*; Chandra Talpade Mohanty, 'Under Western Eyes: Feminist Scholarship and Colonial Discourses'; Gayatri Chakravorty Spivak, 'Can the Subaltern Speak?'
1989	Fall of the Berlin Wall	Shashi Tharoor, *The Great Indian Novel*; Maxine Hong Kingston, *Tripmaster Monkey: His Fake Book*; Bill Ashcroft, Gareth Griffiths and Helen Tiffin, *The Empire Writes Back: Theory and Practice in Post-Colonial Literatures*

	Historical events	Literary events
1990	Release of Nelson Mandela from prison in South Africa; Namibia gains independence; Coup in Haiti	Hanif Kuresihi, *The Buddha of Suburbia*; Dionne Brand, *No Language is Neutral*; Mahesh Dattani, *Tara*; Derek Walcott, *Omeros*; August Wilson, *The Piano Lesson*
1991	First Gulf War begins	Nadine Gordimer awarded the Nobel Prize for Literature; Ben Okri, *The Famished Road*; Rohinton Mistry, *Such a Long Journey*; Mahesh Dattani, *Bravely Fought the Queen*
1992		Derek Walcott awarded the Nobel Prize for Literature; Alice Walker, *Possessing the Secret of Joy*; Michael Ondaatje, *The English Patient*; Mary Louise Pratt, *Imperial Eyes: Travel Writing and Transculturation*; Salman Rushdie, *Imaginary Homelands: Essays and Criticism 1981–1991*
1993	Apartheid ends; violence erupts in India, involving many Muslim deaths in Bombay and Gujarat; Eritrea gains independence following armed struggle with Ethiopia	Toni Morrison awarded the Nobel Prize for Literature; Vikram Seth, *A Suitable Boy*
1994	Nelson Mandela elected president of post-apartheid South Africa	Shyam Selvadurai, *Funny Boy*; Edwidge Danticat, *Breath, Eyes, Memory*; Homi Bhabha, *The Location of Culture*
1995	Inter-ethnic massacres in Rwanda	Rohinton Mistry, *A Fine Balance*; Salman Rushdie, *The Moor's Last Sigh*

	Historical events	Literary events
1996		Junot Díaz, *Drown*; Edwidge Danticat, *Krik? Krak!*; Wilson Harris, *Jonestown*
1997	Hong Kong returned by Britain to China	Arundhati Roy, *The God of Small Things*; Dionne Brand, *Land to Light On*; Hanif Kureishi, *My Son the Fanatic*
1998	Eritrean–Ethiopian War (–2000)	Mahesh Dattani, *On a Muggy Night in Mumbai*
1999		J. M. Coetzee, *Disgrace*; Jhumpa Lahiri, *Interpreter of Maladies*
2000		Zadie Smith, *White Teeth*; Michael Ondaatje, *Anil's Ghost*
2001	September 11 attack on Twin Towers; war in Afghanistan begins by US-led coalition force	V. S. Naipaul awarded the Nobel Prize for Literature; Caryl Phillips, *The Atlantic Sound*
2002	Bali bombings	Hari Kunzru, *The Impressionist*
2003	Invasion of Iraq by US-led coalition forces	J. M. Coetzee awarded the Nobel Prize for Literature; Chimamanda Ngozi Adichie, *Purple Hibiscus;* Caryl Phillips, *A Distant Shore*; Khaled Hosseini, *The Kite Runner*
2004	United Nations stabilisation mission in Haiti	Andrea Levy, *Small Island*; Meena Alexander, *Raw Silk*; Hari Kunzru, *Transmission;* Edwidge Danticat, *The Dew Breaker*
2005	London tube and bus bombings	Kamau Brathwaite, *Born to Slow Horses*; Salman Rushdie, *Shalimar the Clown*; Zadie Smith, *On Beauty*; Dionne Brand, *What We All Long For*

	Historical events	Literary events
2006	Ethiopian intervention in Somalia (–2009)	Chimamanda Ngozi Adichie, *Half of a Yellow Sun*; Ngugi wa Thiong'o, *Wizard of the Crow*; Wilson Harris, *The Ghost of Memory*
2007		Doris Lessing awarded the Nobel Prize for Literature; Junot Díaz, *The Brief Wondrous Life of Oscar Wao*; Mohsin Hamid, *The Reluctant Fundamentalist*; Edwidge Danticat, *Brother, I'm Dying*; Ed Husain, *The Islamist*
2009	Tamil Tigers defeated in Sri Lanka; inauguration of first black president of the United States, Barack Obama	Chimamanda Ngozi Adichie, *The Thing Around Your Neck*; Meena Alexander, *Poetics of Dislocation*; Amit Chaudhuri, *The Immortals*; Kamila Shamsie, *Burnt Shadows*; H. M. Naqvi, *Home Boy: A Novel*
2010	Ivory Coast crisis following elections	Andrea Levy, *The Long Song*; Dionne Brand, *Ossuaries*
2011	Egyptian Revolution	

Further Reading

General Introductions and Key Concepts

Ashcroft, Bill, Gareth Griffiths and Helen Tiffin (eds), *Post-Colonial Studies: The Key Concepts* (London: Routledge, 1998)

A comprehensive glossary that defines key terms in postcolonial studies and includes an extensive bibliography of essential writings in the field

Childs, Peter and R. J. Patrick Williams, *An Introduction to Post-Colonial Theory* (Harlow: Prentice Hall, 1997)

Accessible introduction to key works by Frantz Fanon, Edward Said, Homi Bhabha and Gayatri Chakravorty Spivak

Gandhi, Leela, *Postcolonial Theory: A Critical Introduction* (Edinburgh: Edinburgh University Press, 1998)

Introduction to the work of Edward Said, Gayatri Chakravorty Spivak and Homi Bhabha, also including discussions of Frantz Fanon and Mahatma Gandhi

Loomba, Ania, *Colonialism / Postcolonialism*, 2nd edition (London: Routledge, 2005)

Excellent introduction to colonial discourse, anti-colonialism, sex/gender and debates about globalisation

McLeod, John, *Beginning Postcolonialism*, 2nd edition (Manchester: Manchester University Press, 2010)

Clearly written, accessible introduction to postcolonial literature and theory, including close readings of key literary texts and noted theorists, such as Edward Said, Gayatri Chakravorty Spivak and others

Moore-Gilbert, Bart, *Postcolonial Theory: Contexts, Practices, Politics* (London: Verso, 1997)

Offers an accessible and nuanced introduction to work by Gayatri Chakravorty Spivak, Edward Said and Homi Bhabha

Anthologies, Reference Texts and Essay Collections

General and Thematic

Ashcroft, Bill, Gareth Griffiths and Helen Tiffin (eds), *The Post-Colonial Studies Reader*, 2nd edition (London: Routledge, 2006)
An edited collection of some of the most important and influential essays written by key critics and theorists in the field of postcolonial studies

Bhabha, Homi K. (ed.), *Nation and Narration* (London: Routledge, 1990)
Influential collection of essays by leading critics who explore the connections between the construct of the nation and narration

Connell, Liam and Nicky Marsh (eds), *Literature and Globalization: A Reader* (Abingdon: Routledge, 2011)
Offers various approaches to defining globalisation and the field of studies, including discussions of the relationship between postcolonial and globalising perspectives

DeLoughrey, Elizabeth and George Handley, *Postcolonial Ecologies: Literatures of the Environment* (Oxford: Oxford University Press, 2011)
Brings ecocritical studies into dialogue with postcolonial studies, examining African, Caribbean, Pacific Island and South Asian literatures

Hawley, John Charles (ed.), *Postcolonial, Queer: Theoretical Intersections* (Albany: State University of New York Press, 2001)
Essays addressing the globalisation of Western notions of gay and lesbian identities

Lazarus, Neil (ed.), *The Cambridge Companion to Postcolonial Literary Studies* (Cambridge: Cambridge University Press, 2004)
Essays providing an introduction to the field and various theoretical approaches, including feminist, Marxist and poststructuralist perspectives

Loomba, Ania, Suvir Kaul, Matti Bunzl, Antoinette Burton and Jed Esty (eds), *Postcolonial Studies and Beyond* (Durham, NC: Duke University Press, 2005)
Essays exploring shifting approaches to postcolonial reading practices and theory in a globalising world

Parkinson, Lois Zamora and Wendy B. Faris (eds), *Magical Realism: Theory, History, Community* (Durham, NC: Duke University Press, 1995)

Collection of essays that considers the definition of magical realism and offers close readings of narratives from around the world with a particular emphasis on theory, history and community

Pearson, Nels and Marc Singer (eds), *Detective Fiction in a Postcolonial and Transnational World* (Farnham: Ashgate, 2009)

Collection of essays on postcolonial detective fiction, offering close readings of works by Michael Ondaatje, Vikram Chandra, Mario Vargas Llosa and Lucha Corpi

Quayson, Ato (ed.), *The Cambridge History of Postcolonial Literature* (Cambridge: Cambridge University Press, 2012)

Collection of essays on postcolonial literary history, taking into account various national, cultural, thematic and geo-political contexts

Africa, the African Diaspora and the Caribbean

Donnell, Alison and Sarah Lawson Welsh, *The Routledge Reader in Caribbean Literature* (London: Routledge, 1996)

Offers an introduction to Caribbean literature in the twentieth century through a careful selection of fictional and non-fictional extracts by leading authors

Gates, Henry Louis and Nellie Young (eds), *The Norton Anthology: African American Literature*, 2nd edition (New York: W. W. Norton & Company, 2004)

Essential anthology for the study of African American literature from 1746 to the present

Irele, Abiola F. and Simon Gikandi (eds), *The Cambridge History of African and Caribbean Literature*, volumes one and two (Cambridge: Cambridge University Press, 2004)

Essays on various facets of African and Caribbean literature, including oral and folk traditions, praise poetry, theatre and drama, the novel and key movements, such as the Harlem Renaissance and Negritude

Ouzgane, Lahoucine (ed.), *Men in African Film and Fiction* (Woodbridge, Suffolk: James Currey, 2011)

Collection of essays contributing to the growing field of postcolonial masculinity studies with a focus on the nation and alternative masculinities

Asia and the Asian Diaspora

Aguilar-San Juan, Karin and Annette Jaimes (eds), *The State of Asian America: Activism and Resistance in the 1990s* (Boston, MA: South End Press, 1999)

Essays exploring the links between activism and identity in Asian American culture and literature, including discussions of race, riots, feminism, labour and other social issues

Mehotra, Arvind Krishna (ed.), *A Concise History of Indian Literature in English* (Houndmills: Palgrave, 2009)

Covers two hundred years of literary history from Raja Rammohan Ray to Arundhati Roy, including discussions of key authors such as Rudyard Kipling, Rabindranath Tagore, R. K. Narayan, Nirad C. Chaudhuri and V. S. Naipaul

Australia, New Zealand and Canada

Benson, Eugene and William Toye (eds), *The Oxford Companion to Canadian Literature*, 2nd edition (Toronto: Oxford University Press, 1997)

Reference text that includes more than 300 entries on Canadian literatures

O'Reilly, Nathanael (ed.), *Postcolonial Issues in Australian Literature* (Amherst, NY: Cambria Press, 2010)

Essays on Australian texts from the colonial period to the present, including works by Henry Lawson, Miles Franklin, Patrick White, Xavier Herbert, David Malouf, Peter Carey, Rodney Hall, Andrew McGahan, Elizabeth Jolley, Judith Wright, Kate Grenville, Janette Turner Hospital, Melissa Lucashenko, Kim Scott and Alexis Wright

Robinson, R. and Wattie, N. (eds), *The Oxford Companion to New Zealand Literature* (Auckland: Oxford University Press, 1998)
Reference text that introduces the diverse literatures of New Zealand

Sugars, Cynthia (ed.), *Unhomely States: Theorizing English-Canadian Postcolonialism* (Peterborough: Broadview, 2004)
Collection of essays examining postcolonial Canadian literature in English with discussions of anti-colonial nationalism, the Commonwealth context, the impact of settlers and invaders, debates about postcolonialism in Canada, First Nation subjects and other topics

Webby, Elizabeth (ed.), *The Cambridge Companion to Australian Literature* (Cambridge: Cambridge University Press, 2000)
Important collection of essays that examines indigenous, colonial and postcolonial writing, including discussions of prose, poetry and theatre

Britain

Bassnett, Susan (ed.), *Studying British Cultures*, 2nd edition (London: Routledge, 2003)
Collection of essays that offers an introduction to postcolonial British culture, examining topics such as Irish, Welsh, West Indian and Scottish literatures as well as themes such as mapping and approaches to British cultural studies

Procter, James (ed.), *Writing Black Britain 1948–1998: An Interdisciplinary Anthology* (Manchester: Manchester University Press, 2000)
Anthology of Black British writing that provides a solid introduction to this diverse field of literature

Wambu, Onyekachi (ed.), *Empire Windrush: Fifty Years of Writing about Black Britain* (London: Phoenix, 1999)
Excellent selection of excerpts for studying Black British literature related to *Windrush* migration and the rise of multiracial, multicultural Britain

Critical and Close Readings

General and Thematic

Ashcroft, Bill, Gareth Griffiths and Helen Tiffin, *The Empire Writes Back*, 2nd edition (London: Routledge, 2002)
Landmark text that offers an introduction to postcolonial reading practices, covering topics such as language and textuality in various cultural contexts

Ball, John Clement, *Satire and the Postcolonial Novel: V. S. Naipaul, Chinua Achebe, Salman Rushdie* (London: Routledge, 2003)
Explores the way satire has been used to critique empire, especially through satire's relation to irony, allegory, narrative and the grotesque, offering close readings of key works by Naipaul, Achebe and Rushdie

Boehmer, Elleke, *Colonial and Postcolonial Literature: Migrant Metaphors*, 2nd edition (Oxford: Oxford University Press, 2005)
Offers a comprehensive approach to reading postcolonial literature, covering topics such as imperialism and textuality, colonialist concerns, nationalism, metropolitans and mimics, independence and postcolonial transition

Bromley, Roger, *Narratives for a New Belonging: Diasporic Cultural Fictions* (Edinburgh: Edinburgh University Press, 2000)
Approaches diasporic fiction from multiple angles, including discussions of Chicano, Asian, Cuban, Asian Canadian and Asian and Black British perspectives, with an emphasis on memory, discursive border crossing and silenced or absent histories

Brydon, Diana and Helen Tiffin, *Decolonising Fictions* (Sydney: Dangaroo Press, 1993)
Examines the ways in which literature contributes to the decolonisation of the imaginary and offers incisive close readings of key postcolonial texts

Crow, Brian with Chris Banfield, *An Introduction to Post-Colonial Theatre* (Cambridge: Cambridge University Press, 1996)
Offers close readings and discussions of theatrical works by Derek Walcott, August Wilson, Jack Davis, Wole Soyinka, Athol Fugard, Badal Sircar and Girish Karnad

Lane, Richard, *The Postcolonial Novel* (Cambridge: Polity Press, 2006)

Offers close readings of key postcolonial texts, including Wilson Harris's *Palace of the Peacock*, Chinua Achebe's *Things Fall Apart*, J. M. Coetzee's *Foe* and Margaret Atwood's *Surfacing*

Lionnet, Françoise, *Postcolonial Representations: Women, Literature, Identity* (Ithaca, NY: Cornell University Press, 1995)

Offers readings of works by Michelle Cliff, Maryse Condé, Bessie Head, Nawal Ed Saadawi and others

Patke, Rajeev S., *Postcolonial Poetry in English* (Oxford: Oxford University Press, 2006)

Analyses poetry from around the world, offering excellent close readings with close attention to cultural contexts and aesthetics

Scott, Helen and Joanne Tompkins, *Post-Colonial Drama: Theory, Practice, Politics* (London: Routledge, 1996)

Offers a theoretical framework for reading postcolonial drama, including discussions of counter-discourse, ritual and carnival, postcolonial history, the language of resistance, body politics and neoimperialism

Sharpe, Jenny, *Allegories of Empire: The Figure of Woman in the Colonial Text* (Minneapolis: University of Minnesota Press, 1993)

Brings the historical memory of the 1857 Indian Mutiny to bear upon the theme of rape in British and Anglo-Indian fiction

Africa, the African Diaspora and the Caribbean

Bobb, June D., *Beating a Restless Drum: Poetics of Kamau Brathwaite and Derek Walcott* (Trenton, NJ: Africa Research and Publications, 1998)

Comparative analysis of the work of Walcott and Brathwaite

Boyce Davies, Carole, *Black Women, Writing and Identity: Migrations of the Subject* (London: Routledge, 1994)

Explores the interplay between migration and writing in the field of Black Women's Writing with discussions of subjectivity, uprising, writing home, mobility and language

Dash, Michael J., *The Other America: Caribbean Literature in a New World Context* (Charlottesville: The University Press of Virginia, 1998)

Analysis of Caribbean literature from a geo-political perspective including close readings by key authors

Donnell, Alison, *Twentieth-Century Caribbean Literature: Critical Moments in Anglophone Literary History* (London: Routledge, 2006)

Significant contribution to Caribbean literary history and theory that interrogates canon formation, including discussions of gender and sexual identity, migration and women's writing

Durrant, Sam, *Postcolonial Narrative and the Work of Mourning: J. M. Coetzee, Wilson Harris and Toni Morrison* (New York: State University of New York Press, 2003)

Draws on trauma theory to analyse postcolonial trauma narratives, offering close readings of works by Coetzee, Harris and Morrison

Ferguson, Moira, *Colonialism and Gender Relations from Mary Wollstonecraft to Jamaica Kincaid: East Caribbean Connections* (New York: Columbia University Press, 1993)

Examines the connections between gender and colonial relations in texts by British writers of the eighteenth and nineteenth centuries as well as Caribbean writers of the nineteenth and twentieth centuries, including discussions of Mary Wollstonecraft, Jane Austen, Jean Rhys and Jamaica Kincaid

Gikandi, Simon, *Writing in Limbo: Modernism and Caribbean Literature* (Ithaca, NY: Cornell University Press, 1992)

Influential study of the impact of modernist poetics on authors such as George Lamming, Sam Selvon, Paule Marshall and Merle Hodge

Pollard, Charles W., *New World Modernisms: T. S. Eliot, Derek Walcott and Kamau Brathwaite* (Charlottesville: University of Virginia Press, 2004)

Examines how Walcott and Brathwaite appropriate and transform Eliot's modernist principles in the service of Caribbean writing

Soyinka, Wole, *Myth, Literature and the African World* (Cambridge: Cambridge University Press, 2000)

Collection of essays on morality, aesthetics and social vision in African culture, including an appendix on the notion of the Fourth Stage, which is central to an appreciation of Soyinka's writing

ten Kortenaar, Neil, *Postcolonial Literature and the Impact of Literacy: Reading and Writing in African and Caribbean Fiction* (Cambridge: Cambridge University Press, 2011)

Interrogates the ways in which writers conceive of their own writing practices, including discussions of Chinua Achebe, Wole Soyinka and V. S. Naipaul

Asia and the Asian Diaspora

Brians, Paul, *Modern South Asian Literature in English* (Westport, CT: Greenwood 2003)

Offers close readings of South Asian fiction, including discussions of Jhumpa Lahiri, R. K. Narayan, Anita Desai, Salman Rushdie, Michael Ondaatje and Rohinton Mistry

Gopinath, Gayatri, *Impossible Desires: Queer Diasporas and South Asian Public Cultures* (Durham, NC: Duke University Press, 2005)

Provides theoretically informed close readings of South Asian literature and culture by bringing queer theory to bear on the reading of diaspora, including analyses of works by Hanif Kureishi, V. S. Naipaul, Shani Mootoo and others

Mukherjee, Meenakshi, *The Perishable Empire. Essays on Indian Writing in English* (New Delhi: Oxford University Press, 2000)

Contains essays on nineteenth- and twentieth-century Indian English literature

Nasta, Susheila, *Home Truths: Fictions of the South Asian Diaspora in Britain* (London: Palgrave, 2002)

Excellent introduction to literature of the South Asian Diaspora, including close readings of works by V. S. Naipaul, Salman Rushdie, Romesh Gunesekera, Hanif Kureishi and others

Australia, New Zealand and Canada

Allen, C., *Blood Narrative: Indigenous Identity in American Indian and Maori Literary and Activist Texts* (Durham, NC: Duke University Press, 2002)

Comparative literary and cultural study of post-Second World War literary and activist texts by New Zealand Maori and American Indians

Huggan, Graham, *Australian Literature: Postcolonialism, Racism, Transnationalism* (Oxford: Oxford University Press, 2007)

Examines Australian literature in the context of debates about race, multiculturalism and transnationalism as well as offering close readings by Bruce Dawe, Les Murray, Ray Lawler, David Williamson, Christina Stead, Patrick White, Sally Morgan and Kim Scott

Keown, Michelle, *Pacific Islands Writing: The Postcolonial Literatures of Aotearoa/New Zealand and Oceania* (Oxford: Oxford University Press, 2007)

Offers readings of works by Albert Wendt, Witi Ihimaera, Alan Duff, Patricia Grace, Sia Figiel, Caroline Sinavaiana-Gabbard and Dan Taulapapa McMullin

New, H. W., *A History of Canadian Literature* (Montreal: McGill-Queen's University Press, 2003)

Examines literature from the early records of oral tales to the writing strategies of the 1980s, including discussions of aboriginal storytelling traditions and postcolonial issues

Britain

Dawson, Ashley, *Mongrel Nation: Diasporic Culture and the Making of Postcolonial Britain* (Ann Arbor: The University of Michigan Press, 2007)

Offers historically and culturally informed close readings of works by postcolonial British writers, including analyses of works by Sam Selvon, Linton Kwesi Johnson, Buchi Emecheta, Salman Rushdie and Zadie Smith

Gunning, Dave, *Race and Antiracism in Black British and British Asian Literature* (Liverpool: Liverpool University Press, 2010)

Offers close readings of works on race and the postcolonial critique of racism by Hanif Kureisihi, Zadie Smith, Meera Syal, Caryl Phillips and Nadeem Aslam

Innes, C. L., *A History of Black and Asian Writing in Britain 1700–2000* (Cambridge: Cambridge University Press, 2002)

Beginning with authors who arrived as immigrants or slaves in the mid-eighteenth century, Innes offers a compelling and perceptive analysis of the rise of Asian and Black postcolonial writing in Britain

McLeod, John, *Postcolonial London: Rewriting the Metropolis* (London: Routledge, 2004)

Offers compelling close readings of the postcolonial representation of London, including analyses of works by Sam Selvon, Buchi Emecheta, Salman Rushdie, Hanif Kureishi, Bernardine Evaristo, David Dabydeen and others

Procter, James, *Dwelling Places: Postwar Black British Writing* (Manchester: Manchester University Press, 2003)

Presents innovative and historically informed close readings of Black British writing, including discussions of the socio-political dynamics of housing, suburbia and the street

Upstone, Sara, *British Asian Fiction: Twenty-First Century Voices* (Manchester: Manchester University Press, 2010)

Offers theoretically informed readings of works by Salman Rushie, V. S. Naipaul, Hanif Kureishi, Ravinder Randhawa, Atima Srivastava, Meera Syal, Suhayl Saadi, Monica Ali, Hari Kunzru, Nadeem Aslam, Gautam Malkani, Niven Govinden and Nirpal Singh Dhaliwal

Author Studies

Chinua Achebe

Gikandi, Simon, *Reading Chinua Achebe: Language and Ideology in Fiction* (London: James Currey, 1991)

Offers close readings of key works, including *Things Fall Apart*, *Arrow of God*, *No Longer at Ease*, *A Man of the People* and *Anthills of the Savannah*

Innes, C. L., *Chinua Achebe* (Cambridge: Cambridge University Press, 1990)

Comprehensive approach to the author's works, exploring Achebe's concern with communalism rather than individualism and his transformation of traditional Igbo orature

Morrison, Jago, *The Fiction of Chinua Achebe: A Reader's Guide to Essential Criticism* (Basingstoke: Palgrave Macmillan, 2007)

Introduces critical debates about the author and examines key novels with an emphasis on *Things Fall Apart*

J. M. Coetzee

Attwell, David, *J. M. Coetzee: South Africa and the Politics of Writing* (Berkeley: University of California Press, 1993)

Presents close readings of *Dusklands*, *In the Heart of the Country*, *Waiting for the Barbarians*, *Life and Times of Michael K*, *Foe* and *Age of Iron*

Head, Dominic, *J. M. Coetzee* (Cambridge: Cambridge University Press, 1997)

Introduction to the author's oeuvre with close readings of major works, including *Dusklands*, *In the Heart of the Country*, *Life and Times of Michael K*, *Foe*, *Age of Iron* and *The Master of Petersburg*

Jamaica Kincaid

Ferguson, Moira, *Jamaica Kincaid: Where the Land Meets the Body* (Charlottesville: University Press of Virginia, 1994)

Examines the mother–daughter relationship in the context of empire and offers close readings of *At the Bottom of the River*, *Annie John*, *A Small Place* and *Lucy*

Paravasini-Gebert, Lizabeth, *Jamaica Kincaid: A Critical Companion* (Westport, CT: Greenwood, 1999)

Offers close readings of key works, including *At the Bottom of the River*, *Annie John*, *Lucy* and *The Autobiography of My Mother*

Hanif Kureishi

Moore-Gilbert, Bart, *Hanif Kureishi* (Manchester: Manchester University Press, 2001)

Examines the author's oeuvre, including discussions of drama, film, fiction and short stories, taking into account issues such as gender and sexuality, multiculturalism and globalisation

Ranasinha, Ruvani, *Writers and their Work: Hanif Kureishi* (Plymouth: Northcote House in association with the British Council, 2002)

Comprehensive introduction to the author's works, offering close readings of key texts

Toni Morrison

Matus, Jill, *Toni Morrison* (Manchester: Manchester University Press, 1998)

Examines trauma and cultural memory in Morrison's oeuvre with close readings of key works such as *The Bluest Eye*, *Sula*, *Tar Baby*, *Song of Solomon*, *Beloved*, *Jazz* and *Paradise*

Smith, Valerie, *Toni Morrison: Writing the Moral Imagination* (Hoboken, NJ: Wiley-Blackwell, 2012)

Explores the links between Morrison's aesthetic practice and political vision through an analysis of the key texts as well as her less studied works

Tally, Justine (ed.), *The Cambridge Companion to Toni Morrison* (Cambridge: Cambridge University Press, 2007)

Essays examining the author's oeuvre as a whole with discussions of well known novels as well as the short story, drama, musical and opera

V. S. Naipaul

Dooley, Gillian, *V. S. Naipaul, Man and Writer* (Columbia: University of South Carolina Press, 2006)
Comprehensive study of the author's oeuvre offering close readings of key works

Hayward, Helen, *The Enigma of V. S. Naipaul* (Houndmills: Palgrave, 2002)
Offers close readings of key works and examines themes such as family, auto-fiction, the rewriting of history and postcolonial representation

Salman Rushdie

Gurnah, Abdulrazak (ed.), *The Cambridge Companion to Salman Rushdie* (Cambridge: Cambridge University Press, 2007)
Collection of essays offering close readings, discussions of contexts and analyses of thematic concerns, such as gender and the role of the family, the influence of English writing and the *fatwa*

Teverson, Andrew, *Salman Rushdie* (Manchester: Manchester University Press, 2007)
Presents theoretically informed close readings of Salman Rushdie's works from *Grimus* through to *Shalimar the Clown*

Wole Soyinka

Jeyifo, Biodun (ed.), *Perspectives on Wole Soyinka: Freedom and Complexity* (Jackson: University Press of Mississippi, 2001)
Collection of essays on Soyinka by leading critics in the field

Jeyifo, Biodun, *Wole Soyinka : Politics, Poetics, Postcolonialism* (Cambridge: Cambridge University Press, 2005)
Introduction to the author's work, including discussions of mythopoesis and ritual as well as close readings of key works

Msiska, Mpalive-Hangson, *Wole Soyinka* (Plymouth: Northcote House in association with the British Council, 1998)

Introduction to the author's oeuvre, offering close readings of key works

Derek Walcott

Breslin, Paul, *Nobody's Nation: Reading Derek Walcott* (Chicago: University of Chicago Press, 2001)

Examines Walcott's approach to aesthetics and history, arguing that Walcott sees history as a realm of necessity, something to be confronted, contested and remade through literature, as is evidenced through readings of plays and poetry

Burnett, Paula, *Derek Walcott: Politics and Poetics* (Gainesville: University Press of Florida, 2000)

Discusses Walcott's approach to myth, identity and aesthetics, offering close readings of key works

Thieme, John, *Derek Walcott* (Manchester: Manchester University Press, 1999)

Solid introduction to Walcott's work, which offers especially insightful readings of the author's theatrical works

Other Writers

Grice, Helena, *Maxine Hong Kingston* (Manchester: Manchester University Press, 2006)

Offers close readings of key works, including *The Woman Warrior*, *China Men*, *Tripmaster Monkey* and others

Howells, Coral Ann (ed.), *The Cambridge Companion to Margaret Atwood* (Cambridge: Cambridge University Press, 2006)

Essays discussing various facets of the author's oeuvre, including her contribution to postcolonial literature

Ledent, Benedicte, *Caryl Phillips* (Manchester: Manchester University Press, 2002)

Examines novels from *The Final Passage* to *The Nature of Blood* as well as plays and essays by Phillips

Mondal, Anshuman, *Amitav Ghosh* (Manchester: Manchester University Press, 2007)

Comprehensive introduction to the author's work, taking into account the context of the development of Indian modernity and a modern Bengali vernacular tradition

Spinks, Lee, *Michael Ondaatje* (Manchester: Manchester University Press, 2009)

Introduction to the author's poetry and prose, including readings of *The Collected Works of Billy the Kid*, *Anil's Ghost* and *The English Patient*

Thieme, John, *R. K. Narayan* (Manchester: Manchester University Press, 2007)

Discusses the oeuvre of a founding figure in Indian literature in English

Woodcock, Bruce, *Peter Carey* (Manchester: Manchester University Press, 2003)

Introduces the author's oeuvre and offers close readings of key works

Theoretical and Historical Perspectives

Postcolonial Theory and Critical Perspectives

Bhabha, Homi K., *The Location of Culture* (London: Routledge, 1994)

Influential book of essays discussing issues of hybridity, ambivalence, mimicry and other key concepts for postcolonial literary and cultural studies

Chakrabarty, Dipesh, *Provincializing Europe: Postcolonial Thought and Historical Difference*, new edition (Princeton, NJ: Princeton University Press, 2007)

Offers a Marxist critique of the history of modernity from a postcolonial perspective, which interrogates the 'myth' of Europe, including discussions of domestic cruelty and the birth of the subject, nation and imagination, family, fraternity and labour

Crosby, A. W., *Ecological Imperialism: The Biological Expansion of Europe, 900–1900* (Cambridge: Cambridge University Press, 1986)
Offers a historical analysis of the interplay between imperialism and the environment

Hardt, Michael and Antonio Negri, *Empire* (Cambridge, MA: Harvard University Press, 2001)
Book that sparked debate and controversy concerning the thesis that classical notions of imperialism are being supplanted by a new decentred form of empire related to the intersections of technology, economics and globalisation in the contemporary world order

Parry, Benita, *Postcolonial Studies: A Materialist Critique* (London: Routledge, 2004)
Essays urging postcolonial critics to move towards a more materialist critique of literature that places emphasis on imperial violence and exploitation

Said, Edward, *Orientalism* (New York: Penguin Books, 2003)
Twenty-fifty anniversary edition of the text that is said to have launched postcolonial studies, which presents a critique of colonialist discourses, specifically those relating to the representations of the Middle East

Said, Edward, *Culture and Imperialism* (London: Vintage, 1994)
Offers close readings of literary texts from a postcolonial perspective, including analyses of works by Joseph Conrad, Jane Austen and others as well as his innovative account of contrapuntal reading practices

Spivak, Gayatri Chakravorty, *In Other Worlds: Essays in Cultural Politics* (New York: Methuen, 1987)
Essays on literature and culture, including discussions of Subaltern Studies, French Feminism and reading practices

Spivak, Gayatri Chakravorty, *A Critique of Postcolonial Reason: Toward a History of the Vanishing Present* (Cambridge, MA: Harvard University Press, 1999)
Influential collection of essays in postcolonial studies covering four main areas: philosophy, literature, history and culture

Diaspora and Migration

Brah, Avtar, *Cartographies of Diaspora: Contesting Identities* (London: Routledge, 1996)

Maps theoretical shifts in the study of diversity and difference, including discussions of race, labour and gender in Asian British literature and culture

Chambers, Iain, *Migrancy, Culture, Identity* (London: Routledge, 1994)

Conceptual approach to the literature of migration, including discussions of migrant landscapes, aural innovations and traditions, the city and subjectivity

Rushdie, Salman, *Imaginary Homelands: Essays and Criticism, 1981–91* (London: Penguin, 1992)

Essays on literature, migration and the notion of the homeland

Writing the Nation, Multiculturalism and Transnational Frameworks

Ahmad, Aijaz, *In Theory: Nations, Classes, Literatures* (London: Verso, 1992)

Engages with the work of Fredric Jameson, Edward Said and Salman Rushdie in order to assess the emergence of and directions in postcolonial theory

Anderson, Benedict, *Imagined Communities: Reflections on the Origins and Spread of Nationalism* (London: Verso, 2006)

Essential reading for constructions of the nation, including discussions of language, patriotism, memory, national consciousness and imperialism

Chatterjee, Patricia, *The Nation and its Fragments: Colonial and Postcolonial Histories* (Princeton, NJ: Princeton University Press, 1993)

Analysis of nationalism from a postcolonial perspective, offering many examples drawn from the history of India, in order to demonstrate that anti-colonialist nationalists articulated their own domain of sovereignty by drawing on traditions – especially in the spiritual domain – that preceded colonialist intervention

Gilroy, Paul, *The Black Atlantic: Modernity and Double Consciousness* (London: Verso, 1993)

Reads works of literature from the African diaspora in the light of a transnational framework that focuses on the Black Atlantic as a space of social and cultural construction with an emphasis on hybridity

Gunew, Sneja, *Haunted Nations: The Colonial Dimensions of Multiculturalisms* (London: Routledge, 2004)

Examines the ways in which the transnational discourse of multiculturalism is related to race

Kymlicka, Will, *Multicultural Odysseys: Navigating the New International Politics of Diversity* (Oxford: Oxford University Press, 2007)

Examines the history of multiculturalism from an international perspective and considers debates about diversity and the future of multiculturalism in a globalising world

Puri, Jyoti, *Encountering Nationalism* (Malden, MA: Wiley-Blackwell, 2004)

Provides an excellent introduction to approaches to nationalism, covering colonial, postcolonial and post-9/11 perspectives as well as debates about citizenship

Hybridity, Creolisation and Transculturation

Anzaldúa, Gloria, *Borderlands / La Frontera: The New Mestiza*, 2nd edition (San Francisco: Aunt Lute Books, 1999)

Chicana feminist text exploring the role of a new consciousness associated with the mixed race woman, offering discussions of language, historical reclamation and counter-discourses to patriarchal and racial oppression as well as heteronormative practices and discourses

Brathwaite, Edward (Kamau), *The Development of Creole Society in Jamaica, 1770–1820* (Oxford: Oxford University Press, 1971)

Offers a history and theory of creolisation in Jamaica, which marks a key contribution to the field of creolisation studies

Brathwaite, Kamau, *History of the Voice: The Development of Nation Language in Anglophone Caribbean* (London: New Beacon Books, 1984)

Discusses issues of voice, vernacular expression and postcolonial articulation in a Caribbean context

Glissant, Edouard, *The Poetics of Relation*, Trans. Betsy Wing (Ann Arbor: Unviersity of Michigan Press, 1997)

Essays offering a relational approach to postcolonial identity, drawing primarily on the Caribbean experience as the basis for analysis

Pratt, Mary Louise, *Imperial Eyes: Travel Writing and Transculturation*, 2nd edition (London: Routledge, 2008)

Updated edition of an original study of travel writing and empire which examines the role of representation in the contact zone from the eighteenth century to the contemporary era

Walcott, Derek, *What the Twilight Says* (London: Faber and Faber, 1998)

Essays on postcolonial poetics, including discussions of language, history and creolisation

Young, Robert, *Colonial Desire: Hybridity in Theory, Culture and Race* (London: Routledge, 1995)

Offers a historical account of hybridity and a critique of contemporary theory, taking into account the interplay between discourses of race and sex

Race and Decolonisation

Du Bois, W. E. B., *The Souls of Black Folk* (Oxford: Oxford University Press, 2008)

Seminal book on race and racial uplift in the history of African American letters that was first published in 1903

Fanon, Frantz, *Black Skin, White Masks*, Trans. Richard Philcox (New York: Grove Press, 2008)

Analysis of race thinking by one of the leading postcolonial thinkers in the twentieth century (first published in French in 1952), which had a profound influence on civil rights, anti-colonial and black consciousness movements around the world

Fanon, Frantz, *The Wretched of the Earth*, Trans. Richard Philcox (New York: Grove Press, 2004)

Written during the Algerian struggle for independence, this work considers issues of decolonising the nation and the imaginary

Gilroy, Paul, *Against Race: Imagining Political Culture Beyond the Color Line* (Cambridge, MA: The Belknap Press of Harvard University Press, 2000)

Critical interrogation of race-thinking and call for a new kind of humanism that goes beyond the colour line

Memmi, Albert, *The Colonizer and the Colonized*, Trans. Howard Greenfield (London: Earthscan Publications, 2003)

Describes the psychological effects of colonialism on colonised and coloniser alike, which should be read together with Fanon's *Wretched of the Earth*

Thiong'o, Ngugi wa, *Decolonising the Mind: The Politics of Language in African Literature* (London: James Currey, 1981)

Examines African language, theatre and writing in terms of decolonisation as well as contributing to debates about language in the postcolonial era, arguing for the need to reject the language of the coloniser in favour of local language and cultural traditions

Gender and Sexuality

hooks, bell, *Ain't I a Woman: Black Women and Feminism* (Cambridge, MA: South End Press, 1999)

Influential study of how black women have been oppressed by white men, black men and white women that offers a critique of the limitations of first and second-wave feminisms

Lorde, Audre, *Sister Outsider: Essays and Speeches* (Berkeley, CA: Crossing Press, 2007)

Collection of essays from 1984 on black feminism, the power of the erotic and the need to move beyond prevailing approaches to identity politics

McClintock, Anne, *Imperial Leather: Race, Gender and Sexuality in the Colonial Context* (New York: Routledge, 1995)
Chronicles the interplay between gender, race and class as it came to shape British imperialism and decolonisation

Mohanty, Chandra Talpade, *Feminism Without Borders: Decolonizing Theory, Practicing Solidarity* (Durham, NC: Duke University Press, 2003)
Influential study of postcolonial feminism from a transnational perspective

Phillips, Richard, *Sex, Politics and Empire: A Postcolonial Geography* (Manchester: Manchester University Press, 2006)
Explores the connections between sexual governance and empire, providing a history of sexuality that is informed by an attentiveness to spatiality

Spurlin, William, *Imperialism within the Margins: Queer Representation and the Politics of Culture in Southern Africa* (New York: Palgrave, 2006)
Focuses on the sexual politics that have emerged out of post-apartheid South Africa, considering issues of citizenship, hybridity and borders

Journals

Amerasia
Interdisciplinary journal in Asian American Studies

Ariel: A Review of English Literature
Critical and scholarly study of new and established literatures in English around the world

Callaloo
African diasporic literary journal, including critical analysis and creative writing

Interventions: International Journal of Postcolonial Studies
Offers theoretically orientated discussions of postcolonial literature from around the world

Journal of Postcolonial Writing
Presents essays about literature written in English and published throughout the world, especially strong on close reading

Journal of South Asian Literature
Contributes to the study of South Asian literature with critical and creative submissions

MELUS
Features articles, interviews and reviews encompassing the multi-ethnic scope of American literature past and present

Research in African Literatures
Presents critical analyses of African literatures from around the world, including essays on oral and literary traditions

Small Axe
Focuses on the Caribbean and its diaspora, offering social, cultural, literary and political criticism

The Journal of Commonwealth Literature
Examines aspects Commonwealth and postcolonial literatures from around the world

Transition
Publishes interviews, reviews and essays about postcolonial literatures from around the world

Wasafiri
Literary magazine for postcolonial, migrant and diasporic writing in Britain as well as international contexts

Websites and Online Resources

Colonial and Postcolonial Literary Dialogues
Analysis, links and resources for colonial and postcolonial literatures, histories, topics and theories: http://www.wmich.edu/dialogues/sitepages/home.html

Contemporary Postcolonial and Postimperial Literature in English

Offers introductory information concerning postcolonial literatures and authors from around the world, which are accessible by region/nation: http://www.postcolonialweb.org/

Contemporary Writers in the UK

Up-to-date profiles and introductory critical commentary of many of the United Kingdom and Commonwealth's most important living writers: http://www.contemporarywriters.com/

Repeating Islands

Blog on Caribbean literature, culture and the arts: http://repeatingislands.com/our-blog/

The Imperial Archive

Provides resources for all those interested in the influence of the British imperial process on literature from the nineteenth through to the twenty-first centuries: http://www.qub.ac.uk/schools/SchoolofEnglish/imperial/imperial.htm

Voice of the Shuttle

Provides links to many postcolonial resources, including information about authors, critical theory and special topics: http://vos.ucsb.edu

Index

Index

Acknowledgements

Extracts from:

'The Thing Around Your Neck', taken from *The Thing Around Your Neck* by Chimamamda Ngozi Adichie Copyright © 2009 Chimamanda Ngozi Adichie. All rights reserved. Reprinted by permission of The Wylie Agency (UK) Ltd; Kachifo Limited; Knopf Canada; and HarperCollins Publishers Ltd © Chimamanda Ngozi Adichie 2009

Kamau Braithwaite, excerpts from 'Hawk' from *Born to Slow Horses* © 2005 by Kamau Braithwaite. Reprinted by permission of Wesleyan University Press

Poetry and Protest: A Dennis Brutus Reader (Chicago: Haymarket Books, 2006). Reprinted by permission of Haymarket Books

'Waiting for the Barbarians' by C. P. Cavafy. Copyright © C. P. Cavafy. Reproduced by permission of the author c/o Rogers, Coleridge and White Ltd, 20 Powis Mews, London W11 1JN

THE SOULS OF BLACK FOLK by W. E. B. Du Bois, introduction by Donald B. Gibson, notes by Monica E. Elbert (Penguin Classics, 1989). Copyright © the Estate of W. E. B. Du Bois 1903. Introduction copyright © Viking Penguin, a division of Penguin Books USA, Inc., 1989

THE BONE PEOPLE by Keri Hulme. Copyright © Keri Hulme, 1989. Reprinted by permission of Pan Macmillan UK

M. Butterfly by David Henry Hwang. Reproduced by permission of Paradigm Agency, New York

'Columbus in Chains' from ANNIE JOHN by Jamaica Kincaid. Copyright © 1985 by Jamaica Kincaid. Reproduced by permission of Farrar, Straus and Giroux LLC and The Random House Group

A SMALL PLACE by Jamaica Kincaid. Copyright © 1988 by Jamaica Kincaid. Reproduced by permission of Farrar, Straus and Giroux LLC

THE WOMAN WARRIOR by Maxine Hong Kingston. Copyright © 1976 by Maxine Hong Kingston. Originally appeared in THE WOMAN WARRIOR: MEMOIRS OF A GIRLHOOD AMONG GHOSTS. Reprinted by permission of the author and the Sandra Dijkstra Literary Agency

Sammy and Rosie Get Laid by Hanif Kureishi. Copyright © Hanif Kureishi. Reproduced by permission of the author c/o Rogers, Coleridge and White Ltd, 20 Powis Mews, London W11 1JN

'Sexism: An American Disease in Blackface' and 'Uses of the Erotic: The Erotic as Power' from *Sister Outsider: Essays and Speeches* by Audre Lorde © by the Estate of Audre Lorde, 1984, 2007. Reproduced by kind permission of the Estate of Audre Lorde

THE TABLES OF LAW by Thomas Mann, translated by Helen Lowe-Porter, translation copyright 1945, copyright renewed 1973 by Alfred A. Knopf, a division of Random House, Inc. Used by permission of Alfred A. Knopf, a division of Random House, Inc.

BELOVED by Toni Morrison, published by Chatto & Windus, copyright © 1987 by Toni Morrison. Used by permission of Alfred A. Knopf, a division of Random House, Inc and The Random House Group, Ltd

A Bend in the River by V. S. Naipaul (New York: Vintage International, 1989) Copyright © V. S. Naipaul, 1979. Permission granted by The Wylie Agency (UK) Ltd and Alfred A. Knopf, a division of Random House, Inc.

'Prologue' from 'Ti-Jean and His Brothers' from DREAM ON MONKEY MOUNTAIN by Derek Walcott. Copyright © 1970 by Derek Walcott. Reprinted by permission of Farrar, Straus and Giroux, LLC